*Authoritarian Legacies
and Democracy in Latin America
and Southern Europe*

RECENT TITLES FROM THE HELEN KELLOGG INSTITUTE
FOR INTERNATIONAL STUDIES

Scott Mainwaring, *general editor*

The University of Notre Dame Press gratefully thanks the Hellen Kellogg Institute for International Studies for its support in the publication of titles in this series.

Guillermo O'Donnell
Counterpoints: Selected Essays on Authoritarianism and Democratization (1999)

Howard Handelman and Mark Tessler, eds.
Democracy and Its Limits: Lessons from Asia, Latin America, and the Middle East (1999)

Larissa Adler Lomnitz and Ana Melnick
Chile's Political Culture and Parties: An Anthropological Explanation (2000)

Kevin Healy
Llamas, Weavings, and Organic Chocolate: Multicultural Grassroots Development in the Andes and Amazon of Bolivia (2000)

Ernest J. Bartell, C.S.C., and Alejandro O'Donnell
The Child in Latin America: Health, Development, and Rights (2000)

Vikram K. Chand
Mexico's Political Awakening (2001)

Ruth Berins Collier and David Collier
Shaping the Political Arena (2002)

Glen Biglaiser
Guardians of the Nation? (2002)

Sylvia Borzutzky
Vital Connections (2002)

Alberto Spektorowski
The Origins of Argentina's Revolution of the Right (2003)

Caroline C. Beer
Electoral Competition and Institutional Change in Mexico (2003)

Yemile Mizrahi
From Martyrdom to Power (2003)

Charles D. Kenney
Fujimori's Coup and the Breakdown of Democracy in Latin America (2003)

For a complete list of titles from the Helen Kellogg Institute for International Studies, see http://www.undpress.nd.edu

Authoritarian Legacies and Democracy in Latin America and Southern Europe

KATHERINE HITE & PAOLA CESARINI

editors

Foreword by Nancy Bermeo

University of Notre Dame Press
Notre Dame, Indiana

Manufactured in the United States of America

Library of Congress Cataloging-in-Publication Data
Authoritarian legacies and democracy in Latin America and Southern
Europe / Katherine Hite and Paola Cesarini, editors.
p.   cm.
"Recent titles from the Helen Kellogg Institute for International Studies."
Includes bibliographical references and index.
ISBN 0-268-02019-1 (cloth : alk. paper)
ISBN 0-268-02020-5 (pbk. : alk. paper)
1. Democratization—Case studies.   2. Latin America—Politics and
government—20th century.   3. Authoritarianism—Latin America.
4. Democratization—Latin America.   5. Europe, Southern—Politics and
government—20th century.   6. Authoritarianism—Europe, Southern.
7. Democratization—Europe, Southern.   I. Hite, Katherine.   II. Cesarini,
Paola, 1966–   III. Helen Kellogg Institute for International Studies.
JC423.A837   2004
320.94—dc22

2003024943

∞ *This book is printed on acid-free paper.*

Contents

Foreword

This collection of essays constitutes a daring enterprise. At a time when political scientists are under pressure to focus on subjects that can be easily quantified, an investigation of authoritarian legacies stands out for its boldness. This particular investigation stands out for its precision and its breadth. The editors have taken care to be precise about the many forms that legacies have taken in the real world of politics and in the scholarly literature. They have also taken time to include the whole range of legacies in their case studies. Readers will be enlightened by essays on legacies of authoritarianism that are carried in the hearts and minds of individuals, but they will also learn about legacies that are carried by institutions—especially in laws that empower some and disempower others. Each of the core institutions of concern to scholars of comparative politics is covered in the text—constitutions, political parties, executives, legislatures, militaries, and interest groups, each gets its due—but the book also includes essays on equally important subjects of a less overtly structural nature regarding trust, perception, and citizenship.

The collection's geographic breadth complements the breadth of its subject matter. At a time when the social science community thinks most often in terms of continents and regions, cross-continental comparisons offer some surprising consistencies. The complexities of legacies are not easy to quantify, but they are certainly easy to recognize across a broad range of countries, and they are critically important wherever they are found. After all, the challenges confronting new democracies today are largely the result of what previous regimes have left behind. Weak parties, politicized militaries, compromised judiciaries, corrupt police forces, and pervasive citizen distrust are but a few of the contemporary problems with roots that run deep into the history of previous regimes. These essays on the legacies of authoritarianism give us lenses to see connections with the past, but they also help us see the prospects for the durability of democracy in the future. As a number of these essays illustrate, politicians and ordinary people are capable of learning from past mistakes. Thus authoritarian legacies can be positive as well as negative. Whatever their valence, legacies are consequential. This collection speaks eloquently to the question of consequences and by so doing is sure to stimulate further research.

I should not close, however, without stating that this collection itself is a mixture of legacies. In some senses, and for some of its authors, it is a legacy of personal and painful firsthand experience with an authoritarian regime. For all of the authors and both of its editors, it is the legacy of a more positive association with a vibrant political space within Columbia University's Institute of Latin American and Iberian Studies. Douglas Chalmers, Katie Roberts Hite, and Paola Cesarini are to be commended for using their space so creatively and for providing us with a tangible argument for the merits of inclusion.

Nancy Bermeo
Princeton University

Acknowledgments

The coeditors wish to express their thanks to the Institute of Latin American and Iberian Studies of Columbia University for offering the Authoritarian Legacies Project a supportive institutional home. We also thank the Ford Foundation-Chile and Alexander Wilde in particular, who provided both intellectual stimulus and financial support. Our appreciation also extends to the Casa Italiana of Columbia University for co-hosting our first working group meeting; to the Universidad Torcuato di Tella and to José María Ghio for co-hosting the second series of meetings in Buenos Aires; and to the Cursos de Arrábida and to António Costa Pinto for co-sponsoring the third series of meetings near Lisbon. Further institutional support for the project came from Centro Brasileiro de Análise e Planejamento (CEBRAP) of Brazil, Centro de Investigación y Docencia Económicas (CIDE) of Mexico, the Center for European Studies of Columbia University, the Fundação Oriente of Portugal, and the William and Flora Hewlett Foundation.

This project benefited from the encouragement of some very special people, including Nancy Bermeo, who was unshakable in her support from the beginning and who created the opportunity for our meeting in Portugal. We are also very grateful to Atilio Borón, Margaret Crahan, Douglas Chalmers, Eric Hershberg, Robert Kaufman, Edward Malefakis, Ioannes Sinanoglu, and Alfred Stepan, all of whom contributed to the shaping of the project.

Many others were involved as participants or discussants at various stages of the project. We wish to acknowledge them here: Carlos Acuña, José Antonio Aguilar Rivera, Astrid Arraras, Alexandra Barahona de Brito, Louis Bickford, Rut C. Diamint, Maria Helena Dos Castros Santos, Argelina Figueiredo, Fernando Filgueira, Iván Jaksic, Elizabeth Jelín, Elizabeth Lira, David Lorey, Brian Loveman, Anna Margheritis, Ana María Mustapic, Gabriel Negretto, Gianfranco Pasquino, Enrique Peruzzotti, José Manuel Pureza, Stefano Rodotá, Jorge Rodríguez, Ricardo Salvatore, Catalina Smulovitz, and Pedro Ginestral Tavares de Almeida.

ix

We also thank the political science department of Vassar College for colleagueship and support, the Vassar Research Committee, and the Vassar's Ford Scholars program for funding research assistants José Medina, Lissette Olivares, Sarah Shanley, and Henry Hutten to work on this project. We are grateful to Jan Bindas-Tenney for taking on the index. In addition, we appreciate the encouragement of Scott Mainwaring and the assistance of Jeffrey Gainey, Rebecca DeBoer, and Elisabeth Magnus of the University of Notre Dame Press.

Last but not least, we wish to express our deepest gratitude to all the authors in the volume, who made this project not only a great intellectual adventure but a venue to look forward to, thanks to their openness to intellectual strands and approaches as well as their congeniality and warmth.

Paola Cesarini dedicates this book to her husband, Richard Strasser, for always sharing his strength, joy, and genius. Katherine Hite dedicates the book to her family for their love and patience and to Margaret Crahan for her exceptional colleagueship.

1

Introducing the Concept of
Authoritarian Legacies

PAOLA CESARINI & KATHERINE HITE

The purpose of this volume is to provide a set of interpretive lenses for those interested in the panoply of authoritarian legacies that continue to affect postauthoritarian democracies in Latin America and southern Europe—and in other postauthoritarian regions as well. This introductory chapter offers a critical review of existing approaches to the study of authoritarian legacies. It also introduces a conceptualization of authoritarian legacies, further developed by the authors of this volume, that attempts to highlight key components of legacies in both their formal-legal and their practiced dimensions. Finally, the chapter suggests that the study of authoritarian legacies requires both problematizing and synthesizing a range of disciplinary perspectives to achieve a more robust understanding of legacies' influences on postauthoritarian democracies.

Defining Authoritarian Legacies

Within what was the new and energetic field of modernization studies of the immediate post–World War II period, there was strong concern about authoritarian legacies, characterized primarily as those "inherited" cultural, social, and political traits that were obstacles to economic and political development. For both southern Europe and Latin America, students of the regions attributed widespread poverty and weak democracies (or the outright lack of democracies) to the centuries-old Iberian traditions of authoritarian centralism, Roman Catholicism, and a range of primarily valuative features that limited the scope for modernization. By the late 1960s, however, social scientists had soundly criticized such culturalist explanations, laying bare the ethnocentrism of the Iberian legacy arguments. In a sense, however, the effect of these important critiques was to throw the baby out with the bathwater, and, with a few notable exceptions, little attention has been paid to the notion of authoritarian legacies ever since.

More recently, social science scholars have conceptualized authoritarian legacies within postauthoritarian democratic regimes in essentially three ways: (1) as formal structures and institutions inherited from authoritarian regimes; (2) as the lingering power and influence of traditional/conservative groups; and (3) as cultural or psychological manifestations of authoritarianism (i.e., uncertainty, distrust, fear). In reviewing these conceptualizations, we noted, first, that scholars tend to draw a sharp distinction between the *formal-legal* and the *cultural, practiced, experienced,* or *dispositional* dimensions of authoritarian legacies—with a tendency among political science democratization theorists to emphasize formal-legal dimensions. Thus, for example, Kitschelt et al. (1999) still largely ignore the cultural dimensions of legacies by defining them as "resource endowment and institutions that precede the choice of democratic institutions" (11). Combining social structural and political institutional variables, Elster, Offe, and Preuss (1998) characterize legacies more broadly as "determinants of present outcomes that stem from the (distant) past, such as inherited endowments of actors with material resources, mentalities, and traditions" (293). On the other hand, those such as social psychologist Elizabeth Lira (1996) focus on authoritarian legacies as lingering remnants of fear, alienation, and anxiety within the political-cultural milieu.

Second, we discerned a marked difference in the way scholars of different social science fields *temporalize* authoritarian legacies. Most comparative political science scholarship tends to narrow the investigation to legacies associated with distinct and time-framed recent authoritarian experiences, conceptually eliminating transmissions of legacies from other nondemocratic regimes of the past. Others consider authoritarian legacies part of a country's political culture or historical tradition whose origins far predate recent authoritarian regimes (e.g., Putnam 1993). In general, while political scientists do not deny the influence of authoritarian historical traditions, they argue that conceptually it becomes too unwieldy and imprecise to incorporate the distant past into a useful model linking authoritarian legacies to postauthoritarian politics. Many settle for O'Donnell's characterization of legacies that constitute "an old 'schizophrenia' that predates authoritarianism, on which newer problems are superimposed" (quoted in Agüero 1998, 6).

Third, it becomes apparent that different scholars often detect different legacies—or at least different concentrations of them—within the same country context, depending upon the *definition of democracy* they employ (see also Agüero 1998, 7). For example, Atilio Borón (1998) argues that while Latin American democracies might be considered consolidated in terms of the establishment of formal representative political institutions, the inequalities and lack of opportunities that plague the great majority of the region's population since the Spanish colonization persist. We often found that those espousing essentially formal or procedural notions of democracy are likely to identify different (and definitely fewer) authoritarian legacies than those selecting more participatory, social, or substantive definitions of democracy.[1]

Fourth, it appears that the same legacy is often considered *negative* in the eyes of some but *positive* in those of others. Thus, for example, allowing the military to retain substantial reserved domains has, according to some, facilitated Chile's democratic transition. According to others, such authoritarian enclaves pose an array of judicial and institutional obstacles to that country's political and social reconciliation and, in turn, to full-fledged democratization (Garretón 1995).

Fifth, while we noted a general tendency to consider authoritarian legacies as *continuations* of the past, we found that some also characterize authoritarian legacies as *reactions* to the past. In this volume, Katherine Hite and Leonardo Morlino (chapter 2) suggest that Italy's 1948 constitution created an excessively weak executive mainly in reaction to fascism's excesses. They also suggest that in light of the precariousness of previous democratic experiences, Argentine citizens' comparatively high regard for democracies above all other regimes is a reaction to the repressive, authoritarian years of El Proceso (1976–83). More problematically, however, we noticed that among those interpreting authoritarian legacies as continuations of the past, there is a marked difference between those who limit themselves to showing such continuation as a form of *inertia* that has "little (if anything) to do with intentional causation" (Elster, Offe, and Preuss 1998, 293–94) and those who believe that the persistence of authoritarian legacies requires some kind of *agency* and is therefore something that needs explaining (Thelen 1999).

While some scholars believe that authoritarian legacies constitute either a distraction for new democracies' institution builders or the inevitable product of immutable historical or cultural structures, others hold that authoritarian legacies can also be the result of conscious choice by political actors to promote particular interests. Authoritarian legacies in this sense are the product of "specific historical struggles," and their reproduction is a dynamic process that we can come to understand only if we "know who, exactly, is invested in particular institutional arrangements, how exactly that investment is sustained over time, as well perhaps as how those who are not invested in the institutions are kept out" (Thelen 1999, 32). In her chapter on authoritarian legacies and economic reform for this volume (chapter 3), Frances Hagopian pursues a related line of inquiry, focusing in part on the ways authoritarian political actors have molded institutions to protect their interests.

In light of these observations and as a conceptual framework for the contributions of this collection, we define authoritarian legacies as follows: *Authoritarian legacies are those rules, procedures, norms, patterns, practices, dispositions, relationships, and memories originating in well-defined authoritarian experiences of the past that, as a result of specific historical configurations and/or political struggles, survive democratic transition and intervene in the quality and practice of postauthoritarian democracies.*

Our conceptualization of authoritarian legacies requires a number of clarifications. First, we are acutely aware that it fails to resolve all the problems encountered with previous definitions. At a minimum, however, it seeks to systematize the concept, as well as to provide a common point of reference that might lead scholars to refer to similar phenomena in their research. Each contribution of this volume explores a distinct but related aspect of our conceptual framework.

In our view, authoritarian legacies are not necessarily correlated with "unconsolidated" democracy. Rather, they are likely to be found in most postauthoritarian democracies that display "contradictory or arrhythmic patterns" in both formal institutions and informal practices (Agüero and Stark 1998, ii), present significant social and institutional realms that appear "out of synch" with the rest of the democratic polity (Thelen 1999), or comprise "processes in which the institutionalization, practice and meaning of citizenship are rarely uniform or homogeneous" (Holston and Caldeira 1998, 280), regardless of their degree of consolidation. The authors of this volume highlight an array of authoritarian legacies in what are arguably the most consolidated of democracies as well as in those regimes where democracy is less than consolidated.[2]

We seek to reject the artificial separation between formal and informal authoritarian legacies. Authoritarian legacies consist of the obvious "formal" or readily identifiable structures and institutions inherited from an authoritarian past as well as lived, practiced, and dispositional manifestations (i.e., memories, fear, distrust) and "informal" institutions (i.e., clientelism, *caudillismo*) that can be traced directly to the authoritarian experience. We are aware, of course, that this may pose all sorts of methodological problems, as many of these dimensions of legacies are often difficult to operationalize and measure. To detect dispositional, political-cultural dimensions of legacies, for example, comparativist political scientists have tended to rely on attitudinal survey research. We strongly believe that denying the existence of less empirically graspable dimensions would only limit, and even misguide, scholarly research on legacies.

Our definition of authoritarian legacies espouses a broader, substantive view of democracy rather than a strictly procedural one—as authoritarian legacies often lie in the fissures between formally democratic institutions and the institutionalization of undemocratic practices. In this sense, we agree with Borón (1998) when he states that a procedural notion of democracy reduces the concept to "the establishment of a system of rules and procedures unconcerned with and unrelated to the ethical contents proper of democracy—and indifferent to the implications of deep-seated social contradictions and class inequalities in the political process" (43).

Lingering authoritarian legacies—even when they cannot per se cause authoritarian backlash—nevertheless present a long-term problem for the quality and consistency of postauthoritarian democratic regimes, both at the macrolevel of political and economic institutions' operations and at the microlevel of citizens' perceptions of democracy. Many of the chapters of this volume stress this point.

Regarding the question of temporalization, we believe that although authoritarian legacies are often not the product of the most recent authoritarian regime, it does become necessary, for research's sake, to identify with some degree of precision the historical moments in which the legacies originated, as well as the mechanisms that carried such legacies into the postauthoritarian democratic setting. The closer the authoritarian experience in question, of course, the easier it is to pinpoint the legacy one wishes to analyze. The chapters of this volume tend to recognize conceptually that the authoritarian legacies they are examining are rooted in good part in historical moments that predate the most recent authoritarian regimes. Nevertheless, empirically the chapters tend to focus on legacies that are exacerbated, if not created, by the immediate authoritarian predecessor regimes.

Finally, we would argue that the persistence of legacies as both continuation and reaction requires some form of agency. In other words, even those legacies that most clearly represent continuity with the past are rarely simply the result of inertia. Rather, legacies are often the product of willful agency by democratization's political actors to promote their own agendas and therefore require at least as much explanation as any "rupture" with, or "reaction" to, an authoritarian past. With our definition we intend to argue that it is fundamentally erroneous to understand authoritarian legacies *solely* as the inescapable deadweight of history on the shoulders of postauthoritarian democracies—as authors writing on the subject have done in the past. Rather, the persistence of authoritarian legacies in postauthoritarian democracies is most likely to result from the dynamics among a country's specific historical configuration leading to democratization; conscious choice or manipulation by key political actors to further their own particular goals; and ongoing political struggles among collective actors during critical moments of democratization.

Authoritarian Legacies' Locations

Felipe Agüero (1998) writes that the ways in which authoritarian legacies are conceived greatly influence the kinds of approaches used to study them (4). We agree. Our review of existing literature shows that when authoritarian legacies are defined as formal-legal institutions and rules governing representation, formal institutionalist approaches are likely to constitute the preferred lenses. Here scholars generally attempt to analyze both how and why formal structures and institutions, often transmitted in part by previous authoritarian regimes, shape political actors' behavior, interactions, and incentives in the political, social, and economic arenas in ways that are harmful to democracy.

When authoritarian legacies are conceptualized as the continuing influence of entrenched powers and elites associated with a previous authoritarian regime, a range of sociological approaches is generally preferred, from historico-structuralist to sociological-institutionalist and rational choice approaches. Here scholars seek to explain why and how specific social groups or networks closely associated with former dictatorships (i.e., traditional social and political elites, the military, the Church) continue to be able to maintain power, privileges, hierarchies, and structures that undermine democratic rule even after the transition is formally completed.

Finally, when authoritarian legacies are interpreted as more intersubjective features of society, located in the everyday spheres of political and cultural interaction, social constructivist, culturalist, and psychological approaches are the preferred conceptual lenses. These generally focus on how and why the uncodified, performed psychological and cultural relationships—as shaped by previous authoritarian experiences—constrain actors from engaging "democratically."

In practice, however, things are seldom as clear-cut. Problems associated with inherited authoritarian institutions of the formal kind are, in fact, often created and/or compounded by authoritarian cultural or traditional actors, forces, and patterns in society. Consequently, institutionalist and culturalist analyses are concurrently required to achieve a richer understanding of authoritarian legacies. For example, Holston and Caldeira (1998) effectively show how in Brazil "the population's support for police violence indicates the existence not only of an institutional dysfunction, but also of a pervasive cultural pattern that associates order and authority with the use of violence and that, in turn, contributes to the delegitimation of the justice system and the rule of law" (273). In their analysis of the police and authoritarian legacies in the Southern Cone and Brazil for this volume, Anthony Pereira and Mark Ungar (chapter 7) problematize legacies in a similar vein. Pereira and Ungar trace and analyze the historical, cultural, and political features of Southern Cone and Brazilian authoritarian "law enforcement" institutions and practices, as well as (interestingly counterintuitive) public perceptions of criminality and justice.

The persistence of authoritarian legacies in postauthoritarian democracies may be explained in terms of a combination of socially, culturally, and institutionally induced sets of attitudes, perceptions, motivations, and constraints—that is, from traditions or institutions of the past as well as from present political struggles within formally democratic arrangements. For example, as Consuelo Cruz provocatively argues in chapter 8 of this volume, because civic self-conception at the individual level is largely missing in contemporary Latin American (formal) democracies as a result of their historical development, the public sphere remains monopolized by elites who see themselves as enlightened minorities called upon to lead—often uncontested—subaltern classes and racial groups. As a result, democracy in much of Latin America largely belongs to the realm of constitutions and code books rather than reality.

Finally, it is often difficult to relegate legacies into sole categories of formal-legal institutions, sociological institutions, or cultural manifestations. There is also the risk of confusing legacy as cause with legacy as effect, of folding legacies as independent variables into that which we are trying to explain—

that is, the influences of legacies on the quality of democracy as well as the pace and scope of reform. Each of our authors wrestles head on with such questions. In fact, we would argue that the most innovative contribution of this collection is the authors' deliberate efforts to mesh institutionalist, sociological, and culturalist approaches in their examinations of legacies and their impact on postauthoritarian states and societies.

Legacies as Formal-Legal Institutions

Bucking the earlier actor-process-oriented approaches to transitions from authoritarian rule, the 1990s political science literature on democratic consolidation and reform focused largely on formal institutions, such as codified "rules of the political game," executives and legislatures, and other formal structures of governance. Formal institutional structures may represent authoritarian legacies when they consist of rules and institutions from previous authoritarian regimes that shape the behavior and choices of key political actors in ways that undermine the quality of new democracies. In this sense authoritarian legacies provide, just like any other institution, "a matrix of sanctions and incentives to which rational agents respond" (Hall and Taylor 1996, 937). Furthermore, such legacies may set a country along a suboptimal developmental path toward democratization and therefore may negatively affect the long-term quality and consistency of democracy.

The most glaring example of authoritarian legacies of the formal institutional kind is that of explicit "enclaves," "reserved domains," or other similar formal institutional shelters.[3] Such enclaves allow actors compromised with the previous authoritarian regime to maintain significant political influence in the new democracies—such as those created in Chile by the 1980 constitution, which, in General Augusto Pinochet's phrase, was designed to ensure a "protected democracy." But less obvious examples are also numerous. In Italy, for example—a consolidated democracy for the past fifty years—the 1948 democratic constitution coexisted, until quite recently, with "a great deal of fascist legislation [that] remained largely untouched" (Colarizi and Morlino 1998, 473).

Many political scientists have analyzed the most problematic formal institutions of postauthoritarian democracies, such as strong presidencies, fragmented or weak party systems, and excessively centralized state bureaucracies.[4] A number of scholars have also attempted to link such institutions to authoritarian, oligarchic, and even colonial pasts, arguing that these constitute remnants of previous nondemocratic regimes that somehow survived the democratic transition.

Nevertheless, formal institutionalists often fail to specify the sequence and mechanisms through which the nondemocratic features of these formal institutions were transmitted to the new democratic regimes, as well as which actors (or coalition of actors) continue to champion their survival in the new democracies. There is a tendency, instead, to take notice of similarities or "continuities" between institutions of the present and of the past and then to dedicate analysis to assessing the (generally negative) influence of such institutional legacies on the new democracies. Implicit in these formal institutionalists' work is the notion that proper institutional reengineering will engender healthier democracies and that the histories of these malfunctioning institutions are less important than the retooling of them.[5] Moreover, there is a marked unidirectionality within much of the institutionalist literature. In other words, while institutionalism rightly stresses the fact that institutions shape actors' behavior, it tends to underestimate the extent to which actors also shape institutions in what constitutes a constant feedback process.

A comparatively early notable exception in this regard is the collection of essays edited by John Herz (1982). In that volume, the authors make a collective effort not only to identify legacies of authoritarianism and totalitarianism[6] and link them to a nondemocratic past but also to study the role of outgoing elites and militaries, incoming political actors, and occupying forces in facilitating the preservation of such legacies. In the end, however, the impact of Herz's contribution is weakened by the scarce attention paid to more "informal" authoritarian legacies and to democracy's microfoundations.[7] Institutional engineering cannot alone rebuild such fundamental ingredients of democracy as citizenship and trust. For that, institutional reform needs to be complemented by processes and practices through which "subjects" begin to identify themselves as "citizens" and to trust each other and the government (Varas 1998). In this sense, and as Paola Cesarini argues in chapter 4 of this volume on transitional justice and authoritarian legacies, citizenship and trust provide as much a key foundation for democracy as free and fair elections.

Finally, institutionalist approaches have often been wrong in forecasting that the "right" institutional engineering would bring about successful democratization or economic liberalization. In doing so, in fact, they failed to foresee that the interaction of the new institutions with what survived from previous regimes might instead lead to a disappointing mix with even disastrous consequences (see Stark 1992, 299–304). They also underestimated the possibility that authoritarian legacies might emerge not only from new democracies' failures to eradicate authoritarianism's formal political and economic structures but also from new democratic regimes' inability to confront the more informal authoritarian powers or practices that remain entrenched in the day-to-day operation of the new institutions.

The most egregious failures in this respect belong to neoliberal institutionalists, who predicted early on that political and economic transformations would go hand in hand in the democratizing countries of Latin America and eastern Europe, only to discover later that political democratization would often produce fierce opposition to economic liberalization or that neoliberal reforms would undermine—in practice—the realization of democracy beyond the electoral arena (Pastor and Wise 1999, 35). Neoliberal and rational choice institutionalists also largely distinguished themselves for their failure to anticipate the resistance of groups closely associated with the previous regimes to any institutional reform or their ability to occupy positions of power within the new institutions and, in so doing, to drain the reforms of any practical significance.

Legacies as Social and Political Actors and Forces

What are broadly conceived as sociological approaches to democracy and democratization tend to identify authoritarian legacies in the lingering power and influence of specific social classes, groups, coalitions, or networks associated with previous nondemocratic regimes under the new postauthoritarian democracies. Frances Hagopian (1996) identifies these groups as "traditional power structures"—elite groups that "historically have denied the fruits of full citizenship to . . . lower-class groups through coercive labor systems and various formal and informal political mechanisms that limit mass political representation" (64).

In contrast to those who argue that formal institutions lie at the root of constraints to democracy and good governance, historico-structuralist-oriented scholar Brian Loveman (1993) claims that Latin American authoritarian legacies are due to social structures and political forces, such as political leaders and the military. Since the independence movements of the nineteenth century, Loveman argues, such actors have created, maintained, and manipulated institutions, including constitutional clauses and "regimes of exception," to justify their authoritarian practices. Using a very different methodological lens, rational choice scholars Barbara Geddes (1994) and

Barry Ames (1987) similarly consider politicians and state bureaucrats to be the keys to the perpetuation of antidemocratic practices.

Political scientist Gretchen Casper (1995) argues, broadly, that "the legacies of authoritarian rule are fragile democracies" (5). Joining Latin Americanist scholarship on social institutions in democratization processes, Casper's work on the military and the Church in the Philippines explicitly addresses how authoritarian rule politicized social institutions in ways that far outlive the authoritarian regimes themselves. Other scholars on southern Europe and Latin America have pointed to the Catholic Church as inimical to democracy in the two regions. As one analyst claims, in Latin America "soldiers, priests, and bureaucrats laid the foundations of modern political systems as they competed for power during the sixteenth century. All were men. And they began two dominating legacies: military rule and oligarchy" (Hansis 1997, 220).

In Latin America and southern Europe, aristocratic and landed elites have been indicated as examples of traditional power structures whose continuing predominance constitutes a formidable obstacle for modernization and democratization (Moore 1966; Rueschemeyer, Stephens, and Stephens 1992). Interestingly enough, a number of students of democratic transition initially argued that the direct involvement of traditional and conservative elites in the rebuilding of democratic institutions and processes after authoritarianism would be vital to ensure the "stability" of the new democracies (O'Donnell and Schmitter 1986; Kaufman 1986) because participating in the reestablishment of democracy after authoritarian rule would allow traditional elites to gain direct guarantees for their futures under the new democratic regime, as well as to develop a stake in their own survival.

The transition experiences of Latin American and southern European countries, however, later inspired a reevaluation of elites' involvement in democratization. Scholars drew from Barrington Moore's (1966) claim that failing to rid the social and political order of traditional elites would not bode well for democratization. Hagopian (1996) concludes that where "traditional elites [continue to] dominate the political arena through blunt coercion exercised in the private sphere, through state institutions, through more subtle mechanisms, especially the dispensation of state patronage . . . [and] through highly personalized family-based, clientelistic networks" (64–68), the effectiveness and accountability of the new democratic governments can be severely undermined.[8]

Historico-structuralists Evelyne Huber, Dietrich Rueschemeyer, and John Stephens (1999) point to the balance of class power, state structures, and the international system as the crucial dimensions of politics in which authoritarian legacies persist. While they do not explicitly discuss authoritarian legacies, their analysis emphasizes such social structures and forces as clear hindrances to good democracies. Political scientist Marcus Kurtz (1999) argues in a similar vein. On the basis of a study of land tenure patterns, labor, capital, and political associationalism in the Chilean countryside from the 1960s to the late 1990s, Kurtz claims that successful neoliberalism and democratic consolidation in Chile have come at the expense of active authoritarian, exclusionary legacies in the rural areas. In essence, Kurtz argues that the authoritarian regime resurrected and the post-transition regime sustains a well-documented authoritarian legacy of social and political domination (Loveman 1976; Kaufman 1972). In his study of economic reforms in Latin America, Hector Schamis (1999) argues that the Argentine military's liberalization program created a new set of conditions to compete for the distribution of fiscal resources and finance capital. The program produced powerful, concentrated economic groups who continue to be the winners in contemporary reform projects.

One of the most oft-cited groups likely to pose a problem to democracy is the *military,* due to their record (especially in Latin America) of overthrowing democratic regimes either to establish an oligarchic government or to assume the executive to achieve their own political and societal objectives. Far from being a neutral *poder moderador,* the military constitutes a specialized bureaucracy with its own interests, often inimical to democracy. According to some, the military's identification with and ownership of the state in Latin America are rooted in "birth defects" dating as far back as the Spanish colonial period (see, e.g., Loveman 1993). According to others, the military's lack of sympathy for democracy has been due to the peculiar type of "professionalization" of the military, rooted in anticommunist doctrine and disdainful of "corrupt" civilian politicians' behavior as antithetical to the national interest and to their own interests as institution (Stepan 1971).

In transitions from authoritarian rule, the military often manage to retain, in Alfred Stepan's (1988) terminology, important prerogatives, from representation in government or legislative bodies without being elected, to automatic funding mechanisms, to virtual immunity from civilian justice.[9] The military may also continue to participate, and even control, agencies and organizations whose task is the surveillance of civil society. Finally, the military also may retain a strong influence on democratic politics either by supporting right-wing parties (Payne 2000) or by intervening in the political debate with veiled—and not-so-veiled—threats that encourage acquiescence to their demands.

In this volume, the chapters by Agüero (chapter 6) and Pereira and Ungar (chapter 7) explore the military and the police as "carriers" of authoritarian legacies. Agüero cautions that while the military may represent a logical authoritarian legacy carrier, it is clearly contingent upon institutional and practiced spaces dependent upon nonmilitary actors and institutions. Like Agüero, Pereira and Ungar argue that the status of the police and security forces is closely linked to the civilian side of the evolution of civil-military relations in the Southern Cone and Brazil. Pereira and Ungar find that the continuing authoritarian, violent practices and the institutional shelters for such practices are deeply rooted in the legacies of authoritarian states rather than the immediate predecessor authoritarian regimes per se.

Legacies as Cultural Practices, Lived Experience, and Psychological Dispositions

Culturalist approaches—including works from such disciplines as political science, anthropology, social psychology, and sociology—are essentially concerned with what have been termed the subjective dimensions of politics. Culturalist-oriented scholars locate authoritarian legacies in such dimensions as the range and divergence of everyday political-cultural practices, dispositions, and spaces within societies;[10] questions of power as exercised discursively, symbolically, and practically;[11] and the webs of collective memories,[12] none of which are necessarily codified or embodied in rigidly formal structures. Scholars who incorporate culturalist approaches into their analyses tend to concur on two basic points: (1) that authoritarian regimes exercise a powerful influence on a society's cultures, traditions, norms, and memories; and (2) that such influence is likely to survive long after the installation of a formal democracy.

Latin American postmodernist scholars have explored the "hybridity" of Latin American states and societies that mesh both democratic and decisively authoritarian cultural forms and practices within quite "modern" institutions and spaces (García Canclini 1990). Postmodernists resist what they perceive as a metanarrative emanating from democratization theorists that implies that democratizing regimes can (and should) be moving uniformly toward a modernizing, secularizing, technically rationalizing set of political institutions.[13] In their assessments of the "microphysics" of power, postmodern Latin Americanists argue that the legacies of authoritarian rule themselves contain quite "renewable modern logics of terrorism and fear" that have proved quite compatible with neoliberal modernization programs in the region (Brunner 1995, 42).

In a different vein, southern European and Latin Americanist social scientists have actively resuscitated studies of *citizenship*—that is, of the microfoundations of democratic regimes. Here, the focus is on citizens' awareness of both their rights and their duties and on their interpretations of their roles vis-à-vis other citizens and their democratic institutions. This literature stems, to a great extent, from other approaches' failure to take democracy's microfoundations seriously or to realize that persistent informal authoritarian institutions, networks, and practices can make it very difficult for democratic citizenship to emerge. In the context of democratization, citizenship identities must be re-created, lest the new formal democracies remain exactly that—formal. This is the conceptual focus of chapter 8 of this volume, by Consuelo Cruz, who, paraphrasing Barrington Moore, writes, "No citizens, no true democracy."

A number of works from southern Europe and the Southern Cone have focused on the effects of authoritarianism on "the everyday," or *lo cotidiano*. These are pioneering efforts to reveal how the repression and shutting down of the public sphere over an extended period inevitably takes its toll on citizens' activities and on the understandings or exercises of citizen rights after the public space has been renewed (Jelín et. al. 1996). Lechner (1988, 1992) claims that the most enduring legacies of the Southern Cone dictatorships are the insecurities and fears generated by the erosion of historic collective identities. Such insecurities and fears produce a constant societal demand for political predictability, political certainty, and political order—all of which a democracy may not be in the best position to ensure. Latin American authoritarian regimes' physical emphasis on political order and stability, as well as their discursive drives to emphasize the preauthoritarian periods as chaotic and unstable, resulted in the weakening of people's identities as politically engaged actors—that is, as "citizens" (Lechner 1988). In this volume, drawing from both survey research and intensive studies of political attitudes and perceptions, Hite and Morlino (chapter 2) suggest that for the Southern Cone, fear and alienation are marked legacies of authoritarian rule. In the case of Italy, Hite and Morlino argue that even after democracy was consolidated, Italians continued to be socialized into an idea of politics as bequeathed from above, as passively accepted.

A second and closely related approach in this vein is the burgeoning literature on *trust*. Tyler (1998), among others, argues that "democratic governments need trust of one form or another. . . . There must be some basis for long-term commitments to government and government officials, to facilitate cooperative solutions to collective action problems" (286–87). In turn, without trust, democracy suffers because social interaction becomes an impossible game, and transaction costs are much higher than they would otherwise be (see, among others, Putnam 1993; Gambetta 1993). When one has experienced fear of being spied upon by neighbors, friends, and even family or taken away by a faceless persecuting state to be tortured and—in many cases—murdered, trust in government and one's fellow citizens is harder to come by. Authoritarian legacies, therefore, may effectively prevent new "formal" democratic regimes from rebuilding the necessary *trust* among citizens that is required for democracy to operate properly.

Bridging the realms of political science and psychology, *political learning* approaches also shed light on how authoritarian legacies influence post-authoritarian regimes. This literature focuses on how and why political experience may influence subsequent elite political behavior. In particular, political learning scholars seek explanations of thinking and action that link contextual and institutional variables at the macro level to political behavior at the micro level (McCoy 2000; Aguilar 1996; Bermeo 1992; Higley and Gunther 1992). Nancy Bermeo (1992) defines political learning as a "process of re-evaluation of the nature of political regimes, enemies, goals, and behavior, and the consequential formulation of a changed conception of political goals or measures" (274). On the one hand, as a result of learning, each group may be more amenable to granting greater concessions to their former political adversaries. On the other hand, "learning" may result in a possibly less-than-enthusiastic outlook on democracy. In other words, during the transition political actors may choose democracy as the lesser of two evils and not as their valuative first option. There may be serious limits regarding the extent to which political learning is a "collective" phenomenon. "Lesson drawing" is a contested political process, and there is little assurance (or evidence in our cases) that the lesson drawn will be shared across political actors or will be the "right" one.

In other realms of social and political psychology, authors have argued that authoritarianism activates the fear of death and—associated with it— the fear that things might again be as in the past (see, e.g., Lira 1996, 46–48). This feeling often becomes a psychological burden that creates a real obstacle to policy making, in the sense of making political actors more cautious than they would otherwise be or drastically limiting their array of options (Hite 2000). This represents a distinct set of arguments from those on political learning that imply learning is a positive process. Here the conceptual emphasis is on the silences and ongoing fears based on past experiences rather than on a fundamental revaluation of political beliefs and behavior.

Complementing social psychology perspectives is a vast and growing literature on *social or collective memories. Social memories* here refers to the intersubjective collective representations of (and claims about) the past and the impact of these on the present and future. Such memories are held to be distinct from individual memories but, at the same time, constitutive of the latter. They are, however, neither immutable nor immune from agency but rather amenable to reshaping by social groups (Passerini 1987; Aguilar 2001), often in response to memory entrepreneurship by members of the elite to serve their contingent goals (Hite 1998). In other words, the past is "neither totally precarious nor immutable, but a stable image upon which new elements are intermittently superimposed" (Schwartz 1991, 234).

Memory approaches to authoritarian legacies in postauthoritarian democracies remind us that democratization is not exclusively about the future (i.e., rewriting the rules of the political game, reorganizing rights and obligations, and reshaping relations between state and society). Democratization is *also* in relation to the past, including the ways memories of past traumatic events become reshaped or "reinvented" to serve the process (see Aguilar 1996, 21; Hobsbawm and Ranger 1983). Social memories associated with authoritarian regimes, however, tend to be "sticky"—difficult to eliminate—and often bequeath tangible collective traumas to society (Pennebaker, Paez, and Rimé 1997). Moreover, in countries where irreconcilable versions of the past continue to wage bitter war against each other, a part of society may continue to distrust the new regime, even if it is a democratic one. In some societies, such irreconcilable versions of the past engender "active" silences (Lechner and Guell 1999; Wilde 1999). Similarly, several scholars have engaged the language of a "politics of forgetting" to emphasize silence as performed rather than tacit (Bergero and Reati 1997; Jelín 1998). For the Chilean case, Elizabeth Lira and Brian Loveman (1999) have traced historical patterns of official pardons as a type of politics of forgetting in the wake of authoritarian injustices from the nineteenth century to the present.

The chapters in this volume by Paola Cesarini on Italy and Argentina (chapter 4) and by Paloma Aguilar and Katherine Hite on Spain and Chile (chapter 5) focus on the ways transitional governments have addressed (or failed to address) authoritarian regime atrocities and the memories of such atrocities through transitional justice policies. Cesarini argues that transition periods are crucial moments for constituting "refounding myths" regarding the past and the nation. Such myths can contribute to revitalizing or encouraging public trust in democratic institutions, thereby chipping away at authoritarian legacies. Aguilar and Hite argue that in the absence of domestic (and, in the Spanish case, international) pressures to do otherwise, southern European and Southern Cone political elites have preferred to engage in a politics of forgetting or pardoning rather than a politics of accountability and justice. The authors reveal little consensus regarding either transitional justice policies or how the past should be remembered in the Chilean case, while for Spain transitional justice is simply not a theme for debate, and the dominant sense of the past is "We were all guilty." While consensus is often most divided along ideological lines, for the Spanish case it is also a regionally divided memory between Basque nationalists and much of the rest of Spain. These authors claim that in societies that fail to confront the past adequately, ample room is left for "memory entrepreneurs" to reignite unresolved battles over memory for particularistic purposes. Authoritarian legacies stand a better chance of being eliminated if democratic reforms and democrats themselves seek to contribute to a public sphere that engages in collective debates over memories. This may require adding to formal reforms highly symbolic and discursive dimensions that highlight the need for a true break with the past and renewed trust between citizens and the state.

Comparativist political scientists have tended to shy away from culturalist approaches, as they argue that the variables used in such approaches tend to be hard to measure, quantify, and operationalize. But there are other reasons for comparativists' resistance. In his defense of pursuing the study of parliamentarism versus presidentialism for understanding the challenges to democratization, for example, Juan Linz argued that at least institutions "are about the only variable that can be modified in the short run" (quoted in Ames 1999, 223). Within our own sympathetic working group on authoritarian legacies, we found it quite difficult to work across disciplines, and even subdisciplines, to marry culturalist approaches with more institutionalist or sociological ones. Nevertheless, several of the chapters of this volume pair authors accustomed to working in approaches fairly distinct from one another, as well as authors with distinct country and regional areas of expertise. The result is a promising attempt to convince fellow comparativists of the utility of conceptualizing authoritarian legacies and their influences on democratization and reform in ways heretofore little explored.

Following this chapter, Katherine Hite and Leonardo Morlino's "Problematizing the Links between Authoritarian Legacies and 'Good' Democracy" (chapter 2) deepens our analysis of legacies by forwarding a set of arguments regarding the effects of authoritarian regime "innovation," duration, and mode of transition on democratizing institutions, actors, and norms. The chapter conducts a systematic comparative analysis of these relationships for Italy, Spain, Portugal, Argentina, Brazil, Chile, and Uruguay.

In "Authoritarian Legacies and Market Reforms in Latin America" (chapter 3), Frances Hagopian carefully problematizes the links between authoritarian legacies and economic reforms in Argentina, Brazil, Chile, and Uruguay. She examines legacies as both institutional and actor-centric, and she analyzes their influences on a range of economic reforms from the authoritarian through the postauthoritarian periods.

Chapter 4 by Paola Cesarini, and chapter 5, by Paloma Aguilar and Katherine Hite, examine the ways transitional governments address legacies of human rights atrocities committed under fascist/authoritarian rule for Italy and Argentina (Cesarini) and Spain and Chile (Aguilar and Hite). The authors focus on both the policy-making and the more discursive-symbolic dimensions of traumatic collective memories, and they speculate on these dimensions for quality-of-democracy issues.

Felipe Agüero's "Authoritarian Legacies: The Military's Role" (chapter 6) explores the ways in which the military as institution can be considered a "carrier" of authoritarian legacies in the Southern Cone, Brazil, and southern Europe, while chapter 7, "The Persistence of the *Mano Dura:* Authoritarian Legacies and Policing in Brazil and the Southern Cone," by Anthony Pereira and Mark Ungar, traces and analyzes the deeply entrenched authoritarian legacies within the "law enforcement" agencies of the police and security forces of Argentina, Brazil, Chile, and Uruguay. The chapters assert that authoritarian legacies within the security forces must be understood in relation to both civilian policy-making patterns and choices and public perceptions of criminality and justice. Chapter 8, "Latin American Citizenship: Civic Microfoundations in Historical Perspective," by Consuelo Cruz, is a broad historical discussion of the effects of distorted liberalism and authoritarian legacies on the microfoundations of democracy, particularly the question of citizenship in Latin America.

Cesarini and Hite's conclusion (chapter 9) is a call for a more comprehensive understanding of legacies in postauthoritarian regimes. Each of the contributions urges a long view of authoritarian legacies, in terms of both their historical reach and their impact on even the most consolidated of democratic regimes. The volume advances a rich and systematic examination of authoritarian legacies and their influences on the quality of democracy and the scope of reform.

NOTES

1. The difference here is often characterized as that between "minimalist" and "maximalist" definitions of democracy. "Procedural" democracy emphasizes rules governing representation, including free and fair elections and the separation of powers, while "substantive" democracy emphasizes the full realization of citizenship in the social and economic as well as political realms. For a useful discussion of such differences, see Huber, Reuschemeyer, and Stephens (1997).

2. We recognize that the term *consolidation* is a heavily contested concept, paralleling debates regarding "minimalist" and "maximalist" definitions of democracy. For a review of democratic consolidation debates, see Schedler (1998).

3. Manuel Antonio Garretón (1995) coined the term *authoritarian enclaves* for the Chilean case with his explicit reference to the 1980 Chilean constitution. See also Siavelis (2000).

4. For leading debates and analyses of presidentialism in Latin America, see Mainwaring and Shugart (1997); for these and other debates incorporating a range of regions, see Diamond and Plattner (1993). The Mainwaring and Shugart volume also addresses the question of political party systems; see also Mainwaring and Scully (1995) and Coppedge (1994). For important texts on political institutions in southern Europe, see Morlino (1998); and in western Europe more broadly, see Colomer (1996); for an important institutionalist analysis of challenges to democratic transition and consolidation in southern Europe, South America, and postcommunist Europe, see Linz and Stepan (1996).

5. Interestingly enough, in Mainwaring and Shugart (1997), Julio Faundez's chapter on democratic Chile from 1932 to 1970 points to social-structural variables, including urgent socioeconomic crises from the 1930s to the 1970s, rather than formal institutional variables, as the key to democratic breakdown in Chile. While his is an analysis of democratic rather than authoritarian legacies, it is nonetheless a useful historical check on "presentist" institutionalist debates (Faundez 1997).

6. Herz's list includes problems of authoritarian monarchs, elites, judiciaries, and militaries; problems of lower-level bureaucrats and other collaborators of the regime (i.e., problem of purges); problems of constitution writing; problems of social and economic restructuring; and problems related to nonregime authoritarian structures such as churches and educational institutions.

7. In all fairness, in his conclusion to the volume Herz (1982) does mention in passing the problems of "traditional authoritarianism" and of the "subject culture" associated with it (284–85) and the issue of establishing "positive consensual democratic value systems" (287).

8. In a different vein, Edward Gibson (1996) analyzes the evolution of similarly historic supporters of authoritarianism into conservative but democratic actors in the postauthoritarian period. While he does not make this claim for Brazil, he makes it for Argentina and Chile, two countries central to our study.

9. There is a healthy set of debates on the status of the military in democratizing societies in Latin America. See, among others, Hunter (1997), Norden (1996), Stepan (1988), and, of course, Felipe Agüero in chapter 6 of this volume.

10. We are using the term *culturalist* very broadly, to include more traditional comparativist political science studies of political culture that focus on citizens' attitudes and perspectives toward politics, as well as contemporary debates in anthropology regarding the relationships among culture, history, and power.

11. Beginning in the 1980s, what is now a vast range of studies of Latin America in this vein includes works influenced primarily by such thinkers as Antonio Gramsci, Michel Foucault, and Jürgen Habermas. For a useful synthesis of the evolution of understandings of power and culture, see Dirks, Eley, and Ortner (1994).

12. For ambitious literature reviews on social and collective memory studies, see Olick and Robbins (1998) and Carr (1986).

13. For a very useful reference on postmodernism in Latin America, see Beverley, Oviedo, and Aronna (1995), particularly Beverley and Oviedo's introduction and the chapters by José Joaquín Brunner, Néstor García Canclini, Norbert Lechner, and Nelly Richards.

REFERENCES

Agüero, Felipe. 1998. "Conflicting Assessments of Democratization: Exploring the Fault Lines." In Felipe Agüero and Jeffrey Stark, eds., *Fault Lines of Democracy in Post-Transition Latin America* (pp. 1–20). Coral Gables, Fla.: North-South Center Press.

Agüero, Felipe, and Jeffrey Stark, eds. 1998. *Fault Lines of Democracy in Post-Transition Latin America.* Coral Gables, Fla.: North-South Center Press.

Aguilar, Paloma. 1996. *La memoria histórica de la guerra civil española (1936–39): Un proceso de aprendizaje político.* Madrid: Alianza Editorial.

———. 2001. "Justicia, política, y memoria: Los legados del Franquismo en la transición española." Estudio/Working Paper 2001/163, Instituto Juan March de Estudios e Investigaciones, Madrid.

Ames, Barry. 1987. *Political Survival: Politicians and Public Policy in Latin America.* Berkeley: University of California Press.

———. 1999. "Approaches to the Study of Institutions in Latin American Politics." *Latin American Research Review* 34, no. 1: 221–36.

Bergero, Adriana J., and Fernando Reati, eds. 1997. *Memoria colectiva y políticas de olvido: Argentina y Uruguay, 1970–1990.* Buenos Aires: Beatriz Viterbo Editora.

Bermeo, Nancy. 1992. "Democracy and the Lessons of Dictatorship." *Comparative Politics* 24, no. 3: 273–91.

Beverley, John, José Oviedo, and Michael Aronna, eds. 1995. *The Postmodernism Debate in Latin America.* Durham, N.C.: Duke University Press.

Borón, Atilio. 1998. "Faulty Democracies? A Reflection on the Capitalist 'Fault Lines' in Latin America." In Felipe Agüero and Jeffery Stark, eds., *Fault Lines of Democracy in Post-Transition Latin America.* Coral Gables, Fla: North-South Center Press.

Brunner, José Joaquín. 1995. "Notes on Modernity and Postmodernity in Latin American Culture." In John Beverley, José Oviedo, and Michael Aronna, eds., *The Postmodernism Debate in Latin America* (pp. 34–54). Durham, N.C.: Duke University Press.

Carr, David. 1986. *Time, Narrative and History.* Bloomington: Indiana University Press.

Casper, Gretchen. 1995. *Fragile Democracies: The Legacies of Authoritarian Rule.* Pittsburgh, Pa.: University of Pittsburgh Press.

Colarizi, Simona, and Leonardo Morlino. 1998. "Italy after Fascism: An Overview of the Fascist Legacy." In Stein Ugelvik Larsen, ed., *Modern Europe after Fascism, 1943–1980s* (pp. 457–75). New York: Columbia University Press.

Colomer, Josep, ed. 1996. *Political Institutions in Europe.* New York: Routledge.

Coppedge, Michael. 1994. *Strong Parties and Lame Ducks: Presidential Partyarchy and Factionalism in Venezuela.* Stanford, Calif.: Stanford University Press.

Diamond, Larry, and Marc F. Plattner, eds. 1993. *The Global Resurgence of Democracy.* Baltimore, Md.: Johns Hopkins University Press.

Dirks, Nicholas, Geoff Eley, and Sherry Ortner, eds. 1996. *Culture/Power/History: A Reader in Contemporary Social Theory.* Princeton, N.J.: Princeton University Press.

Elster, Jon, Claus Offe, and Ulrich K. Preuss. 1998. *Institutional Design in Post-Communist Societies: Rebuilding the Ship at Sea.* New York: Cambridge University Press.

Faundez, Julio. 1997. "In Defense of Presidentialism: The Case of Chile, 1932–70." In Scott Mainwaring and Matthew Soberg Shugart, eds., *Presidentialism and Democracy in Latin America.* New York: Cambridge University Press.

Gambetta, Diego. 1993. *The Sicilian Mafia: The Business of Private Protection.* Cambridge, Mass.: Harvard University Press.

García Canclini, Néstor. 1990. *Culturas híbridas: Estrategias para entrar y salir de la modernidad.* Mexico, D.F.: Grijalbo.

Garretón, Manuel Antonio. 1995. "Redemocratization in Chile." *Journal of Democracy* 6, no. 1:146–58.

Geddes, Barbara. 1994. *Politician's Dilemma: Building State Capacity in Latin America.* Berkeley: University of California Press.

Gibson, Edward L. 1996. "Conservative Party Politics in Latin America: Patterns of Electoral Mobilization in the 1980s and 1990s." In Jorge I. Domínguez and

Abraham F. Lowenthal, eds., *Constructing Democratic Governance: Latin America and the Caribbean in the 1990s—Themes and Issues.* Baltimore, Md.: Johns Hopkins University Press.

Hagopian, Frances. 1996. "Traditional Power Structures and Democratic Governance in Latin America." In Jorge I. Domínguez and Abraham F. Lowenthal, eds., *Constructing Democratic Governance: Latin America and the Caribbean in the 1990s—Themes and Issues.* Baltimore, Md.: Johns Hopkins University Press.

Hall, Peter, and Rosemary Taylor. 1996. "Political Science and the Three New Institutionalisms." *Political Studies* 44:936–57.

Hansis, Randall. 1997. *The Latin Americans: Understanding Their Legacy.* Boston: McGraw-Hill.

Herz, John, ed. 1982. *From Dictatorship to Democracy: Coping with the Legacies of Authoritarianism and Totalitarianism.* Westport, Conn.: Greenwood Press.

Higley, John, and Richard Gunther, eds. 1992. *Elites and Democratic Consolidation in Latin America and Southern Europe.* New York: Cambridge University Press.

Hite, Katherine. 1998. "The Status of Memory in Political Science" Paper presented as Social Science Research Council Workshop, "Collective Memory of Repression in the Southern Cone in the Context of Democratization Processes," 16–17 November, Montevideo, Uruguay.

———. 2000. *When the Romance Ended: Leaders of the Chilean Left, 1968–1998.* New York: Columbia University Press.

Hobsbawm, Eric, and T. Ranger, eds. 1983. *The Invention of Tradition.* New York: Cambridge University Press.

Holston, James, and Teresa Caldeira. 1998. "Democracy, Law, and Violence: Disjunctions of Brazilian Citizenship." In Felipe Agüero and Jeffrey Stark, eds., *Fault Lines of Democracy in Post-Transition Latin America.* Coral Gables, Fla.: North-South Center Press.

Huber, Evelyne, Dietrich Rueschemeyer, and John D. Stephens. 1997. "The Paradoxes of Contemporary Democracy: Formal, Participatory, and Social Dimensions." *Comparative Politics* 30 (April): 323–41.

Hunter, Wendy. 1997. *Eroding Military Influence in Brazil: Politicians against Soldiers.* Chapel Hill, N.C.: University of North Carolina Press.

Jelín, Elizabeth. 1998. "The Minefields of Memory." *NACLA Newsletter* 32, no. 2: 23–29.

Jelín, Elizabeth, Laura Gingold, Susana G. Kaufman, Marcelo Leiras, Silvia Rabich de Galperín, and Lucas Rabinich. 1996. *Vida cotidiana y control institucional en la Argentina de los '90.* Buenos Aires: Nuevohacer.

Kaufman, Robert. 1972. *The Politics of Land Reform in Chile.* New York: Cambridge University Press.

——— 1986. "Liberalization and Democratization in South America: Perspectives from the 1970s." In Guillermo O'Donnell, Philippe C. Schmitter, and Laurence Whitehead, eds., *Transitions from Authoritarian Rule: Comparative Perspectives.* Baltimore, Md.: Johns Hopkins University Press.

Kitschelt, Herbert, Peter Lange, Gary Marks, and John D. Stephens, eds. 1999. *Continuity and Change in Contemporary Capitalism*. New York: Cambridge University Press.

Kurtz, Marcus. 1999. "Free Markets and Democratic Consolidation in Chile: The National Politics of Rural Transformation." *Politics and Society* 27, no. 2:275–301.

Lechner, Norbert. 1988. *Los patios interiores de la democracia: Subjetividad y política*. Santiago: Facultad Latinoamericana de Ciencias Sociales.

———. 1992. "Some People Die of Fear: Fear as a Political Problem." In Juan Corradi, Patricia Weiss Fagen, and Manuel Antonio Garretón, eds., *Fear at the Edge: State Terror and Resistance in Latin America*. Berkeley: University of California Press.

Lechner, Norbert, and Pedro Guell. 1999. "Construcción social de las memorias en la transición chilena." In Ampara Menéndez-Carrión and Alfredo Joignant, eds., *La caja de Pandora: El retorno de la transición chilena*. Santiago: Planeta/Ariel.

Linz, Juan, and Alfred Stepan. 1996. *Problems of Democratic Transition and Consolidation: Southern Europe, South America, and Post-Communist Europe*. Baltimore, Md.: Johns Hopkins University Press.

Lira, Elizabeth. 1996. "Y a los ojos que se me asomara la vida que ya viví." In Alejandro González, Andrés Domínguez, Miguel Kottow, Eduardo Llanas, Hernán Montealegre, Carolina Rivas, and José Rodriguez eds., *IV Concurso Nacional de Ensaya: Por una cultura de respeto a los drrechos humanos* (29–68). Santiago: Corporación Nacional de Reparación y Reconciliación.

Lira, Elizabeth, and Brian Loveman. 1999. *Las suaves cenizas del olvido*. Santiago: LOM Editores.

Loveman, Brian. 1976. *Chile: The Legacy of Hispanic Capitalism*. New York: Oxford University Press.

———. 1993. *The Constitution of Tyranny: Regimes of Exception in Spanish America*. Pittsburgh, Pa.: University of Pittsburgh Press.

Mainwaring, Scott, and Timothy Scully, eds. 1995. *Building Democratic Institutions: Party Systems in Latin America*. Stanford, Calif.: Stanford University Press.

Mainwaring, Scott, and Matthew Soberg Shugart, eds. 1997. *Presidentialism and Democracy in Latin America*. New York: Cambridge University Press.

McCoy, Jennifer, ed. 2000. *Political Learning and Redemocratization in Latin America: Do Politicians Learn from Political Crises?* Coral Gables, Fla.: North-South Center Press.

Moore, Barrington. 1966. *Social Origins of Dictatorship and Democracy: Lord and Peasant in the Making of the Modern World*. New York: Beacon Press.

Morlino, Leonardo. 1998. *Democracy between Consolidation and Crisis*. New York: Oxford University Press.

Norden, Deborah. 1996. *Military Rebellion: Between Coups and Consolidation in Argentina*. Lincoln: University of Nebraska Press.

O'Donnell, Guillermo, and Philippe Schmitter. 1986. *Transitions from Authoritarian Rule: Tentative Conclusions about Uncertain Democracies*. Baltimore, Md.: Johns Hopkins University Press.

Olick, Jeffrey K., and Joyce Robbins. 1998. "Social Memory Studies: From 'Collective Memory' to the Historical Sociology of Mnemonic Practices." *Annual Review of Sociology* 24:105–40.

Passerini, Luisa. 1987. *Fascism in Popular Memory*. New York: Cambridge University Press.

Pastor, Manuel, and Carol Wise. 1999. *The Post-NAFTA Political Economy: Mexico and the Western Hemisphere*. University Park: Pennsylvania State University Press.

Payne, Leigh. 2000. *Uncivil Movements: The Armed Right Wing and Democracy in Latin America*. Baltimore, Md.: Johns Hopkins University Press.

Pennebaker, James, Dario Paez, and Bernard Rimé. 1997. *Collective Memory of Political Events*. Mahwah, N.J.: Lawrence Erlbaum.

Putnam, Robert. 1993. *Making Democracy Work: Civic Traditions in Modern Italy*. Princeton, N.J.: Princeton University Press.

Rueschemeyer, Dietrich, Eleanor Stephens, and John D. Stephens. 1992. *Capitalist Development and Democracy*. Chicago: University of Chicago Press.

Schamis, Hector. 1999. "Distributional Coalitions and the Politics of Economic Reform in Latin America." *World Politics* 51, no. 2: 236–68.

Schedler, Andreas. 1998. "What Is Democratic Consolidation?" *Journal of Democracy* 9, no. 2: 91–107.

Schwartz, Barry. 1991. "Social Change and Collective Memory: The Democratization of George Washington." *American Sociological Review* 56 (April): 221–36.

Siavelis, Peter. 2000. *The President and Congress in Postauthoritarian Chile: Institutional Constraints to Democratic Consolidation*. University Park: Pennsylvania State University Press.

Stark, David. 1992. "From System Identity to Organizational Diversity: Analyzing Social Change in Eastern Europe." *Contemporary Sociology* (Symposium: The Great Transformation? Social Change in Eastern Europe) 21, no. 3: 299–304.

Stepan, Alfred. 1971. *The Military in Politics: Changing Patterns in Brazil*. Princeton, N.J.: Princeton University Press.

———. 1988. *Rethinking Military Politics: Brazil and the Southern Cone*. Princeton, N.J.: Princeton University Press.

Thelen, Kathleen. 1999. "Historical Institutionalism in Comparative Politics." *Annual Review of Political Science* 2:369–404.

Tyler, Tom. 1998. "Trust and Democratic Governance." In Valerie Braithwaite and Margaret Levi, eds., *Trust and Governance*. New York: Russell Sage Foundation.

Varas, Augusto. 1998. "Democratization in Latin America: A Citizen Responsibility." In Felipe Agüero and Jeffrey Stark, eds., *Fault Lines of Democracy in Post-Transition Latin America*. Coral Gables, Fla.: North-South Center Press.

Wilde, Alexander. 1999. "Irruptions of Memory: Expressive Politics in Chile's Transition to Democracy." *Journal of Latin American Studies* 31:473–500.

2

Problematizing the Links between Authoritarian Legacies and "Good" Democracy

KATHERINE HITE *&* LEONARDO MORLINO

This chapter joins efforts to understand the complex forces that influence the quality of democracy in postauthoritarian regimes in southern Europe and the Southern Cone and Brazil. Crucial to this understanding are the authoritarian legacies that affect the interplay among political institutions, social and political identities, and interests. We argue that the influences of authoritarian legacies on the quality of democracy can be assessed by analyzing three variables: (1) the durability of the previous authoritarian regime; (2) the institutional innovation of that regime; and (3) the mode of transition from authoritarianism. Simply stated, the more durable and institutionally innovative the previous authoritarian regime, the greater the potential influence of authoritarian legacies. The more privileged the authoritarian incumbents in the mode of transition from authoritarian rule, the greater the potential influence of authoritarian legacies.

In the first part of our chapter, we define what we mean by a "good" democracy, discuss salient authoritarian legacies, and suggest theoretical links between such legacies and hindrances to good democracy. We then analyze specific cases from southern Europe and the Southern Cone and Brazil to illustrate the kinds of legacies that constrain good democracy. Finally, we compare the cases, highlighting the most important legacies and the possible processes by which authoritarian legacies fade away in the democracies under study.

Defining a "Good" Democracy

Over the past several years there has been a good deal of debate within the democratization literature regarding how to conceptualize and temporalize democratization processes, from how best to define and demarcate transitions from authoritarian rule (for a synopsis, see Hartlyn 1998) to whether and when democracies are deemed consolidated (Linz and Stepan 1996; Schedler 1998; Morlino 1998a). Debates over these conceptualizations often rest on how scholars are relating means to ends, how democracy as an "end" is defined, and, therefore, how close, or "complete," or flawed a democratic regime is and why. Democratization processes have produced ambiguous regimes, where the presence of democratic rules, such as elections and multiparty systems, is not accompanied by the praxis of democracy. Different concepts have been developed to attempt to grasp these ambiguities, such as the notions of delegative democracy (O'Donnell 1994), electoral democracy (Diamond 1999), and defective democracy (Merkl 1999).

A "good democracy" is a stable, consolidated democracy with a high level of decisional efficacy and administrative efficiency regarding policy implementation. A good democracy is both politically responsive and accountable. It might include highly autonomous local or regional institutions. A good democracy is not a minimal democracy; rather, it is a regime that provides the best political opportunities for the implementation of democratic values, such as freedom and equality.

Following T. H. Marshall's (1950) classic conceptualization, we focus on democracy in terms of the extent to which civil, political, and social rights are implemented. More precisely, building on research developed regarding the quality of democracy in Great Britain (Weir and Beetham 1999) and Italy (Della Porta and Morlino 2001), Table 2.1 summarizes the main dimensions and the related questions that are essential to assessing a good democracy.

Salient Authoritarian Legacies

Echoing the definition advanced by Cesarini and Hite in chapter 1 of this volume, we define authoritarian legacies as all behavioral patterns, rules, relationships, social and political situations, norms, procedures, and institutions either introduced or patently strengthened by the immediately preceding authoritarian regime. Authoritarian legacies influence a broad range of political, economic, and social institutions (see, in this volume, Aguilar and Hite,

TABLE 2.1   Dimensions and Issues of a "Good" Democracy

I.   Citizenship, Law, and Rights
1.   Nationhood and citizenship: Is government accountable to the people and their representatives?
2.   The rule of law: Are state and society consistently subject to the law?
3.   Civil and political rights: Are civil and political rights equally guaranteed for all?
4.   Economic and social rights: Are economic and social rights equally guaranteed for all?

II.   Representative and Accountable Government
5.   Free and fair elections: Do elections give the people control over governments and their policies?
6.   Democratic role of political parties: Does the party system assist the working of democracy?
7.   Government effectiveness and accountability: Is government accountable to the people and their representatives?
8.   Civilian control of the military and police: Are the military and police forces under civilian control?
9.   Minimizing corruption: Are public officials free from corruption?
10.   The media and open government: Do the media operate in a way that sustains democratic values?

III.   Participation and Government Responsiveness
11.   Political participation: Is there full citizen participation in public life?
12.   Government responsiveness: Is government responsive to the concerns of its citizens?

IV.   Democracy beyond the State
13.   International dimensions of democracy: Are the country's external relations conducted in accordance with democratic norms?

Source: adapted from Beetham (1994, 25–43).

chapter 5; Cesarini, chapter 4; Hagopian, chapter 3; and Cruz, chapter 8). They are often most visible in the workings and behavior of the security forces (see, in this volume, Agüero, chapter 6, and Pereira and Ungar, chapter 7). They also include patterns of social domination, as well as highly unequal access to legal and political institutions. Authoritarian legacies may take the form of repressed memories that are latent but activated and manipulated by social and political actors at particular moments. They may be supported by specific actors, interests, or identities.

Several aspects of legacies must be highlighted. First, an authoritarian legacy carries three key internal dimensions that are strongly related but may be present only in part in the new democratic arrangement. They are (1) a set of beliefs, values, and attitudes; (2) one or more public institutions, agencies, or simple organizations; and (3) the subsequent behaviors emanating from the relationships between the first two dimensions. In processes of political change, these dimensions internal to legacies produce several scenarios: the beliefs, values, and attitudes may fade away or disappear under the democratic establishment while the institutions or organizations with their vested interests persist; the beliefs may persist in spite of the change of regime while the institutions disappear; or behavior may persist because of inertia when beliefs, institutions, or both have disappeared. Of course, the higher the number of dimensions that persist, the stronger the legacies, and the slower and more difficult the fading away.

Second, as suggested by the above definition, there are two fundamental kinds of legacies: (1) those that refer to values, institutions, and behavior introduced by the authoritarian regime; and (2) those that reinforce, strengthen, or entrench previous values and institutions. The latter tend to be well embedded in political culture and are usually stronger and more persistent. As authoritarian regimes are often the institutional transposition of conservative coalitions (Linz 1964), this second kind of legacy is also a more recurrent one. From an empirical perspective, to be considered an authoritarian legacy, the second, more historically embedded kind of legacy must have been clearly supported by the decisions and policies of the immediately preceding authoritarian regime.

Third, a legacy always implies continuity with a previously existing phenomenon. In broader terms, however, a legacy can also be a reaction to that phenomenon. For example, state-crafters of the democratizing regime clearly perceive the need to differentiate the new regime from the previous one, and this specific reaction, while discontinuous, is also a form of legacy. The Italian Constitutional Charter represents a case in point. As suggested by the debates in the committee that drafted it, several of the proposals and decisions represented attempts to make governmental institutions as different as possible from those of the fascist regime. One key outcome in this regard was the enormous role of Parliament vis-à-vis the cabinet, resulting in decisional inefficacy once the dominant role of the Christian Democratic Party (DC) ended in the mid-1950s. As suggested by Bermeo (1992) and Pridham (2000), such a reaction may be more appropriately labeled "political learning." While legacies chiefly involve continuities from the past, it is often difficult to analytically disentangle political learning processes from legacies.

We argue that authoritarian legacies are located both in formal-legal institutions and, perhaps just as importantly for our cases, in those interstices between civil society, political society and the state, including cultural practices and "lived" experiences (Dirks, Eley, and Ortner 1996). Thus, in addition to discussing authoritarian enclaves that continue to pervade formal political institutions, we will examine the influence of authoritarian legacies on both organized and unorganized interests or identities in political and civil society. We will encourage the exploration of authoritarian legacies in what Anthony Giddens (1984) terms the "structuration" or routinization of everyday life, as reflected through political consciousness, discourse, and practice.

We emphasize this latter exploration of authoritarian legacies and structuration because it may be here that authoritarian legacies are the deepest and most enduring, at the level of personal autonomy as a civil and political right and as a fundamental condition for democratic citizenship and the rule of law (O'Donnell 1999b; Held 1997; Giddens 1984). In the case of Brazil, for example, legacies of hierarchical, authoritarian patronage, exacerbated by the 1964–85 military regime, continue to plague democratic practice. In Argentina, the violent reach into citizens' lives and consciousness during the 1976–83 *Proceso* went far beyond previous military regimes, and twenty years later Argentina continues to wrestle politically with the consequences of the horrors. In Chile and Uruguay, the lengthy suspension of democratic politics and the reach of repression were historically unprecedented, contributing to a continuing political caution regarding the parameters for action and debate. Such sobriety was quite clear in the Spanish transition as well.

Remnants and memories of these regimes present an interesting set of paradoxes. On the one hand, memories of repressive patterns and action continue to inhibit political discourse, political participation, and individual notions of political efficacy, associability, and trust. On the other hand, for the cases of Brazil, Chile, Portugal, and Spain, memories of the military regimes also evoke associations with a desire for order, efficiency, and predictability, often in the economic as well as political arenas. In attitudinal surveys, citizens' support for democracy as always preferable to any other form of government continues to hover below 50 percent in Brazil and Chile. For the three southern European cases, partially positive attitudes toward the authoritarian pasts still fluctuate above 40 percent.

To varying degrees, authoritarian regimes have overseen the restructuring of labor-state or capital-labor-state relationships, as well as the restructuring of the political representation of labor. In Italy and Portugal, authoritarian regimes created corporatist arrangements. In the Southern Cone, however, military regimes weakened the social safety net for democratic regimes, and during the authoritarian period a demobilization of labor and popular sector groups occurred in Argentina, Chile, and Uruguay. In those countries, while organized labor has recently reawakened, it is still far weaker than in the pre-authoritarian periods. In contrast, Brazilian labor experienced a strong period of mobilization during the gradualist transition. On the whole, however, in the Southern Cone, restructuring of interest groups meant the weakening of the organized labor force and the strengthening of large commercial national and international political as well as social representation.

Authoritarian legacies as "silencers" are difficult to operationalize, yet they have permitted the continuation of a structural violence that weighs heavily (though unequally) on the polity and society (Habermas 1986). Preferences for stability and order over debate and dissent reflect a lingering fear of polarization under previous democratic regimes and of brutal state response to conflict. Moreover, as José María Maravall (1981) has suggested for the Spanish case, it is quite rational for citizens of the Southern Cone to turn away from politics in the wake of political abuses of power—from the chaotic, conflictive periods of the 1960s and 1970s to the frightening abuses of power under the dictatorships.

Theoretical Links between Authoritarian Legacies and Democracy

We cannot assume that every authoritarian legacy limits democratic expression. On the contrary, there are legacies such as that of efficiency or the building of an effective civil service that are positively related to a "good" democracy. Not every legacy impedes a good democracy. Thus our key question is: When do authoritarian legacies constrain or impede the best expressions of democracy?

We argue that the influence of authoritarian legacies on the quality of democracy depends upon three basic variables, or sites, for strategic action: (1) the durability of the previous authoritarian regime; (2) the innovation of that regime; and (3) the mode of transition from authoritarianism.

By *innovation* under authoritarianism, we mean the degree of transformation and institutionalization of authoritarian rules, patterns, relationships, and norms, often symbolized by a new constitution (Agüero 1998b); the establishment of new institutions; and the degree of strengthening or weakening of particular organized interests or identities (Hagopian 1995). The more institutionally innovative authoritarian regimes are those with totalitarian features, such as Italian fascism or the Chilean military regime. In this chapter, we will explore the range of authoritarian "exacerbations" and "breaks" with the past in terms of the relationships among the state, political parties and other organized political and social interests, and civil society.

By *mode of transition*, we mean the ways in which the transition from authoritarian rule privileged particular incumbents and/or challengers, altered (or left in place) authoritarian institutional rules and procedures, influenced political elite appeals to their constituencies (Munck and Leff 1997; Linz and Stepan 1996; Karl and Schmitter 1991), and/or were characterized by some degree of violence that made discontinuity more probable. Here we will highlight prerogatives for the military and other authoritarian incumbents, pact making, rules governing elections and political parties, and the roles and positioning of organized and unorganized civil society interests in the transition process. We argue that continuous or discontinuous modes of transition mediate whether and how authoritarian legacies endure.

By *durability*, we mean the span of time of the authoritarian regime. If a regime is innovative, then the span of time is less relevant. If, on the other hand, the regime is not innovative, then the regime must be in power for at least fifteen to twenty years—that is, for at least a generation—for timespan to be a salient dimension. While we do not examine this here, we are conscious of the importance of exploring transformations in the sites of traditional political socialization under authoritarian regimes, including family, church, and educational institutions, which become the primary referents for political socialization in the absence of a public sphere. We argue that the intensity of authoritarian legacies in the post-transition period depends in good part on the enduring shock and penetration of authoritarian rules, norms, and practices in the private sphere as well as the public sphere.

There are also important connections between innovation and the mode of transition from authoritarianism. If the transition is discontinuous, institutional innovation may be less salient, as the new political elite transforms the previous authoritarian institutions. If the transition is continuous, then authoritarian regime innovation is much more relevant, for path dependency may essentially be established.

Our task now becomes to relate the key variables of regime innovation, duration, and mode of transition to the quality of democracy in the post-transition period. We will focus on how such legacies have affected the new democratic institutions as well as the modes of political incorporation. We will primarily examine and analyze political parties, including internal party organization and the relationships between parties and interests (see Morlino 1998a). We will also explore a range of indicators regarding citizens' assessments of their democracies and specific political institutions, as well as their sense of efficacy and investment in their governments' decision-making processes regarding the economy and other key issues. Moreover, we will explore the state and reach of political discourse and of discursive practices as indicators of the parameters and constraints on a democratic public sphere (Arendt 1958). When possible, we will examine the links between contemporary political organization and action and authoritarian legacies, including strategies for ameliorating or working with the constraints that particular authoritarian legacies have represented.

One difficulty stems from including the exacerbation of historical patterns of egregious social domination as authoritarian legacies, for while we can recognize such patterns as far from democratic, this may be more appropriately framed as a classic question of social inequality and its relationship to political institutions and practices. For example, the contrast between the strong presence of authoritarian legacies in Brazil and their weaker presence in Uruguay forces us to ask whether the establishment of a politically responsive social welfare state in Uruguay in the early twentieth century has more explanatory power than authoritarian regime durability, regime innovation, or modes of transition. It raises a basic question regarding the relationship between the enduring presence of authoritarian legacies and structural inequality.

This suggests that we should focus on the ways in which the most notorious legacies for each case are present in the postauthoritarian regime politics. Such legacies may include but are not limited to historical patterns of social domination. We argue that authoritarian ideologies or mentalities (Linz 1964) and leaders' decisions mark the beginning of the creation of norms or formal rules and institutions that may continue in postauthoritarian settings and, therefore, that the persistence of authoritarian legacies in a succeeding regime is achieved by elites' managing and manipulation of those legacies.

Table 2.2 lists some of the main legacies that authoritarian regimes may transmit to democracies, focusing attention on the quality of the new regimes. We suggest rough categories of regime institutions and rules, elite actors, social groups, political culture, and the mass level. For each domain, we suggest legacies that constrain good democracies. For example, a statist authoritarian tradition is largely present in the new democracies of southern

TABLE 2.2   Authoritarian Legacies as Constraints to a "Good" Democracy

Dimension	Legacy
Regime institutions and norms	Authoritarian legal rules Poor or no rule of law Barely independent judiciary Large public sector of economy (not in Southern Cone)
Elite actors	High military prerogatives Poor or no efficiency of police Radical rightist groups No party elite accountability
Social groups/ institutions	Gleichschaltung[a]
Culture and mass level	Statism (not in the Southern Cone) Passivity/conformism/cynicism Fear/alienation from politics Nondemocratic attitudes Rightist radical party/ies

[a] This term is intended to refer to the extreme leveling of cultural/social differences, a policy carried out by the Nazi regime.

Europe (Morlino 1998a), resulting in low political interest and participation. Poor or no rule of law may have already existed in the countries' pasts. In both Giolittean Italy at the beginning of this century and Vargas's Brazil of the 1930s and 1940s, there was a similar saying: "For friends what they want, for enemies the law." Yet both the Italian and Brazilian authoritarian regimes strengthened such inequality regarding due process, and it thus persists as a key legacy that makes the guarantee of equal political and civil rights for all citizens far more difficult.

Comparative Analysis

To flesh out our conceptualization of authoritarian legacies and their influence on the quality of democracy in postauthoritarian regimes, we will examine and compare cases from southern Europe and Latin America. We will analyze Italy, Spain, Portugal, Chile, Argentina, Uruguay, and Brazil. We excluded Greece, for the Greek authoritarian experience between 1967 and 1973 is neither long enough nor institutionally innovative or meaningful enough to be considered here. Political leader Constantinos Karamanlis, who reestablished democracy in July 1973, was already a prominent politician during the previous limited democracy, and he immediately moved to hold the military accountable. Trials, condemnations, and convictions were conducted in the months immediately following democratic reestablishment. The symbolic and real impact of the Greek court decisions were both deeply felt and very effective. We will thus start with southern Europe, a region whose experience and distance in time from transitions provide meaningful fields for research regarding both authoritarian legacies and their fading away.

Southern Europe

The three southern European cases are relatively more distant in time than those of Latin America. As such, the legacies concerning the possible continuity of the political elite and civil servants—that is, short-run legacies—are intentionally excluded from this analysis. Rather, we analyze the authoritarian legacies outlined in Table 2.2. Authoritarian legacies in southern Europe thus include authoritarian legal institutions, a statist economy, the persistence of military prerogatives, labor restructuring, large radical rightist groups or parties, and passivity and widespread nondemocratic attitudes—all with a major negative impact on the actual working of democracy. The differences among the three countries depend on the characteristics of authoritarianism and modes of transition, as well as on reasons idiosyncratic to each of the countries.

Italy

For the Italian case, the innovation and durability of the fascist regime are more important dimensions than the mode of transition, in spite of fascism's military defeat in World War II. There are several reasons for this, from the mobilizational project and highly pervasive features of fascism, to fascism's capacity to build new institutions and the fact that the role of democratic elites is stronger in some regions than others. Once the heroic moments were over, the old habits, attitudes, behaviors, institutions, and individuals of the fascist regime reappeared. Thus, during democratic consolidation and for decades later, several legacies highlighted in Table 2.2 persisted.

Italian fascism proved both preoccupied with and adept at developing authoritarian legal procedures, norms, and institutions. Once democracy was established, such authoritarian legacies were compounded under democracy by consistently poor implementation of the law, especially in parts of the south. At the elite level, the army disintegrated at the end of World War II, and the country was invaded and split in two for several crucial months. During the moments of both democratic establishment and consolidation, the army had no role. There has thus been no legacy in terms of military prerogatives, as in other southern European and Southern Cone countries. At the level of social groups, in spite of the regime's totalitarian features, there was no real *gleichschaltung,* or leveling, of associations, social structures, and cultural diversity. On the contrary, during the twenty years of fascist rule, Catholic associations and the lower middle classes became more powerful.

On the whole, Italian authoritarian legacies contextualized and strengthened other, more subtle, yet persistent legacies. These include various dimensions of political incorporation, such as passivity, alienation from politics, and nondemocratic and radical attitudes. They also include the organization of fascist opinion and ideology in a democracy by an anti-system, neofascist party (the Italian Social Movement—MSI) and the persistence of a corporatist mode of authoritarian representation in agriculture.

To account for the first set of legacies, the fascist regime established and consolidated mass politics in areas where politics had formerly been only an elite experience. Fascist politics "taught" the importance of an organized mass party for the creation and sustaining of popular participation and mobilization from above. The state played a strongly hegemonic role, advancing a politics whose form and contents were decided by "those who know." Paradoxically, this granted more room for an irresponsible ideological radicalism.

Mass politics was not a clearly established reality in Italy before fascism. In contrast, by 1945, mass politics was well established. One of the main explanations for the activation and large diffusion of mass participation in the mid-1940s is the collective mobilization that took place during the Resistance and at the end of the war. The saliency of these experiences lies at the core of Italian democracy. In particular, the alliance of democratic parties in the National Liberation Committee (CLN) played a central role in the democratic coalition that generated the democratic regime. This has frequently been emphasized and requires no further comment.

In addition, however, the most relevant changes between the prefascist period and the postwar years were the change from an unstructured party system to a structured one; the increase in voter turnout in 1946 and in the following elections, in comparison to previous elections; the spread of mass politics to southern Italy in and after the fascist period, and thus the disappearance of the previous North-South imbalance in electoral participation; and the creation of strengthened or new collective political party identities, that is, Christian Democracy (DC), the Italian Socialist Party (PSI), and the Italian Communist Party (PCI), particularly in the south, compounded by the disappearance in 1946–48 of the oligarchic parties (see Morlino 1998b).

Transition to a Structured Party System. In 1912, the Italian government dramatically extended male suffrage, increasing the electorate from 2,930,473 potential voters in 1909 to 8,443,205 in 1913. In addition, between 1913 and 1919, the population grew by about three million (see official statistics, Mitchell 1980; Flora and Heidenheimer 1981), and in 1919 the government decreased the voting age to twenty-one.[1] Electoral reforms and population growth laid the groundwork for mass political incorporation.

Amidst industrialization, urbanization, and the development of public education, the second key factor to trigger mass politics was large-scale mobilization brought about by World War I. As in other European countries, the war had a major impact on the formation of the Italian party system (Lipset and Rokkan 1968). Nevertheless, while mass politics had begun to develop, the Italian party system failed to be restructured until the establishment of the fascist regime. Measures of electoral volatility show the unstructured nature of the party system until 1924 and the drastic change after 1946: the 1919–21 average volatility was 51.1, whereas the average for 1946–48 was 32.6.

In some areas of northern and central Italy one can also discern the formation of so-called political subcultures as early as the 1920s, and in some cases before World War I (see, in general, Farneti 1971, 275ff.). These subcultures emerged in an integrated, homogeneous society and shared a set of their own autonomous values at the local level. They became politicized, either leftist or Catholic, and were the strongholds of the respective parties after fascism.[2] Before World War I one can trace a leftist subcultural area in Emilia and a Catholic subcultural area in Venice (the latter having only 25 percent of the vote). By 1919–21, there appeared to be leftist or Catholic subcultures in Piedmont and Lombardy—that is, in most of the northwest—and in Venice, Emilia, Tuscany, and Umbria. Dramatic party subcultural expansion, however, did not take place until 1946, when one could define the entire northwest, together with Liguria, and the northeast (Venice, Trentino, and Friuli), as well as Marche, Emilia, Tuscany, and Umbria, as subcultural areas. Subsequently, these areas extended to include the entire northeast for the Catholics but remained the same for the socialists and communists. The expansion of DC's electoral strength in the northwest and south was remarkable (see official electoral statistics but also Farneti 1983, 101–2).

This demonstrates the limits of the argument that prefascist party subcultures, revitalized after 1946, underlie Italian voting stability and party penetration. Such a hypothesis may hold for much of the northwest of the country, yet DC strength emerged in the northeast, northwest, and south after the 1948 elections. Thus the limited existence of subcultures before 1946 is of no use as an explanatory variable for nationwide party system structuring after 1948.

Increased Political Participation.   First, it is well known that the political role of women was acknowledged under fascism with the establishment of women's organizations, albeit within a traditional notion of the role of women. Although there were legislative proposals to extend the vote to women as early as 1905 and then again in 1919 and 1922, these never became law. Thus, in spite of previous attempts, Italian women had their first political roles, albeit formal, passive, subordinate, and complementary, during fascism's two decades. By 1945, women's political citizenship in a democratic context appears to have been taken for granted.

Second, as mentioned above, the high voter turnout in 1946 is accounted for by the mobilization following the collapse of the fascist regime and the Resistance. But even here, the fascist legacy has some responsibility, shown by the electoral turnout of 1929 and 1934 (89.9 percent and 96.5 percent). The high level of electoral participation had already been experienced in a nondemocratic context, and thus it was much easier to attain the same result in a different, and democratic, context. Union participation was also very high, with a total membership at the end of 1940s of close to five million (see Feltrin 1991).

Furthermore, there is no continuity between the prefascist and the postfascist electorates. This is not only because of the difference in voter turnout between the two periods but also and primarily because of the difference in the electorate itself. In the last prefascist democratic elections of 1921, the electorate stood at 11,239,326, whereas in 1946 this figure had risen to 25,832,170. If one takes into account the total mortality rate in the intervening twenty-five years, a total of 20,000,000 people (see population statistics by age in Mitchell

1980) who had been politically educated or reeducated under fascism, including women, became voters for the first time in 1945–46. Thus, in this limited and partial way, the fascist experience is at least as important as the experience of its collapse and of the Resistance, which did not take place in the south.

The Spread of Mass Politics to Southern Italy. With some exceptions in Apulia and Sicily, there was virtually no mass politics in the south until the fascist period. But after 1946, the imbalance in voter turnout in the southern regions almost disappeared. The spread of mass politics occurred in these regions for the first time with the establishment of the National Fascist Party, the PNF (see particularly De Felice 1966, 8–11 and 407ff.). At this time many members of the traditional southern elite joined the PNF, together with the lower middle classes, who were to a great extent politically socialized during this period. Here the ideas of parties as public agencies and politics as a state affair imposed from above were established for the first time in Italy. These were recurring features of nondemocratic mass politics and were maintained in the subsequent democratic period.

The "integrating" role of the PNF in the diffusion of mass politics in southern Italy is also demonstrated in that it occurred in those regions where the mobilizational opportunities provided by the Resistance were lacking. As stated, the breakdown of fascism itself had a mobilizational impact. But fascism created habits of political participation that were largely formal and passive. In other words, in the political socialization of at least an entire generation, the external, public, passive features of politics prevailed. When fascism broke down, some democratic leaders were highly aware of the empty space left by the disappearance of the regime and the fascist party, mainly for the middle classes. De Gasperi, the leader of the DC, was one of these leaders, and he explicitly raised the problem of winning the consensus—and the support—of groups educated into politics during fascism. As Scoppola (1977, 31ff., 67–68) points out, some cautious, moderate, and conservative choices within DC during the 1940s, as well as a few conflicts between the prefascist generation of *Popolari* and the new Catholic generation educated during fascism, can be explained only if one considers the persistence of traditional, nondemocratic attitudes in the middle classes and the maintenance of visions of politics learned during the fascist years from youth, visions that were very difficult to forget.

The Creation of New Collective Political Identities. Fascism may also be considered responsible for contributing to new party identities and to the habit of party identification in nonprivate daily life, above all for the middle classes who entered politics mainly through the first middle-class mass party formed in Italy, the PNF (see also Petersen 1975). In 1943, the regime broke down, and the desire to eliminate and forget the broad-based and resolute consensus around fascism that had provoked the war, as well as all the subsequent disasters, became quite pronounced. In such a situation, the void in the political arena left by the sudden disappearance of the PNF gave the democratic parties the best conditions for attaining and maintaining the widespread support of the Italian population. Thus the void was easily filled. In other words, three strongly related factors eventually led civil society toward the same goals and results: first, the habit of political identification; second, the disappearance of the object of previous identification; and third, the necessity of erasing the experience of the war and the regime that had provoked it. For the democratic parties these were the best foundations.

For a better understanding of this point, let us consider a completely different hypothesis, that of a fascist regime that does not promote political participation, however passive and controlled, and where the party and its ancillary organizations do not play a relevant role. In this situation there would be no mass participation and the role of the party as the organizer of consensus would not be crucial. This is the hypothesis of fascism as a *demobilizational regime,* as in some Latin American regimes during the past decades. Had this been the case, mobilization from 1943 to 1946 would still have been massive but would not have been strengthened by those habits of collective identification already mentioned, and it would probably have been more difficult to institutionalize them. The south would have experienced neither mass politics nor the conditions for developing new democratic parties. Even DC would have been much more difficult to establish than was actually the case.

Galli (1966) emphasizes that even if the socialist union was the first mass organization before fascism, the first party with a membership of several million individuals was the PNF (148). In the early 1940s, PNF membership totaled 12 percent of the population, approximately the same percentage that joined new democratic parties after the breakdown of fascism. In this sense, the PNF was a model of (1) a governmental party; (2) a mass party that appealed across social classes, a sort of catch-all party seeking broad-based social consensus; and (3) an organized party formed by personnel who made politics their profession, with a large network of ancillary organizations. In the aftermath of the fascist breakdown, it was obviously impossible to find democratic party leaders who openly acknowledged that the fascist party was a model to imitate. Thus it is also impossible to find strong, direct empirical evidence to support this hypothesis.

Nevertheless, we can explore the influence of the PNF as an organizational model for the democratic opposition. The importance and meaning of a mass party were clear to democratic opponents of fascism from the days of the fascist takeover. For example, in the mid-1930s, Rosselli, in his *Quaderni di Giustizia e Libertá* (an underground, rare journal published in Florence; see, e.g., n. 10, February 1934, or n. 12, January 1935), analyzed the characteristics of both the fascist regime and its mass party, as well as the subsequent problems for the democratic opposition.

It is possible that PCI leader Togliatti's notion of a "new party" reflects this lesson instead of either the Italian communist or the Bolshevik tradition. His penetrating analysis of the fascist party raises this possibility. Togliatti clearly saw the mass component of fascism, even if characterized by a reactionary politics. At the same time, he criticized his own party (as well as the entire democratic opposition) for ignoring the dissatisfaction of the petit bourgeoisie and for underestimating the fascists (Togliatti [1933] 1973, 111ff.). In addition, Togliatti stressed the great political relevance of a mass organization that addressed working-class leisure time, the *dopolavoro:* "[T]he *dopolavoro* is one of the most complex organizations in fascist dictatorship" (Togliatti [1933] 1973, 170). Consequently perhaps, Togliatti substituted the basically militant and elitist Leninist tradition of the party as "the vanguard of the proletariat" with a quite different notion of mass party.

In a famous speech of April 1944 and on several other occasions ([1994] 1972, 71ff.; Spriano 1975, 386ff.), Togliatti addressed the problem of the transformation of the PCI from an underground militant party to a mass party, thus allowing it to compete in the electoral arena alongside other parties of the future democracy. The communist leader focused on working toward a national, not strictly working-class, mass-based party capable of governing in a democratic context (Togliatti [1944] 1972, 71ff.). Today's "new party" is not directly inspired by the fascist experience. However, it is difficult to avoid the conclusion that the lesson afforded by the experience of the fascist party in the early 1920s, with its legal seizure of power and its creation of organizational structures to reach and maintain consensus, underlies Togliatti's convictions regarding the need to make the PCI a mass party.

Furthermore, communist leaders' understandings of the fascist experience and its impact on the masses conditioned PCI organization and strategy. Secchia, the leader in charge of organization during the postwar years, on many occasions complained that the fascist regime had deeply affected the education and the habits of the younger generation, above all in their being accustomed to obeying orders from above without questioning them (Poggi 1968, 37). During the same years, Togliatti ([1944] 1972, 87) also mentions this aspect and its relevance to mass politics. If we also consider all the members of the PNF who subsequently joined the PCI, even if only for protection, or who joined other parties, it is again very difficult to avoid coming to the same conclusion, namely the importance of the fascist mass party experience for the new democratic mass parties and their leaders.

Regarding DC, one can conclude that there was no model of a mass party in the mind of its leaders to parallel that of the left. During the 1930s, De Gasperi did not even have the idea of building a true party of all Catholics (Scoppola 1977, 96–97). Later, the points of strength of DC became the Catholic ancillary organizations. However, the interclass mass appeal, which had also been a characteristic of the Partito Popolare in prefascist years and the PNF later, reemerged very strongly. In addition, during the early 1940s, DC leaders frequently advocated strong continuity—building a governmental party of all Catholics that would simply succeed the fascist regime (Scoppola 1977, 37ff.).

On the whole, there is no direct evidence that the PNF was a model for the democratic leaders. In addition, those who had spent their exile in France or the United States would have had the experiences of other democratic models. The very relationship of PCI militants and leaders in exile within the popular front strategy, again particularly in France, since the mid-1930s, could be considered an alternative source of inspiration for the notion and the experience of a mass party as well as the need for alliances. But the Italian fascist experience (and the mistakes made by the democratic forces in the early 1920s) was a lesson for new and old democratic leaders. Given the proximity in time and the penetration of the fascist party model, we cannot exclude the possibility of its imitation by the new democratic leaders and party structures.

■

To summarize, we maintain that legacies at the mass level and a learning process at the elite level are interwoven: at the mass level there are clearly characteristics of democratic politics that are related to attitudes and habits acquired during fascism, such as the idea of politics as practiced by an elite, a politics that is imposed from above and must be passively accepted and to which the very idea of accountability is extraneous. And for the democratic elite who suffered the fascist suppression, the PNF de facto became an organizational model to imitate in a different context. These hypotheses account for the attitudes of apathy, passivity, and indifference uncovered by survey analyses of Italians in the 1950s (see, e.g., Almond and Verba 1963).

There is, in fact, a more specific, openly declared legacy at the mass and elite levels: the neofascist MSI, with its mass organization and leaders who came directly from the previous experience, particularly that of the Italian Social Republic. This party was the organization and the channel for carrying over the beliefs and the political attitudes of the previous experience to a democratic context. Its electoral strength was around 8 percent for decades and then declined in the 1980s. Nevertheless, public opinion polls documented strong, antidemocratic attitudes at approximately 70 percent of the population through the end of 1950s. La Palombara and Waters (1961), for example, found that 68.4 percent of antidemocratic attitudes in 1958 were also profascist attitudes. Later in the mid-1980s, Morlino and Mattei (1992, 142) found that authoritarian opinion was supported by about 16 percent of Italian voters and that about 4 percent still explicitly referrred to the old fascist experience forty years later. It is not necessary here to analyze the values, programs, and organizational characteristics of the MSI. Both its continuity with fascism and its anti-system positions are openly declared. The most relevant point is to clarify why the MSI contributed to democracy of a lower quality, together with the features examined above.

The MSI was a party with major success in southern Italy, traditionally in Apulia and several southern towns, particularly during the first decades of democracy. If to this we add the large, widespread affinity for authoritarianism, it is easy to understand why DC was heavily influenced in its policy positions by the neofascist right and at the same time why fear of the right, in this case compounded by fear of the communist left, maintained a large electorate totally frozen in its vote for DC. In other words, the anti-system and antidemocratic components of Italian politics "condemned" DC to govern for decades until their breakdown in 1993–94, and the party made alternation or even semialternation impossible. This also rendered impossible every serious form of party accountability or political responsiveness. And this was also one of the heavier constraints on Italian democracy, where there was no full right to vote—that is, to choose the governing party or coalition.

Spain

In Spain there is no electorally significant anti-regime party with strong links to the past. In fact, during the first years of democratic transition and consolidation, the right performed poorly at the polls: in the first election of 1977, the Spanish right won one seat. Only when the consolidation process was largely over was a more moderate, center-rightist party, the Partido Popular, led by a man with no personal links to the authoritarian past, able to win the elections of both 1996 and 2000. In fact, until the late 1980s, the Spanish Socialist Party (PSOE) enjoyed a dominant position, in part due to the presence of the right-wing Alianza Popular, led by Manuel Fraga, a Francoist minister, as well as by other former high officials from the Franco regime. Thus, during the 1980s, there was no possibility of alternation, and consequently, no possibility of accountability.

In this country, where every family was in some way deeply affected by the civil war (1936–39) and where there were almost forty years of authoritarian rule (1939–76), the obsessive anticommunist propaganda was complemented by a demobilizational policy to control all opposition, democratic or otherwise. The dictatorship was not institutionally innovative. It lasted for a long time but did not restructure political institutions and was virtually devoid of the totalitarian features of fascism (Linz 1964).

The democratic transition, however, presented strong features of continuity: this was the goal pursued by the moderate leaders, and the presence of a monarchy seemed the best guarantee of that continuity. Thus, given authoritarian regime durability and the mode of transition, there should be ample space for strong legacies; but such legacies are again much subtler than the simple persistence of the National Industrial Institute (IN), the state economic agency, and a magistracy recruited and formed during Francoism. The important legacies are centered in the beliefs and attitudes that have characterized Spanish politics. In this regard, the parallel with Italy is only partial, as the years of the Spanish Second Republic (1931–36) were a period of mass politics and, in a very extreme way, mass conflict during the subsequent years of civil war. Consequently, as suggested above, the Franco regime viewed the problem as one of demobilizing those involved in the war, rather than the opposite one, that of incorporating people into constrained participation, as in fascist Italy.

In spite of the existing empirical problems, Spanish authoritarian legacies can be detected through the following analytical steps: (1) a review of some of the main features of mass democratic politics after Franco; (2) defining the main characteristics of Francoist politics; and (3) a search for the possible, perhaps problematic links.

Main Features of Mass Democratic Politics after Franco.   In a 1985 survey and other research on Spain, the most positive attitudes toward politics, such as interest, commitment, enthusiasm, and passion, were rather low: only 29 percent of respondents maintained these positive attitudes. Negative feelings, such as irritation and disgust, were declared by 10 percent. But above all, Spaniards expressed very high levels of indifference toward politics: 54 percent (see Morlino 1998a, 125). When left-right self-placement as a control variable was introduced, the same basic pattern could be observed: respondents on the left were more positive in their feelings about politics, while those on the right were more negative, and centrist and center-right respondents were less involved with politics—that is, political indifference was comparatively more widespread among rightists. To what extent were these largely affective evaluations complemented by parallel cognitive orientations and were these attitudes related to perceptions of personal efficacy—that is, to respondents' assessments of their own capacities to influence politics? To address these issues, an "index of political alienation" was constructed, combining responses to three questionnaire items regarding "internal" and "external" efficacy.[3] The resulting data revealed a high degree of alienation from and negative attitudes toward politics and political elites among 43 percent of the sample and no alienation among only 8 percent (see Morlino and Montero 1995, 252).

These data suggest some specificity in Spanish, and southern European, political culture that is consistent with Malefakis's (1995) analysis of political and socioeconomic "contours" of southern European history. The findings on attitudes toward politics and the related index of alienation are also consistent with those of other research. Maravall (1981) and, more recently, Botella (1992, 121–36) similarly have described Spain's political culture as characterized by a lack of popular interest, perceptions of inefficacy, a critical skepticism, and a lack of confidence in political elites. Maravall referred to this combination of attitudes as "democratic cynicism," while Botella described it as "cynical democratism." Maravall further argued that a cynical view of politics has long been a central trait of southern European political culture and that this trait could even be a rational judgment based on a long experience of politics as the abuse of power.

Main Features of Politics during the Franco Period. In the mid-1960s, when demands for some form of opening became stronger, including pressure from the democratic opposition who were in exile or underground, the reaction of the regime was to allow a *concurrencia de pareceres* (proposals of different opinions) to accommodate some kind of pluralism within the Franco regime. The key point is that for decades there was highly negative propaganda portraying a multiparty system as the source of hatred, division, unnecessary conflict, decisional inefficacy, personalism, and corruption. For decades, the experience of political participation during the previous period was criticized, and only political conformism was encouraged. At the same time, it was suggested that the important component of political decisions was technical and that people had to trust the wisdom of the *caudillísimo* Francisco Franco, who was responsible for grassroots economic development and the Spaniards' growing material well-being.

Links between Present and Past and Empirical Support for Legacies. During the democratic phase, Spanish people had largely accepted the new democratic regime: in 1985, for example, two out of three people expressed a preference for democracy, whereas one out of ten would have preferred an authoritarian regime in some cases; and two-thirds of all respondents believed that democracy worked (see Morlino 1998a, 119). When, however, opinions about the past authoritarian experience were requested, the picture became much more intriguing: among southern Europeans, Spaniards possessed the most positive attitudes regarding their previous regime. In Morlino's (1998a) survey in 1985, assessments of the past regime were very positive. In 1985, 17 percent of respondents showed a positive evaluation of Francoism; even more telling, 44 percent considered that past "partly good." These findings match those of other studies, showing that most of those who had positive attitudes toward Franco and were ideologically identified with Francoism also accepted the new democratic regime: only 4 percent of respondents interviewed by Data Spain in 1981 totally identified with Francoism and maintained clearly antidemocratic positions (see Linz et al. 1981, 614). Linz et al. also stressed that in 1978, 39.6 percent of Spaniards considered Franco's regime positively or fairly positively (589). That percentage became even higher, very close to 50 percent, in a survey conducted the following year, 1979, during a crisis of legitimation of Spanish democracy (see Gunther, Sani, and Shabad 1986). Between 1985 and 1992, those polled in EC countries who stated that they preferred democracy increased from 70 to 78 percent in Spain. At the same time, the preference for authoritarianism remained basically stable: in Spain it went from 10 to 9 percent.

In this sense the explanation is the same as that given for Italy: not refusal of the past but an adaptation to a new, different situation that was democratic. There was, in addition, a widespread consciousness, even among most of the main elites who had supported Franco, that the past was over and that there was no alternative to a democratic institutional arrangement. The death of Franco marked the turning point at which most Spaniards began to regard change as unavoidable. Yet high praise of the past and widespread negative sentiment about contemporary democratic politics suggested that the acceptance of the new politics was likely to be superficial.

The links between Francoist politics and the new politics emerge very clearly. Statism, conformism, alienation, indifference, passivity, and cynicism were closely related and were introduced during the demobilizing authoritarian years. Authoritarian regime propaganda obsessively emphasized the so-called technical content of politics, as well as the divisive, conflictive and unnecessary role played by parties. The regime also suppressed alternative opinion. Positive opinions about the past represent the link that allows us to connect attitudes of the authoritarian past with analogous tendencies in the democratic present.

Again, Morlino's (1998a) survey confirms a phenomenon that also began to appear in the 1958 survey of Italy (see La Palombara and Waters 1961), where the left appeared more democratic than the right. That is, the left had more positive attitudes toward democracy than the right. The speculation is related to what has been affirmed above: the left had learned the positive features of democracy through the experience of harsh suppression by rightist, authoritarian regimes. In an important sense, what represented a legacy for some sectors of the population was a learning process for other sectors. This becomes clearer in light of the moderation of the left, primarily the Spanish Communist Party (PCE), and of the organized working class, who accepted both the monarchy and the social pacts of 1978 (see Pérez Díaz 1987; Fishman 1990). The profound presence of memories of the radicalization of the Second Republic and the subsequent Spanish civil war contributed to such moderation (Aguilar 1996). There is thus an interweaving of different experiences to shape a more complex set of legacies. In part, the same set of political attitudes that we relate to Francoism account for a low quality of politics, with passivity, conformism, and so on. At the same time, such attitudes—passivity, cultural deference toward the elite and conformism related to the past—have contributed to a democratic consolidation that otherwise would have been much more difficult and dangerous.

The tentative conclusions suggested by the Spanish case are (1) that there is an interweaving of legacies and learning process and (2) that there are features of authoritarian legacies at the mass political culture level that may be extremely positive and useful for democratic consolidation but at the same time negative for the development of the quality of democracy. The conclusions seem to point in opposite directions. There are important parallels between the Spanish and Chilean cases in this regard.

Portugal

We will now stress how powerful the potential authoritarian legacies are in Portugal, where the authoritarian regime lasted for forty-eight years. The almost half-century of authoritarian rule distinguished the regime as one of the most durable in contemporary history. In addition, the Portuguese regime was particularly innovative in terms of institutions, such that building on the fascist example became the applied model of authoritarian corporatism. Although the corporatist system was not actually implemented until the 1950s, this did not change the profound impact of this set of institutional arrangements. They were lucidly conceived by Salazar beginning in the early 1930s (de Lucena 1976), and they had profound social and economic consequences and, accordingly, potentially profound legacies.

The strong potential legacies of Salazarism are, however, contrasted and eventually powerfully undermined by the similarly strong discontinuity of the transition, one that was not a conscious transition to democracy, during the first years after the military coup and the successful "Revolution of the Carnations" of April 1974. The Manifesto of Captains, proclaimed by those who launched the coup, had a strong social content in terms of agrarian reform and nationalizations that ran against everything that Salazarism and later Caetanism were in terms of domestic and foreign policies as well as in terms of institutions. The clash between the two forces was similarly strong, making authoritarian legacies difficult to detect after the constitutional revisions of 1982, when the army was compelled to let go of its grip on the emerging democracy and accept regime civilianization, and after 1989, when private property and capitalism again became part of that democracy, with the subsequent repeal of key agrarian reform laws, the return of several properties, and the privatization of banks and industrial firms.

Four authoritarian legacies clearly related to the quality of democracy can be highlighted. The first was short term: the maintenance of military prerogatives for a few years until the very divisions of the army and the consolidation of parties abolished most of them. The second was related to mass politics in the new democratic context as compared to the previous authoritarian setting. The third concerned international isolation. Finally, the fourth concerned corporatist traditions in the organization of interests.

The fading away of the political role of military officers represents a necessary condition for a democratic regime. In Portugal, the legacy of prolonged military involvement in politics was largely an outgrowth of the mode of transition led by the captains. The process of achieving civilian control was gradual and lasted about a decade (1976–86). As late as 1979, a military officer attacked Parliament for refusing the proposed military budget. By 1980, however, there was no longer a military officer as minister of defense and by 1981, the president of the republic was no longer also the chief of general staff. On October 30, 1982, the Council of the Revolution, the key body through which the soldier-authors of the new regime attempted to "protect" their hybrid creature, met for the last time. In November 1982, the Law of National Defense was eventually approved despite being vetoed by President Ramalho Eanes, and civilian control was openly declared and shaped through it. With the 1985 elections Eanes de facto accepted the civilianization of his political designs by forming a centrist movement, which achieved strong electoral results.

By 1986, with the election of the socialist leader Mario Soares, the president of the republic was no longer a military officer. This basically concluded the process of establishing civilian control. This list of episodes leaves out several events, such as the transformation of the size of the armed forces (from 282,000 people in 1974 to 83,000 six years later and 63,000 in 1986) and a drastic reduction of the related budget (Graham 1993, 65, 77) as well as the late 1980s' creation of the Ministry of Defense (Graham 1993, 67–68). This is not the place to explain the achieved civilian control over the army. However, the role played by moderate, democratic officers should be stressed, for the belief in the legitimacy of the institution these democratic officers created represents a key aspect of the explanation (see Morlino 1998a, 72).

Overcoming the legacy of military dominance was an essential component of democratization. There is large room for ambiguity where the role of the army is more implicit and de facto than openly suggested by the law. The difference between the existence of a formal democracy and the improvement of its quality is less distinct. Here, overcoming the legacy of international isolation was crucial: the help of western European countries, such as Germany, and the related acceptance of the European model of democracy were essential steps for both democratic consolidation and improving the quality of democracy. The Portuguese political elite fully understood the importance of overcoming this legacy, and it consciously pursued and later achieved accession to the European Union in 1986.

Thus both the legacy of military dominance and the legacy of international isolation were profoundly influential, but conscious political elites were able to overcome them and achieve good results in terms of both the consolidation and the quality of democracy. In contrast, the widespread legacy at a mass level concerning the beliefs and attitudes toward democratic institutions has been much more difficult to overcome. In Portugal there is no previous, even limited, democratic experience of mass politics, as in Spain or Italy. More precisely, the preauthoritarian years are virtually irrelevant for Portugal because of temporal distance from the republic, the lack of an experience of consolidated mass politics complemented by the lack of major episodes of civil war or bloody conflicts and deaths, and the durability of authoritarianism. The authoritarian establishment with the coup of 1926 anticipated a possible forthcoming transition toward some kind of liberal democracy. Despite some mobilizational policies that resembled fascist policies, the institutional solution was a corporatist one with a hierarchical conception, a culture of deference toward the political and social elites, strong statism, and a population quite distant from politics.

As in Spain, in Portugal the positive evaluation of the past has been fairly high. In 1978, 35 percent still considered that Salazar and Caetano had governed the country best (Bruneau 1984, 113; Bruneau and Macleod 1986, 93). By 1984, 35 percent still praised Salazar and Caetano's governments (Bruneau and Mcleod 1986, 94). In a 1985 survey, the percentage of positive evaluations of the past in Portugal dropped to 13 percent (Morlino 1998a, 118). Between 1985 and 1992, the percentage of those who stated that they preferred democracy increased from 61 to 83 percent. At the same time, the preference for authoritarianism remained basically stable at 9 percent (see Morlino and Montero 1995, 238). Thus, as in Spain, the links with the past and the related socialization of the people in authoritarian politics have been very strong.

Consequently, we should not be surprised to find negative public attitudes toward politics, higher than in Spain (16 percent compared to 10 percent), and similar high percentages of those expressing feelings of indifference, diffidence, and boredom toward politics: 52 percent (see Morlino 1998a, 125). Even by 1988, a passive acceptance—not active support—of democracy was expressed by 51.3 percent of Portuguese (Heimer, Vala-Salvador, and Leite Viegas 1990). The extent of political alienation from and negative attitudes toward politics and political elites is also very high, at 57 percent; while no alienation is declared by only 3 percent of Portuguese (see Morlino and Montero 1995, 252). As in Spain, preference for democracy is stronger on the left than on the right (see Morlino 1998a, 124).

Portuguese political culture, however, presents a few specific features that should be emphasized for a better understanding of the kinds of legacies we are analyzing. First of all, preference for democracy is lower than in the other southern European countries, as are positive attitudes toward politics (see Morlino 1998a, 118, 125). Second, in Morlino's 1985 survey (Morlino 1998a) the percentage of nonresponse was the highest, together with a large number of responses reflecting noninvolvement with politics. In the Eurobarometer surveys, the highest indifference toward the European Union—ironically—has been shown by the Portuguese. These characteristics are better understood when related to authoritarian and nonauthoritarian politics where there is no experience of either mobilization from above or civic participation.

The corporatist tradition in the structuration of interests can be considered both a constraining and an enhancing legacy in terms of democratic quality. On the one hand, every definition of corporatism, even within a democratic context (see, e.g., Schmitter 1974), includes a lack of competition, hegemonic positions, hierarchy, deferential culture at a mass level, and the strong role of the state. However, such a legacy has to be very strong to become a real possible constraint to democratic quality. This is the case for neither Italy nor Spain, both of which have had corporatist traditions. For contemporary Portugal, the question is partially open: the strong corporatist past is only partially mirrored by the present situation in the way interests are actually articulated and in the existing institutions, such as the Permanent Council of Social Concertation. When complemented with other channels and forms of interest articulation, the corporatist mode may have democratic value regarding the protection of large social groups (see Schmitter 1983). Consequently, corporatism might be a vehicle for greater democratic quality. From this perspective, an apparently negative legacy may become a positive or very positive one for a "better" democracy. Moreover, at the end of the 1980s, while the massive privatization program ended the large role of the public sector in the economy, neocorporatist politics continued.

Analysis of the three southern European countries points to several problematic issues involved in the study of authoritarian legacies. They include the interweaving of a range of previous legacies, particularly where complex historical events have profoundly scarred the political culture of a country; the mutual exchange and influence between legacies and reactions to legacies or learning, at both mass and elite levels; and the opposite effects that a set of legacies may have with regard to democratic consolidation and to the quality of democracy (i.e., that the same legacies may both contribute to democratic consolidation and act as powerful constraints on the development of "better" democracies).

Southern Cone and Brazil

The more recent authoritarian experiences of the Southern Cone provide a useful comparison for understanding authoritarian legacies' influence on the quality of democracy. One of the most notable contrasts between southern Europe and the Southern Cone and Brazil was the mobilizational project of two of the three southern European authoritarian regimes and the demobilizational project of the Latin American cases (with Spain more similar to the Southern Cone cases in this regard).

Chile

The Chilean case has presented an interesting paradox, in that democratic stability and economic progress have made Chile a model of redemocratization, yet authoritarian enclaves remain codified in the military regime-sponsored 1980 Chilean constitution and continue to pervade Chilean politics. It is the Chilean case that most exemplifies the impact of authoritarian legacies as potential silencers and as severe constraints on the development of a rich, deliberative, inclusive public sphere.

In terms of authoritarian regime durability, only Brazil (twenty-one years) surpasses Chile (seventeen years) among our Latin American cases. In terms of innovation, the Chilean dictatorship fundamentally transformed historic relationships among the state, the polity, the economy, and society. Regarding the modes of transition, in both Chile and Brazil, authoritarian incumbents oversaw fundamental aspects of the transition, including the timing of change and the degree of autonomy afforded the military branches. Yet while attention to authoritarian legacies in the Brazilian case will focus on state patronage, social domination, and the unrule of law within a fragmented political party system, attention in Chile must focus on transformations in the quality of political incorporation within a strong and highly institutionalized party system.

Perhaps in no Southern Cone case is the contrast between pre- and postauthoritarian regime inclusion so clear as in the Chilean case. As Arturo Valenzuela (1979) attests, such forms of incorporation as electoral registration, political party recruitment, worker unionization, popular sector organizing, and political mobilization historically represented "a deliberate policy on the part of the government to include people who had been left behind" (33). Between 1949 and 1973, for example, the percentage of registered voters due to electoral reforms increased from 9.0 percent of the population to 44.1 percent (Scully 1992, 144).

Valenzuela (1979, 33) suggests that from the early 1950s through the mid-1960s, governmental policies of inclusion provided a good example of Gabriel Almond's notion of "responsive performance," a key positive normative underpinning of a good democracy. The chief symbols of political inclusion were the electoral reforms, including granting women the right to vote, guaranteeing a secret ballot, lowering the voting-age requirement, and removing the literacy requirement. Inclusion also involved new unionization rights for workers in the countryside. Political parties actively recruited, organized, and mobilized new political constituencies. As long as the Chilean political elite practiced accommodationist politics in the halls of the executive and legislature, political inclusion could be valued as a promising sign of civil society–based political participation and a legitimation of the political system.

From the late 1960s through the 1970–73 Popular Unity administration of Salvador Allende, popular mobilization proved one of the most visible features of an incorporating, albeit increasingly polarized, society. The Popular Unity government incorporated new social and political actors and organizations, including neighborhood committees, shopfloor organizations, and peasant cooperatives, into the workings and administration of society. Yet highly conflictive, large-scale pro- and antigovernment protests marked the Allende years, symbolizing both intense support for and resistance to the reach and meaning of popular sector incorporation. Sectoral strikes shut down vital production and transportation networks.

High on the agenda of the Pinochet dictatorship was to demobilize Chilean society, to bring an end to the politics of inclusion. Pinochet's brutality struck at the core of an inclusionary project. During the first year of rule, the military junta closed the Chilean Congress, replaced local elected officials, nullified the electoral rolls, replaced university presidents with military men, suspended trade unions, and banned all political parties and organizations. The dictatorship brought a dramatic halt to the expansive trends in voter participation, political party organization, unionization, and other forms of popular sector incorporation. While accommodationist politics among Chile's political elite has returned to postauthoritarian Chile, popular sector inclusion has not. This is arguably the most enduring legacy of authoritarian rule and merits considerable attention.

Much of the Latin Americanist social science literature has pointed to the uniqueness of the ideological innovation of the Pinochet regime. While there is some debate regarding how to characterize the regime ideologically (Schamis 1991; Hunneeus 2001), scholars focus on the peculiar mix of extreme repression, neoliberalism, technocracy, *gremialismo*, and conservative Catholic social doctrine. Moreover, while most hold that the military regime was authoritarian, the Pinochet regime also possessed totalitarian elements, particularly in terms of the reach of the repressive mechanisms of the state in society and its comparatively developed ideological scheme (Linz 2000).

The authoritarian regime instituted an extreme presidentialist system, thereby weakening the Congress, and it created a powerful set of nonelected governing bodies (Siavelis 2000). In addition to the most notorious authoritarian legacies of the Chilean constitution, which uphold a "political guardianship" role for the military, the constitution shrank the number of popularly elected representatives in both the Chamber of Deputies and the Senate and created an electoral system that has notably weakened political diversity (Ensalaco 1994). Moreover, the complicated binomial majoritarian electoral system, designed to overrepresent the Chilean right, continues to reflect authoritarianism's "disdain of popular sovereignty" (Ensalaco 1994, 418–20), its politics of exclusion rather than inclusion.

Chilean sociologists and social psychologists make a convincing case that the brutality that ended incoporationist trends instilled deep-seated and lasting fears regarding individual security, collective identities, and participation in the public sphere (Lechner 1988, 1992; Salimovich, Lira, and Weinstein 1992). Targeted, direct repression in the workplace, the universities, the poor neighborhoods, the city, and the countryside had a multiplier effect: kidnapping, torturing, and "disappearing" one person affected the many. Here the conceptual language of Giddens (1984) and Habermas (1975) becomes quite useful, for it lends a markedly psychological dimension to understanding the production and reproduction of social and political systems. Using their terms, authoritarian repression hit at the heart of Chile's traditional "identity-securing" systems (Habermas 1975), breaking down both individual and collective routines, or "anxiety diffusing mechanisms" (Giddens 1984; Erikson 1967). Under the dictatorship, political stability came at the expense of anxiety diffusion. Collective routines were shrunk, reduced to the private sphere, practiced with caution. The repressive atmosphere that guaranteed political stability produced rather than diffused anxiety.

In the Chilean case, we would argue that the legacies of transformed notions of political stability as anxiety producing endure. The United Nations

Development Programme [UNDP], in its *Desarrollo humano en Chile 1998*, pointed to a series of indicators that reveal an exaggerated personal insecurity. Based on extensive surveys, focus groups, and empirical data on national conditions, the UNDP (1998) report argued that Chileans today, in comparison to those of the past, harbor a good deal of fear: "fear of the other, fear of social exclusion, and fear of that which makes no sense" (22). The report found that Chileans do not discuss political issues except with close friends and family. Politics as openly expressed in the public sphere is thus anxiety producing—a legacy of authoritarian rule. Moreover, according to Latinobarómetro, Chileans today are among the Latin Americans least inclined to participate in public demonstrations (cited in UNDP 1998, 144). Argument, debate, dissent, even protest take the form of "irruptions" in an otherwise "agreeable" routinization of politics (Wilde 1999).

In addition, Chileans sense that there is a good deal they do not know. While 69.8 percent of Chileans surveyed say they follow the news every day, and another 12.6 percent say they follow the news from four to six days a week, 64.2 percent say they feel little informed or uninformed about the facts that affect their lives (UNDP 1998, 150). There is little sense among Chileans regarding a shared or collectively communicated knowledge. Chileans feel "in the dark" beyond their immediate circles of family and close friends.

Recent trends in voter participation tend to confirm Chileans' alienation from politics. During two of the climactic moments of the Chilean transition, namely the 1988 plebiscite and the 1989 congressional and presidential elections, voter registration and participation were at record levels. Since 1989, voter registration and participation have dropped, not just steadily, but dramatically. Among the most "disenchanted" of the voting-age population are Chilean youth, over a million of whom failed to register as newly eligible voters in the December 1997 elections. In addition, over a quarter of the votes cast by registered voters in the December 1997 elections were either abstentions or null and void. As Felipe Agüero (1998a) writes, "In all, about 3.7 million people, of a total of 9.6 million of voting age, chose not to express any preference. Government officials promptly recognized this as a protest vote" (69). In the structuration of everyday life, disenchantment actively pervades Chilean political consciousness.

Regarding participation in organizations, a more recent UNDP (2000) survey reports that fully two-thirds of Chilean society participate in no organizations, whether social, religious, or political. The primary type of organization for those who do participate is religious. The majority of participants report that their activity is limited to sporadic participation, usually in the form of attendance at a public event or a financial contribution. Ongoing, civic-minded participation is simply not a feature of Chileans' routines.

Regarding *political* participation specifically, a public opinion poll conducted by the Centro de Estudios de la Realidad Contemporánea (CERC) in December 1997 during the congressional election campaigns found that "eight out of ten respondents received written information about the candidates, one out of every two watched political campaign 'infomercials' (*franjas*) on television at some point, and one in ten participated in some campaign act or demonstration" (cited in UNDP 1998, 144). In the language of Chilean sociologist Tomás Moulián (1997, 1998), it is a "consumption-oriented" rather than a participatory-oriented politics.

Evidence indicates that political party membership has also declined, from an average of between 9 and 11 percent between 1961 and 1973 to a mere 2 percent in 1996 (earlier polls conducted by Eduardo Hamuy, 1996 poll by Latinobarómetro, both cited in UNDP 1998, 142–44). Regarding political party identification more generally, Chile's Centro de Estudios Públicos reports that the percentage of "those who do not identify with any political party has increased from 21% in December 1991 to 42% in November 1996" (quoted in Agüero 1998a, 68). An October 1995 survey of 1,900 respondents conducted across the country by the Chilean public relations firm FEEDBACK Comunicaciones placed the percentage of those who neither "sympathized nor identified with any party in particular" at an even higher 60.4 percent (FEEDBACK Comunicaciones 1995).

How do we explain the dramatic decline in voter participation and in other forms of citizenship? After all, there was a resurgence of participation in the 1980s to defeat (and defend) the dictatorship. We would argue that the authoritarian regime dealt a serious blow to upward trends in political incorporation and that the demobilizing legacy reinforced an ultimately cautious approach among the opposition leadership to the mode of transition. The 1990s was marked by continuining elitist, insular tendencies among political party leaders, who remained fearful, or at least hesitant, regarding the consequences of incorporation (see Hite 2000).

If we examine the patterns of political incorporation, particularly patterns of mass political mobilization, from the preauthoritarian years to the present, we find a general pattern of gradual political incorporation from the 1950s to the mid-1960s, growing more intense and mobilizational from the mid-1960s to the coup. Political incorporation came to an abrupt end from the coup d'état to the mid-1980s. In 1983, after ten years of authoritarian rule, sectors of the opposition regrouped to initiate a mobilizational protest period against the dictatorship, and mobilizational efforts ebbed and flowed from the mid-1980s to the 1988 plebiscite. The opposition leadership mounted a final mobilizational effort for the 1989 national elections. During the decade of the 1990s, political leaders steered away from mobilizational politics, shifting their campaign efforts toward "spins" and "spots" in the national media.

Within the mobilizational period from the mid-1980s to the 1988 plebiscite, it is important to distinguish certain features. The mobilizing against the dictatorship from the first mass protests in 1983 to the protests of 1986 represented a moment in which much of the political opposition believed a mobilizational strategy might bring an end to the dictatorship. By 1986, this sense had dissipated. The military regime successfully mounted a carrot-and-stick approach to confront its opposition: The regime offered economic concessions to sectoral organizations representing the Chilean middle class; but the Chilean poor, including the working poor who risked losing their jobs for their participation in the protests, faced brutal crackdowns in their neighborhoods (Hunneeus 1986). Such regime innovation in the face of political and economic crisis proved effective at many levels. It showed that the regime could ultimately provide the flexibility in the economic arena that the middle class demanded, and it reinforced a sense of economic insecurity, dependency, and fear among the Chilean poor. Significant sectors of the opposition leadership began to accept and plan for the transition timetable dictated by the military and outlined in the transitional clauses of the 1980 constitution, including the 1988 plebiscite to determine whether Pinochet would remain as president until 1997. Mobilizational politics shifted from protest against the dictatorship to mass efforts to register Chilean voters in preparation for the plebiscite.

Despite attempts to proceed otherwise, the mode of transition was determined primarily by the military regime itself. While Pinochet lost the 1988 plebiscite, the transitional clauses spelled out the procedures following such an outcome and continued to guarantee tremendous military autonomy, an electoral system overrepresenting former supporters of the authoritarian regime, and a powerful set of legal obstacles to block constitutional reform. Equally important, after negotiating a series of amendments, the opposition accepted the legitimacy of the 1980 constitution as well as last-minute authoritarian regime decrees (*amarres*). Moreover, opposition leaders of the political center and center-left, haunted by memories of past errors and the atrocities of the dictatorship, proved loath to confront the military and hold it accountable for its past crimes (Hite 2000).

Chilean citizens perceive political elite behavior in negative terms: polls conducted between 1991 and 1994 by Participa found that those who considered political parties "indispensable for democracy" declined from 63 percent in 1991 to 55.4 percent in 1994. Those who felt that political parties "function well" declined from 39.8 percent to 24.8 percent, and those who felt that "[i]n Chile parties only pursue their own interests" increased from 50 percent to 65.1 percent (cited in UNDP 1998, 143). Thus, while Chile boasts a highly institutionalized political party system as a key component of a good democracy, it does not enjoy the high degree of legitimacy it once possessed as a system for political representation.

Beyond the legacies of direct repression of organization and association are the shutting down and reinvention of political discourse and debate. Through the formal promulgation of a new constitution, the major media, and everyday forms of discursive practices, the dictatorship "introduced" a series of decrees, laws, messages, euphemisms, and silences that continue to influence political communication as well as the balance of power in both subtle and not-so-subtle ways.

One important indicator of the parameters of discourse is the practice of censorship, as well as the more difficult-to-measure practice (or consequence) of self-censorship. In Human Rights Watch's study *The Limits of Tolerance: Freedom of Expression and the Public Debate in Chile* (1998), the group documented the cases of twenty-five individual journalists charged with "defamation of a public authority," Article 6(b) of the State Security Law, since the 1990 transition. Several were charges brought by different branches of the military against newspaper, magazine, and television reporters and their editors. While some of these "seditious" investigative reports focused on military actions under the dictatorship, most concerned current investigations into military corruption. Human Rights Watch also documented cases of self-censorship by the major media and printed press, which decide not to run stories for fear of costly legal battles (and perhaps more). In April 1999, journalist Alejandra Matus left Chile to avoid arrest under Article 6 for her writing of the "Black Book of Chilean Justice," a detailed account of the judiciary's failure to recognize the hundreds of writs of habeas corpus filed by human rights victims and their families during the dictatorship. In May 2001, the Chilean government partially amended the censorship laws.

In spite of this record, the October 1998 arrest of Pinochet has considerably altered aspects of the political and legal playing field. The Frei government actively pursued Pinochet's release and return to Chile, concerned that if it did not do so, the institutional carriers of authoritarian legacies could prove destabilizing. Over time, however, Pinochet's eighteen-month stay under household arrest in London opened space for members of the judiciary to proceed with investigations and indictments of orchestrators of Chilean disappearances (see Aguilar and Hite, chapter 5 of this volume). In the December 1999 presidential elections, the once outspoken Pinochet loyalist candidate Joaquín Lavín distanced himself from Pinochet. Once considered absolutely immune from prosecution, Pinochet faced the possibility he would be held responsible for covering up criminal acts on Chilean soil. While the Chilean Supreme Court ultimately ruled him mentally unfit to stand trial, thus avoiding his prosecution, the ruling made it untenable for Pinochet to return to his Senate seat.

Authoritarian legacies continue to plague democracy in Chile, narrowing the parameters of political behavior, political participation, and political discourse. The duration and innovation of the authoritarian regime transformed fundamental patterns of political incorporation. Seventeen years of authoritarian discourse condemning the behaviors of parties and politicians of the past took a toll on the Chilean citizenry, who today in the polls show only lukewarm support for democracy as a political system preferable to any other. Fear of political conflict continues to pervade both leaders and citizens. Formal authoritarian enclaves in the Chilean constitution restrict the representativeness of elected officials and grant the military autonomy from executive authority. The mode of transition was predominantly defined by the authoritarian regime. These variables have deeply influenced the extent of postauthoritarian political incorporation of the citizenry, negatively affecting the quality of democracy in Chile today. This situation is aggravated even further by the abusiveness of the police (see Pereira and Ungar, chapter 7 of this volume).

Nevertheless, symbolic gestures by president Ricardo Lagos (2000–06) indicate his awareness of how insulated Chilean leaders are from the citizenry and of his interest in garnering civil society support for democratic political reform. On his first day in the presidential palace, for example, Lagos announced that the palace doors would be open to all citizens, and for the first time in almost half a century, the gates to the palace remain open each working day. The judiciary is changing considerably. Chilean courts have moved decisively against dozens of officers responsible for human rights violations under the authoritarian regime (see Aguilar and Hite, chapter 5 of this volume). Such acts may foretell a new period of political work to lessen the burden of authoritarian legacies on democracy.

Brazil

For the Brazilian case, we can trace the exacerbation of traditional authoritarian legacies by a durable and innovative authoritarian regime (1964–85), as well as the continued active presence of such legacies given the Brazilian mode of transition from authoritarian rule. We join Frances Hagopian (chapter 3) and Anthony Pereira and Mark Ungar (chapter 7) in this volume, who argue that authoritarian legacies in Brazil have been reproduced in state agencies that are largely unresponsive and unaccountable. Brazilian authoritarian legacies are also manifest in what is a very weak system of political representation.

One can locate the obstacles to democratic deepening in the more distant moments of the founding of the republic and in the Getulio Vargas regime, reemphasizing Latin American claims that modernization and nation-state building in the region have been extremely authoritarian (Murilo de Carvalho 1990; Andrews 1991; Diacon 1991; Borón 1995; Cruz 1998). For our purposes, it is useful to focus on particular types of authoritarian legacies, including patriarchal social domination (O'Donnell 1992), traditional political privileging (Hagopian 1996a), military prerogatives (Zaverucha 1999; Stepan 1988), and the unrule of law (Holston and Caldeira 1998; Pinheiro 1997).

There is considerable debate on just how "new" Brazilian authoritarian legacies are, though disagreement is more a question of degree than substance. Many highlight the 1964–85 Brazilian military regime's authoritarian breaks and exacerbations as keys to understanding obstacles to the quality of democracy. Such actions include (but are not limited to) the military's redistricting of the electoral system to overrepresent the north and northeastern states and underrepresent the industrialized center-south; the overrepresentation of the military in the cabinet; the institutionalized practice of decree laws; and the tremendous power and insulation of the state military police forces (Pereira 1997).

In terms of military regime innovation and durability, it could be argued that the Brazilian military's decision to permit ongoing, albeit limited, political contestation contributed to a distorted political socialization process that has undermined the legitimacy of the relationship between electoral institutions and democracy. Under the military, the national Congress continued to function, and the regime staged direct elections for mayors and many governorships. The Brazilian citizenry, therefore, does not disassociate electoral choice from authoritarian regimes. In fact, Brazilians may perceive little difference between authoritarianism and democracy in crucial local and regional-level elections and dynamics.

Frances Hagopian (1996b) argues that to understand hindrances to democratic representation in Brazil, the military's strengthening of political features continued from the preauthoritarian period may be as significant as the military's breaks or innovations. Hagopian traces the role of the traditional political elite, an elite defined primarily by territorial interests and clientelist practices. She claims that the military regime strengthened the traditional political elite at the expense of progressive and more democratic-minded politicians and movements, and that this dynamic has remained a central feature of Brazilian democracy in spite of the recent dramatic victory of Partido de los Trabahladores candidate Luís Inácio Lula da Silva, or Lula, in his fourth run for the presidency.

The lengthy mode of transition favored the perseverance of authoritarian legacies, for the military as well as the traditional political elite, in the postauthoritarian period. The military guarded their roles as dominant actors in the country's national security, broadly defined, including issues of presidential succession, internal order as well as external defense, and directions in economic development (Stepan 1988). As in Chile, the Brazilian military "executed transitions without compromise" (Agüero 1998b, 10). While the high prerogatives afforded the Brazilian military have not been fully exercised, successive administrations have appeased the military on several fronts (Agüero 1998b, 17).

The 1988 constitution contributed to the formal institutionalization of a far-reaching internal mission for the military. This mission has been exercised powerfully, if unevenly, in the post-transition period. Some important national and regional political elites (chiefly in the state of São Paulo) have actively contested such power, while in many regions and among the country's poor majority, military justice is clearly the main form of justice exercised (see, e.g., Zaverucha 1999, on the state of Pernambuco).

Brazilians remember the military regime both as the guarantor of order and as comparatively nonrepressive. This has contributed to the comparatively low levels of legitimacy for democracy as preferable above all else (never reaching over 50 percent of those surveyed by Latinobarómetro between 1995 and 1998, for example; Caldeira 1996). The majority of Brazilians attribute high levels of crime and everyday violence to weak authority. Yet citizens also perceive the military police as corrupt, unjust, and above the law (Caldeira 1996, 205). Thus, while there is indifference and even support for harsh treatment of alleged criminals, there is also a strong sense that "justice is a joke" and "immunity is widespread" (Caldeira 1996, 205).

This sense that corruption and the lack of accountability are widespread is not reserved solely for the military police. Brazilians hold little regard for the justice system as a whole (Linz and Stepan 1996, 179), and they view politicians in general as unabashedly self-serving and corrupt (Weyland 1997, 110). And as the 1992 impeachment of President Collor and more recent high-level scandals attest, Brazilians have a good deal of justification for such views. Although Collor was impeached in a very democratic process, "state officials often violate the laws with impunity" (Linz and Stepan 1996, 179).

The connection between social exclusion and violence in the post-transition period has broadened and deepened. Far from encouraging a politics of wide-ranging incorporation or the practice of citizenship, Brazil possesses a highly exclusionary, unequal system regarding basic human rights. Paulo Sergio Pinheiro (1997, esp. 270–71) argues that institutionalized violence against the poor and disenfranchised is a structural feature of the Brazilian reality.

Many claim that the new democratic rules of the game have in fact furthered political fragmentation, bureaucratic bottlenecks, and general patronage politics (Weyland 1997; Linz and Stepan 1996; Mainwaring 1995). Linz and Stepan (1996, 184) argue that the political party system exacerbates political party fragmentation, where political candidates perceive their vote as a "personal vote," not a "party vote." Guillermo O'Donnell (1992) argues that the basic obstacle to democracy in Brazil is "the predominant style of doing politics" (36).

A political style which is predominantly clientelistic and prebendalist may be normal in an oligarchical republic based on a predominantly agrarian society, where capitalist social relations are not widespread and where there is little organization and mobilization of the popular sector. The politics practiced in such contexts consists of "conversations among gentlemen," which scarcely conceive of party discipline. Relations with the subordinated classes are clientelistic. With regard to the state apparatus, these relations are based on the distribution or appropriation of sinecures; relations among politicians consist mostly of the exchange of support and "favors" for the (mostly regionalist) interests which they embody. This oligarchical style was the predominant style of politics practiced in Brazil prior to the coup of 1964. It is still the case today. (O'Donnell 1992, 34–35)

Finally, in comparison to the Southern Cone cases, Brazil's large public sector of the economy has tended to prove intractable to reforms (see Hagopian, Chapter 3 of this volume). Authoritarian legacies actively pervade Brazilian democracy, legacies that have in good part been structural and that were exacerbated by the military regime.

Uruguay

The presence of authoritarian legacies is comparatively weak in the Uruguayan case. If we examine the durability of the Uruguayan authoritarian regime (1973–85) and the mode of transition from authoritarian rule, there are indicators that authoritarian legacies should be more enduring than they appear. In addition, while the Uruguayan military was unsuccessful in establishing a new constitution or in transforming the economy, certainly the repressive break and degree of penetration by the dictatorship into the private sphere was just as dramatic and in some ways even more dramatic than in the Chilean case. The Uruguayan military classified each citizen as A, B, or C, on the basis of the individual's perceived threat to the regime. During the late 1970s, Uruguay possessed the highest per capita incarceration and torture rate in the world.

In terms of the mode of transition, the democratic opposition ceded to the majority of the military's demands. The August 1984 Club Naval negotiations between the military and the opposition political elite (with the important exception of the National Party) represented a pact both proscribing two major political opposition figures from participating in the presidential elections and assuring the military that the future Colorado-led government would not press for military accountability for the past (De Brito 1997). The Uruguayan mode of transition, therefore, initiated a legacy of impunity for human rights violators and privileged the authoritarian incumbents' limiting of the parameters for political contestation.

The military regime practiced an unprecedented, systematic pattern of human rights violations that contributed to a form of continuity in security force practices through the democratic period (see Pereira and Ungar, chapter 7 of this volume). Nevertheless, the military failed to be institutionally innovative. In an attempt to mimic the victory of the Chilean military referendum on their 1980 constitution, the Uruguayan military staged a referendum to approve a constitution representing their version of a protected democracy. In November 1980, amidst continuing repression, including high levels of censorhip, Uruguayan voters rejected the military constitutional reform project. More importantly, perhaps, and again unlike the Chilean authoritarians, the Uruguayan military junta oversaw no fundamental changes to the economy and were not viewed by the Uruguayans as successful economic managers.

In a crucial contrast to the Chilean case, there were virtually no Uruguayan right-wing leaders or parties that adamantly supported the military during the authoritarian regime's tenure. While Uruguayan political and civil society was largely silent under the repression of the dictatorship, the 1980 anti-military vote reflected strong support for redemocratization. During the transition and the postauthoritarian period, the organized expressions of Uruguayan military positions have been limited to the military officers clubs and their families—a real contrast to the Chilean case. While transitional president and Colorado Party leader Julio Sanguinetti (1985–89) refused to undertake any kind of truth and reconciliation policy, Sanguinetti did not defend the military's record. The vast majority of Uruguayan society never accepted the framing of the authoritarian period as a war against communist aggression, as did a significant sector of Chilean society.

Thus, in spite of the ability of the Uruguayan military to remain cohesive and in control during its eleven-year reign, authoritarian legacies seem to have had comparatively little effect upon postauthoritarian political incorporation. The military's lack of significant innovation outweighed the effects of regime durability. Its lack of support among important elites and citizenry weakened its ability to exercise its prerogatives, even though political leaders did not press for regime accountability for past human rights atrocities. In contrast to the Chilean case where there is a rupture between pre- and postauthoritarian incorporating politics, Uruguay has generally returned to the preauthoritarian modes of democratic political inclusion.

Three components of this inclusion figure prominently: The first is the nature of the historically dominant political parties. As Hagopian (1996b) argues, while Uruguay's historic dominant parties have always represented the traditional elites, they have also incorporated popular interests, together championing "the most progressive package of social welfare policies in the hemisphere" (69). In addition, the most recent presidential elections demonstrated the major strength of a comparatively new political force, the Frente Amplio, an alliance of left parties and factions. Since 1990, the Frente Amplio has governed Montevideo, home to roughly half of the country's population. Frente Amplio leader, the Montevideo intendant Tabaré Vásquez, forced a runoff in the 1999 presidential elections, and he was ultimately defeated by an alliance of the two traditionally dominant parties. In the post-authoritarian period, new parties and party alliances have thus challenged and broadened organized political expression and representation (Winn and Ferro-Clérico 1997).

The second institutionalized mechanism and tradition of political inclusion is the Uruguayan referendum, which has allowed both government and opposition to educate and mobilize citizens around key issues. The process of signature gathering, as well as the use of the media and public forums to present both the "yes" and the "no," garner important attention and debate for contentious policies. The Uruguayan human rights movement and its allies engaged in a more than two-year bitter struggle to win the right to a referendum on the December 1986 Ley de Caducidad, a virtual blanket amnesty law (De Brito 1997). While the movement was disappointed by the "yes" outcome of the April 1989 plebiscite, human rights activists recognized the opportunity the referendum afforded to educate their fellow citizens about basic civil, political, and social rights as well as about the grim legacy of abuse. Demands for an investigation into the forced disappearances under the military have recently returned to center stage, and current president Jorge Battle is the first since the transition to support such efforts.

The third component of political incorporation is both old and new social movements' level of institutional access to corporate bodies of the state. Trade unions serve on decision-making councils. A new movement of Uruguayan retirees banded with established groups and political party factions to defeat major pension and social security reforms. The retirees also won a seat at the decision-making table regarding future reforms (Filgueira and Papadopulos 1997). In addition, after more than a decade-long hiatus, the Uruguayan executive assumed its responsibility regarding investigation of the fate of forced disappearances and announced financial compensation for families of the victims.

Uruguayan civil society has demanded and political society and the state have ceded important political space to Uruguayan citizens regarding such issues as accountability for human rights violations of the past, privatization, and social security. Such traditions and practices sustain democratic legitimacy in the face of difficult battles over reform (Blake 1998), overriding the influence of authoritarian legacies.

Argentina

There are important parallels between the Argentine and the Uruguayan cases regarding failed authoritarian regime innovation, thus producing weaker authoritarian legacies than in Brazil and Chile. Like the Uruguayan military, the Argentine military juntas (1976–83) conducted historically unprecedented, systematic violations of human rights, trouncing the Argentine left and the organized working class. Such massive repression contributed to a silent, fearful public. And like the Uruguayan military, the Argentine authoritarians failed to transform the badly performing Argentine economy. This led both to tensions within the military as institution and to the disastrous decision to confront England over the Malvinas/Falkland territory. The Argentine mode of transition through collapse turned the tables on the balance of power between authoritarian incumbents and the opposition. As Felipe Agüero discusses in chapter 6 of this volume, the Argentine mode of transition allowed postauthoritarian administrations to reform the military, thereby weakening the armed forces as carriers of authoritarian legacies.

Considered in the context of authoritarian legacies and a political learning process with reference to continuity of these legacies and reaction against them, reactions to authoritarianism (for better and for worse) in the post-transition period offer a particularly interesting perspective on political consciousness, public political debate, and political behavior. The profound *desprestigio* of the armed forces granted politicians comparatively ample space to reclaim democratic civilian authority. In addition, for the first time in twentieth-century Argentine history, the Argentine upper classes channeled considerable energy into democratic party politics. No longer skeptical about playing by the democratic rules of the game, the Argentine upper strata formed the Unión del Centro Democrático (UCEDE), a political party to champion neoliberal reform through electoral mobilization (Gibson 1992).

While the Argentine executive chose not to sustain punishment of the military for the past, the general antiauthoritarian reaction within Argentine society has remained at consistently high levels. This reaction can be measured in several ways. First, according to Latinobarómetro, public opinion preference for democracy over authoritarianism has averaged roughly 73 percent through the 1990s (exceeded in South America only by Uruguay, which averages 80 percent over the same period). This is in spite of quite negative, conflictive preauthoritarian democratic experiences. Thus, while comparable data are not available for the pre-1976 period, the volatility of Argentine regimes into the 1970s would suggest that the high and sustained legitimacy for democracy in the post-1983 period is a strong and potentially enduring reaction to the *Proceso*.

Another set of measures of the Argentine reaction is survey data regarding what to do with the repressors, including public opinion data on amnesty laws, accountability, and sentencing of the generals. Surveys show that in spite of Raúl Alfonsín's and Carlos Menem's actions, a strong majority of Argentine citizens felt amnesty would be "very negative" for the country, that "all those in the military who violated human rights are responsible, regardless of rank," and that the ex-commanders "should not be freed" (Landi and González Bombal 1995, 158, 170, 174). Argentines felt strongly that holding the military accountable for the past was crucial to subordinating the military in the post-transition period, as well as to ensuring that such violations would never happen again.

A good deal of debate among Argentine scholars has centered on the trials of the ex-commanders and related events as crucial instances for analysis of both the transition and the mediation of authoritarian legacies between the state and society. While many pointed to the Argentine trials and their aftermath as far too debilitating a method for addressing the authoritarian past (Ackerman 1992), other scholars have emphasized several positive outcomes for the quality of Argentine democracy. The first such outcome has been the state's (namely the judiciary's) lesson to the military that authoritarian regressions would be met with punishments that posed potentially irreparable damage to the military as an institution (Acuña and Smulovitz 1995).

Another positive outcome of the trials has been transformed discursive practices and perceptions regarding the legitimacy of the Argentine judiciary (Jelín et al. 1996). In a series of intensive interviews, Jelín et al. found that the trials made Argentine citizens perceive formal institutions of justice and the rule of law as more credible and conferred a new legitimacy on a judiciary conventionally viewed as inaccessible and elitist (129–30). The authors also suggested a correlation between observation of the judiciary's handling of the powerful elite—the generals—and citizens' subsequent recourse to judiciary institutions for redress of grievances.

A second "reaction" that has also been the subject of debate is that of the legacy of the human rights movement. Scholars credit the Argentine human rights movement for inserting an agenda inclusive of human rights issues into existing social and political groups (see, e.g., González Bombal 1988). They also see human rights groups as the precursors for today's civil society activism around such issues as government transparency and accountability (Landi and González Bombal 1995; Jelín et al. 1996).

Some suggest that the human rights movement has contributed to a pluralization of collective action in the post-transition period (Peruzzotti 1998). Others have questioned just how "democratic" the intraorganizational practices of the new social movement groups have proved to be. Evidence indicates that the practices within these organizations are just as authoritarian as those of more traditional political groups, if not more so, given the extreme conditions in which the new organizations first emerged and operated (Crahan and Armony 1998).

There has been a good deal of debate in the Argentine case regarding the use of executive decree laws to override the Congress. Under the Menem administrations, the president practiced unprecedented use of such powers. As Paola Cesarini documents in chapter 4 of this volume, Menem also worked to undermine judicial independence (see also Larkins 1998). While some have argued that the resort to executive decrees may constitute a mechanism for unpopular but necessary reforms, Cesarini suggests that such behavior represents an executive's drawing upon authoritarian legacies that will not bode well for the quality of democracy.

The Argentine case powerfully reminds us that "forgetting the past," particularly one so brutal for so many, is unviable, and therefore that how political leaders and institutions negotiate authoritarian legacies is crucial to the potential erosion of as well as support for democratic political institutions. The postauthoritarian administrations of Alfonsín and Menem ultimately performed a political calculus of trading off prosecution of the military for important military reforms, including budget cuts and subordination of the military to civilian authority (Roniger and Sznajder 2000). Yet like her neighbors of the Southern Cone, Argentina has had to face the continual "resurfacing of the repressors" and radical rightist groups (Feitlowitz 1998; Payne 2000). There have been numerous (and quite bizarre) instances, from the circumstances surrounding the dozen or more public confessions of complicity in the repression to the discovery that active-duty officers were in line for major promotions and positions (including elected ones) in spite of their dark human rights records. The confessions and revelations have evoked extreme, even violent, reactions from a range of both public and anonymous actors, contributing to fleeting moments of tension and uncertainty around such reactions (Feitlowitz 1998, esp. 193–255). Moreover, there are important continuities between authoritarian and postauthoritarian police practices, well documented by Pereira and Ungar in chapter 7 of this volume.

As the Chilean case also reveals, the "wheels of justice" move slowly and as such are subject to shifts in the political and legal climate over time. In June 1998, on the basis of a judicial case begun by the Grandmothers of the Plaza de Mayo in 1985, an Argentine judge ordered the arrest of Lieutenant General Jorge Videla for his role in the "kidnapping" of five babies born to political prisoners in capitivity in the 1970s. While Menem attempted to dismiss many of the revelations as an unnecessary revisiting of the past, these instances represent open wounds, "wild cards" in terms of their effects on citizens' senses of personal security and autonomy.

The repressors' stories and behavior in the post-transition period resurrect painful memories and trigger sometimes violent responses from a handful of anonymous extremists (or mercenaries or *mafiosos*). Yet the emergence of the repressors into full public view, the public expressions of disgust for the ex-commanders, and the public debates surrounding the meaning of these personified authoritarian legacies represent an active public sphere, engaged in a public soul searching. This has only very recently begun to happen in Chile, for example, where for close to a decade public silence was more the norm than the exception.

Conclusion

In this chapter, we have attempted to identify authoritarian legacies that are hindrances to the quality of democracy. Before entering into a comparative discussion of such legacies, we will review the contextual dimensions that influence and condition the authoritarian legacies in each country. Table 2.3 lays out the presence and the salience of these dimensions. We use a capital X to indicate what we judge to be the stronger salience of the dimension and a small x to indicate when the dimension is less salient but nonetheless present. An empty cell indicates the absence of any saliency of the dimension.

The "durability" dimension is particularly relevant for Portugal, Chile, Spain, and Brazil, and, as anticipated at the beginning of the chapter, it is more relevant when it is accompanied by institutional innovation, as is the case in Portugal and Chile. For Uruguay, the durability-related cell is empty. While Uruguay's twelve-year authoritarian regime span was unprecedented for a country with such a long history of democracy, in comparative terms, it was nonetheless a short period, and authoritarian socializing institutions were not set in motion.

Regarding institutional innovation—the chief aspect of innovation we consider—again, Portugal and Chile stand out as highly innovative regimes. Curiously, for both cases, there was a recurring reference to Italian fascism— that is, to the third case where there was strong innovation. Spain and Brazil were also fairly innovative regimes, though to a lesser extent in comparative terms. In both cases, again, durability works to enhance the strength of the

TABLE 2.3   Dimensions Influencing Authoritarian Legacies, per Country

Factors	Italy	Spain	Portugal	Chile	Brazil	Uruguay	Argentina
Durability	X	X	X	X	X		
Institutional innovation	X	X	X	X	X	x	x
Continuous transition		X		X	X	X	

relative innovation. Uruguay and Argentina were innovative regimes in sinister ways, that is, the two regimes restructured the security apparatuses of repression and engaged in unprecedented abuse.

Finally, for Spain and for three of the four Latin American countries, the modes of transition are continuous. And again, as expected, this is an important dimension when we account for the presence of authoritarian legacies. On the whole, on the basis of our dimensions, we expected to have a stronger, more salient set of legacies in Chile, first, but also in Spain and Brazil, with Portugal and Italy ranking second and Uruguay and Argentina ranking a more distant third. Such expectations are confirmed by our empirical analyses, as we will see below.

Regarding specific, expected authoritarian legacies themselves (see Table 2.2), we discern legacies both in the formal rules of governance and in dramatic, explicit assertions of power by unequivocal authoritarian actors. But legacies are also less easy to detect—and even more difficult to measure—in the day-to-day political patterns and practices that condition democratic representation and participation. In fact, authoritarian legacies pervade most societies, and in spite of the difficulties, attempts to identify them have to be pursued: particular authoritarian legacies become serious hindrances to democracies when agents give legacies unchallenged or unchecked expression, visibility, or power. Table 2.4 provides one summary of our analysis.

The dimension concerning *gleichschaltung*, or the leveling of cultural/social/economic differences, is present in Table 2.2 but not in Table 2.4. This is so because in none of the cases we examined was this kind of phenomenon—recurrent in totalitarian regimes—empirically evident. For many years the Franco regime attempted to suppress the ethnic, language, and cultural differences in Catalonia and the Basque Countries particularly. The only real result

TABLE 2.4   Authoritarian Legacies as Constraints to a "Good" Democracy, per Country

Dimension	Legacy	Italy	Spain	Portugal	Chile	Brazil	Uruguay	Argentina
Regime institutions and norms	Authoritarian legal rules	X			X	X		
	Poor or no rule of law					X		x
	Barely independent judiciary				x	X		x
	Large public sector of economy	X		X		X		
Elite actors	High military prerogatives			X	X	X	X	
	Poor or no efficiency of police				X	X	X	
	Radical rightist groups	X						X
	No party elite accountability	X	X	X			X	X
Culture and mass level	Statism	X	X	X	X	X	X	X
	Passivity/conformism/cynicism	X	X	X	X	X	X	X
	Fear/alienation from politics				X	X		X
	Nondemocratic attitudes	X	X	X	X	X	X	
	Rightist radical party/ies	X			X	X	X	

was to fuel and further radicalize the violent factions among Basque nationalists in their demands for independence (see also Aguilar 2001). In Chile, while it was unsuccessful, the Pinochet regime similarly attempted to annul the political left. This, too, created a violent organized response from the ultraleft. Pinochet's attempt to abolish the left is illustrated by Spanish judge Baltasár Garzón's charge of genocide against Pinochet, and a socialist leader has returned to become president of Chile.

Regarding regime institutions and norms, Italy, Brazil, and Chile are countries where authoritarian legal rules remain present in the postauthoritarian period. The obvious example of this for the Chilean case is the 1980 constitution. O'Donnell's (1999a) analysis of the poor rule of law is confirmed here in terms of legacies for Brazil and Argentina, albeit in distinct ways regarding the extent of the "unrule" of law. A barely independent judiciary is a legacy in three of the four Latin American countries. For Chile, a more independent judiciary is beginning to emerge and has been a focus of reform for successive democratic administrations. The Argentine judiciary has been engaged in a fitful process of establishing independence from the executive. We find the legacy of a large public sector of the economy in Brazil, Italy, and Portugal. During Portugal's 1974–82 transition there was massive nationalization of the economy, later transformed radically by Cavaco Silva in the late 1980s. Italy and Brazil possessed resilient, large public sectors that have been shrunk only recently.

Undoubtedly, the lack of full civilian control of the army over a sustained period is one of the most important legacies. This is the case for Portugal for virtually a decade after the establishment of a different regime; for Uruguay, given the pacted mode of transition to democracy; for Brazil, with the role of the armed forces in the Brazilian state, in addition to the continuous mode of transition; and for Chile, where the political role of the armed forces has been even longer-lasting and more profound (see Agüero, chapter 6 of this volume). The inefficiency of police, so relevant for the guarantee of civil rights, also emerges as an important legacy (see Pereira and Ungar, chapter 7 of this volume). While inefficiency of the police has been a constant throughout modern Latin America, it is clear that the military regimes exacerbated this legacy. The rightist radical groups are strongly relevant and influential in the Italian political arena. For Argentina, the *carapintadas* were extremely active during the transition, and select leaders are still active today (Payne 2000).

If we consider elite accountability in terms of the possibility of alternation and incumbency, then in different ways Italy, Spain, and Portugal showed no or low accountability. In Italy, there was no real possibility of alternation until the breakdown of Christian Democracy in the early 1990s. In Spain, there was a long period of socialist dominance, given that the right was seen as contaminated by its association with the Franco regime. And in Portugal there was an even longer period of no alternation until the mid-1990s.

The third set of legacies are cultural. These legacies are deeper and more pervasive and refer to the basic problems of the modes of incorporation, or the ways citizens have been involved and socialized into politics. By *statism*, we refer to the constant, continuous reference to public institutions, as well as to people's expectations that the state will initiate and be responsible for every aspect of their lives. Statism has been highly related to the lengthy authoritarian experiences of southern Europe and Brazil. Passivity, conformism, and cynicism represent the single set of attitudes toward politics that is most widespread throughout the seven countries under analysis. These two aspects together—statism and passivity—make accountability much more difficult to achieve. Accountability assumes the existence of an active civil society.

Of course, statism and passivity were also well embedded in the pre-authoritarian regime political cultures of all these countries. Nevertheless, the authoritarian experiences exacerbated these dimensions. Moreover, politics in the Latin American countries analyzed were characterized by fear and alienation, and this is undoubtedly related to the repressive component of the four military regimes.

In survey studies, we find widespread nondemocratic attitudes across the three southern European countries as well as in Chile and Brazil. This is so in different ways and to a different extent in each of the cases. In Italy, for example, such attitudes have been present for years, including well into the 1990s. In Brazil, in spite of the considerable differences among states within the country, nondemocratic attitudes are quite widespread. Italian radical right parties were present until the late 1980s and early 1990s (Morlino 1996). All three features converge to produce political cultures less than conducive to civic democracy (see also Cruz, chapter 8 of this volume).

It is worth noting that Uruguay possessed a long democratic tradition prior to authoritarian rule, and the absence of nondemocratic attitudes is quite consistent with this past. In Argentina, on the contrary, there is an ironic inconsistency that should be noted. The lack of nondemocratic attitudes in the new democratic regime is incongruent with the negative experiences with previous democracies, characterized by high polarization, conflict, corruption, and the frequent recourse to military force. High ratings for democracy in Argentina thus attest to the potential saliency of an authoritarian legacy in the form of a reaction to the country's authoritarian past.

On the whole, this analysis confirms that both the contextual dimensions and the content of legacies show how numerous the hindrances to a good democracy were and still partially are in Chile and Brazil, but also in Italy for a lengthy period. Argentina and Uruguay present favorable contextual dimensions but less favorable substantive hindrances to a good democracy. Our main conclusion must be that there is no necessary consistency between contextual dimensions and legacies themselves.

Throughout our analysis, we faced analytical challenges that were very difficult to disentangle. We wish to emphasize at least two of them. First, as we have pointed out, authoritarian legacies are often related to preauthoritarian experiences. It is impossible, for example, to analyze the beliefs, attitudes, and behavior at the mass level in Spain and Chile developed under authoritarianism without considering the Second Spanish Republic and civil war in Spain and the Allende period in Chile. This may also account for positive assessments of the authoritarian past during the present democratic regimes.

Second, on several occasions, for all seven countries, it was difficult to separate analytically the influence of authoritarian legacies from the influence of political learning on democratization processes. Such was the case of Italy in the first year after the war, but this is also relevant for the Spanish case, as well as for Uruguay and Argentina, given the contexts of severe repression under authoritarianism.

The question of the fading away of legacies is problematic. First, the fading away itself cannot be taken for granted. The kinds of attitudes and beliefs at the mass level that we describe in Table 2.4 may continue, even when the elapsed time would suggest their disappearance. Such attitudes and beliefs continue, not because of fascism, Salazarism, Francoism, or the various military experiences, but rather because of new features of modernity. Passivity, conformism, cynicism, and alienation are features that are shared and reproduced in contemporary democracies as well as authoritarian regimes. In Italy, the same passivity, indifference, and negative feelings toward politics are perpetuated because they are part of specific cultural traditions and are reproduced by the anti-politics of the new millennium. Similar mechanisms can be envisaged in other countries, including Spain and Brazil. On the other hand, the statism that was characteristic of some authoritarian regimes and that is not reproduced by dominant contemporary cultural and economic paradigms tends to disappear.

Ultimately, we cannot be sure that the fading away of the legacies discussed above is always positive. It cannot be taken for granted that the moderation and low radicalism that have been fundamental components of Spanish and Chilean democratic consolidation are not inextricably related to the indifference and passivity that have been ever-present tendencies within these complex political cultures. The fading away of the latter may imply the disappearance of the former. However, it is well known that those who have no memories of the past lose their identities and are condemned to make the same mistakes (see, among others, Bendix 1984). Thus when we emphasize that some legacies, although hindrances to a "better" democracy, were helpful or very helpful for democratic consolidation, one could conclude that it is wiser to maintain those legacies or—even better—strong memories of them.

NOTES

1. In fact, even in 1913 all male citizens over thirty and some male citizens over twenty-one (i.e., those who had completed military service, who had a primary school diploma, who paid a minimum tax, or who exercised official functions) were entitled to vote. In 1919 only an additional 6.8 percent of the population was enfranchised: from 42.0 percent in 1913 to 48.8 percent in 1919, while in 1909 the electorate was 15.0 percent of the population. The electoral reform of 1919 was more important in terms of the electoral system, which was changed from a single-member majoritarian system to a multimember constituency system with proportional representation and the application of the D'Hondt formula.

2. To establish the existence and diffusion of subcultural areas, we have taken the electoral strength of the class-oriented leftist parties and of the Catholic Party as the main and politically relevant indicator of a subculture, using a vote threshold of about 40 percent. Such an indicator is, of course, fairly limited, and there are others that would be very interesting to analyze, such as association membership. After reviewing them, however, we concluded that the electoral indicator was satisfactory for our purposes and that the use of the others would not lead to substantially different conclusions.

3. The three statements that served as the basis for the index were (1) "Politicians do not worry about people like me"; (2) "Politics is so complicated that people like me don't know what is going on"; and (3) "Those in power always follow their personal interests" (see Morlino and Montero 1995, 250–53). The definition of political alienation follows Finifter's (1970, 389–410; 1972) notion, particularly with reference to the dimension of political powerlessness. This focus on inefficacy is clearly distinct from several related concepts, including the more negative concept of Gam-

son (1968, 56–57), according to which authorities are regarded as "incompetent and stupid"; various scholars' conceptualizations of "social" alienation; or Schwartz's (1973) concept of "estrangement"—the "perception that one does not identify oneself with the political system" (7). See also Citrin and McClosky et al. (1975, 1–31) and Wright (1976).

REFERENCES

Ackerman, Bruce. 1992. *The Future of Liberal Revolution*. New Haven, Conn.: Yale University Press.

Acuña, Carlos, and Catalina Smulovitz. 1995. "Militares en la transición argentina: Del gobierno a la subordinación constitucional." In Carlos Acuña, Inés González Bombal, Elizabeth Jelín, Oscar Landi, Luís Alberto Quevedo, Catalina Smulovitz, and Adriana Vacchieri, *Juicio, castigos y memorias: Derechos humanos y justicia en la política argentina*. Buenos Aires, Argentina: Ediciones Nueva Vision.

Agüero, Felipe. 1998a. "Chile's Lingering Authoritarian Legacy." *Current History* 97, no. 616:66–70.

———. 1998b. "Legacies of Transitions: Institutionalization, the Military, and New Democracies in South America." Paper presented at "Confronting Non-Democratic Legacies during Democratic Deepening: Latin America and Southern Europe in Comparative Perspective," 29 August, Columbia University–Universidad Torcuato di Tella, Buenos Aires.

Aguilar, Paloma. 1996. *Memoria y olvido de la guerra civil española*. Madrid: Alianza Editorial.

———. 2001. "Justicia, política, y memoria: Los legados del Franquismo en la transición española." Estudio/Working Paper 163, Instituto Juan March de Estudios e Investigaciones, Madrid.

Almond, Gabriel A., and Sidney Verba. 1963. *The Civic Culture: Political Attitudes and Democracy in Five Nations*. Princeton, N.J.: Princeton University Press.

Andrews, George Reid. 1991. *Blacks and Whites in São Paulo, Brazil, 1888–1988*. Madison: University of Wisconsin Press.

Arendt, Hannah. 1958. *The Human Condition*. Chicago: University of Chicago Press.

Beetham, David. 1994. "Key Principles and Indices for a Democratic Audit." In David Beetham, ed., *Defining and Measuring Democracy* (pp. 25–43). Thousand Oaks, Calif.: Sage Publications.

Bendix, Reinhard. 1984. *Force, Fate and Freedom: An Historical Sociology*. Berkeley: University of California Press.

Bermeo, Nancy. 1992. "Democracy and the Lessons of Dictatorship." *Comparative Politics*, 24, no. 3:273–91.

Blake, Charles. 1998. "Economic Reform and Democratization in Argentina and Uruguay: The Tortoise and the Hare Revisited?" *Journal of Interamerican Studies and World Affairs* 40, no. 3:1–26.

Borón, Atilio. 1989. *Authoritarian Ideological Traditions and Transition: Towards Democracy in Argentina*. Papers on Latin America, no. 8. New York: Institute of Latin American and Iberian Studies, Columbia University.

———. 1995. *State, Capitalism, and Democracy in Latin America*. Boulder, Colo.: Lynne Rienner.

Botella, Joan. 1992. "La cultura política en la España democrática." In Ramón Cotarelo, ed. *Transición política y consolidación democrática en España* (pp. 121–36). Madrid: Centro de Investigaciones Sociológicas.

Bruneau, Thomas C. 1984. *Portugal in Development: Emigration, Industrialization, the European Community*. Ottawa: University of Ottawa Press.

Bruneau, Thomas C., and Alex Macleod. 1986. *Politics in Contemporary Portugal: Parties and the Consolidation of Democracy*. Boulder, Colo.: Lynne Rienner.

Brunner, José Joaquín. 1985. "Cultura autoritaria y cultura escolar." In José Joaquín Brunner and Gonzalo Catalán, eds., *Cinco estudios sobre cultura y sociedad*. Santiago: Facultad Latinoamericana de Ciencias Sociales.

Caldeira, Teresa. 1996. "Crime and Individual Rights: Reframing the Question of Violence in Latin America." In Elizabeth Jelín and Eric Hershberg, eds., *Constructing Democracy: Human Rights, Citizenship, and Society in Latin America* (pp. 197–214). Boulder, Colo.: Westview Press.

Citrin, J., Herbert McClosky, J. Merrill Shanks, and Paul M. Sniderman. 1975. "Personal and Political Sources of Political Alienation." *British Journal of Political Science* 5:1–31.

Crahan, Margaret, and Ariel Armony. 1998. "A Note of Caution on Civil Society and Transitions from Authoritarianism." Paper presented at "Confronting Non-Democratic Legacies during Democratic Deepening: Latin America and Southern Europe in Comparative Perspective," 28 August, Columbia University–Universidad Torcuato di Tella, Buenos Aires.

Cruz, Consuelo. 1998. "Neither Gentlemen nor Citizens: First World Models of Democracy and Third World Products." Paper presented at "Confronting Non-Democratic Legacies during Democratic Deepening: Latin America and Southern Europe in Comparative Perspective," 27 August, Columbia University–Universidad Torcuato di Tella, Buenos Aires.

De Brito, Alexandra Barahona. 1997. *Human Rights and Democratization in Latin America: Uruguay and Chile*. New York: Oxford University Press.

De Felice, Renzo. 1966. *Mussolini il fascista*. Vol. 1 *La conquista del potere 1921–25*. Turin: Einaudi.

De Lucena, Manuel. 1976. *A evoluçao do sistema corporativo português*. 2 vols. Lisbon: Perspectivas & Realidades.

Della Porta, Donatella, and Morlino, Leonardo. 2001. *Rights and the Quality of Democracy in Italy: A Research Report*. Stockholm: International Institute for Democracy and Electoral Assistance.

Diacon, Todd. 1991. *Millenarian Vision, Capitalist Reality: Brazil's Contestado Rebellion, 1912–1916*. Durham, N.C.: Duke University Press.

Diamond, Larry. 1999. *Developing Democracy toward Consolidation*. Baltimore, Md.: Johns Hopkins University Press.

Dirks, Nicholas, Geoff Eley, and Sherry Ortner, eds. 1996. *Culture/Power/History: A Reader in Contemporary Social Theory*. Princeton, N.J.: Princeton University Press.

Ensalaco, Mark. 1994. "In with the New, Out with the Old? The Democratising Impact of Constitutional Reform in Chile." *Journal of Latin American Studies* 26:409–29.

Erikson, Erik. 1967. *Identity and the Life Cycle*. New York: International Universities Press.

Farneti, Paolo. 1971. *Il sistema politico e società civile: Saggi di teoria e ricerca politica*. Turin: Giappichelli.

———. 1983. *Il sistema dei partiti in Italia 1946–1979*. Bologna: Il Mulino.

FEEDBACK Comunicaciones. 1995. *Evaluación anual del gobierno*. Encuesta secc. no. 8, December. Santiago: Feedback Comunicaciones.

Feitlowitz, Marguerite. 1998. *A Lexicon of Terror: Argentina and the Legacies of Torture*. New York: Oxford University Press.

Feltrin, Paolo. 1991. "Partiti e sindacati: Simbiosi o dominio?" In Leonardo Morlino, ed., *Costruire la democrazia: Gruppi e partiti in Italia* (pp. 293–366). Bologna: Il Mulino.

Filgueira, Fernando, and Jorge Papadapulos. 1997. "Putting Conservativism to Good Use? Long Crisis and Vetoed Alternatives in Uruguay." In Douglas Chalmers, Carlos Vilas, Katherine Hite, Scott Martin, Kerianne Piester, and Monique Segarra, eds., *The New Politics of Inequality in Latin America: Rethinking Participation and Representation*. New York: Oxford University Press.

Finifter, Ada. 1970. "Dimensions of Political Alienation." *American Political Science Review* 64:389–410.

———. 1972. *Alienation and the Political System*. New York: John Wiley.

Fishman, Robert M. 1990. *Working-Class Organization and the Return to Democracy in Spain*. Ithaca, N.Y.: Cornell University Press.

Flora, Peter, and Arnold Heidenheimer. 1981. *The Development of Welfare States in Europe and in America*. New Brunswick, N.J.: Transaction Books.

Galli, Giorgio. 1966. *Il bipartitismo imperfetto*. Bologna: Il Mulino.

Gamson, William A. 1968. *Power and Discontent*. Homewood, Ill.: Dorsey Press.

Gibson, Edward L. 1992. "Conservative Electoral Movements and Democratic Politics: Core Constituencies, Coalition Building, and the Latin American Electoral

Right." In Douglas A. Chalmers, Maria do Carmo, Campello de Souza, and Atilio A. Borón, eds., *The Right and Democracy in Latin America.* New York: Praeger.

Giddens, Anthony. 1984. *The Constitution of Society.* Berkeley: University of California Press.

González Bombal, Inés. 1988. *Los vecinazos: Las protestas barriales en el Gran Buenos Aires, 1982–1983.* Buenos Aires: Ediciones del IDES.

Graham, Larry S. 1993. *Representation and Party Politics in a Comparative Perspective.* Oxford, England: Blackwell.

Gunther, Richard, Giacomo Sani, and Goldie Shabad. 1986. *Spain after Franco: The Making of a Competitive Party System.* Berkeley: University of California Press.

Habermas, Jürgen. 1975. *The Legitimation Crisis.* Boston: Beacon Press.

———. 1986. "Hannah Arendt's Communications Concept of Power." In Steven Lukes, ed., *Power* (pp. 75–93). New York: New York University Press.

Hagopian, Frances. 1995. "After Regime Change: Authoritarian Legacies, Political Representation, and the Democratic Future of South America." *World Politics* 45 (April): 464–500.

———. 1996a. *Traditional Politics and Regime Change in Brazil.* New York: Cambridge University Press.

———. 1996b. "Traditional Power Structures and Democratic Governance in Latin America." In Jorge Dominguez and Abraham Lowenthal, eds., *Constructing Democratic Governance: Latin America and the Caribbean in the 1990s—Themes and Issues.* Baltimore, Md.: Johns Hopkins University Press.

Hartlyn, Jonathan. 1998. "Political Continuities, Missed Opportunities, and Institutional Rigidities: Another Look at Democratic Transitions in Latin America." In Scott Mainwaring and Arturo Valenzuela, eds., *Politics, Society, and Democracy: Latin America.* Boulder, Colo.: Lynne Rienner.

Heimer, Franz-Wilhelm, Jorge Vala-Salvador, and José Manuel Leite Viegas. 1990. "Padrões de cultura política em Portugal: Atitudes em relaçao à democracia." *Análise Social* 25:105–6.

Held, David. 1997. *Models of Democracy.* Stanford, Calif.: Stanford University Press.

Hite, Katherine. 2000. *When the Romance Ended: Leaders of the Chilean Left, 1968–1998.* New York: Columbia University Press.

Holston, James, and Teresa P. R. Caldeira. 1998. "Democracy, Law, and Violence: Disjunctions of Brazilian Citizenship." In Felipe Agüero and Jeffrey Stark, eds., *Fault Lines of Democracy in Post-Transition Latin America* (pp. 263–98). Coral Gables, Fla.: North-South Center Press.

Human Rights Watch. 1998. *The Limits of Tolerance: Freedom of Expression and the Public Debate in Chile.* New York: Human Rights Watch.

Hunneeus, Carlos. 1986. "La dinámica de los 'nuevos autoritarismos': Chile en una perspectiva comparada." *Revista de Estudios Políticos* 54:105–58.

———. 2001. *El régimen de Pinochet.* Santiago: Editorial Sudamericana.

Jelín, Elizabeth, Laura Gingold, Susana G. Kaufman, Marcelo Leiras, Silvia Rabich de Galperín, and Lucas Rubinich. 1996. *Vida cotidiana y control institucional en la Argentina de los '90.* Buenos Aires: Grupo Editor Latinoamericano.

Karl, Terry Lynn, and Philippe Schmitter. 1991. "Modes of Transition in Latin America, Southern Europe and Eastern Europe." *International Social Science Journal* 128 (May): 269–84.

Kaufman, Robert. 1972. *The Politics of Land Reform in Chile.* Cambridge, Mass.: Harvard University Press.

Kurtz, Marcus J. 1999. "Free Markets and Democratic Consolidation in Chile: The National Politics of Rural Transformation." *Politics and Society* 27, no. 2:275–301.

La Palombara, Joseph, and Jerry B. Waters. 1961. "Values, Expectations and Political Predisposition of Italian Youth." *Midwest Journal of Political Science* 5, no. 1:39–58.

Lagos, Marta. 1996. "The Latinobarómetro: Media and Political Attitudes in South America." Paper presented at the annual meeting of the American Political Science Association, 29 August, San Francisco.

Landi, Oscar, and Inés González Bombal. 1995. "Los derechos en la cultura política." In Carlos Acuña, Inés González Bombal, Elizabeth Jelín, Oscar Landi, Luís Alberto Quevedo, Catalina Smulovitz, and Adriana Vacchieri, *Juicio, castigos y memorias: Derechos humanos y justicia en la política argentina.* Buenos Aires: Ediciones Nueva Visión.

Larkins, Christopher. 1998. "The Judiciary and Delegative Democracy in Argentina." *Comparative Politics* 30, no. 4:423–42.

Lechner, Norbert. 1988. *Los patios interiores de la democracia: Subjetividad y política.* Santiago: Facultad Latinoamericana de Ciencias Sociales.

———. 1992. "Some People Die of Fear: Fear as a Political Problem." In Juan Corradi, Patricia Weiss Fagen, and Manuel Antonio Garretón, eds., *Fear at the Edge: State Terror and Resistance in Latin America* (pp. 26–38). Berkeley: University of California Press.

Linz, Juan J. 1964. "An Authoritarian Regime: The Case of Spain." In E. Allardt and Y. Littunen, eds., *Cleavages, Ideologies and Party System* (pp. 291–342). Helsinki: Westermarck Society.

———. 2000. *Totalitarian and Authoritarian Regimes.* Boulder, Colo.: Lynne Rienner.

Linz, Juan, and Alfred C. Stepan. 1996. *Problems of Democratic Transition and Consolidation.* Baltimore, Md.: Johns Hopkins University Press.

Linz, Juan J., Manuel Gomez-Reino, Francisco A. Orizo, and Dario Vila. 1981. *Informe sociológico sobre el cambio político en España 1975–1981.* Madrid: Euramerica.

Lipset, Seymour M., and Stein Rokkan. 1968. "Cleavage Structures, Party Systems and Voter Alignments: An Introduction." In Seymour M. Lipset and Stein Rokkan, *Party Systems and Voter Alignments.* New York: Free Press.

Loveman, Brian. 1976. *Chile: The Legacy of Hispanic Capitalism.* New York: Oxford University Press.

Mainwaring, Scott. 1995. "Brazil: Weak Parties, Feckless Democracy." In Scott Mainwaring and Timothy Scully, eds., *Building Democratic Institutions: Party Systems in Latin America* (pp. 354–98). Stanford, Calif.: Stanford University Press.

Malefakis, Edward. 1995. "The Political and Socioeconomic Contours of Southern European History." In Richard Gunther, P. Nikiforos Diamandouros, and Hans-Jürgen Pahle, eds., *The Politcs of Democratic Consolidation: Southern Europe in Comparative Perspective.* Baltimore, Md.: Johns Hopkins University Press.

Maravall, José María. 1981. *La política de la transición.* Madrid: Taurus.

Marshall, T. H. 1950. *Citizenship and Social Class, and Other Essays.* Cambridge, England: Cambridge University Press.

Matus, Alejandra. 1999. *El libro negro de la justicia chilena.* Santiago: Editorial Planeta.

Méndez, Juan, Guillermo O'Donnell, and Paulo Sergio Pinheiro. 1999. *The (Un)Rule of Law and the Underprivileged in Latin America.* Notre Dame, Ind: University of Notre Dame Press.

Merkl, Peter H. 1999. *The Federal Republic of Germany at Fifty: The End of a Century of Turmoil.* New York: New York University Press.

Mitchell, Brian R. 1980. *European Historical Statistics, 1750–1975.* 2d rev. ed. New York: Facts on File.

Morlino, Leonardo. 1996. "Crisis of Parties and Change of Party System in Italy." *Party Politics* 2, no. 1:5–30.

———. 1998a. *Democracy between Consolidation and Crisis: Parties, Groups and Citizens in Southern Europe.* New York: Oxford University Press.

———. 1998b. "Is There Another Side to the Fascist Legacy?" In Stein Larsen, ed., *Modern Europe after Fascism,* vol. 1. Boulder, Colo.: Social Science Monographs.

Morlino, Leonardo, and Franco Mattei. 1992. "Vecchio e nuovo autoritarismo nell' Europa mediterranea." *Rivista Italiana di Scienza Politica* 22, no.1:137–60.

Morlino, Leonardo, and José Ramon Montero. 1995. "Legitimacy and Democracy in Southern Europe." In Richard Gunther, Nikiforos Diamandouros, and Hans-Jürgen Puhle, eds., *The Politics of Democratic Consolidation: Southern Europe in a Comparative Perspective* (pp. 231–60). Baltimore, Md.: Johns Hopkins University Press.

Moulián, Tomás. 1997. *Chile actual: Anatomía de un mito.* Santiago: LOM-Arcis.

———. 1998. *El consumo me consume.* Santiago: LOM-Arcis.

Munck, Gerardo, and Carol Skalnik Leff. 1997. "Modes of Transition and Democratization: South America and Eastern Europe in Comparative Perspective." *Comparative Politics* 29, no. 3:343–62.

Murilo de Cavalho, José. 1990. *A formacao das almas: O imaginario da Republica no Brasil.* São Paulo: Companhia das Letras.

O'Donnell, Guillermo. 1992. "Transitions, Continuities, and Paradoxes." In Scott Mainwaring, Guillermo O'Donnell, and J. Samuel Valenzuela, eds., *Issues in Democratic Consolidation: The New South American Democracies in Comparative Perspective.* Notre Dame, Ind.: University of Notre Dame Press.

———. 1994. "Delegative Democracy." *Journal of Democracy* 5, no. 1:55–69.

——— 1999a. *Counterpoint: Selected Essays on Authoritarianism and Democratization.* Notre Dame, Ind.: University of Notre Dame Press.

———. 1999b. "Polyarchies and the (Un)rule of Law in Latin America: A Partial Conclusion." In Juan Méndez, Guillermo O'Donnell, and Paulo Sergio Pinheiro, eds., *The (Un)Rule of Law and the Underprivileged in Latin America* (pp. 303–37). Notre Dame, Ind: University of Notre Dame Press.

Payne, Leigh. 2000. *Uncivil Movements: The Armed Right Wing and Democracy in Latin America.* Baltimore, Md.: Johns Hopkins University Press.

Pereira, Anthony. 1997. "Brazil." Memo prepared for Authoritarian Legacies Working Group Meeting, October, Columbia University.

Pereira, Anthony, and Mark Ungar. 1998. "State Security Forces and Democracy in Chile, Argentina and Brazil." Paper presented at "Confronting Non-Democratic Legacies during Democratic Deepening: Latin America and Southern Europe in Comparative Perspective," 29 August, Columbia University–Universidad Torcuato di Tella, Buenos Aires.

Pérez Díaz, Victor V. 1987. *El retorno de la sociedad civil: Respuestas sociales a la transición politica, la crisis económica y los cambios culturales de España 1975–1985.* Madrid: Instituto de Estudios Económicos.

———. 1993. *La primacía de la sociedad civil.* Madrid: Alianza Editorial.

———. 1996. *España puesta a prueba 1976–1996.* Madrid: Alianza Editorial.

Peruzzotti, Enrique. 1998. "Eroding Authoritarian Legacies: Collective Learning and Cultural Innovation in Contemporary Argentina." Paper presented at "Confronting Non-Democratic Legacies during Democratic Deepening: Latin America and Southern Europe in Comparative Perspective," 28 August, Columbia University–Universidad Torcuato di Tella, Buenos Aires.

Petersen, J. 1975. "Elettorato e base sociale del fascismo italiano negli anni venti." *Studi Storici* 16, no. 3:627–69.

Pinheiro, Paulo Sergio. 1997. "Popular Responses to State-Sponsored Violence in Brazil." In Douglas Chalmers, Carlos Vilas, Katherine Hite, Scott Martin, Kerianne Piester, and Monique Segarra, eds., *The New Politics of Inequality in Latin America: Rethinking Participation and Representation* (pp. 261–80). New York: Oxford University Press.

Poggi, Gianfranco, ed. 1968. *L'organizzazione partitica del PCI e della DC.* Bologna: Il Mulino.

Pridham, Geoffrey. 2000. "Confining Conditions and Breaking with the Past: Historical Legacies and Political Learning in Transitions to Democracy." *Democratization* 9:36–64.

Roniger, Luis, and Mario Sznajder. 2000. *The Legacy of Human Rights Violations in the Southern Cone: Argentina, Chile, and Uruguay.* New York: Oxford University Press.

Salimovich, Sofia, Elizabeth Lira, and Eugenia Weinstein. 1992. "Victims of Fear: The Social Psychology of Repression." In Juan Corradi, Patricia Weiss Fagen, and Manuel Antonio Garretón, eds., *Fear at the Edge: State Terror and Resistance in Latin America* (pp. 72–89). Berkeley: University of California Press.

Schamis, Hector. 1991. "Reconceptualizing Latin American Authoritarianism in the 1970s: From Bureaucratic Authoritarianism to Neoconservatism." *Comparative Politics* 23, no. 2:201–20.

Schedler, Andreas. 1998. "What Is Democratic Consolidation?" *Journal of Democracy* 9:91–107.

Schmitter, Philippe. 1974. "Still the Century of Corporatism?" *Review of Politics* 36, no. 1:85–131.

———. 1983. *Democratic Theory and Neo-Corporalist Practice.* Florence: European University Institute.

Schwartz, David C. 1973. *Political Alienation and Political Behavior.* Chicago: Aldine.

Scoppola, Pietro. 1977. *La proposta politica di De Gasperi.* Bologna: Il Mulino.

Scully, Timothy. 1992. *Rethinking the Center: Party Politics in Nineteenth- and Twentieth-Century Chile.* Stanford, Calif.: Stanford University Press.

Siavelis, Peter. 2000. *The President and Congress in Postauthoritarian Chile: Institutional Constraints to Democratic Consolidation.* University Park: Pennsylvania State University Press.

Silva, Eduardo. 1996. "From Dictatorship to Democracy: The Business-State Nexus in Chile's Economic Transformation, 1975–1994." *Comparative Politics* 28, no. 3:299–320.

Spriano, Paolo. 1975. *La Resistenza, Togliatti e il partito nuovo.* Turin: Einaudi.

Stepan, Alfred. 1988. *Rethinking Military Politics: Brazil and the Southern Cone.* Princeton, N.J.: Princeton University Press.

Togliatti, Palmiro. [1933] 1973. "Lezioni sul fascismo." In *Opere: A cura di Ernesto Ragionieri,* vol. 3. Rome: Editori Riuniti.

———. [1944] 1972. *La via italiana al socialismo.* Rome: Editori Riuniti.

Trigilia, Carlo. 1986. *Grandi partiti e piccole imprese: Comunisti e democristiani nelle regioni a economia diffusa.* Bologna: Il Mulino.

United Nations Development Programme. 1998. *Desarrollo humano en Chile 1998.* Santiago: Programa de las Naciones Unidas para el Desarrollo.

———. 2000. *Desarrollo humano en Chile 2000.* Santiago: Programa de las Naciones Unidas para el Desarrollo.

Valenzuela, Arturo. 1979. *The Breakdown of Democratic Regimes: Chile.* Baltimore, Md.: Johns Hopkins University Press.

Weinstein, Barbara. 1994. "Not the Republic of Their Dreams: Historical Obstacles to Political and Social Democracy in Brazil." *Latin American Research Review* 29, no. 2:262–75.

Weir, Stuart, and David Beetham. 1999. *Political Power and Democratic Control in Britain.* New York: Routledge.

Weyland, Kurt. 1996. "Obstacles to Social Reform in Brazil's New Democracy." *Comparative Politics* 29, no. 1:1–22.

———. 1997. "The Politics of Corruption in Latin America." *Journal of Democracy* 9, no. 2:108–21.

Wilde, Alexander. 1999. "Irruptions of Memory: Expressive Politics in Chile's Transition to Democracy." *Journal of Latin American Studies* 31:473–500.

Winn, Peter, and Lilia Ferro-Clérico. 1997. "Can a Leftist Government Make a Difference? The Frente Amplio Administration of Montevideo, 1990–94." In Douglas Chalmers, Carlos Vilas, Katherine Hite, Scott Martin, Kerianne Piester, and Monique Segarra, eds., *The New Politics of Inequality in Latin America: Rethinking Participation and Representation* (pp. 447–68). New York: Oxford University Press.

Wright, James D. 1976. *The Dissent of the Governed: Alienation and Democracy in America.* New York: Academic Press.

Zaverucha, Jorge. 1999. "Military Justice in the State of Pernambuco after the Brazilian Military Regime: An Authoritarian Legacy." *Latin American Research Review* 34, no. 2:43–73.

3

Authoritarian Legacies and Market Reforms in Latin America

FRANCES HAGOPIAN

One of the most daunting challenges facing new democracies in Latin America seeking to enhance effective and accountable governance has been to reform states and to extend the reach of markets in economic life. For nearly a half-century, state resources and institutions in the most advanced countries in the region were marshaled to compensate for market failures in promoting industrialization and distributing welfare by intervening in the productive sector of the economy, regulating trade and domestic markets, and distributing a wide range of social services. When economic crisis manifested itself in the 1980s so vividly in unprecedented levels of external indebtedness and four-digit rates of annual inflation, states suddenly appeared to be part of the problem rather than the solution and thus in dire need of reorganization. A policy consensus slowly emerged not only that stabilization and trade liberalization were necessary but also that state-owned enterprises in the productive and infrastructural sectors should be transferred to the private sectors; key markets, such as the financial and labor markets, had to be deregulated; such social responsibilities as social security and health care should be shared by the private sector; and the spending of subnational governments should be brought under control, even as local and provincial governments should become democratized, invite more participation, and assume more responsibilities.

This consensus aside, state and market reform was not achieved smoothly and in some areas was hardly achieved at all. In many cases, reforms proceeded only after lengthy delays and after they had been significantly watered down. Against the pressure of international creditors and inflation-weary populations, the state-interventionist model was entrenched in an impressive array of institutions. The path to market-oriented reforms that entailed reforming precisely these state structures was blocked, most observers believe, by too-strong vested interests that stood to lose from reform. In addition to bureaucrats of the central state administration and managers of state-owned enterprises (Waterbury 1990, 303–4), most notable among the rent seekers that benefited from these arrangements were industrialists and workers in protected industries (Rodrik 1994, 64–66), as well as politicians who based their successful careers on the distribution of state patronage (Geddes 1995).

When governments are successful against these odds, most analysts contend that they are able to advance reforms for one of two reasons. The first is that reform is abetted by severe economic crisis (Haggard and Kaufman 1995). This is so because economic constraints cause bankrupt states to succumb to the dictates of international creditors (Stallings 1992, 41–88), cause one group to surrender and pay the cost of stabilization (Alesina and Drazen 1991, 1171), cause a consensus to form around policy change (Rodrik 1994, 79), and cause private sector elites to shift their preferences and embrace the lesser evil of trade liberalization against the more potent threat of expropriation (Tornell 1991, 53–73). These approaches understand economic transitions to be effected when and because economic actors shift their preferences or tactical positions, which they do, in turn, when they recognize that their power has been diminished in light of changed economic realities.

Since most economic reform has taken place amid crises of inflation, external debt, investment, and state bankruptcy, such views hold an intrinsic appeal. Yet upon closer examination, the depth of economic crisis alone, as measured by the rate of inflation or any other indicator, cannot explain the willingness of actors to surrender, compromise, or shift their preferences to support market-oriented reforms. If high inflation triggered a shift in preferences toward economic policy, Brazil's strategic interests should have surrendered to economic liberalization long before they did. As Rodrik (2000) put it, "South Korea's politicians are ready to change course at the slightest hint of a crisis, while Brazil's will bring their economy to the brink of hyperinflation several times before they tackle the problem" (66). Research indicates that the general relationship between economic conditions and policy responses in a number of countries is weak (Bates and Krueger 1993, 454), and the capacity of organized interests to resist reform outright has probably been overstated (Naim 1993; Geddes 1995). Indeed, the piece of economic reform that has proceeded most smoothly and immediately in almost every country in Latin America has been trade liberalization (Morley, Machado, and Pettinato 1999; Inter-American Development Bank [IADB] 1997, 49), despite the fact that dismantling protection is the reform that most affects society's powerful vested interests: organized workers and industrialists. If economic liberalization has advanced virtually across Latin America in the past fifteen years, moreover, it has not done so uniformly. There are clear variations in the pace, timing, sequence, and design of state and market reforms that are not easily reducible to levels of external crises.

The alternative claim is that the configuration of political institutions might constrain or facilitate the implementation of a presidential reform agenda. In this view, economic reform might have been easier in Mexico in the 1980s (and, for that matter, Argentina in the 1990s), where presidents enjoyed a relatively high degree of partisan powers in the Congress, than in Brazil, where presidents by and large could not count on the support of disciplined legislative majorities. This framework has obvious merit and should be incorporated into any explanation of reform. But as a sole explanatory factor, it may be inadequate. In particular, arguments about reform that rely on institutionalist explanations rarely adjudicate which institutions are important, and they almost never consider the origins of those institutions, despite the fact that institutional design itself might be an epiphenomenon of culture or power. Moreover, relatively stable institutional settings alone cannot explain why some aspects of reform are accomplished more readily than are others and why some are passed eventually without institutional reform or an election with radically different results. The incentives and constraints posed by institutions say little about the capacities of actors to exert influence in the institutional arena.

From both perspectives, economic policy change follows—or not— according to the calculus of individuals given certain institutional constraints, independently of the influence of a preceding regime. The argument I will advance in this chapter is that the depth, design, and results of economic reform programs are shaped to a much larger degree than generally acknowledged by economic, institutional, and political legacies bequeathed by authoritarian regimes to their democratic successors. This impact is exercised directly by establishing the threshold and framework for reform and indirectly by influencing the ability and strategies of government reformers and representatives of social and political groups to negotiate economic change. There is growing consensus that such negotiations play a key role in the latter stages of reform, when state structures are reformed and labor markets deregulated (cf. Haggard and Kaufman 1992, 19–20; Nelson 1993, 438–42) and that organized interests may be, not automatic opponents of reform, but potential supporters (Przeworski 1991, 180; Nelson 1993, 442). I argue that the bargaining positions of actors with respect to these reforms do not automatically follow from market conditions or electoral systems but rather are profoundly influenced by the policies, institutions, and political strategies of authoritarian rulers as well as democratic governments.

I examine the extent of the impact of the economic, institutional, and political legacies of authoritarian regimes on state and market reform in four South American countries: Argentina, Brazil, Chile, and Uruguay. All four countries were governed in the recent past by military regimes: Brazil, from 1964 to 1985; Chile, from 1973 to 1990; Uruguay, from 1973 to 1985; and Argentina, from 1966 to 1973 and again from 1976 to 1983. Although all four have liberalized their economies to an impressive extent, they did so to differing degrees and according to different designs during and after military rule. Chile had substantially reformed its economy by the time that power was transferred to civilians, Uruguay had experienced partial reform, and Argentina had taken only inconsistent steps in the direction of neoliberal reform. Brazil's military, by contrast, had expanded the role of the state in the economy. Since the transition to democracy, Chile's center-left coalition government has hardly tampered with military-era market-oriented policies, whereas Argentina's Peronists have succeeded to an impressive degree in scaling back the scope of state intervention in a number of important areas. In Uruguay the introduction of market-oriented reforms has advanced but the reform of the state's contribution to social insurance has not, and Brazil lagged behind its neighbors in most areas for many years. Although successive Brazilian governments liberalized trade, stabilized prices, and accelerated the pace of the privatization of state-owned enterprises in the mid- to late 1990s, they faltered in carrying out a key fiscal reform, the reforms of social security and state administration, and in controlling the spending of subnational governments. Beyond the simple facts that authoritarian legacies served to constrain severely the process of state reform in Brazil in the 1990s as well as any attempt to reverse the market-oriented reforms already undertaken during dictatorship in Chile, what the evidence will suggest is that these legacies bolstered or constrained the bargaining positions of actors in ways that shaped the patterns and sequence of economic liberalization in all four countries. The regulatory environment, the design of social insurance, and even the instruments of federal fiscal policy have been profoundly influenced in all four countries by authoritarian policies and politics. Yet there is ample evidence that authoritarian legacies are not permanent yokes, and the theoretical challenge is to be able to specify when and why these legacies constrain future policy and politics and when they do not.

This chapter proceeds as follows. First, I briefly describe the scope, pace, and design of market-oriented reforms in Argentina, Brazil, Chile, and Uruguay. Next, I present a model of the impact of authoritarian legacies on market and state reform that encompasses the direct and indirect effects of inherited economic conditions, economic and regulatory institutions, and authoritarian economic policies, institutions, and politics on the agenda and arena of economic reform and negotiations over that reform. In subsequent sections, I examine the three sets of authoritarian legacies: the economic policies undertaken by military regimes that survived transitions to democracy, particularly with respect to the roles of the state in production and provision of infrastructure, regulating markets, and distribution; the institutions created or destroyed that managed the state's policies; and the impact of authoritarian politics on the representatives of social and political groups. I then consider the indirect effect of these legacies on the ability and propensity of social and political actors to negotiate reform under democratic regimes in four areas: privatization of state-owned enterprises, fiscal decentralization, pension reform, and labor market reform. Finally, I provide a comparative discussion of the implications of authoritarian legacies for national diversity in state structures, economic policy, and democratic institutions.

Mapping Market Reforms

The recent shift toward economic liberalization represents a sharp U turn from the strategy of economic development in Latin America in the postwar period, which was spearheaded by massive state intervention in the fiscal, regulatory, and productive sectors of the economy and was managed politically through state employment and extensive state distribution of social welfare. Such paradigmatic shifts of development models, embedded as they are in capital and labor markets, state institutions, electoral cleavages, and social organizations, are not undertaken readily and without cost and often tend to occur in fits and starts. While widely adopted, market-oriented reforms are not implemented according to a uniform template of sequence or design, and they are not guaranteed similar rates of success. Generally, trade liberalization has proceeded more rapidly and completely than financial sector reform, tax reform, and the privatization of state-owned enterprises, and labor market reform has been the most difficult.[1] Before we can begin to explain this variation, we must establish the benchmark of progress toward reform in the four cases under study.

To begin, I consider market reforms to be policies that liberalize key markets and recover the fiscal solvency of the state. These might include trade liberalization and reforming labor and financial markets as examples of the former and privatizing state-owned enterprises and reducing the fiscal burden of providing social insurance as examples of the latter. There are at least two ways to judge the progress countries have made toward reforming their economies. One is by the results (e.g., maximum tariff levels, deposit/ lending requirements, cost of dismissal of employees, levels of government spending). The drawback of such an approach is that a more extensive privatization program in one country may not result in an economy in which private enterprise plays as large a role in generating product, employment, and investment as a less extensive program in a country that has already been substantially reformed or did not need to be. It is of course easier to complete the job of deregulating markets and reducing state financial commitments in an economy that has been less subject to state intervention than in one that has been branded "state capitalist." The second approach is to measure the amount of reform undertaken in a given time period. However, such an approach could distort the record of a country such as Chile, which completed a rapid conversion to market economics before several other countries had begun. If we were to examine reform in the 1990s, Chile would not stand out for its progress in relation to its late-blooming neighbors. Table 3.1 reports both the extent of economic liberalization across five areas and the distances countries traveled on the path to reform under both authoritarian and democratic regimes. It also provides two composite measures of reform, which, too, produce very different portraits of which reformers are the pioneers and which are the laggards, depending on which measures are privileged in the indexes. The Economic Commission on Latin America and the Caribbean (ECLAC) index of commercial, financial, and tax reform, capital account liberalization, and privatization shows Chile moving from .309 in 1972 to .768 in 1990 (with a score of 1 being the most reformed), and Uruguay, moving from .380 to .815 (Morley, Machado, and Pettinato 1999). This index suggests that Uruguay has made substantial progress toward reform and could hardly be considered a laggard. Yet if just one measure of structural policy reform—labor reform—was substituted for capital account liberalization, as it is in the IADB index, the results would appear somewhat different. Now, Uruguay is characterized as a "below average gradual reformer," still better than Brazil (a "below average slow reformer") but not

TABLE 3.1 Indexes of Structural Reform

Index	Commercial	Financial Reform	Capital Account Liberalization	Privatization	Tax Reform	General Reform (ECLAC Index)	IADB Structural Policy Index[a]
Brazil							
1972[b]	.583	.301	.600	.810	.473	.553	
1985[c]	.485	.313	.420	.798	.444	.492	.348
1990[d]	.770	.965	.461	.745	.678	.724	.512
1995	.930	.971	.639	.813	.674	.805	.584
Argentina							
1975[b]	.445	.000	.423	.794	.387	.410	
1983[c]	.753	.480	.380	.874	.435	.584	.367[e]
1989[d]	.795	.905	.700	.840	.427	.733	.371
1995	.934	.986	.986	1.000	.534	.888	.679
Chile							
1972[b]	.237	.496	.311	.383	.118	.309	
1990[c]	.961	.986	.567[f]	.635	.691	.768	.596
1995	.984	.983	.745	.840	.663	.843	.628
Uruguay							
1972[b]	.000	.240	.596	.816	.249	.380	
1985[c]	.776	.925	.800	.868	.703	.815	.486
1990[d]	.848	.886	.800	.942	.746	.844	.511
1995	.957	.943	.840	.945	.769	.891	.573

Sources: Morley, Machado, and Pettinato (1999, 29–34); IADB (1997, 96).

Note: Each index is normalized to be between 0 and 1, with 1 being the most reformed or free from distortion or government intervention.

[a] Includes trade policy, tax policy, financial policy, privatization, and labor legislation.

[b] Last full year of democratic government before authoritarian regimes were installed in Argentina, Chile, and Uruguay. Data from Brazil, 1972, are provided to compare cases in same world time.

[c] First year of postauthoritarian democratic government.

[d] First year of second democratic government.

[e] 1985.

[f] Was .731 in 1979; reform reversed after 1981 financial collapse.

as impressive as Argentina and Chile ("above average early reformers") (IADB 1997, 50).

Combining these approaches would suggest that whereas Chile and Uruguay made substantial progress during military rule toward structural reform and Argentina modest progress, Brazil was "less reformed" in 1985 than it was in 1972 (Tables 3.1 to 3.3). Although Remmer (1989, 175) characterized efforts at economic liberalization by the Uruguayan military as "limited" and scholars generally view Uruguay as "highly resistant to change" (Filgueira and Papadópulos 1997, 360), the Uruguayan military in fact undertook a dramatic commercial opening, financial reform, and tax reform and modestly liberalized its capital accounts. Uruguay's reputation as a resister of reform was probably earned by the reluctance of both the military and general public to advance the privatization of state-owned enterprises and to dismantle the Battlista welfare state. After the restoration of civilian government, popular referenda in the late 1980s blocked pension reform and reversed an early government bill launching key privatizations.

Argentina lagged behind both Chile and Uruguay in embracing the path of market reforms, but once it did, it proceeded swiftly, steadily, and extensively. Privatizations in the first half of the 1990s represented 6.9 percent of GDP, the highest of any country in Latin America (Table 3.2). By 1995, Argentina had the most privatized economy in the region (Table 3.1). Similarly, market reforms were instituted in a wide range of activities and services, including the financial sector, the external sector, the pension system, and even the deregulation of health care (Table 3.3).

By contrast, Brazilian chief executives were slow not only to propose market-oriented reforms but also, critically, to achieve success in implementing them. The first and second democratic governments liberalized trade, reformed the financial sector, and undertook a partial fiscal reform, but the level of public ownership of enterprises was roughly the same in 1995 as it was in 1972. Most of the sale of state-owned enterprises and other significant reforms would have to wait until after the election of Fernando Henrique Cardoso, more than a decade after the transition to democracy and years after Brazil's neighbors had already reaped some benefits from their experiments in reform. Since 1996, the pace of privatization has increased markedly, with 1997 and 1998 by far being the best years.

In sum, Chile's embrace of market-oriented reforms occurred substantially by 1990, before the restoration of democratic governance. Uruguay's reform can be viewed as proceeding in two stages, the first during military

TABLE 3.2. Toward Economic Liberalism

	Argentina	Brazil	Chile	Uruguay
Privatization (1990–95)				
No. of transactions	123	45	14	7
Revenues (U.S.$ million)	18,446	9,136	1,259	17
Revenues (% GDP)	1.21	.27	.51	.02
Revenues (% central government expenditure)	6.9	.84	2.1	.12
External Sector				
Average tariff (simple avg., 1995, %)	13.9	12.7	11.4	9.6
Imports subject to nontariff barriers (% of value), postreform, ca. 1994	3.1	14.3	.4	N/A
Pension System (1995)				
Retirement age, private sector (men/women)	(60)62/(55)57	65/60	65/60	60/(55)60[a]
Social security contribution rate (employee/employer) (%)	11/16	9/20	13/none	11.5/14.5[a]
Role for private pension funds	Complement public pillar	None (but FGTS)	Mandatory	Complement public pillar[a]
Labor Market (1996)				
Layoff expenses:				
After 1 year of work	"More rigid"	"More rigid"	"Intermediate"	"More flexible"
After 10 years of work	"Intermediate"	"More rigid"	"Intermediate"	"More flexible"
Flexibility of contracts	"Intermediate"	"Intermediate"	"Intermediate"	"More rigid"
Social security contributions	"More rigid"	"More rigid"	"Intermediate"	"More rigid"
Workday and overtime	"More flexible"	"More flexible"	"More flexible"	"More rigid"

TABLE 3.2. Toward Economic Liberalism (*cont.*)

	Argentina	Brazil	Chile	Uruguay
Financial Market Regulations				
De facto central bank independence	More independent	About the same	Much more independent	More independent
Commercial bank supervision	Reasonable	Reasonable	Reasonable	Reasonable
% targeted credit	1–49	1–49	100	0
% share of loan market privatized	15	0	0	10–15
Reserve requirements	Much lower	Much higher	Same	Much lower
Modern capital markets law	Yes	Yes	Yes	No
Modern bank law	Yes	No	No	Yes

Sources: IADB (1996, 89–90, 144–47, 171, 173–75, 188); World Bank, 1993; De la Balze (1995).
ª Uruguayan social security system reformed in 1996.

rule and the second under its third democratic government in the second half of the 1990s. Argentina's economy was perhaps the most thoroughly reformed, and reforms took place essentially in the first half of the 1990s, under Argentina's second democratic government. Finally, Brazil's reforms were launched in earnest in the second half of the 1990s, under its fourth democratic government.

Authoritarian Legacies and Market Reforms

The Argument

The principal questions for research this chapter raises are why, after authoritarianism, economic reform in Brazil lagged behind Argentina; why economic reform was not reversed in Chile; and why Uruguay implemented a considerable degree of market-oriented but not necessarily neoliberal economic reform. Brazil and Argentina exited from military rule in roughly the same time period (1983–85); both were saddled with extraordinarily high lev-

TABLE 3.3   Economic Reform in Argentina, Brazil, Chile, and Uruguay

	Argentina	Brazil	Chile	Uruguay
Stabilization	1991	1994	1975, 1985	1978, 1991
Trade liberalization	1978, 1989–91	1990–94	1975, 1985	1978, 1991
Price deregulation	1989–91	1990–92		
Financial sector reform[a]	"Major," 1992–98	"Some," 1988–89	"Some," 1989	"Major," 1985
Liberalization of foreign investment	1989	1995		
Privatization (biggest 3 years)	1992–94	1997–98, 2002[b]		
Fiscal reform	1990–92	—		
Fiscal pact with provinces	1992–93	—		
Social security reform	1994	1998	1981	1996
Labor market reform	1991	1988		
Public sector employment/civil service reform	—	1997–98		

[a] As classified by the IADB (1996, 85, 145–47, 150).
[b] See BNDES (2002).

els of debt and inflation; they shared federalism and open-list proportional representation; and both initially dallied in their reform efforts. Argentina in 1989 embraced market-oriented reforms, but Brazil's president in 1990 could not advance his reform agenda. While one may question why Chile would want to return to inflation and protected markets, there is an open question about why the privatization program, the pension and labor policies, and the extensive deregulation inherited from the military should not have been reformed by a center-left democratic government. The "Uruguayan" question begs for an unpacking of the bundle of "market reforms" and forces us to ask not merely who is blocking reform but why some reforms are more acceptable than others and why some designs win out over others.[2]

The first theoretical challenge raised by the divergent outcomes of reform is this: How do we know when authoritarian legacies work to reinforce institutions and policies established during authoritarian regimes and when they serve as a catalyst to change? It is not simply the case that all authoritarian legacies weigh on the future forever and can never be cast aside. Nor is it true that good authoritarian policies and institutions were preserved and bad ones overturned. From the standpoint of stability, the relatively "good" constraints on state government spending imposed by the Brazilian military were lifted by democratic reformers reacting to authoritarian centralization. On the other hand, the "bad" institution of senators-for-life in Chile was retained. The fact that no outcome can be assumed means that "path-dependency," an analytic tool of choice in any study of the legacies of antecedent authoritarian regimes, cannot in and of itself explain outcomes. If we are to avoid post hoc explanations for political outcomes, an auxiliary theory is necessary.

Such a theory cannot rest simply on the distinction between legacies that were embedded formally in institutions or constitutions and those that were not. Although the Chilean generals wrote a constitution that bound subsequent civilian administrations to an independent central bank and appointed senators, and the constitution proved to be a serious constraint on revising political institutions in democratic Chile, in Brazil the authoritarian constitution was shelved altogether and a democratic one promulgated within a few years of the departure of the military. Nor can we merely extend O'Donnell's (1992) "paradox of success"[3] to contend that because the Chilean military regime was ultimately judged to have achieved economic success and the Argentine military presided over an abject failure, it was more possible to revise the economic and political institutions of the Argentine state inherited by civilians than their Chilean counterparts. Such a thesis could not account for the six-year delay in the onset of state and market reforms in Argentina. In fact, reform eventually took virtually the precise course of the military's botched attempt at liberalization known as the "capitalist revolution."

One possible avenue is to expand on an argument made by Karl (1990) and Huntington (1991) that transitions that followed collapses of the authoritarian regime (as in Argentina) permitted more change than those that were organized and led by incumbents of the authoritarian regime, as I argued was the case in Brazil (Hagopian 1990).[4] Such a line of argument has been applied to market-oriented reforms by Stark and Bruzst (1998) in the East European context. But the nature of political transitions alone will not serve to explain divergent outcomes in the four cases under examination in this chapter. Reform proceeded in these cases and elsewhere in fits and starts in some areas and more quickly and directly in others.

If the question of which authoritarian legacies should have analytical power and which are ultimately marginal cannot be settled exclusively by the nature of the transition, then how is their influence on market-oriented reform and efficient democracy to be understood? My argument is that these legacies exercise their impact both directly and indirectly and that they set the parameters for change or resistance to change in particular ways. The *direct effects* of authoritarian rule encompass the state of the economy, including existing productive structures, degree of openness to the world economy, and fiscal solvency of the state, as well as the economic and regulatory institutions that democratic governments inherit. In some cases, the challenge of economic reform was made a great deal more difficult by the policies pursued by authoritarian regimes; in others, it was made infinitely easier. Authoritarian regimes also created, preserved, or redesigned state and political institutions that govern the money supply, provide social insurance, and regulate labor markets.

But authoritarian legacies also exercise *indirect effects* on the process of economic liberalization that are perhaps more interesting for their long-term impact on states and markets. Three sets of authoritarian legacies in particular constrain and shape the pace and design of economic reform by strengthening or weakening social and political actors and the networks through which their interests are represented before state authorities. First, economic policies of the antecedent regime shape the power of actors to resist, surrender to, or negotiate reform. Labor unions decimated by recessionary policies may be less able to negotiate stock ownership plans in privatized industries than those that emerged from authoritarian rule relatively unscathed. The second legacy is the nature of the political institutions that serve as the venue through which economic reform must take place. The levels of actor strength or weakness required for reform itself vary according to whether a reform can take place by decree or whether it requires a supermajority in the legislature. If congressional action is required, then the impact of authoritarian rule on political parties and the party system can be consequential, and these, in turn, affect the prospects for negotiated reform.

The third is the way in which authoritarian politics affected the power and calculus of actors who must approve the reorganization of the state and economy, or the preferences of those actors with respect to reform and their political strength to resist or modify the new arrangements.[5] Authoritarian strategies to decapitate the labor movement or privilege politicians of the right affect the capabilities of different actors to undertake collective action and to form alliances within and outside government and the party system

FIGURE 3.1 The Impact of Authoritarian Legacies

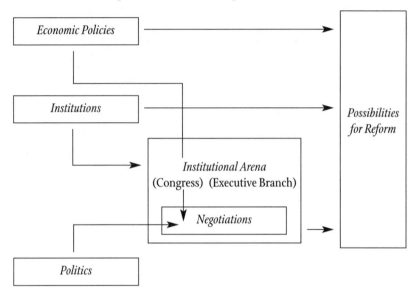

for or against economic reforms. Authoritarian policies also privileged or undermined particular networks of representation through which leaders negotiate economic reforms and enforce agreements with their constituents. The vitality of the channels for mediation between states and societies, embedded in such institutions as political parties and labor unions, in turn exercised an impact on the strength and weakness of various social and political forces, their negotiating positions, and their own aspirations and priorities at the moment of economic transition. This argument presumes that reforms, particularly after the first steps toward stabilization and trade liberalization, are undertaken, not by shock tactics, but gradually and by negotiation between government reformers and representatives of political interests and social groups. The model of the direct and indirect impact of authoritarian legacies is illustrated in Figure 3.1. The model of negotiated economic transitions is presented in Figure 3.2.

This approach raises a theoretical challenge of its own: Which of these authoritarian legacies should be accorded analytical supremacy? That is, if two legacies were to work in one direction and a third in the opposite direction, how could we predict the outcome? Must all legacies pull in the same direction? If not, which legacy trumps the others? My response is to assert

FIGURE 3.2 Propensities to Negotiate

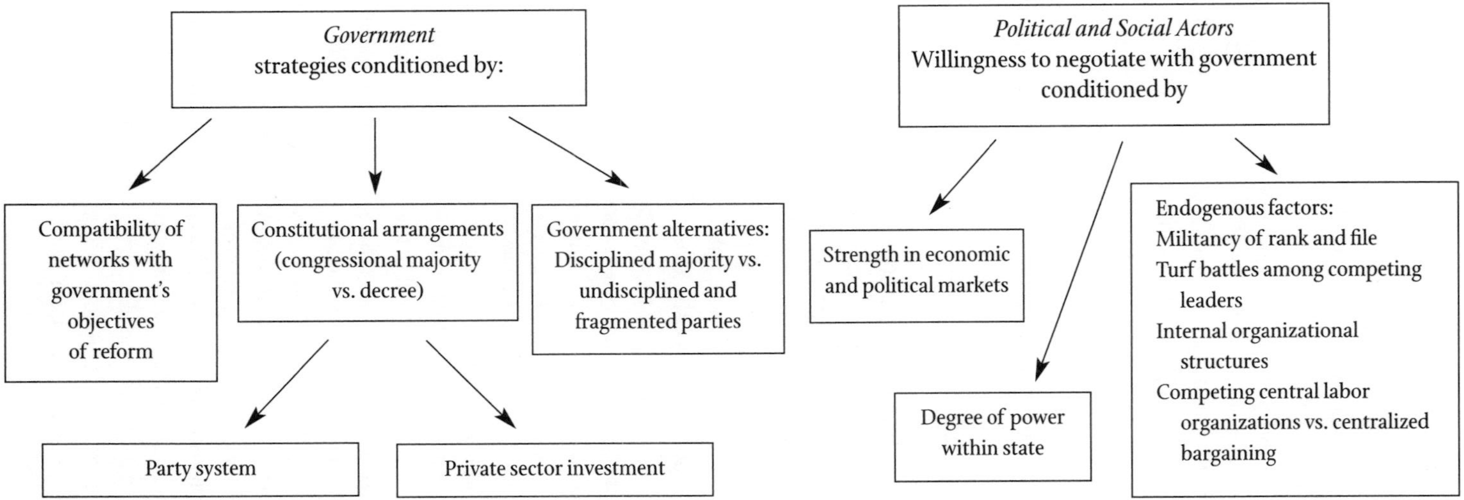

Political and Social Actors
Willingness to negotiate with government conditioned by

Endogenous factors:
Militancy of rank and file
Turf battles among competing leaders
Internal organizational structures
Competing central labor organizations *vs.* centralized bargaining

Strength in economic and political markets

Degree of power within state

Government
strategies conditioned by:

Government alternatives: Disciplined majority *vs.* undisciplined and fragmented parties

Constitutional arrangements (congressional majority *vs.* decree)

Compatibility of networks with government's objectives of reform

Private sector investment

Party system

that the direct effects of the authoritarian regime's economic legacy are the most readily overcome. Whether a democratic governments needs to sell off seventeen enterprises or thirty-seven worth 1 percent of gross domestic product or 2.5 percent, or whether it needs to reduce employer contributions to social insurance schemes by 10 percent or 20 percent, is ultimately less consequential for whether reform advances or is scuttled than are the effects of political legacies on the propensity and capacity of actors to negotiate reform. The institutional legacies of authoritarian regimes set the parameters for reform and dictate the political strategies that social actors must pursue. Within this setting, the capacity for negotiation and priorities of social actors, alongside government motivations and power, determine the outcome of reform.

Objections to the Argument

The objection might be raised that the "path" outlined here is too long and blurry. It is true that this framework cannot well specify, let alone measure, the effects of authoritarian-era policies on the negotiating capacity and propensities of social and political actors in democratic settings. It also does not pretend to model formally a prediction of when reforms will take place.

A second possible objection is that in Argentina and Brazil, severe economic crisis and institutional obstacles to reform could be considered as much legacies of founding democratic regimes as of their authoritarian predecessors. Proponents of such a view might contend that in the 1980s the underlying fiscal crises of these states not only were not dealt with but were in fact exacerbated by the first democratic governments in both countries: Raul Alfonsín (1983–89) in Argentina and José Sarney (1985–90) in Brazil. Such an argument would find support in the heterodox economic policies of the Alfonsín and Sarney administrations and their own legacies of hyperinflation; the relaxation of party laws in Brazil in the aftermath of the democratic transition; and the impetus to spending on the part of subnational governments in both countries, but especially codified in provisions of the democratic Brazilian Constitution of 1988, which more than doubled the fiscal revenue of the subnational governments at the expense of the central government without a corresponding devolution of fiscal responsibilities.[6] In Brazil, the payrolls and hence fiscal obligations of the federal and state governments were inflated by civilian politicians in the 1980s.[7] In Argentina, although Alfonsín did not pursue the same lax fiscal policy as did Sarney and is not considered a populist, public employment was maintained at high levels, and with economic crisis there was even pressure to expand provincial spending from 1986 to 1988

(Novaro 1994, 97–98). Alfonsín's administration ended amid runaway inflation, food riots, and the bankruptcy of the Argentine state. The extent of the
economic emergency, as manifested in the trauma of the July 1989 hyperinflation, may have converted the minds of the mass public and then the Congress against state interventionism. Such an argument has some support in the
documented shift in public opinion regarding the appropriate role of the state
in the economy,[8] the change in government months ahead of schedule, and
the Congress's delegation of extraordinary powers to the executive in the Economic Emergency Law and the Law of the Reform of the State. These powers
arguably permitted the launch of the kind of profound economic reforms that
had eluded successive Brazilian governments for so long.

If the policies of democratic governments in the 1980s undoubtedly aggravated the economic crisis, we must ask why these policies were adopted.
Were they the mere result of gross incompetence and mismanagement, or
were there deeper, underlying reasons for what in retrospect were serious
policy mistakes? It is just as likely that Raul Alfonsín and José Sarney turned
to untested and ultimately inadequate heterodox stabilization solutions because of authoritarian legacies. Alfonsín lacked links to organized labor,
as did Sarney, who also lacked a stable base of support in the legislature
(the mammoth victory of the Partido do Movimento Democrático Brasileiro
[PMDB] in the 1986 congressional elections followed the reflation of the
Cruzado Plan).

Second, in Brazil, fiscal federalism of the order enacted by the Brazilian
Constituent Assembly in 1987–88 could not have become a reality merely
with the support of democrats who favored decentralization against what was
perceived as the excessive centralization of the authoritarian state and pro-
moters of municipal interests. Rather, it was made possible by the endorse-
ment of the state political machines organized by regionally based political elites who stood to gain from the injection of federal transfers into state
coffers—a boon to their patronage war chests. The hand of these politicians
had itself been strengthened during military rule. They were permitted to administer state patronage as a means of marshaling electoral victories for the
military regime, which in turn reinforced their own power. They thus found
themselves at the close of the authoritarian regime in a powerful position to influence the transition to democracy and post-transition political institutions,
especially political parties and the Congress. Stepan (2000) contends that the
balance of power in this and other Congresses was shaped by military-era
decisions. "Participation in the constituent assemblies of 1946 and 1988 was
largely based on the seat allocation rules crafted by the immediately preceding

authoritarian regime for its own purposes" (156). I return to this theme below in my discussion of institutional legacies of authoritarian rule.

Seen in this light, the state's fiscal crisis cannot be understood without reference to military-era policies and, more importantly, could not apparently be revised because of the configuration of political institutions inherited from the authoritarian regime. It is to these factors that I now turn.

Authoritarian Legacies I: Economic Policies

During the period of authoritarian rule in South America, Brazil's military produced an "economic miracle" founded on a model of extensive state intervention in the economy as a means of promoting advanced consumer durable and capital goods industries. The Chilean, Uruguayan, and second Argentine (1976–83) military regimes took the opposite tack, albeit to different degrees, in scaling back the state's role in production and the distribution of social services and in promoting neoliberal commercial policies.

Brazil

Under authoritarian rule in Brazil, the military strengthened the state apparatus and harnessed it to engineer growth. In its first decade, the military overhauled the income tax system, established a Workers' Pension Fund (FGTS) to capture investment for construction (funneled through a new National Housing Bank), created a National Social Security Institute (INPS), and vastly expanded the parastatal sector. By 1983, public sector companies accounted for three-quarters of the net assets and half of the sales, profits, and employment of the two hundred largest nonfinancial corporations in Brazil ("Quem e quem" 1983, 431, 23) and over half (51.2 percent) of the net assets of Brazil's financial sector. These institutions, moreover, were by far the most important source of investment capital for the private sector. In 1974, state-owned enterprises alone accounted for more than 26 percent of all investment in the economy, and the combined contribution of the public sector (state enterprises plus government investment) to investment exceeded 60 percent (Coutinho and Reichstul 1977, 63). With the gross tax burden (27 percent in 1973 and 28 percent in 1981) the highest in Latin America, state expenditure rose in real terms, on a per capita basis, and in relation to the gross product. Government expenditures represented 37.6 percent of GDP in 1985, by far the highest of the four cases (Table 3.4).

TABLE 3.4   Economic Legacies of Authoritarian Rule

	Brazil (1985)	Argentina (1983)	Chile (1990)	Uruguay (1984)
General Indicators				
Average growth (total GDP), 1970–80[a]	8.8	2.5	2.6	3.0
Manufacturing product (% GDP)[b]	26.4	24.1	20.8	20.8
Consumer prices[c]	226.9	345.0	26.0	56.8
External Sector				
Total disbursed external debt (U.S. $ billions)[d]	105.9	45.9	19.1	3.3
Interest payments due/exports[e]	40.0	58.2	17.8	24.6
Debt service ratio[f]	40.8	73.3	26.8	38.8
Average tariffs[g]	45 (1986 avg.)	0–38 (1986, range)	10 (1979–82) 20 (1986)	0–15 (1985–86 range)
Ratio of trade/GDP[h]	15.2	18.5	56.0	34.8
State Sector				
Nonfinancial public sector balance (% of GDP)[i]	−4.4	−9.6	1.4	−4.8
Central government overall surplus/deficit[j]	−11.1	−14.1	+1.4	−5.8
Government spending % of GDP[k]	37.6	20.0	25.2	20.5
Total state (public enterprise) employment/pop.[l]	3.5 (s/d)	5.7 (4.8)	2.5 (1.8)	8.1 (6.2)
National spending/ total spending[m]		52.3 (1983)	87.3 (1992)	

TABLE 3.4   Economic Legacies of Authoritarian Rule (*cont.*)

	Brazil (1985)	Argentina (1983)	Chile (1990)	Uruguay (1984)
Employment trends				
Manufacturing				
employment[n]				
(% of workforce, 1965)	20	34	29	29
(% of workforce, 1980)	27	34	25	29
Unemployment	6.8	3.4	15.0	10.6
(1978–84 avg.)[o]				
Unionization rates			19.1	
			(1980–89)	

[a] IADB (1992, 286).
[b] Wilkie, Ochoa, and Lorey (1990, 1051). Figure for Chile is for 1987.
[c] IADB (1992, 331).
[d] IADB (1992, 324).
[e] Smith, Gamarra, and Acuña (1995, 30, 150, 216); IADB (1992, 177).
[f] IADB (1992, 329).
[g] Wilkie, Ochoa, and Larey (1990, 672).
[h] (Combined value of exports and imports of goods and services/GDP (IADB 1992, 286, 289).
[i] IADB (1996, 403, 408, 409, 427). Figures for Argentina, Brazil, and Uruguay are for 1986, and for Chile, 1990.
[j] IADB (1992, 298); IADB (1994, 253). Category excludes state and local governments, and decentralized agencies. Argentine data refers to "national administration" and include decentralized agencies. Chilean data correspond to "general government concept."
[k] IADB (1992, 297); IADB (1994, 252).
[l] Marshall (1990), cited in Filgueira and Papadópulos (1997, 386).
[m] IADB (1994, 203, 212). For Argentina, 72.1 includes public debt and government-owned companies. In Chile, the figure for 1970 was 95.3.
[n] Wilkie, Ochoa, and Lorey (1990, 347).
[o] Drake (1996, 39).

The net effect of such state expansion and promotion of industrial development was an increase in growth, industrial product, and industrial employment. Brazil's double-digit growth rates in the late 1960s and early 1970s earned it the reputation of having achieved an economic miracle. Overall, during the 1970s, GDP grew on average by 8.8 percent per year, even despite two oil shocks. The percentage of the workforce employed in manufacturing rose from 20 percent in 1965 to 27 percent in 1980; Brazil was the only country in this study to have experienced an increase. By 1985, Brazil was the most industrialized of the Southern Cone cases, as measured by the percentage of GDP accounted for by manufacturing product (26.4).

These positive developments in overall growth, growth of manufacturing product, and employment aside, in other ways the Brazilian military bequeathed to its successors an essentially unreformed economy plagued by high levels of external debt and inflation. Borrowing to stoke the economy in the late 1970s rather than adjusting to two oil shocks, in conjunction with a dramatic increase in international interest rates, led to an astronomical rise in the level of foreign indebtedness. In 1985, the year in which Brazil's civilian government took office, Brazil's total external disbursed debt reached U.S.$105.9 billion, and interest payments represented 40 percent of export revenues. The nonfinancial public sector deficit represented 4.4 percent of GDP, and the central government's budget deficit stood at over 11 percent. Debt service and deficit spending fueled an annual inflation rate of 226.9 percent. Although the military promoted exports in the 1980s to service the external debt, it continued to protect the economy. Average tariffs in 1986 were 45 percent, and Brazil was one of the least open economies in the region, as measured by its ratio of trade/GDP (15.2 percent).

Chile

The design of economic policy was very different under military rule in Chile than it was in Brazil. In Chile, the military regime reduced the state sector to a minimum, opened the economy to international trade to a degree not witnessed in Latin America since the Great Depression, deregulated the financial sector, privatized the social security system (except for military personnel), and decentralized the administration of education and a range of other public services. Although the military program (and especially an overvalued exchange rate) initially produced intolerable levels of unemployment and a financial debacle in the years from 1981 to 1983, a corrected, less dogmatic course eventually resulted in what most observers agree was one of the healthiest economies in Latin America to be inherited by civilians in the 1980s and 1990s.

The Chilean military government diminished both the functions and spending of the central government and the state enterprise sector. Government spending as a percentage of GDP fell precipitously throughout military rule, from 40.8 percent of GDP in 1970 (IADB 1987, 437) to a mere 25.2 percent in 1990. With the 1979–81 "seven modernizations" program, the Chilean military reduced to a minimum the state's role in the provision of health care and social security that it had performed since 1952. The new regime allowed employees to opt for private sector health care institutions (known as ISAPRES) at the same time that it cut funding to the National Health Service (SNS), and it transferred the provision of social security from the public sector to privately managed funds (known as AFPs). It also transferred the administration and funding of primary and secondary education to local government institutions (Morales 1989, 175–79, 183–96, 297–308). The military also sharply scaled back the state's role in production. The hundreds of state enterprises expropriated during the Allende government (1970–73) were restored to their former owners in the first years after the coup, but more radically, the ownership of firms established in earlier decades by the public sector corporation CORFO were also transferred to the private sector. By 1980, there were only twenty-four state enterprises remaining in Chile.

The reduction of the role of the state in economic production, distribution, and regulation no doubt contributed to a condition of macroeconomic health. Chile's central government was the only one of our four cases to be running a budget surplus at the time of transition. In 1990, the surplus was 1.4 percent; in 1989, the last full year of military rule, it was as high as 5 percent. Inflation, moreover, was contained to a level of 26 percent. The debt service burden, too, was the most manageable of the Southern Cone countries, with a ratio of interest payments to exports of 17.8 percent and a debt service ratio of 26.8. Finally, the military opened Chile's market to the world economy earlier and more completely than any other Latin American country; by 1979, a uniform tariff rate of 10 percent was in place. In 1990, it was one of the most open economies in the region, with a ratio of trade/GDP of 56 percent. Trade liberalization, however, decimated protected industries and caused a drop in the number of industrial workers from 29 percent of the workforce in 1965 to 25 percent in 1980.

Argentina

In Argentina, the military regime that took power in 1976 concluded that its predecessors had not been sufficiently radical in their approach to reorienting the economy. Accordingly, José Martínez de Hoz was appointed economy minister to preside over the "Process of National Reorganization." The military set out to reduce real wages to a level about 40 percent below the average of the previous five years; eliminate export taxes on agricultural and livestock products; cut import tariffs in half (from 80 to 40 percent); abolish subsidies promoting nontraditional manufactured export goods; liberalize foreign exchange markets and reform the financial sector; raise public sector prices; and cut back state activities, especially by reducing public expenditure for social welfare and by privatizing some state enterprises (Smith 1989, 235). Although we know that the implementation of the economic program of the Argentine military was highly uneven (Remmer 1989, 175), one of the most dramatic impacts of this policy package was a deindustrialization of the Argentine economy. The manufacturing share of GDP fell from 28 percent in 1970 to 24 percent in 1983, and overall, growth averaged 2.5 percent in the 1970s, a figure three times lower than that for neighboring Brazil (Table 3.4).

Despite its neoliberal pretensions, the authoritarian government did not bequeath to its democratic successors an economy reformed to the same degree as the Chilean. Average tariffs ranged as high as 38 percent, and the ratio of trade/GDP was 18.5 percent, only slightly higher than in unreformed Brazil. Moreover, when power was acceded to civilians in 1983, consumer prices rose by 345 percent, the debt service ratio stood at 73.3, and the central government (including decentralized enterprises) ran a 14.1 percent deficit.

Uruguay

The Uruguayan military has been characterized as "less avid" than its Chilean or Argentine counterparts in its adherence to free-market economics (Drake 1996, 99). The privatization of state-owned enterprises was blocked by the nationalist sectors of the armed forces, which often saw state industries as geopolitical resources. It has been claimed that military "interference" with his privatization program may have prompted the technocratic economy minister Alejandro Végh Villegas to resign his post in 1976 (Gillespie 1991, 57–58). In Uruguay, unlike Chile and Argentina, manufacturing did not shrink under the military in the 1970s. To the contrary, between 1973 and 1980, it grew by 6 percent per year, a rate that surpassed that for agriculture and services. Before the same downturn that plagued Chile and Argentina in 1982, the population employed in manufacturing dropped only slightly, from 21 to 19 percent (Drake 1996, 99–100).

The Uruguayan military did liberalize trade. In 1985, average tariffs ranged up to 15 percent, and of our four cases, only Chile's economy was more open (the ratio of trade/GDP in Uruguay was 34.8). Although the central government ran a deficit in 1984 of 5.8 percent, inflation was contained to 56.8 percent, high by today's standards but considerably lower than in Brazil and Argentina in the comparable period. Its debt service ratio was 38.8 percent—high by international standards but more manageable than that for many

Latin American countries, and its ratio of interest payments due/exports was 24.6 percent.

■

In sum, economic legacies of authoritarian regimes constrained democratic governments in particular ways. Any Brazilian government seeking to introduce market reforms would have to undo not only postwar import substitution policies but also the military-era expansion of parastatal enterprises and regulatory capacity. It would have to do so, moreover, with a high debt burden and high levels of inflation. Democratic Argentine governments may have inherited a proportionally smaller public sector than the Brazilian, but they also inherited a higher debt-to-export ratio and a public sector in even greater deficit. Civilian governments in Uruguay faced a more mixed picture. On the one hand, inflation was moderate, and trade was reasonably liberalized. The debt service burden was high but left some room for maneuvering. On the other hand, the state was essentially unreformed; with no movement on privatization of production and social welfare, the state's fiscal burden was severe. As is commonly understood to be the case, Chilean civilians inherited an already reformed economy with its key macroeconomic indicators—consumer prices, central government deficit—as well as its degree of openness to world trade in fine shape.

Authoritarian Legacies II: Institutions

Most analysts today agree that institutions shape the possibility for reforming states and markets. What is still open to contention is which institutions are most important in constraining or enabling an executive to promote his or her administrative and legislative economic agenda. Less well studied are the origins of institutions and why institutional constraints are sometimes overcome and sometimes cannot be relaxed.

Which Institutions?

The IADB (1997) analyzed the impact of a number of institutional variables on fiscal decision making at the national and subnational levels. Although our focus is not on everyday fiscal decision making per se, many of the same variables can be claimed to apply to the process of reform. The bank considered two kinds of institutions—political and administrative. The political variables related to electoral systems and included type of electoral system (plurality vs. proportional representation), electoral cycle, district magnitude, number of effective parties, and the size of the president's party/coalition in the legislature. The administrative variables referred to procedures and constraints regarding government spending. The most important of the political variables turned out to be district magnitude, and the most important administrative ones were budgetary institutions and the borrowing autonomy of subnational governments. Less important were the type of electoral system, the permissiveness of the legislation governing the formation of political parties, and constitutional arrangements governing intergovernmental transfers. These findings suggest that Brazil's familiar demons— open-list proportional representation, permissive legislation governing political parties, and constitutionally mandated transfers from the central to state and municipal governments—actually contribute less to Brazil's woes than commonly assumed.

District magnitude affects the effective number of parties, which in turn influences the support that the executive has in Parliament. A high district magnitude leads to a larger number of parties. Party fragmentation, in turn, tends to undermine fiscal discipline. Generally, countries with high district magnitudes have larger government size, deficits, and debt. Specifically, a country with a district magnitude of 10 is expected to have government spending 2.5 to 5 percentage points of GDP above, a budget surplus nearly 2 percent of GDP below, and a debt-to-GDP ratio 30 percentage points above, a country with a district magnitude of 1 (a plurality system) (IABD 1997, 130). Of our cases, the highest district magnitude was Brazil (19), followed by Argentina (10.3), Uruguay (5.2), and Chile (2.0) (IADB 1997, 127). Brazil's high district magnitude is reflected in the number of effective parties in the Chamber of Deputies—8.16 (Table 3.5).

Budget institutions, or the set of rules and procedures by which budgets are drafted in the executive branch, modified and approved by Congress, and then carried out, and that affect the transparency of the process, are also demonstrated to have a significant impact on these same variables. Elements of an index of budget institutions (IBI) prepared by the IADB were constitutional constraints on fiscal deficits; macroeconomic program constraints on the budget process; debt ceiling constraints on the budget process; authority

TABLE 3.5 Institutional Legacies of Authoritarian Rule

	Brazil	Argentina	Chile	Uruguay
Reigning Constitution Executive-Legislative Relations[a]	1988 "Proactive"	1994 "Potentially dominant"	1980 "Potentially dominant"	1967/89/97 "Reactive"
Configuration of presidential powers	decree, weak veto, exclusive introduction	decree, strong veto	decree, strong veto, exclusive introduction	strong veto, exclusive introduction
President's partisan powers[b]	Very low	Medium high	Very low	Medium high
Mean share of congressional seats:[c]				
(%) president's party (lower chamber)	26.9 (1985–90)	48.3	31.7	45.6
(%) president's coalition (lower chamber)	37.0 (85–90)/13.6 (1994)	49.1	58.3	n/a
% president's party (upper chamber)	25.6 (85–90)/13.6 (1994)	52.0	28.3	43.8
% president's coalition (upper chamber)	35.4 (85–90)/42.0 (1994)	52.0	46.3	n/a
Electoral/Party System[d]				
District magnitude (lower chamber)	19.0	10.3	2.0	5.2
District magnitude (upper chamber)	3.0	2.9	2.0	31.0
Effective number of parties (lower chamber)	8.16	2.82	4.95	3.30
Absolute number of parties (lower chamber)	18	16	8	4

TABLE 3.5 Institutional Legacies of Authoritarian Rule (*cont.*)

	Brazil	Argentina	Chile	Uruguay
Budget Institutions[e]				
Index	.57	.50	.73	.62
Vertical fiscal imbalance	.33	.56	.61	.17
Borrowing autonomy (subnational governments)	2.9	3.0	0.0	1.0
Decentralization (subnational/ total government spending):				
1995	45.6	49.3	13.6	14.2[f]
1985 (approximate)	44.0	33.5	4.5	9

[a] From Mainwaring and Shugart (1997, 49).
[b] From Mainwaring and Shugart (1997, 432).
[c] From Mainwaring and Shugart (1997, 400–401).
[d] From IADB (1997, 127).
[e] From IADB (1997, 141).

of the finance minister in the drafting stage; scope of amendments permitted by Congress; relationship of government and Congress in the approval stage; revisions to the budget permitted in the implementation stage; contingent liabilities (whether the central government typically assumes debt originally contracted by other public agencies); and the scope for deviations from the approved budget (whether the government is legally empowered to cut spending after the budget has been approved). On this index, Chile's budget institutions were the most constrained (.73); Uruguay's (.62) and Argentina's (.57) were intermediate; and Brazil's were the least constrained (.50) (IADB 1997, 141). These scores are potentially tremendously significant given that "countries with high IBI have average to primary surpluses that are 4 percent of GDP and debt-to-revenue ratios that are half the size of those observed in countries with low IBI." More concretely, "a country with an IBI of .45 is expected to have an average budget surplus nearly three percentage points of GDP below that of a country with an index of .65," with the quantitative impact stronger for the primary budget surplus than for the overall surplus, (IADB 1997, 141).

One of the most daunting challenges facing states struggling to reform in Latin America has been dealing with subnational governments. The two most decentralized systems in Latin America are Argentina and Brazil, where 49.3 and 45.6 percent, respectively, of total government spending is accounted for by subnational (state and local) governments. In federal systems where state and local governments have considerable budgetary autonomy, an asymmetry between expenditure responsibilities and the capacity to generate revenues generates a gap that the IADB has called a "vertical imbalance." The central government transfers that bridge this imbalance represent a considerable drain on the budget surplus. Among the cases under study here, this problem is more acute for Brazil and Argentina, which score 45.6 and 49.3, respectively, on the "decentralization" index (Table 3.5), than for Chile and Uruguay (13.6 and 14.2). But most important is whether subnational governments are allowed to borrow (Chilean subnational governments are not), whether these borrowing decisions are autonomous, how subnational debt is guaranteed, whether there are numerical constraints on subnational borrowing, and especially whether subnational governments own banks. Argentina and Brazil (along with Colombia) are the only countries in Latin America where subnational governments own banks. On the IADB's (1997) index of borrowing autonomy (176), Argentina and Brazil scored the highest (3.0 and 2.9, respectively). Uruguay scored a 1, and Chile, 0.

Institutional Origins and the Permanence of Constraint

Thus far, we have considered only whether there are institutional constraints on legislative discipline and government spending at various levels. We have not considered whether these institutional configurations are necessarily *authoritarian* legacies, and indeed, they often are not. The reigning constitution in Chile (1980) is a military-era document, but those in Brazil (1988), Argentina (1994), and Uruguay (1967, with constitutional reform approved by plebiscite in 1989 and 1997) were promulgated under democratic governments. The real villain of fiscal indiscipline in Brazil—the state government-owned banking system—predates democratic *and* authoritarian rule.[9]

What, then, were the institutional legacies of authoritarian rule? And how might these affect the ability—and need—of states to reform their instruments of economic policy making and resource allocation? What is most relevant is how authoritarian regimes altered the patterns of executive-legislative relations, a country's party and electoral laws, and budgetary institutions. Also of crucial importance is whether authoritarian-era institutional reforms could themselves be easily reformed. Consistent with its larger project to harness the capabilities of the state to promote economic modernization and growth, the Brazilian military created economic and political institutions to strengthen state and executive capacity and to extend the state's regulatory reach into the economy, but it did not constrain the future spending autonomy of subnational governments. In Chile, the military substantially abdicated the state's regulatory instruments but imposed hard budget constraints on future governments. It also enacted electoral system reform and created appointed senators-for-life and a National Security Council—two important sets of institutional legacies that would make future reform harder. In Argentina and Uruguay, by contrast, however harsh military rule might have been, it did not substantially alter the institutions governing branches of government, political parties, and state spending.

As a result of military rule, the Brazilian executive gained some authority—principally decree authority[10]—but did not gain control over the levers of legislative action. The president's partisan powers are characterized as "very low" (Table 3.5), as the president's party and coalition at virtually no time since the transition from authoritarian rule have assembled anything close to a stable majority. Legislative compliance with the executive's agenda in Brazil is complicated not merely by the fragmentation and lack of cohesion of parties, however. It is also shaped to a remarkable degree by a territorial divide between the less developed north, northeast, and center-west on the one hand and the south and southeast on the other. As a result of authoritarian rule, the former are vastly overrepresented in both houses of the Brazilian Congress. Late in its tenure in office, the military created two new states—Mato Grosso do Sul (1978) and Rondônia (1982)—and eliminated an opposition state by combining Guanabara and Rio de Janeiro. As a result, twelve new federal deputies and six new federal senators were created in the proauthoritarian north and center-west, and the developed southeast (where the opposition was strong) lost three senators. The military also altered the formula for new federal representation to the lower chamber (by setting a floor of seven deputies per state and a ceiling of seventy), causing a further underrepresentation of the population from the larger states (Stepan 2000, 156–57). On balance, the states of the north, northeast, and center-west, with 40 percent of the population, controlled 52 percent of the votes during the Constituent Assembly. This bloc then voted to admit three new states— Tocantins, Roraima, and Amapá—from the same regions. To the extent that votes from these states are key in blocking such reforms as the control of subnational government spending, the balance of power in the legislative arena cannot be divorced from its authoritarian legacy.

With respect to budgetary institutions, the Brazilian military government granted autonomy to the indirect administration, apparently to enhance efficiency. Acting on the belief that the direct administration was more rigid than the decentralized administration, Decree Law 200 of 1967 transferred activities related to the production of goods and services to semiautonomous agencies, foundations, and state-owned corporations. In the decentralized units, employees were hired under the Consolidated Labor Laws. As Bresser Pereira (1997) has pointed out, Decree Law 200 had two unsuspected and undesirable consequences: by permitting the hiring of employees without competitive examinations, it facilitated the survival of clientelism, and by neglecting the training of senior civil servants in the central state administration, it weakened the "strategic core" of the state (9). At the same time, Brazil did not establish an independent central bank, as did other Latin American countries, including Chile. Most seriously, it did not constrain future spending by subnational governments and particularly state government-owned banks. This turned out to be a more important source of fiscal indiscipline than the much-discussed transfers from the federal to state and municipal governments. In fact, there was actually little change in expenditure decentralization between 1985 and 1995 (IADB 1997, 158).

In Chile, the executive was strengthened over the pre-1973 period. Authoritarian institutions also dramatically shaped the ideological, programmatic, and organizational reorganization of the political parties, particularly on the left but generally across the political spectrum. The electoral formula for selecting the Congress handed down by the authoritarian constitution has enhanced the power of party leaders, attenuated partisan competition, and provoked the realignment of the party system into two major blocs that, according to recent research, also behave as legislative coalitions (Carey 2002). The electoral formula handed down by the dictator Pinochet—Article 109 of the Political Party and Elections Law—provides that two candidates from the same list will be elected not only when they receive the most votes but also when the total of their votes is more than double that of the list or candidate that comes in next in the balloting. If no list wins both seats, then one place will go to each of the lists or candidates that obtains the two highest majorities of the total votes. Similarly, a president must be elected with more than half of the "validly cast" votes (excluding blank as well as null votes). The effect of this law has been to reward electoral coalitions, provide a strong disincentive to a proliferation of lists, and overrepresent the minority list, which happens to be the right. It also enhances the power of party leaders, who, in negotiations with their coalition partners, in effect exercise a great deal of control over the party nomination process. The "bionic" senators confer upon the parties of the right a majority in the Senate that endows the right with a veto over government policy.

Also significantly affecting the capacity of the Congress either to tamper with fiscal policy or to "reform the reforms" are the significant changes to the budget process and the manner in which bills are drafted (Siavelis 1997, 330). Assembly proposals are unlikely to be considered, let alone enacted into law. As part of a decentralization program, many responsibilities have been transferred downward to subnational branches of the Chilean state, although not all have been adequately funded. Chilean subnational governments may not borrow. They have substantially increased their share of spending without taking on any new spending responsibilities (IADB 1997, 160). A third area of institutional change bequeathed to the civilian government of Chile by Articles 97 and 98 of the authoritarian constitution was an independent central bank.

The final question refers to those institutions that make other institutional reform either easier or harder to achieve. It is very clear that political and institutional reform in Chile has been made more difficult, if not impossible, by the appointed senators and the institutional presence of military commanders from the authoritarian period. The constitution provides for appointment to the Senate of the ex-presidents of the republic, two ex-ministers of the Supreme Court, one ex-controller general, one ex-commander of each of the armed forces (army, navy, and air force) and the police, an ex-rector of a state university, and one ex-minister of state. Similarly, a powerful National Security Council (composed of the president, presidents of the Senate and Supreme Court, commanders of the armed forces and police, controller general, ministers of the interior, foreign relations, national defense, economy, and finance, and the military chief of staff) looms as a potential veto player in the political system.

In contrast to the deep changes wrought by the Brazilian and Chilean militaries, the Argentine and Uruguayan militaries did not substantially alter the framework in which state institutions function. In Argentina, unlike Brazil and Chile, the military did not attempt to write a new constitution. The most controversial, if useful, devices employed by the Menem presidency in the 1990s to accelerate economic reform—the executive decrees of need and urgency, the presidential veto, and packing of the Supreme Court—were all expansions by the president of constitutionally bounded authority, not legacies of military rule changes. With their quick exit after their military and economic defeats, Argentina's authoritarian rulers also did not revise Argentina's party or electoral laws. In sharp contrast to neighboring Chile, the military also did not rein in public spending during its own tenure, and it did not design budget institutions to do so in the future.

By all accounts, the Uruguayan military was profoundly ambivalent about political parties and any possible structures to replace them, and the governing structures that were altered during military rule were resurrected once the military-proposed constitution was defeated in a 1980 plebiscite. Most important, the military-created "Council of State" was replaced with the "quasi-presidential" system that had been established with the 1967 constitution.[11] It has been called "quasi-presidential" (González 1991, 19–23) because, as in a parliamentary system, the legislature may censure and remove ministers, and the president may (at least theoretically) dissolve the legislature, but the institutional power of the president is stronger than that of a prime minister. The president remains in charge during his entire mandate and may not be removed for political reasons. Similarly, the military suspended the activity of political parties but did not bequeath a new electoral system to its civilian successors. Rather, closed-list proportional representation in which voters choose at the same time for a party and for a specific set of can-

didates within the party from among several party lists (the "double simul-
taneous vote" [DSV]) was reinstated after the transition to democracy. The
DSV was eliminated for presidential elections only a decade after redemocratization. Thus extreme fractionalization of the political parties persisted as
a distinguishing feature of Uruguayan politics. As Gillespie (1991) put it, the
military's "attempt at institutionalization was to prove a failure. The traditional forms of Uruguay's polity resisted efforts by the military to 'reengineer' the political system from above" (50–51).

Uruguay's budget institutions are second only to Chile's in their degree
of effectiveness in controlling the size of the public sector deficit. Uruguay
has the highest degree of political autonomy and civic participation at subnational levels of all Latin American countries (IADB 1997, 164), and the gap
between the level of spending required to carry out the responsibilities
assigned to subnational governments and the revenues that the subnational
levels generate themselves is small. Finally, in Uruguay, the mass public has
recourse to an extraordinary device, the plebiscite, to reverse decisions of
its government, and as we shall see, citizens have made effective use of the
popular referendum in various aspects of economic policy. This peculiarly
Uruguayan institution, not eliminated by military rule, makes politics all the
more important.

Authoritarian Legacies III: Politics

I have argued that the ability to carry out economic reform depended on
the strength of the interests of various actors to promote economic reform, resist it, or shape it to their advantage. Within the constraints imposed by the economic policies and political institutions where reform has
to take place, the strength and preferences of these actors were profoundly
influenced by the politics of authoritarian regimes. In this section I examine the impact on authoritarian politics on three sets of actors (labor, business, and national party and provincial politicians) and networks of representation (corporatism, clientelism, and party organizations) in the four
countries under study.

Labor and Business: Corporatism

In Brazil and Argentina prior to military rule, the state had regulated labor
markets through the institutions of corporatism. In Brazil, the Consolidated

Labor Code of 1943 created noncompetitive labor unions, conferred monopoly status on them, and established avenues of representation leading directly from these unions to state institutions in the Ministry of Labor, the labor courts, and the social security institutes. Labor leaders, content to negotiate for the best wage settlements they could achieve in state labor courts, allied themselves with politicians in the Brazilian Labor Party and state bureaucrats. In exchange for mobilizing the votes of their members and forfeiting union autonomy, they received state financing for their unions, generous benefits for their members (which they administered), and secure positions for themselves. In Argentina, Juan Perón reorganized and brought under state control already established and militant unions. From 1945 to 1953, a system of labor relations and collective bargaining was codified that permitted a centralized pattern of wage bargaining by branch of economic activity, conducted primarily through a "majority union" of the branch designated by the Ministry of Labor (Buchanan 1985, 64–65; Etchemendy 1994, 2). Because Perón depended upon the political support of labor in his confrontations with the agro-exporting elite, labor gained the most generous regulations and benefits on the continent and a considerable degree of power vis-à-vis the state. Corporatism and trade protection in Argentina were more radical than in Brazil, which had a labor surplus (Waisman 1987).

In Chile and Uruguay, the state similarly sought to create weak, dependent labor movements through preemptive and cooptative strikes. Arturo Alessandri legalized Chilean unions in 1924 but did not rely on them for political support. Chilean labor was highly constrained for decades until a powerful political left captured its allegiance in the years before the 1973 coup d'état (Collier and Collier 1979, 974). In Uruguay, labor's corporatist ties to the state were similarly weak. The Batlle-led Colorado Party early in the century introduced major labor reforms to cultivate the anarchist working class as a political constituency. Following a period of conservative restoration (1933–42) and a new period of reform, the Colorados retained the labor vote but had only weak organizational ties to the labor movement (Collier and Collier 1991, 271, 439). In the mid-1960s, the labor movement came together in a single, powerful trade union organization (Filgueira and Papadópulos 1997, 369), and the period from 1968 to 1973 brought an important change in the relationship between labor and the state. Amid a prolonged crisis of economic stagnation, the Colorado president Jorge Pacheco ended the wage councils that had existed since the 1940s in favor of an employer-dominated council and embraced an International Monetary Fund (IMF)-style stabilization program with predictably negative effects on labor.

There were over three hundred private sector strikes and five hundred public sector strikes between June and December of 1968 alone, and in the late 1960s and early 1970s, worker protest reached such a magnitude that the government responded by evoking emergency powers and initiating a state of siege. The confrontation between the state and labor has been identified as a major factor in the 1973 coup (Collier and Collier 1991, 639, 646–47, 655–56).

Military dictatorships in Argentina, Brazil, Chile, and Uruguay shared an agenda to undermine the power of labor, but the effects of their policies on labor and the systems that organized labor interests varied. In Brazil, where rapid economic growth swelled the ranks of industrial workers, military strategy entailed using the institutions of corporatist mediation that had secured the support of labor for populist governments in previous decades to intervene in union leadership and attempt to repress labor organizations (Mericle 1977). Although the regime may have intended for the working class and labor unions to grow under state control (Drake 1996, 33), the essential ingredient of paternalistic co-optation that had kept labor leaders and rank-and-file unionists within the state corporatist fold was withdrawn and the illusion of state benevolence was shattered (Cohen 1982) when labor leaders were denied their traditional access to the state through the Ministry of Labor and Social Security Institutes (Malloy 1979) and the regime stole wages from labor by manipulating the inflation index to which wage and salary adjustments were pegged. Labor leaders in the 1970s looked to the shop floor to build new bases of strength on the foundation of their relationship with their rank and file, and a "new unionism" took shape (Keck 1989, 256–59; Tavares de Almeida 1983; Antunes 1991). The union movement received a further boost during the *distensão* ("relaxation") of the Geisel administration (1974–78). Paradoxically, one of the weaker labor movements in Latin America on the eve of the military coup of 1964 gained in strength under military rule from robust industrial sector growth, institutional factors, and authoritarian politics.

The Southern Cone cases present a stark contrast to the Brazilian. As Drake (1996) puts it, "The Southern Cone governments meshed a policy to atomize and shrink the proletariat with an economic program that reduced industry and employment. . . . The debilitated labor movements became less militant and more moderate than they had been before the coup" (33). In Argentina, the Onganía administration (1966–70) suspended collective bargaining, limited the right to strike, and introduced measures to make the use of the labor force more flexible. The regime's intention to harden the state's role in corporatist mediation doomed whatever intentions veteran Peronist leaders like Augusto Vandor had of putting the shattered Peronist state-labor coalition back together again. In May 1969, blue- and white-collar workers beyond the control of the Peronist leadership erupted in protest in the industrial city of Córdoba, and after that the military evidently lost control of Argentine society. As a response, and to lay the basis for its "Process of National Reorganization," the hard-line military regime that seized power in 1976 undertook a campaign of state-sponsored murder to decapitate the labor movement. The hard-line military regime that seized power in 1976 dismantled the system of collective bargaining ushered in by Perón (Ferro 1995, 46–48). The military's trade policies caused the number of production workers in medium-sized and large firms in urban areas to decrease by 39 percent between 1975 and 1982 and the self-employed sector in greater Buenos Aires to expand by 25 percent from 1974 to 1980. There was a substantial increase in those living in poverty from 1974 to 1982 occasioned by a 24 percent decline in wages (Waisman 1992, 237–38). While some industries were relocated and a handful of interior provinces such as Tierra del Fuego were the beneficiaries of industrial promotion schemes, it is unlikely that they generated sufficient employment to compensate for those jobs lost in the large metropolitan areas, and unions as a result undoubtedly suffered.

In Chile, where labor unions were closely associated with programmatic political parties of the left and center left, harsh repression and economic adjustment also severely weakened labor organization. Between 1971 and 1984, the number of workers in mining, manufacturing, and construction plummeted from 660,500 to 290,700. In 1971, these workers represented 22.3 percent of the labor force; in 1984 only 7.5 percent (Tironi 1988, 76). With the shift in status for many workers from wage earners to self-employed and the steep rise in official unemployment from 3.1 to 22.6 percent of the labor force, unions were weakened. From a high of 679,910 affiliated members in 1972, the unionized population declined to 320,903 in 1983, with the steepest sector declines registered in the manufacturing and construction industries (Campero and Valenzuela 1984, 158). Government decrees that deliberately weakened the bargaining position of labor vis-à-vis their employers further undermined a union movement already crippled by the economic policies pursued by the regime. After years of outright repression, the Chilean military in 1979 succumbed to labor unrest and international pressure and implemented a Labor Plan, which eventually became one of the so-called "Seven Modernizations." The plan established a new legal framework for labor organizations and collective bargaining. The draconian legislation eliminated closed shops, allowed employer lockouts, and regulated strikes on terms favorable to employers—during strikes, which were limited to sixty days, employers could hire replacement workers, and when the strike period ended, they could dismiss workers (Remmer 1989, 161). Drake (1996) classified Chile's labor movement at the end of the period of military rule as the weakest of our four cases (Table 3.6); before the coup, only the Argentine labor movement was considered stronger.

The authoritarian regime in Uruguay set out in a fashion similar to its Argentine and Chilean counterparts to shift the basis of labor organization from corporatism to what Paul Drake (1996) has called "atomization." Although the regime was reasonably successful at political repression, it was less successful at re-creating the basis for labor organization in Uruguay. In terms of structural factors (industry strength, employment) and political factors (ties to parties and role in government), the Uruguayan labor movement emerged from authoritarian rule stronger than its counterparts in Argentina and Chile. Institutionally, however, it was weakened (Table 3.6). Yet even so, after the passage of labor legislation in 1981, labor reconstituted itself by forming unions at the enterprise level, then revivifying the traditional union structure, and without legal authority creating an Interunion Plenary of Workers (PIT) in 1983 (Drake 1996, 103).

For economic elites, authoritarian rule was a double-edged sword. Although business stood to gain from economic and political measures that disciplined labor, business leaders protested what they perceived to be their diminished access to government decision makers, and they too became a target of some harsh policies. In their attack on corporatist representation, Argentina's military did not spare the entrepreneurial elite. To carry out their "capitalist revolution," the military establishment and its technocratic allies perceived that it was necessary to "neutralize" the traditional pressures that business had exerted on the state through corporatist channels and lobbying activities. Accordingly, the military government abolished the General Economic Confederation (CGE) and its member confederations in 1976 and expropriated their assets a year later. The Argentine Industrial Union (UIA) was permitted to function but was placed under the control of an army officer (Acuña 1995, 7–8). When coupled with economic mismanagement and the Malvinas fiasco, the political attack on the Argentine economic elite finally persuaded it to abandon its penchant for authoritarian solutions and embrace democracy. The Argentine economic elite recovered its main organization by an act of Congress in 1984, but nonetheless the CGE was weakened. The UIA, which took a greater role in representing business interests, did so unevenly and considered its input insufficiently valued by the Radical

TABLE 3.6 Authoritarian Legacies and Labor Strength

Ratings of Factors Affecting Strength of Precoup Labor Movements

Factor	Brazil	Uruguay	Chile	Argentina
Structural factors				
Industry strength	Low	Medium	Medium	High
Employment	Medium	Medium	High	High
Institutional factors				
Union density	Low	High	High	High
Federals and confederations	Low	Medium	Medium	High
Unity	Low	Medium	Medium	High
Independence	Low	High	Medium	High
Political factors				
Party ties	Low	Medium	High	High
Party strength	Low	Low	Medium	High
Role in government	Medium	Low	High	High

Country Ratings with Regard to Factors Affecting the Strength of Precoup Labor Movements

Factor	Best ←			→ Worst
Structural conditions	Argentina	Chile	Uruguay	Brazil
Institutional features	Argentina	Chile	Uruguay	Brazil
Party assets	Argentina	Chile	Uruguay	Brazil
Roles in government	Chile	Argentina	Brazil	Uruguay

Factors Affecting the Evolution of Labor Movements under Authoritarianism

Factor	Brazil	Uruguay	Chile	Argentina
Level of repression	Low	Medium	High	High
Structural conditions				
Changes in industrialization	↑	↓	↓	↓
Level of unemployment	Low[a]	High[a]	High[a]	Low[a]

TABLE 3.6 Authoritarian Legacies and Labor Strength (*cont.*)

Factors Affecting the Evolution of Labor Movements under Authoritarianism (*cont.*)

Factor	Brazil	Uruguay	Chile	Argentina
Institutional conditions				
Labor system	Corporatism	Atomization	Atomization	Atomization
Union density	Medium	Medium	Low	High
Labor response	Infiltration	Abstention	Abstention	Abstention
Political result	Radicalization	Moderation	Moderation	Moderation

Country Ratings with Regard to Factors Affecting the Strength of Postcoup Labor Movements

Factor	Best ◄———————————————► Worst			
Structural conditions	Brazil	Uruguay	Argentina	Chile
Institutional features	Brazil	Argentina	Uruguay	Chile
Political factors	Brazil	Uruguay	Argentina	Chile

Source: Drake (1996, 12, 13, 31, 32).

[a] An up arrow indicates increased industrialization; a down arrow indicates deindustrialization.

government. In one of the most dramatic political turns in Latin America in decades, Argentine business began to work with Peronist governments, prompting one prominent Argentine intellectual to pronounce optimistically that the "future no longer is what it used to be" (Acuña 1994, 31).

In Chile, where the military is alleged to have trampled on the economic interests of the economic elite in exchange for guarding its political interests—defeating the Marxist left—the military actually provided compensatory policies for entrepreneurs through dealings with the long-established Industrial Promotion Society (SOFOFA) and the National Agricultural Society (SNA) (Edwards and Lederman 1998). In fact, although it is widely believed that reform in Chile was imposed on society, business leaders negotiated significant alterations in the economic model in the 1980s and even in the 1970s (Silva 1993). Business remained loyal to the military throughout its rule and supported publicly the authoritarian regime in the

1980 and 1988 plebiscites. Democratic rule began with the business community deeply skeptical of the center-left government but hardly weakened.

In Brazil, disgruntled by what was perceived as excessive productive and regulatory activities of the state under authoritarian rule, leading segments of the business community in the mid-1970s waged in succession "antistatism" and "liberalization" campaigns (Stepan 1985). Although once Brazilian labor became stronger and staged a series of flamboyant strikes, the business community retreated from its newfound progressive stances (Cardoso 1986), it nonetheless geared up to influence the new constitution and subsequent legislation (Payne 1994). That these early efforts under democratic governance were disappointing (Kingstone 1999) is a testament to the fact that organizationally and economically, Brazilian business was not as strong as its Chilean counterpart.

In Uruguay, where the big business sector was very small—in 1978, only 310 firms had more than one hundred employees (Rama 1991, 115–17)—relations between business associations and military rulers were allegedly "intimate" (Gillespie 1991, 61–62). One study found that the number of "rent-seeking actions" (lobbying by manufacturers to seek a higher tariff for a particular good or raising the reference prices on which tariffs and subsidies were calculated) rose sharply following the beginning of trade liberalization in 1974 (Rama 1991, 115–17). Yet business representatives did not "go out of their way to make public demonstrations of support for the regime" (Gillespie 1991, 61–62), and they particularly did not endorse a "yes" vote in the 1980 plebiscite but rather adopted a position of official neutrality (Stepan 1985).

Thus at the time when each country emerged from authoritarianism and embarked on its path toward economic liberalization, the capacity of labor and business organizations to unify the policy preferences of their various sectors and to represent those preferences effectively in the formulation of public policy differed across the four cases. Corporatist networks of negotiation were weakest in Brazil. Brazilian unions chose to flex their newly acquired muscle to achieve gains for their members denied to them during military rule, and Brazilian business was disorganized in its dealings with state authorities. It lacked the two ingredients that Schneider (1997) deems essential for effective negotiations over reform between government reformers and business: a major formal association for the entire private sector and a well-articulated organization for the very largest producers. In Argentina, a weakened labor movement kept its distance from a Radical administration that it distrusted, but it eventually was more pliant with a Peronist government. Business elites, however, had a cooperative relationship with Peronist governments for the first time ever. In Uruguay, labor unions were no more supportive of reform than their Brazilian counterparts, and they had legislative and mass public support. In Chile, while labor organizations were flattened, business remained strong, well organized, and capable of influencing policy.

National and Provincial Politicians: Clientelism and Parties

Before authoritarian rule, there were vivid contrasts in party systems in these countries and in the intensity of partisanship. On the basis of the indicators of regularity of party competition (as measured by electoral volatility), the stability of party roots in society (as measured by the difference between presidential and legislative voting), the legitimacy of the electoral process, and the strength of party organization, Mainwaring and Scully (1995, 6–17) classified Chile's and Uruguay's party systems as among the most institutionalized in Latin America. Argentina's party system also received a classification of "institutionalized," but Brazil's was labeled "inchoate."

Traditionally, Southern Cone politicians based their strength as representatives on principally one of two pillars: their parties as organizers of political identities and programs and their role as distributors of state patronage. Political clientelism in the era of state intervention in the economy became an integral component of structures of political representation in the region, particularly but not exclusively for those whom corporatism left behind. It was an especially important form of interest representation in Brazil and Uruguay. Nearly all Brazilian parties competed electorally and governed during the postwar period on the basis of state clientelism, and in Uruguay, parties alternately competed to deliver and share patronage through state jobs and public services. Although these political systems were better noted for the pervasiveness of clientelistic practices, one sees evidence of a "clientelism of notables" as well in the nonindustrial provinces of Argentina; state resources were distributed personally by leaders, and clients had little or no capacity to act and formulate demands autonomously. Most, but not all, of these networks were found in the provincial Peronist parties (Novaro 1994, 74; Gibson 1997, 432–46; Gibson and Calvo 1997, 2, 4). In Chile, programmatic political parties competed ferociously along ideological lines in national politics, but at the local level they also relied primarily on brokerage strategies. Frequently tacked onto substantive legislation were particularistic appropriations for a deputy's home district (Valenzuela and Wilde 1979).

Military regimes repressed political parties, as they did labor movements, with varying degrees of zeal. The Brazilian military permitted political parties to function, though it abolished existing parties in 1965 and created two new ones—a proregime and an official opposition party—out of a highly fragmented multiparty system. After its electoral advantage eroded in the 1970s, it reverted to a multiparty system in order to divide the opposition; five parties were registered by the time the military transferred power to civilians in early 1985. The Uruguayan military suspended the activities of first the left and then even the traditional political parties. In 1976, it suspended for fifteen years the political rights of fifteen thousand politicians, including all those who had been successful candidates for legislative office in the 1971 and 1966 elections and unsuccessful for executive office. Both the Argentine and Chilean militaries banned elections and attacked the militants of parties of labor and the left. In Argentina, thousands of Peronist militants lost their lives. In Chile, the military conducted a campaign to devalue political parties and end their monopoly as the central organizers of political, social, and economic life to the point that today voter turnout and the public evaluation of political parties are at comparatively very low levels.

Beyond levels of repression toward elections and activists, these authoritarian regimes tolerated party activity to different degrees and with varying effects. In Brazil, the channels for distributing state patronage remained open during authoritarianism, probably because the authoritarian regime that permitted elections needed a means to rally voters to the candidacies of government party representatives. Especially in the second decade of military rule, the military relied on the capacity of regional political elites to mobilize electoral support for the regime through the exercise of state clientelism. This political strategy allowed the particular politicians who distributed these benefits to remain electorally competitive in the years after authoritarianism, to retain their seats at higher than the average rates of turnover (Ames 1987; Hagopian 1996), and even to project their power onto the national political stage. Fernando Collor de Mello owed his presidency to these political networks (Ames 1994, 95–111), and presumably Fernando Henrique Cardoso did as well. The military's strategy also devolved political power to subnational levels of government that were not easy for a democratic central government to recapture. After the transfer of power to civilians, these elites in Brazil were in a position—either directly or through federal deputies—to resist any efforts to diminish their public resource base.

In Uruguay, another system that traditionally was balanced on the broad use of patronage, the military took the opposite approach. Although clientelism as a political practice may have survived in the rural areas to the extent that it was based on private resources, the patronage networks of the traditional (National and Colorado) parties in urban areas that had operated on the basis of their access to state resources were unable to operate during military rule, and electoral machines ground to a halt (Gillespie 1991, 62). Also in Uruguay, unlike Brazil, the military did not attempt to create a new, progovernment party, and it did not attempt to mobilize support through the existing parties. Its failure to organize alternatives may have permitted the parties to survive, but whether the clientelistic basis of Uruguayan politics survived military rule is another question. The military failed to insulate institutionally the distribution of public services from political criteria. But the turnover of politicians cut off from their patronage machines was higher than in Brazil: in 1984, half the members of the new legislature had no previous experience in elective office, and only one-third had been legislators before the coup (González 1991, 60). Juan Rial (1986) had little doubt that the displaced politicians were the old clientelistic leaders, and he predicted that a strongly rejuvenated political class would be less prone to clientelistic politics, even in the provinces. "Although these new politicos might want to use the old methods," he wrote, they would "encounter severe limitations on the practice of traditional politics" (257–58). In the years after Rial's essay was written, the leftist Broad Front did markedly improve its electoral performance at the expense of the traditional parties.

In Argentina, military rulers generally suspended clientelism along with political party activity. Traditional *caudillos* in the peripheral provinces in the 1980s led the "renewal" movements and maintained control of party networks through dispensing state patronage. However, because provincial politicians were subordinate to, and could not likely survive independently of, national party leaders, they were vulnerable.

In Chile, the ability to dispense patronage had already been curtailed in the 1960s, but any possibility of local brokerage politics was all but eliminated under the dictatorship, with Congress and political parties in recess and politicians held in contempt. As the state retreated from a number of social and economic functions, the opportunities for political representatives to maintain these channels of communication with their constituents atrophied. Important institutional changes in the 1980 constitution also undermined traditional channels of local brokerage politics. In the preauthoritarian period, "personalism and the satisfaction of constituent demands were essential to [congressional] reelection" (Siavelis 1997, 329). Tapia Valdes (cited in Siavelis 1997, 329–30) estimated that between 1938 and 1958 more than 55 percent of legislation dealt with personalistic issues. As a result of limitations imposed by budget restrictions, exclusive executive initiative, and presidential urgencies (Siavelis 1997, 330), the range of possible congressional actions in satisfying these personalistic demands became limited.

Partly as a result of these distinctive strategies, the impact of military rule on the fortunes of political parties also varied. The party system that experienced the least disruption following its period of military rule, at least initially, was Uruguay. From the last precoup election (1971) to the first post-coup election (1984), the index of party system discontinuity (the sum of the changes in the vote shares of the major parties [those receiving more than 5 percent of the vote] and the minor parties [those receiving less than 5 percent]) was only 10.2 (Remmer 1989, 53, 55). By contrast, Brazil received a score of 168.8 between 1962, its last precoup election, and 1986, its first post-coup presidential and congressional election year. Argentina's party system was only moderately disrupted between 1965 and 1973 (48.3), but much more so between 1973 and 1983, reflecting the repression of the Peronists and the shift of the electorate toward the Radicals in the 1983 presidential elections. Of course, in the years that followed, the Peronist Party regained its historical electoral advantage, whereas in Uruguay, the two traditional parties could not halt the advance of the Broad Front, which today enjoys the support of one-third of the Uruguayan electorate. Nonetheless, military rule clearly created new parties in Brazil, shifted the party landscape somewhat in Chile,[12] and left Argentine parties pretty much as they had been. The rise of the leftist Frepaso coalition in the 1990s, and its alliance with the Radical Party at the end of the decade, cannot credibly be attributed to military rule.

But the shifting fortunes of particular political parties tells us only part of the story; what we want to know, apart from the degree of fractionalization of the parties in Congress, is the positions that these parties and politicians take on state reform. In some cases, we may know this directly through surveys of members of Congress; in others, we may ascertain this by proxy by the left-right positions of the political parties (though these may shift during times of national crisis). In Uruguay, Luis González's 1986 survey of legislators (González 1991, 80) shows that in the first years after military rule, slightly more than half of the Uruguayan Congress supported a major role for the state in the economy.[13] In Brazil, the parties that represented labor interests and that were opposed to virtually all market-oriented economic reforms, including the Workers' Party and the smaller Communist and Socialist Parties, represented only from 10 to 15 percent of the Congress in the first decade after military rule. Yet in the Brazilian case, most politicians representing centrist and even rightist parties, whom one might expect would support a government seeking to implement market-oriented reforms, are not committed political and economic liberals. They have generally not cast their votes according to programmatic considerations, and when they have, they have often done so in a "bloc" that unites deputies on issues of common interest across party lines. They are also highly motivated to vote to preserve their sources of state patronage, a tendency that might enable them to support some market reforms but not reforms of the state itself.

The representatives of political parties that were more programmatic than clientelistic in Chile and Argentina emerged from authoritarian rule more amenable to market reforms. In Chile, even former Marxist parties have accepted the commercial opening and fiscal discipline and have limited the scope of their disagreement with Pinochet-era market reforms to financial and environmental regulatory policies. In Argentina, the Peronist Party was slower to adapt but did in the early 1990s back Menem's reforms to a remarkable degree and certainly in comparison with virtually all Brazilian parties.

■

These patterns of organizing political representation influenced the strategies, propensities, and capacities of actors to navigate within institutional arenas as they entered into negotiations over market reforms. In some cases, they constrained the efforts of state reformers to redirect national economies to allow a greater role for markets; in others, they provided governments with crucial, if conditional, support for economic liberalization. When governments turned to negotiate market-oriented reforms with representatives of social groups and political parties, they found more pliant negotiating partners in Argentina than in Uruguay and especially in Brazil. Both Argentine labor and business were humbled, and political party and patronage networks were ripe for takeover. In Brazil, the Collor, Franco, and, to some extent, even Cardoso governments had available no effective channels to labor and business and could rely only on the votes of members of Congress who answered not to the government but to regionally based politicians with national political power that had a stake in postponing state reform. In Uruguay, the obstacles were comparable, yet distinctive: its labor movement was not as strong as in Brazil but still strong enough to resist effectively various market reforms. Political clientelism did not flourish to the same degree in the postauthoritarian period as in Brazil, but the left made significant electoral advances, rendering the extension of reform a doubly difficult task. In Chile, conditions were virtually ideal for sustaining reform. Market reforms were embedded not only in institutions but also in the positions of key social and political actors: labor was weakened, business was well organized, and opportunities for clientelism were structurally diminished.

Explaining Economic Reforms

My argument is that authoritarian legacies affect negotiations over market reforms. Economic legacies shape the *agenda* of reform. Institutional legacies determine the arena within which reform must proceed and shape the *strategies* for negotiation these actors develop and adopt to push or oppose reform. Political legacies, and particularly the impact of authoritarian rule on labor and business organizations, and on party and electoral systems, influence the *propensity* and *capacity* of these actors to negotiate.

For the purposes of analysis, I consider the preservation, advancement, or reversal of reform in four select areas: (1) the privatization of state-owned enterprises; (2) financial decentralization; (3) pension reform; and (4) labor reform. I have privileged these areas over such other reforms as stabilization, trade liberalization, financial sector reform, and fiscal reform for a number of reasons. First, stabilization and trade liberalization are among the first reforms, they have been successfully implemented in nearly every country, and hence they provide little variation. Second, there is not a consensus on the desirable degree of financial sector reform or capital account liberalization, and hence it does not seem reasonable to brand Chile, for example, as a laggard for imposing capital controls in the mid-1990s, which several economists seem to feel helped to insulate Chile from the "tequila effect." Debates over fiscal reform continue in reformed economies, as the debates over value-added taxes and appropriate levels continue, even in advanced industrial society. Third, privatizations, pension and labor market reforms, and the reform of subnational government finances afford the opportunity to consider the responses of a wide array of societal and political interests in areas that present real variation. Labor market reforms involve the representation of business and labor interests; the reform of subnational government financing brings national- and especially provincial-level politicians into conflict with government reformers. The privatization of state-owned enterprises pits government reformers against public sector employees. Labor market reforms, especially measures to lower labor costs by decentralizing collective bargaining, making it easier to dismiss redundant workers, and by limiting compensation for work-related accidents, have been intrinsically among the more contentious issues on the reform agenda everywhere in Latin America, and certainly among the most difficult to achieve.

Chile

Chile's reforms were implemented during the authoritarian regime, but this does not constitute a sufficient explanation for why the reforms themselves could not have been reformed or reversed. Indeed, the privatization of state-owned enterprises and the decentralization of government undertaken by the military had been extreme, and labor market and pension reforms were on the political agenda when the new democratic government took office. How authoritarian legacies affected reforms in these areas, therefore, deserves to be addressed.

What the record shows is that military-era reforms were hardly altered at all. No enterprises or services that had been privatized were returned to the public domain; on the contrary, the privatization program was extended further. Those hoping for even more public control of private pension funds were disappointed, as were those critical of authoritarian-era labor market policies. Why this was the case may be attributed to institutional barriers to reform and to the weakened position of labor and the parties that represented it in the political arena.

Privatization of State-Owned Enterprises
The military handed to civilians a substantially depleted state productive sector. As we have seen, by 1980, only twenty-four enterprises remained in the public sector. Beginning in 1985, the regime introduced a program to extend its privatization program, reprivatizing companies that had been brought down by the severe economic crisis of the early 1980s. It did so adopting a "popular capitalist" approach that opened up stock ownership of privatized firms to fifty thousand small investors by selling them shares at preferential prices (fifteen years of interest-free loans with a 30 percent discount if payments were made on time) (IADB 1996, 81; Piñera 1991, 22). Piñera justified these subsidies on the grounds that "widespread ownership was good in itself"; in other words, that it would make it very difficult for any future government of the left to renationalize the firms.

After the transition to civilian government, not only was this strategy successful in the sense that no privatized enterprises were returned to the public sector, but the privatization program was continued, especially in the public utilities and mining sectors. Another fourteen enterprises were privatized from 1990 to 1995, representing 2.1 percent of GDP (Table 3.2), a level much higher than in Brazil and Uruguay.

Fiscal Decentralization

Chile is a unitary state. During the military regime, the central government created a new organization of territorial politics. It abolished existing districts and created a new apparatus of thirteen regions, fifty-one provinces, and 325 municipalities. The regions were administered by an intendant (appointed by the president) and a regional development council; the provinces, by an appointed governor, who was under the authority of the regional intendant. The municipalities were similarly governed by an appointed mayor and a local council. Under the authoritarian regime, national government spending was reduced from 95.3 percent of total government spending in 1970 to 87.3 percent in 1992. Local government spending increased in the same period from 4.7 to 11.5 percent, and regional governments in the latter year accounted for 1.2 percent of total government spending (IADB 1994, 211). The central government transferred to local governments the responsibility for primary and secondary education, as well as basic health.

Despite the explicit policy of decentralization, the authoritarian legacy was in fact highly centralized. The central government retained a monopoly over almost all spending responsibilities; all powers to establish, administer, and collect taxes; and ultimately all principal regulatory functions (IADB 1994, 209). Local governments were not awarded greater independence for deciding to which programs to apply funds and how to apply them but rather were enlisted to target beneficiaries and administer programs designed and financed by the central government.

With the transition to democracy, the constitution was amended to allow for the direct election of mayors and municipal councils. Yet intendants and governors are still appointed, and the regional and provincial units do not correspond with the electoral constituencies of senators and deputies. More significantly, there has been little change in the overall financing structure of lower levels of government. The only independent sources of municipal revenue are license fees, which accounted for about 28 percent of municipal revenue in 1992. Local governments were dependent for the lion's share of their revenues on unconditional and conditional transfers (38.8 and 32.7 percent, respectively). Subnational governments may not establish taxes, borrow money, or even in many cases design their own programs. In the judgment of the IADB (1994, 210), the intermediate regional and provincial administrations do not enjoy the "minimum degree of independence" to be considered a level of government distinct from the central government.

Pension Reform

Chile's military in 1981 was the first to abandon the government-run pay-as-you-go system in favor of a system based on individual contributions to privately managed funds (the AFPs). Workers deposit 10 percent of their monthly earnings in a savings account managed by a private fund that the worker is free to choose. Upon retirement, the funds are converted into indexed annuities. The retirement age for all workers had been raised prior to the reform. For the self-employed, contributions are voluntary. The state guarantees a minimum pension for workers whose contributions are insufficient to finance that level directly. In contrast to other pension reforms that followed in Latin America, no public pension fund was maintained to offer a choice to workers (except for the military). By late 1994, pension funds amounted to more than $20 billion, or, 40 percent of GDP (Cortázar 1997, 245).

Relieved of a major fiscal burden, the center-left Concertación government did not propose an expansion of the public sector responsibility for administering social security. Rather, it only decried the lack of contributor oversight of private pension fund managers and the ample administrative fees that their firms charged.

Labor Market Reform

The first approach of the military government in Chile to the labor market was to control it directly. From 1973 to 1979, collective bargaining and the right to strike were suspended, and government authorities set wage readjustments. In 1979, under pressure from the international labor movement (which threatened a boycott of Chile), the military reformed labor legislation. It authorized the right to unionize, the freedom to affiliate, and a set of procedures for the election of union leaders. But it also denied the right to strike to public sector workers and temporary agricultural workers and legal existence to national confederations of workers, and it failed to provide protection against arbitrary dismissals to union leaders (who were also limited in the number of hours that they could devote to union activities). Collective bargaining could take place only within firms, and no agreement with employers could cover workers of more than one company. If a strike took place, workers could be replaced temporarily by the employer from the first day, and after a strike had lasted sixty days, striking workers could be permanently replaced. Finally, restrictions on individual contracts (which enabled subcontracting) were lifted, and severance payments were reduced to a maximum of five months (Cortázar 1997, 236–37, 242–44).

The restrictions imposed on strikes and collective bargaining, and the lack of protection against arbitrary dismissal and the reduction of severance pay, made the reform of the labor market initiated under authoritarianism an object of reform under the succeeding democratic government. The Concertación government came to power promising "to introduce profound changes in labor institutions" (Henríquez Riquelme 1999, 93). The Aylwin government proposed changes to the labor law that were much more ambitious than envisaged at the time of the presidential elections in December 1989 and that were described in the election manifesto. Compensation for dismissals would have been established at the level of one month of pay for each year in the job, without an upper limit, and with an additional penalty on the employer for unjustified dismissals. Strikes would be allowed for indefinite periods with no replacement of workers. Industry-wide collective bargaining would be allowed for firms with fewer than fifty employees. Liberal provisions for the formation of unions and union federations and for the payment of union fees would have been established.

In the end, however, the Aylwin government and its opposition in Congress agreed to a series of changes to the law that were less ambitious. In terms of job security, the final draft set a limit of twelve months to the month-per-year dismissal compensation plus a surcharge on the employer of 20 percent for unfair dismissal. Strikes for unlimited periods were allowed, but employers retained the right to replace workers as long as their final offer was at least as high as the previous year's inflation rate. Industry-wide collective bargaining was allowed, subject to prior agreement on it having been reached between employer and employees (Hojman 1993, 84–85). Even these changes were enabled in great part due to the fortunate circumstance of the defection of one appointed independent senator from the Pinochet coalition (Londregan 2002).

Argentina

Argentina is one of the few countries that carried out extensive market-oriented reforms under democratic governance in Latin America. Many early analyses presumed that the government of Carlos Menem carried out authoritarian-like reforms through the use of decrees of dubious constitutionality. Despite his reputation as a personalistic chief executive of a delegative democracy, earned by issuing hundreds of these decrees and circumventing his own party during his first two years in office (Ferreira Rubio and Goretti 1998), Carlos Menem on most occasions chose to proceed with the broad-ranging reform of the state and the deregulation of markets by negotiating with at least three sets of representatives of Argentine society—leaders of corporate groups, politicians in Congress, and provincial politicians. How did authoritarian legacies affect the story of Argentine market reforms, if at all?

Because the authoritarian regime weakened, but did not eliminate, Peronist unions and did not reconstitute the party system on an alternative foundation, as did the Brazilian military, I argue that it bequeathed to the Menem government crucial corporate and party networks of representation through which to negotiate state reform. The authoritarian-era weakening of labor may have facilitated the propensity of Peronist union leaders to negotiate economic reform with a Peronist government, an argument echoed by Waisman (1992, 237–38). Menem also assumed the leadership of a formidable party organization that included the network of the Buenos Aires metropolitan area and those of provincial Peronist and allied parties. Once at the helm, Menem refashioned the Peronist Party. He left to flounder during hard economic times in the first two years of his administration the traditional clientelistic politicians of the provinces of the interior; at times, he even intervened in the provinces to remove them from office (Palermo and Novaro 1996, 375). Once politicians more loyal to him had taken the place of the old *caudillos* (like the Saadi family in Catamarca) in the provinces, Menem found that provincial politicians could be useful allies in rounding up the votes of general electors and of their state delegations in the national Congress (Gibson and Calvo 1997). At the national level, after marginalizing from the party executive many center-left Peronist leaders associated with the Cafiero wing of the party in favor of many right-wing politicians, long-time Menem allies from the president's home province of La Rioja, and well-known (often non-Peronist) personalities (Levitsky 1998; Acuña 1994, 54), Menem turned to his party representatives to negotiate the next phase of economic reform (Corrales 2000, 136–39). With the promise of financial stability and a hardening of positions on the part of those government supporters that had initially acceded to the national emergency, he repaired his relations with Peronist legislators in particular by granting Congress several prerogatives in the reform process. These networks enabled the Argentine president to privatize state-owned enterprises and partially social security, reform the labor market, and reach a fiscal pact with the provinces.

Privatization of State-Owned Enterprises

In Argentina, all parties signed onto the privatization of state-owned enterprises in the years after the Economic Emergency Law. The Argentine private sector, and especially the dozen largest holding groups in the country, which had made fortunes through multimillion-dollar public works contracts with the state (the group known as the *patria contratistas*), dropped their resistance to privatization when the government offered them such "rents-as-baits" as sheltered markets, new subsidies, and select tariff increases (Corrales 1998, 7–8, 18–19, 22–23; Schamis 1999, 260–65). Similarly, the government overcame the resistance of the labor movement to the sale of their companies to private sector buyers largely by handing unions up to a tenth of the shares of the newly privatized companies, half of the profits, and representation on the board of directors under the Program for Property Participation (PPP). Several unions, notably those representing workers in the privatized electric and gas companies, railroads, and petroleum sector, opted to participate (Murillo 2000; Gerchunoff and Torre 1996, 29). Finally, to counter any potential resistance from Congress to the sale of the national oil company, its shares were distributed to some provincial governments, thereby "facilitating the support of their deputies in congress" (Gerchunoff and Torre 1996, 32).

Fiscal Decentralization

The pressure to reform the spending of subnational governments in Argentina was strong. Argentina had one of Latin America's most federal systems, and the provinces contributed on average 40 percent to the fiscal primary deficit of the 1980s (World Bank 1993, 125, 129). Moreover, provincial public sector employment had increased by almost 40 percent overall from 1983 to 1990 (and by 70 percent in the "low-density" provinces of the interior).

The 1992 Fiscal Pact with the provinces and the August 1993 Federal Pact for Employment, Production, and Growth (also known as the Fiscal Pact) were negotiated between the central government and provincial politicians, some of whom had been replaced by Menem. Provincial governments agreed to accept a reduced percentage in the transfer payment from the central government (which was still high in historic terms due to the windfall from the improvement in national fiscal accounts following the success of the 1991 Convertibility Plan) and to eliminate provincial taxes that affected the competitiveness of exports. These concessions enabled the federal government to finance social security deficits and generally secure provincial government compliance with what was for it a priority—securing fiscal solvency. In exchange, provincial social security systems, a key piece of the clientelistic system, would remain untouched and specifically not subject to the reform of the national social security system; provincial public enterprises and banks (which often financed provincial governments) would not be privatized; and public employment in the provinces could keep growing (Gerchunoff and Torre 1996, 36; Gibson and Calvo 1997, 8–9).[14]

Pension Reform

The partial privatization of the nation's social security system in 1993 (it took effect in 1994) was also enabled by negotiations between the executive and Congress. The government's initial proposal to replace the pay-as-you-go system with privately administered individual savings accounts, modeled after the Chilean program introduced after 1979 by the Pinochet dictatorship, was initially rejected by the Confederación General de Trabajadores (CGT) (reunified in March 1992) and subsequently substantially modified in the Argentine Congress due largely to the efforts of labor representatives (Gerchunoff and Torre 1996, 32). Congress increased the minimum universal benefit, reduced the retirement age for women from sixty-five to sixty years of age, and permitted contributors to choose between the new private and existing public system and to actually go back and forth between the two.

Labor Market Reform

Since 1989, Argentine union leaders have cooperated with government reformers on permitting the flexibilization of individual labor contracts as a necessary price to pay in order to maintain the centralized system of collective bargaining and a privileged, if diluted, role for unions in the distribution of health care benefits. Nonetheless, progress on labor market reform was slower than in other areas, in no small part because these reforms tend to pit corporate interests against one another as well as labor against government. Under the terms of the 1994 Model Accord (Acuerdo Marco), employers gained concessions from unions on further flexibility in labor contracts (the unions admitted de facto the possibility of a more decentralized system of wage bargaining in Argentina, but they did not concede so formally, nor did they consent to eliminating the principle of *ultra actividad,* which leaves in effect the terms of a lapsed collective bargaining agreement until a new one is achieved), separate legislation for the small and medium-sized enterprise sector, the suspension of labor obligations in bankrupt firms, and limits on litigation in cases of work-related accidents. In exchange, labor won the government's commitment to withdraw the 1993 Labor Market Reform Bill and to sponsor legislation that would grant unions the right to inspect company books as well as facilitate the extension of employee stock ownership plans to private sector firms (Etchemendy and Palermo n.d., 13–14).

Labor interests in labor market reform were represented in these years of bargaining not only by the main labor organization, the CGT, in corporatist bargaining with business and government, but also in the political sphere by labor representatives in the Peronist delegation in the Chamber of Deputies. Despite seeing a slide in the size of the "labor" delegation in the chamber from thirty-five to ten deputies, labor representatives held onto their positions on the Committee on Labor Law, through which at least 80 percent of draft labor legislation passed. When negotiations between labor and government stalled, Peronist union deputies on the Labor Committee froze executive initiatives (Gerchunoff and Torre 1996, 34; Etchemendy and Palermo n.d., 38–39).

Uruguay

With a close-to-universal consensus that the Uruguayan state and society were organized to support social welfare, it is hardly surprising that while commercial and financial liberalization might go forward, pension and labor reform would be more difficult for democratic governments to pursue. Following traditional understandings of the strength of Uruguayan social actors, Filgueira and Papadópulos (1997, 381–82) contend that neoliberal pension and labor market reform were made impossible in Uruguay due to high historical levels of both social and political incorporation and that the privatization of state-owned enterprises was also scuttled by political leaders and representatives who wished to protect their basis for engaging clients. Focusing to a greater extent on political institutions, Brooks (2001) attributes the late, partial reform of social security to the broad range of bargaining partners in the reform process (sixteen partners) resulting from the structure of semiautonomous fractions within Uruguay's political parties, as well as to the credible threat of popular referenda to overturn unpopular reforms. Both arguments have a great deal of merit. A perspective that privileges authoritarian legacies can build on, rather than attempt to supplant, these analyses. Specifically, it may help to explain why executive-branch actors were compelled to negotiate with various political and social representatives and why historically powerful actors, in turn, would have retained the institutional and organizational capacity to influence the design of reform. My argument is that facing serious institutional constraints (no recourse to executive decree; fractionalized, if highly disciplined, parties; and the very real threat of popular referendum initiatives), social and political actors in Uruguay had an increased propensity and capacity to negotiate with government reformers. These actors could draw from a great deal of mobilizational capacity, as well as very well-developed corporatist, clientelist, and party-based networks of representation. Although the military dictatorship did aggressively reform several sectors of the economy, its ambivalence toward an alternative political project, and the public rejection of its proposed constitution in 1980, limited its political legacies. With the economy already partially reformed, and preauthoritarian networks of representation substantially unaltered, Uruguayan civil and political society seized the initiative to limit the scope of neoliberal market reform.

Privatization of State-Owned Enterprises

Of all areas of economic reform, the military dictatorship in Uruguay made no attempt to modify the property regime governing public enterprises. Indeed, this remained the least reformed area of the Uruguayan economy (Tables 3.1 and 3.2). According to Filgueira and Papadópulos (1997, 376–77), the Sanguinetti administration sought to (1) control social spending; (2) eliminate hiring additional state employees; (3) close deficit-ridden public enterprises; and (4) transfer some healthy public enterprises to the private sector or to public-private partnerships. Although limited progress was made toward achieving the first two objectives (through budget control and a civil service law), the government "failed to achieve even a parliamentary debate" for its proposals to reform the public gasoline, alcohol, and port enterprises or the state airline.

The Lacalle government (1990–95) proposed a Law of Privatization of Public Enterprises, which not only slated some of the most important state enterprises for privatization but also gave the executive broad authorization to carry out subsequent privatizations. The law passed Parliament with the support of opposition (Colorado) legislators. But in a dramatic turnaround, 70 percent of Uruguayan voters in a 1993 popular referendum rejected—and overturned—the law of privatizations,[15] supported by many Colorado members of Congress who had voted for the original legislation (Filgueira and Papadópulos 1997, 377–78), effectively burying the privatization project.

Fiscal Decentralization

Uruguay, like Chile, is a unitary state. Thus gaining control of the fiscal policies of subnational governments was not as high a priority of democratic

Uruguayan governments as it was of Argentine and Brazilian administrations. Essentially, Uruguay's nineteen departments retain the sources of tax revenue accorded to them in the 1967 constitution, as well as their right to borrow funds. A decentralization policy also provides the opportunity for the central government to transfer to the interior of the country for the purpose of developing the interior a share of national tax revenue, provided this transfer has been initiated by the president, approved by both houses of Congress, and budgeted in advance in the national budget.

Pension Reform

With one-quarter of the population of retirement age, pension reform was perhaps the most urgent market reform on the agenda of successive Uruguayan administrations. The percentage of public spending devoted to social security rose from 10 percent of GDP in 1989 to 17 percent by the end of 1994 (Filgueira and Papadópulos 1997, 363; Brooks 2001). As Brooks (2001) noted, the geometric growth of the pension system costs in the early 1990s meant that by 1995 some type of reform was practically unavoidable. Yet pension reform was painfully slow in coming in Uruguay. In fact, six attempts at reform on the part of the president were turned back, either by legislative action or by popular referendum. The reform that was ultimately passed in September 1995, moreover, was one of the most generous toward pensioners in Latin America.

Attempts at pension reform began almost immediately after the democratic transition. Under the dictatorship, the quality and level of benefits had declined while the system's deficit had increased (Filgueira and Papadópulos 1997, 364). Facing the necessity of adjustment policies, the first Sanguinetti administration (1985–90) cut benefits further. But its proposal to reform the system in 1987 was blocked by a coalition of various fractions of the political parties, trade unions, and new associations of retirees. The latter organized a plebiscite to coincide with the 1989 elections that would automatically index benefits to the average index of salaries; the referendum passed with the support of 82 percent of Uruguayan voters. The Lacalle government (1990–95) failed to enact subsequent reform initiatives in 1990, 1991, 1992, and 1993. The overwhelmingly negative reaction to the 1992 reform inspired a plebiscite in 1994 that overturned the reform and legislated that pension reforms could not be enacted through the budget process (Brooks 2001).

The reform that was ultimately approved in 1995 was praised by the World Bank as an important first step to address evasion in contributions and artificially inflated pensions (the latter by extending to twenty years the period used to compute the salary that determines pensions). Nonetheless, it does not conform to the model "neoliberal" reform. As in Argentina, reform in Uruguay produced a mixed public and private system, but it was one that was only 40 percent privatized, by Brooks's calculations. Unlike other reforms in Latin America, "the Uruguayan reform kept the state-promised benefits at the same level as in the old public system," and "the pension system was designed in such a way that low-income workers would fare better by participating in the capitalization scheme than they did in the public system" (Brooks 2001). This claim is confirmed by the success of the capitalization scheme in attracting new contributors. Although the government expected that fifty-thousand workers would join the capitalization system in 1996, close to four times that number had joined voluntarily within the first two months of the new system's existence (World Bank 1996).

Labor Market Reform

Reflecting the triumph of political over institutional legacies, the first Sanguinetti administration restored the institutional framework regulating labor markets that used to be in place before the authoritarian regime. In particular, tripartite wage councils reminiscent of societal corporatism began to operate again for private sector workers.

Since the transition to democracy, there has been little advance in labor market reform. Lacalle's plans to regulate the right to strike and move to a decentralized system of wage bargaining without the participation of the state were stymied by three general strikes. Not surprisingly, there have been no significant changes in the provision of Uruguayan law involving procedures for hiring and dismissing workers, which by regional standards are considered especially advanced (Tables 3.2 and 3.6). Some reform in the areas of labor market flexibilization and wage bargaining did take place (Filgueira and Papadópulos 1997, 368), not through executive decrees or legislation but through private sector negotiations between labor and capital (Filgueira and Filgueira n.d., 34). These agreements have proceeded to a greater extent in those sectors of the economy with a strong export orientation.

Brazil

Of the four South American cases represented in this work, Brazil's reform process clearly has the reputation for being the most stubborn. An empirical assessment suggests that this reputation is essentially deserved. After trade liberalization and a surprisingly difficult road to stabilization, progress toward market reforms was painstaking. The question for this chapter is how a focus on authoritarian legacies can help to explain both Brazil's slowness to reform and the pattern of reform that has been achieved.

In contrast to the somewhat contradictory legacies of authoritarian rule in Argentina and Uruguay, in Brazil, most authoritarian legacies pulled in the same direction—to make reform more difficult. A military unconvinced by neoliberal economics left an enlarged state sector and a full agenda of economic reform. Manufacturing growth, the new unionism, and the rise of the Workers' Party produced a stronger labor movement at the same time that business did not become better organized. The absence of a major business association to negotiate on behalf of a diverse range of interests has also been offered as an explanation for why Brazil's road to trade liberalization was bumpier than Mexico's (Schneider 1997) and might be as well for Brazil's slow progress toward the privatization of state-owned enterprises and even pension and labor market reform. Similarly, after authoritarian rule, national and regional politicians who flourished during the era of military-sponsored elections because of their adept manipulation of state resources through patronage channels were important players during negotiations over state reform, not least due to the overrepresentation of their states in Congress.

Authoritarian legacies left the Brazilian government with weak leverage with corporate groups, party leaders, and even individual politicians in the Congress. The state lacked effective channels of intermediation through which to negotiate its retreat in the areas of pension reform, labor market flexibilization, and the privatization of public enterprises with a strengthened labor movement that was linked to parties of opposition, not government (as in Argentina). Regional political elites seeking to preserve their access to patronage resources joined the new governing coalition and effectively resisted in the 1990s government efforts to trim the state payroll, reform the pension system, and gain control of subnational government finances. The Chamber of Deputies passed the first phase of the administrative reform, which dismantled job protection for most civil service workers, only in late 1997, when the currency was under international attack. These politicians enjoyed such veto power because most market reforms had to be enacted by constitutional amendment, not ordinary legislation. Amending the constitution, in turn, required a three-fifths majority (on two separate occasions) in both houses of Congress. Against the backdrop of a high number of effective congressional parties and their relative lack of discipline, Brazilian presidents struggled to secure congressional support and to construct any kind of stable majority coalitions in Congress. With the president's own party of Brazilian Social Democracy commanding only 12.5 percent of the seats after the 1994 elections, each step taken toward state reform in Brazil had to be negotiated with the representatives of the party of the Brazilian Democratic Movement and the party of the Liberal Front (together nearly 40 percent of Congress). Because reform in Brazil had to be negotiated in so many areas with regional and national-level politicians, the effects of each set of transactions spilled over into negotiations over other areas. The financial and political cost of negotiations to eliminate the public monopoly over investment in strategic national resources in 1995, for instance, further delayed state reform. In exchange for the preliminary agreement of Congress to reform the 1988 constitution to permit foreign investment in the petroleum and other sensitive sectors, the Cardoso government made a series of other concessions that would have the effect of delaying the fiscal reform of the state.

Privatization of State-Owned Enterprises

The privatization program of the Brazilian government had a slow start. While the Mexican and Argentine governments raced ahead with ambitious programs to sell off state assets in the early 1990s (Table 3.2), the Collor and Franco governments made little progress aside from the sale of a handful of steel companies.

In the second half of the 1990s, however, the Cardoso government made great strides in its privatization program, with the best years being 1997, 1998, and 2000. The leading sectors were telecommunications and electricity, each representing 32 percent and 30 percent, respectively, of total privatization revenues (Banco de Desenvolvimiento e Social [BNDES], 2002). With a successful effort in late 1996 to mobilize business support for Cardoso's reform program (Kingstone 1999, 222–23), politicians of the center right could back the government's privatization project, especially given their strong preference to resist reform of those segments of the state that were the source of their patronage resources.

Fiscal Decentralization

Just as pension reform must be considered the greatest challenge faced by Uruguayan democratic governments, so for Brazilian governments in the 1990s the profligacy of state governments, which rolled up a collective debt estimated to be in the vicinity of $100 billion, represented the gravest threat to fiscal stability. When it came to the spending autonomy of subnational governments, center-right politicians in the government coalition could hardly have been counted as allies of the government. Deputies who were far more often dependent on state-level politicians for their careers than on national party leaders (Samuels and Abrucio 2000) made it extraordinarily difficult for the central government to put its fiscal accounts to order at the expense of the state governments. To make even temporary progress on either front, governments had to dispense rewards from the state's coffers, which further undermined fiscal stability.

The government's agreement with congressional politicians of the center and right that in 1995 permitted foreign investment in petroleum in exchange for postponing payment on the debts of landowners (estimated at from $1.8 billion to $5.0 billion) for two years (Mainwaring 1997, 105) also rejected any reduction in the size of the transfers to subnational governments mandated by the 1988 constitution. Provincial politicians defended state governments who resisted proposals to limit the resources and fiscal autonomy of state governments and almost any attempt to repay the debts created by state government–owned banks. To gain necessary votes to renew the Social Emergency Fund (later renamed, more accurately, the Fund for Fiscal Stabilization) in late 1996 for a period of eighteen months (Kingstone 1999), the Cardoso government offered deals to roll over state-level debts.[16] In November 1996, the federal government finally achieved an agreement with the government of the state of São Paulo to reschedule $43.9 of the $60 billion debt owed by the state to the federal government, of which $20.6 billion was in state debts to the state development bank, Banespa. Under the terms of the accord, the state of São Paulo agreed to reduce its holding in Banespa (which had been under central bank administration for two years) from 66 to 15 percent, while the federal government assumed a 51 percent controlling share of the bank (Kingstone 1999). In 2000, these shares were transferred to the private sector.

Pension Reform

In Brazil, there has been only parametric, not structural, reform of social security, and there has been no privatization of the system. The government's modest goals at the outset of what turned out to be four years of negotiation were to remove the details of benefit calculation from the text of the constitution and to establish a minimum age at which workers could retire (Brooks 2001). Early on, the government suffered demoralizing defeats of its agenda. Somewhat unexpectedly, it lost in early 1996 a key vote in Congress to proceed with pension reform when approximately forty to fifty government allies defected on the vote. The government was even forced to accept a modification of the social security reform that protected public sector employees from any changes for at least two years.

When the issue of pension reform was put back on the political agenda following the Asian financial crisis, reductions of benefits were strenuously opposed by public sector worker unions, allied with the Central Workers' Union (CUT) and the Partido de Trebalhadores (PT) delegation in Congress. Although a pension reform amendment was approved in the months between March and May 1998 that was reported to have cost the government between U.S. $10 and $20 million to gain the support of resistant deputies, it did not reduce the pension benefit for public sector workers (100 percent of their final wage) (Brooks 2001). Following the crisis of the Brazilian currency in August– September 1998 and the $41.5 billion IMF adjustment package, the government won a crucial vote on capping state-guaranteed benefits for public sector workers in November 1998. As Brooks (2001) has indicated, to ensure the attendance of the 178 deputies that composed the rural bloc (necessary for a quorum), the government promised more than 670 million *reais* in benefits for the rural sector (including the early release for funds for housing and municipal projects, a delay for seven years of the payment of large landowner debts to the Bank of Brazil, and promises to support financially the production and purchase of ethanol). In sum, the government garnered support for what were minimal reforms to the public pension system through an extensive scaling back of its reform agenda, and through the liberation of massive sums of resources to particularistic interests (Brooks 2001).

Labor Market Reform

After authoritarianism, Brazilian labor came to be represented by two organizations, the CUT, founded in 1983, and Força Sindical, founded in 1991. Although Força Sindical differed from the CUT in adopting a moderate, conciliatory stance in its negotiations with employers, it, like the CUT, favored direct collective bargaining between capital and labor over state intervention in the labor market (Martins Rodrigues 1990, 86, 89). The CUT lent support to the Workers' Party, whereas Força Sindical upheld a bread-and-butter unionism that steered clear of parties. The labor movement, strengthened during authoritarianism, was able constitutionally to free unions from some of the most constraining features of Brazilian corporatism, including the right to strike, without forfeiting state financing. A pattern of labor militancy, evident at the close of the military regime, continued after the transition to democracy.[17]

With urgent need to attend to the fiscal solvency of the Brazilian state to defend and consolidate the gains made in the mid-1990s toward price stability, limited negotiating capacity with labor unions, and the absence of strong pressure from employers to make the labor market more flexible, the government relegated labor market reform to the back burner.

Authoritarian Legacies, Markets, and Democratic Institutions

This chapter has attempted to trace the influence of authoritarian-era economic, institutional, and political legacies on market-oriented reforms in four South American countries. We know because of the strange timing of reform that these countries do not undertake reforms as an automatic response to market or even crisis conditions, and within-country variation across reform areas should lead us to suspect that they do not do so merely as a function of the number of political parties or the electoral rules. I have attempted to show—through four Latin American cases—that authoritarian legacies play a role in explaining why some countries have reformed states and markets to a greater degree than others. The application of the authoritarian legacies framework to the area of economic reform is a difficult subject area in which to make the case. It is particularly challenging to establish causal significance in a chain of events that would lead a country to react within or against any particular set of constraints imposed by a regime long gone. But the complexity and difficulty of tracing the impact of these legacies on contemporary policy reform of such great significance do not excuse us from the need to attempt to do so if, as I have argued, that influence is very real and very powerful.

In Chile, budgetary institutions inherited from the authoritarian era did not accord much leeway to democratic governments to overspend, and subnational governments were prohibited outright from borrowing. At the same time, a weakened labor movement could not overcome the institutional legacies of appointed senators-for-life and an electoral system that overrepresented the right to reform the labor reform beyond a limited extent. Authoritarian legacies were constraining, not merely or especially because the policies of the Pinochet regime were "successful," as the familiar argument goes, but because of the specific institutional and political legacies that overlay the economic inheritance of the Concertación government.

A focus on authoritarian legacies may also help to explain the vagaries of the Brazilian reform process. Brazil's stubborn denials of economic constraints, even amid a tumbling currency, have led observers to explain its reluctance to reform in terms of its political institutions and particularly its party system. This analysis places that institutional analysis in a larger context. I claim not only that labor market reform and indeed reform across the board were slowed by a strengthened labor movement but that the reform of the pension system and subnational government finance has been more difficult than that of allowing the privatization of key state enterprises because of the role played by key political actors. The formal institutions and informal arrangements that were part of Brazil's authoritarian legacy elevated regional political elites to the role of veto players in the drive of the 1990s to gain control of the state's finances. Although these elites permitted their state's delegations to approve reforms designed at inviting foreign investment into strategic sectors such as petroleum exploration, they offered resistance to key areas of state reform.

In Uruguay and Argentina, the effects of authoritarian rule appear to be less enduring, principally because they were not embedded in state and political institutions and because the military did not refashion the electoral and party systems. In Uruguay, the commercial, financial, and fiscal reform that was achieved under authoritarian rule was preserved. But those areas that the military chose not to tamper with have been reformed only moderately at best. Pension reform was far more generous to workers than in Chile and even Argentina, and the privatization of state-owned enterprises and labor market reform has been slow. Against the backdrop of thin institutional and political legacies from the authoritarian period and no profound breaks in the political order, the political and social consensus around a welfare state makes it very difficult to reform.

Twenty years after the surrender of the Argentine military at Port Stanley, Argentina has perhaps traveled farthest of the four South American cases under review here to cast off its authoritarian legacies. The military that governed from 1976 through 1983 set out to liberalize the economy and downsize the state but had a record of mixed implementation and success. It also did not create permanent new state and political institutions, nor did it recast the party system or renovate the political class. In this sense, authoritarian legacies constrained both market and state reform less in Argentina than in the other countries. However, we should also consider that labor and business leaders, provincial politicians, and national party politicians were willing and able to negotiate reform with the Argentine government because of the particular way in which they emerged from authoritarian rule. Business had substantial incentives to cooperate with a civilian government, and labor was weakened to the point that it found negotiation fruitful. National politicians, on the other hand, emerged from military rule with electoral institutions untouched and their party organizations and voter loyalties more or less intact. Confident of voter support, they were able to risk embracing liberalizing policies and legislation.

The objection may be raised, of course, that what is being described is just a vagary in a process structured by the global economy. But even if market reforms were to receive an unexpected, immediate boost in, say, Brazil, the lengthy delay in implementing the government's legislative reform agenda carried such a high price that it must be treated as more than an inconsequential lag. Because the government was forced to maintain a high real exchange rate and issue debt in order to limit the inflow of capital to balance the current accounts, it not only put domestic producers at a serious disadvantage but provoked the attack on the *real* following the crisis in Asian financial markets in November 1997. Moreover, once institutions are designed in defining moments, they take on a life of their own and provide incentives to which political actors in the future respond. Although the limited impact of authoritarian legacies in Uruguay appears to have permitted that country to resume its status as an exemplary social democracy, the picture in Chile is not so clear. With informal and formal restrictions on the functioning of democratic institutions for at least a decade, most observers would agreed that the legacy of dictator Augusto Pinochet served to restrict rights in postauthoritarian Chile. There is now in Brazil built-in resistance to reforming basic party and electoral legislation that might make governmental institutions more effective, parties more representative, and elected officials more accountable.

Many Argentine scholars have argued that the nature of the reform process in its early years, however, also weakened Congress, the courts, and the institutions that enforce state regulation. Yet political institutions such as Congress have reasserted their authority in recent years, and the Radical Party that appeared to be on the verge of extinction in 1995 staged an electoral comeback in alliance with the Frepaso to recapture the presidency. Before the challenge of high unemployment and a highly constrained currency system snapped the banking system, a vital party system and quiescent military had led most observers to maintain faith that Argentina had a promising path to democratic consolidation.

Clearly, the blurry chain of causation and the sheer impermanence of these legacies place limits on an "authoritarian legacies" approach. But however limited it may be, an approach that illuminates the way in which authoritarian regimes influenced particular parties, politicians, and constituencies also compensates for the deficiencies of both structural and institutional analyses. Such an approach illuminates when and how fiscal crises trigger reform and when they fail to do so, and how state and political institutions do and do not accommodate major policy shifts. We have seen that in the Southern Cone, for instance, programmatic parties were able to adapt more readily to market-oriented reforms than those steeped in clientelistic practices that depended on parastatal and central government budgets. To the extent that authoritarian regimes strengthened or weakened those parties, countries have been more or less able to cast off their authoritarian legacies. Perhaps the most important lesson of this analysis is that the creation of markets requires well-designed democratic institutions and willing political and social actors. Neither institutions nor actors begin with a blank slate; the legacies of authoritarian regimes are written all over them.

NOTES

1. According to the Inter-American Development Bank (1997, 49), between 1985 and 1995, on a measure of change in the index, divided by 1, minus the value of the index in 1985, trade had been reformed 80 percent; the financial sector, 56 percent; taxation policies, 30 percent; privatizations, 29 percent; and labor markets, 5 percent.

2. For an excellent recent treatment of the diversity of the design of pension, health care, and education policies under authoritarian and democratic regimes in Chile and Uruguay, see Castiglioni (2002). She attributes the speed and design of reform to the ideological position of decision makers, the degree of power concentration, and the role of social actors and interest groups.

3. For O'Donnell (1992), the economic success and low degree of repression of the Brazilian military relative to the Argentine paradoxically made the consolidation of democracy more problematic because the collective memory of authoritarianism wasn't all that bad.

4. In chapter 2 of this volume, Hite and Morlino similarly identify this as one of three dimensions that influence the intensity of authoritarian legacies on the quality of democracy.

5. The ability of policy-making elites to marshal reform coalitions among the potential beneficiaries of reform has been viewed as an important factor in successful reform (Schamis 1999, 237–38; Silva 1993, 527), and the ability of the winners of early reform to block future reform, an impediment (Hellman 1998). But these analysts have not given us a handle on when governments have been able to mobilize successfully large private investment groups, as they did in Chile and Argentina, and

when they have not, as in Brazil and Uruguay. They also cannot account for when the early winners can be successful in stalling the economy in a partial reform equilibrium, as in Russia, and when they cannot, as in Argentina, where reforms went forward, and in Uruguay, where the losers of the first round of reform mobilized to reverse course on reform.

6. The new constitution required that 21.5 percent of the income tax and the tax on the circulation of goods be delivered to the state and 22.5 percent to the municipal governments by 1993, with no strings attached. With these provisions, the subnational governments accelerated the steady fiscal gains made since the mid-1970s. Whereas in 1980, the share of the country's main tax revenues that accrued to Brazil's states and cities was a mere 20 percent, in 1990, they controlled 46 percent of total tax revenues and accounted for 60 percent of government consumption. One former finance minister, Mailson da Nobrega, once called this constitution the "greatest fiscal disaster in the history of our country."

7. In Brazil, former finance and planning minister Delfim Neto calculated that between 1984 and 1987, government payroll spending at the federal, state, and municipal levels rose by 67 percent in real terms, three times as fast as GDP ("Drunk, Not Sick" 1991, 7). Within two years, the cities' payroll spending went up 32 percent in real terms ("Drunk, Not Sick" 1991, 9), and by the late 1980s, salaries and wages of public employees in several states of the northeast accounted for over 100 percent of government revenue (Mainwaring 1999, 205).

8. One of Argentina's leading surveyors of public opinion, Manuel Mora y Araujo (1993, 308–9), detected a major shift in public opinion during the years from 1985 to 1992 away from the values of statism, nationalism, and union organization. His contention is that this shift preceded Menem's reform efforts. Whereas in 1982–83, 35 percent of Argentines could be characterized as "corporatists" (sympathetic to unions, statism, and nationalism) and 30 percent as "social democrats" (valuing political parties, pluralism, universalism, and social concerns) but only 20 percent as "individualists" (believers in the individual and economic liberty) and 10 percent as "traditionalists" (concerned primarily with the family and morals), by 1992 only approximately 10 percent of the population still supported the values of statism and unionism. About 17 percent now opposed the power of unions but still supported a role for the state in the economy. Almost three-quarters of the electorate in the later year favored a predominantly private-sector economy, with the majority opposed to a strong role for unions, and only about a fifth favored preserving the place of unions in Argentine society.

9. The state government bank of São Paulo, Banespa, was established in 1909. In serious need of a bailout, it transferred a percentage of its shares to the central government in 1996, and in 2000, it was privatized.

10. Decree laws in Brazil have their antecedents in the provisional governments of 1889 and the authoritarian "New State" of Getúlio Vargas (1937–45), but

they were absent in Brazil between 1945 and 1964. They were brought back by the military in Institutional Acts 2 and 4 and the 1967 constitution. The Constituent Assembly of 1987–88 returned the decree in the guise of "provisional measures" and infused the Congress with the authority to more easily veto them (Power 1998, 198–203).

11. The Council of the Nation, which consisted of the Council of State and the junta of generals, was created in 1976 at the onset of the most repressive phase of the Uruguayan dictatorship by Institutional Act 2. The "collegial" executive was reminiscent of the 1918–33 and 1942–66 periods in Uruguayan history.

12. The most important new parties are the center-left Party for Democracy (PPD) and the rightist Independent Democratic Union (UDI). Now with five major parties and two party blocs, the degree to which the party landscape has been altered has been a matter of some debate. See Carey (2002).

13. Thirty percent favored an "important public sector, including nationalizations to develop selected areas of the economy"; 20.5 percent favored state control of "the main areas of the economy, including investment"; and 1.6 percent supported "full, direct control of the economy." On the other side, 26 percent favored providing incentives for private firms in selected areas and maintaining a small public sector, 11.6 percent favored providing "economic guidance for the private sector," and only 10 percent supported "free enterprise" and reducing "state intervention to a minimum" (González 1991, 80).

14. According to Gibson and Calvo (1997, 10–11, 13, 15), total federal transfers (composed of automatic transfers known as coparticipation funds and discretionary flows) to the provinces doubled between 1990 and 1995; discretionary transfers to the "metropolitan" provinces (Buenos Aires, Córdoba, Mendoza, and Santa Fe) increased by 31 percent, whereas those to the politically important "peripheral" provinces (all the rest) increased by 76 percent, and these transfers were politically productive for the government: the correlation between discretionary federal spending and votes for the Peronist Party in 1995 was .793.

15. Popular sentiment in Uruguay in favor of maintaining state enterprise ownership was deep and consistent. In a 1988 survey, 82.9 percent of Uruguayans polled expressed a preference for greater government activity in the economy (Blake 1998, 14).

16. The fund, created in 1994 with congressional approval, recovered 20 percent of the federal government's revenues for "social emergencies" for a period of two years in order to contain Brazil's fiscal deficit. The expectation was that a temporary victory over inflation would be consolidated through deeper reform of the public sector.

17. In 1988, there were 1,914 strikes in Brazil, in which more than sixty-three million workdays were lost (Antunes 1991, 19). General strikes were called in 1986, 1987, and 1989.

REFERENCES

Acuña, Carlos H. 1994. "Politics and Economics in the Argentina of the Nineties (Or, Why the Future No Longer Is What It Used to Be)." In William C. Smith, Carlos H. Acuña, and Eduardo A. Gamarra, eds., *Democracy, Markets, and Structural Reform in Latin America: Argentina, Bolivia, Brazil, Chile, and Mexico* (pp. 31–73). Miami, Fla.: North South Center.

———. 1995. "Business Interests, Dictatorship, and Democracy in Argentina." In Ernest Bartell, and Leigh A. Payne, eds., *Business and Democracy in Latin America* (pp. 3–48). Pittsburgh, Pa.: University of Pittsburgh Press.

Alesina, Alberto, and Allan Drazen. 1991. "Why Are Stabilizations Delayed?" *American Economic Review* 81, no. 5: 1170–88.

Ames, Barry. 1987. *Political Survival: Politicians and Public Policy in Latin America*. Berkeley: University of California Press.

———. 1994. "The Reverse Coattails Effect: Local Party Organization in the 1989 Presidential Election." *American Political Science Review* 88, no. 1: 95–111.

Antunes, Ricardo. 1991. *O novo sindicalismo*. São Paulo: Urgente.

Banco de Desenvolvimento Economico e Social. 2002. "Privatization: History." Retrieved May 8, 2003, from www.bndes.gov.br/english/history.asp.

Bates, Robert H., and Anne O. Krueger. 1993. "Generalizations Arising from the Case Studies." In Robert H. Bates and Anne O. Krueger, eds., *Political and Economic Interactions in Economic Policy Reform: Evidence from Eight Countries* (pp. 444–72). Cambridge, Mass.: Basil Blackwell.

Blake, Charles H. 1998. "Economic Reform and Democratization in Argentina and Uruguay: The Tortoise and the Hare Revisited?" *Journal of Interamerican Studies and World Affairs* 40, no. 3:1–26.

Bresser Pereira, Luiz Carlos. 1997. "Managerial Reform in Brazil's Public Administration." Paper presented at the Congress of the International Political Science Association, August, Seoul, Korea.

Brooks, Sarah. 2001. "Social Protection and the Market: The Politics of Pension Reform in Latin America." Ph.D. diss., Duke University.

Buchanan, Paul G. 1985. "State Corporatism in Argentina: Labor Administration under Perón and Onganía." *Latin American Research Review* 20, no. 1:61–96.

Campero, Guillermo, and José A. Valenzuela. 1984. *El movimiento sindical en el regimen militar chileno, 1973–1981*. Santiago, Chile: Instituto Latinoamericano de Estudios Transnacionales.

Cardoso, Fernando Henrique. 1986. "Entrepreneurs and the Transition Process: The Brazilian Case." In Guillermo O'Donnell, Philippe C. Schmitter, and Laurence Whitehead, eds., *Transitions from Authoritarian Rule: Comparative Perspectives* (pp. 137–53). Baltimore, Md.: Johns Hopkins University Press.

Carey, John M. 2002. "Parties, Coalitions, and the Chilean Congress in the 1990s." In Scott Morgenstern and Benito Nacif, eds., *Legislative Politics in Latin America* (pp. 222–53). New York: Cambridge University Press.

Castiglioni, Rossana. 2002. "Retrenchment versus Maintenance: The Politics of Welfare State Reform in Chile and Uruguay, 1973–1998." Ph.D. diss., University of Notre Dame.

Cohen, Youssef. 1982. "The 'Benevolent Leviathan': Political Consciousness among Urban Workers under State Corporatism." *American Political Science Review* 76 (March): 46–59.

Collier, Ruth Berins, and David Collier. 1979. "Inducements versus Constraints: Disaggregating Corporatism." *American Political Science Review* 73, no. 4:967–83.

———. 1991. *Shaping the Political Arena: Critical Junctures, the Labor Movement, and Regime Dynamics in Latin America.* Princeton, N.J.: Princeton University Press.

Corrales, Javier. 1998. "Coalitions and Corporate Choices in Argentina, 1976–1994: The Recent Private Sector Support of Privatization." *Studies in Comparative International Development* 32, no. 4:24–51.

———. 2000. "Presidents, Ruling Parties, and Party Rules: A Theory on the Politics of Economic Reform in Latin America." *Comparative Politics* 33, no. 2:127–49.

Cortázar, René. 1997. "Chile: The Evolution and Reform of the Labor Market." In Sebastián Edwards and Nora Lustig, eds., *Labor Markets in Latin America: Combining Social Protection with Market Flexibility* (pp. 235–60). Washington, D.C.: Brookings Institution Press.

Coutinho, Luciano G., and Henri-Philippe Reichstul. 1977. "O setor produtivo estatal e o ciclo." In Carlos Estevam Martins, ed., *Estado e capitalismo no Brasil* (pp. 55–93). São Paulo: Humanismo, Ciências e Tecnologia and Centro Brasileiro de Análise e Planejamento.

De la Balze, Felipe A. M. 1995. *Remaking the Argentine Economy.* New York: Council on Foreign Relations.

Drake, Paul. 1996. *Labor Movements and Dictatorship: The Southern Cone in Comparative Perspective.* Baltimore, Md.: Johns Hopkins University Press.

"Drunk, Not Sick: A Survey of Brazil." 1991. *Economist,* 7 December, 1–24.

Edwards, Sebastián, and Daniel Lederman. 1998. "The Political Economy of Unilateral Trade Liberalization: The Case of Chile." Working Paper 6510, April. National Bureau of Economic Research, Cambridge, Mass.

Etchemendy, Sebastián. 1994. "Límites al decisionismo? El poder ejecutivo y la formulación de la legislación laboral (1983–1994)." Paper presented at Instituto de Investigación, Facultad de Ciencias Sociales, December, Universidad de Buenos Aires.

Etchemendy, Sebastián, and Vicente Palermo. n.d. "Gobierno, sindicatos, empresarios, y la cuestión de la reforma laboral en Argentina (1989–95)." Unpublished manuscript. Buenos Aires/Rio de Janeiro, Universidad de Buenos Aires–Universidad Torcuato di Tella/Instituto Universitario de Pesquisas do Rio de Janeiro.

Ferreira Rubio, Delia, and Matteo Goretti. 1998. "When the President Governs Alone: The *Decretazo* in Argentina, 1989–93." In John M. Carey and Matthew Soberg Shugart, eds., *Executive Decree Authority* (pp. 33–61). New York: Cambridge University Press.

Ferro, Horacio. 1995. *La negociación colectiva hoy: Vigencia y desafíos.* Buenos Aires: Corregidor.

Filgueira, Carlos, and Fernando Filgueira. n.d. "Taming Market Reform: The Politics of Social State Reform in Uruguay." Unpublished paper, University of Notre Dame.

Filgueira, Fernando, and Jorge Papadópulos. 1997. "Putting Conservatism to Good Use? Long Crisis and Vetoed Alternatives in Uruguay." In Douglas Chalmers, Carlos M. Vilas, Katherine Hite, Scott B. Martin, Kerianne Piester, and Monique Segarra, eds., *The New Politics of Inequality in Latin America* (pp. 360–87). New York: Oxford University Press.

Geddes, Barbara. 1995. "The Politics of Economic Liberalization." *Latin American Research Review* 30, no. 2:195–214.

Gerchunoff, Pablo, and Juan Carlos Torre. 1996. "Argentina: La liberalización económica bajo un gobierno de base popular." Unpublished manuscript, Buenos Aires, Instituto Torcuato di Tella.

Gibson, Edward. 1997. "The Populist Road to Market Reform: Policy and Electoral Coalitions in Mexico and Argentina." *World Politics* 49, no. 3:342–46.

Gibson, Edward, and Ernesto Calvo. 1997. "Electoral Coalitions and Market Reforms: Evidence from Argentina." Paper presented at the Twentieth International Congress of the Latin American Studies Association, 17–20 April, Guadalajara, Mexico.

Gillespie, Charles Guy. 1991. *Negotiating Democracy: Politicians and Generals in Uruguay.* New York: Cambridge University Press.

González, Luis E. 1991. *Political Structures and Democracy in Uruguay.* Notre Dame, Ind.: University of Notre Dame Press.

Haggard, Stephan, and Robert R. Kaufman. 1992. "Institutions and Economic Adjustment." In Stephan Haggard and Robert R. Kaufman, eds., *The Politics of Economic Adjustment: International Constraints, Distributive Conflicts, and the State* (pp. 3–37). Princeton, N.J.: Princeton University Press.

———. 1995. *The Political Economy of Democratic Transitions.* Princeton, N.J.: Princeton University Press.

Hagopian, Frances. 1990. "'Democracy by Undemocratic Means'? Elites, Political Pacts, and Regime Transition in Brazil." *Comparative Political Studies* 23 (July): 147–70.

———. 1996. *Traditional Politics and Regime Change in Brazil.* New York: Cambridge University Press.

Hellman, Joel. 1998. "Winners Take All: The Politics of Partial Reform in Post-communist Transitions." *World Politics* 50, no. 2:203–34.

Henríquez Riquelme, Hélia. 1999. "Las relaciones laborales en Chile: Un sistema colectivo o un amplio espacio para la dispersión?" In Paul Drake and Iván Jaksic, eds., *El modelo chileno: Democracia y desarrollo en los noventa* (pp. 93–123). Santiago: LOM Colección sin Norte.

Hojman, David E. 1993. *Chile: The Political Economy of Development and Democracy in the 1990s.* Pittsburgh, Pa.: University of Pittsburgh Press.

Huntington, Samuel P. 1991. *The Third Wave: Democratization in the Late Twentieth Century.* Norman: University of Oklahoma Press.

Inter-American Development Bank. 1987. *Economic and Social Progress in Latin America: 1987 Report.* Washington, D.C.: Inter-American Development Bank.

———. 1992. *Economic and Social Progress in Latin America: 1992 Report.* Washington, D.C.: Inter-American Development Bank.

———. 1994. *Economic and Social Progress in Latin America: 1994 Report.* Washington, D.C.: Inter-American Development Bank.

———. 1996. *Economic and Social Progress in Latin America: 1996 Report.* Washington, D.C.: Inter-American Development Bank.

———. 1997. *Economic and Social Progress in Latin America: 1997 Report.* Washington, D.C.: Inter-American Development Bank.

Karl, Terry Lynn. 1990. "Dilemmas of Democratization in Latin America." *Comparative Politics* 23, no. 1:1–21.

Keck, Margaret. 1989. "The New Unionism in the Brazilian Transition." In Alfred Stepan, ed., *Democratizing Brazil: Problems of Transition and Consolidation* (pp. 252–96). New York: Oxford University Press.

Kingstone, Peter. 1999. *Crafting Coalitions for Reform: Business Preferences, Political Institutions, and Neoliberal Reform in Brazil.* University Park: Pennsylvania State University Press.

Levitsky, Steven. 1998. "Crisis, Party Adaptation, and Regime Stability in Argentina: The Case of Peronism, 1989–1995." *Party Politics* 4, no. 4:445–70.

Londregan, John. 2002. "Appointment, Reelection, and Autonomy in the Senate of Chile." In Scott Morgenstern and Benito Nacif, eds., *Legislative Politics in Latin America* (pp. 341–76). New York: Cambridge University Press.

Mainwaring, Scott. 1997. "Multipartism, Robust Federalism, and Presidentialism in Brazil." In Scott Mainwaring and Matthew Soberg Shugart, eds., *Presidentialism and Democracy in Latin America* (pp. 55–109). New York: Cambridge University Press.

———. 1999. *Rethinking Party Systems in the Third Wave of Democratization: The Case of Brazil.* Stanford, Calif.: Stanford University Press.

Mainwaring, Scott, and Timothy R. Scully. 1995. "Introduction: Party Systems in Latin America." In Scott Mainwaring and Timothy R. Scully, eds., *Building Democratic Institutions: Party Systems in Latin America* (pp. 1–34). Stanford, Calif.: Stanford University Press.

Mainwaring, Scott, and Matthew Siberg Shugart. 1997. *Presidentialism and Democracy in Latin America.* New York: Cambridge University Press.

Malloy, James. 1979. *The Politics of Social Security in Brazil.* Pittsburgh, Pa: University of Pittsburgh Press.

Martins Rodrigues, Leôncio. 1990. *CUT: Os militantes e a ideologia.* São Paulo: Paz e Terra.

Mericle, Kenneth S. 1977. "Corporatist Control of the Working Class: Authoritarian Brazil Since 1964." In James M. Malloy, ed., *Authoritarianism and Corporatism in Latin America* (pp. 303–38). Pittsburgh, Pa.: University of Pittsburgh Press.

Mora y Araujo, Manuel. 1993. "Las demandas sociales y la legitimidad de la política de ajuste." In Felipe A. M. de la Balze, ed., *Reforma y convergencia: Ensayos sobre la transformación de la economía argentina* (pp. 301–33). Buenos Aires: CARI-ADEBA.

Morales, Eduardo. 1989 "Salud/previsión/vivienda/medio ambiente." In Manuel Antonio Garretón, ed., *Propuestas políticas y demandas sociales,* vol. 2 (pp. 173–519). Santiago: Facultad Latinoamericana de Ciencias Sociales.

Morley, Samuel A., Robert Machado, and Stefano Pettinato. 1999. *Indexes of Structural Reform in Latin America.* Serie Reformas Económicas no. 12. Santiago: United Nations Economic Commission for Latin America and the Caribbean.

Murillo, M. Victoria. 2000. "From Populism to Neoliberalism: Labor Unions and Market Reforms in Latin America." *World Politics* 52, no. 2:135–74.

Naim, Moises. 1993. *Paper Tigers and Minotaurs.* Washington, D.C.: Carnegie Endowment.

Nelson, Joan M. 1993. "The Politics of Economic Transformation: Is Third World Experience Relevant in Eastern Europe?" *World Politics* 45, no. 3:433–63.

Novaro, Marcos. 1994. *Pilotos de tormentas: Crisis de representación y personalización de la política en Argentina (1989–1993).* Santos Dumont, Argentina: Ediciones Letra Buena.

O'Donnell, Guillermo. 1992. "Transitions, Continuities, and Paradoxes." In Scott Mainwaring, Guillermo O'Donnell, and J. Samuel Valenzuela, eds., *Issues in Democratic Consolidation: The New South American Democracies in Comparative Perspective* (pp. 17–56). Notre Dame, Ind.: University of Notre Dame Press.

Palermo, Vicente, and Marcos Novaro. 1996. *Política y poder en el gobierno de Menem.* Buenos Aires: Norma.

Payne, Leigh A. 1994. *Brazilian Industrialists and Democratic Change.* Baltimore, Md.: Johns Hopkins University Press.

Piñera, José. 1991. "The Path to Privatization in Chile." In William Glade, ed., *Privatization of Public Enterprises in Latin America* (pp. 19–27). San Francisco: International Center for Economic Growth, the Institute of the Americas, and the Center for U.S.–Mexican Studies.

Power, Timothy J. 1998. "The Pen Is Mightier Than the Congress: Presidential Decree Power in Brazil." In John M. Carey and Matthew Soberg Shugart, eds., *Executive Decree Authority* (pp. 197–239). New York: Cambridge University Press.

Przeworski, Adam. 1991. *Democracy and the Market.* New York: Cambridge University Press.

"Quem é quem na economia brasileira." 1983. *Visão* 32, no. 35A (August 31).

Rama, Martín. 1991. "Economic Growth and Stagnation in Uruguay." In Magnus Blomström and Patricio Meller, eds., *Diverging Paths: Comparing a Century of Scandinavian and Latin American Development* (pp. 99–125). Washington, D.C.: Inter-American Development Bank.

Remmer, Karen. 1989. *Military Rule in Latin America.* Boston: Unwin Hyman.

Rial, Juan. 1986. "The Uruguayan Elections of 1984: A Triumph of the Center." In Paul W. Drake and Eduardo Silva, eds., *Elections and Democratization in Latin America, 1980–85* (pp. 245–71). San Diego: Center for Iberian and Latin American Studies, University of California, San Diego.

Rodrik, Dani. 1994. "The Rush to Free Trade in the Developing World: Why So Late? Why Now? Will It Last?" In Stephan Haggard and Steven B. Webb, eds., *Voting for Reform: Democracy, Political Liberalization, and Economic Adjustment* (pp. 61–88). New York: Oxford University Press.

———. 2000. "Understanding Economic Policy Reform." In Jeffry Frieden, Manuel Pastor, Jr., and Michael Tomz, eds., *Modern Political Economy and Latin America: Theory and Policy* (pp. 59–70). Boulder, Colo.: Westview Press.

Samuels, David, and Fernando Luiz Abrucio. 2000. "Federalism and Democratic Transitions: The 'New' Politics of the Governors in Brazil." *Publius: The Journal of Federalism* 20, no. 2:43–61.

Schamis, Hector E. 1999. "Distributional Coalitions and the Politics of Economic Reform in Latin America." *World Politics* 51, no. 2:236–68.

Schneider, Ben Ross. 1997. "Big Business and the Politics of Economic Reform: Confidence and Concertation in Brazil and Mexico." In Sylvia Maxfield and Ben Ross Schneider, eds., *Business and the State in Developing Countries.* Ithaca, N.Y.: Cornell University Press.

Siavelis, Peter M. 1997. "Executive-Legislative Relations in Post-Pinochet Chile: A Preliminary Assessment." In Scott Mainwaring and Matthew Soberg Shugart, eds., *Presidentialism and Democracy in Latin America* (pp. 321–62). New York: Cambridge University Press.

Silva, Eduardo. 1993. "Capitalist Coalitions, the State, and Neoliberal Economic Restructuring: Chile, 1973–88." *World Politics* 45, no. 4:526–59.

Smith, William C. 1989. *Authoritarianism and the Crisis of the Argentine Political Economy.* Stanford, Calif.: Stanford University Press.

Stallings, Barbara. 1992. "International Influence on Economic Policy: Debt, Stabilization, and Structural Reform." In Stephan Haggard and Robert R. Kaufman, eds,. *The Politics of Economic Adjustment* (pp. 412–88). Princeton, N.J.: Princeton University Press.

Stark, David, and László Bruzst. 1998. *Postsocialist Pathways: Transforming Politics and Property in East Central Europe.* New York: Cambridge University Press.

Stepan, Alfred. 1985. "State Power and the Strength of Civil Society in the Southern Cone of Latin America." In Peter Evans, Dietrich Rueschemeyer, and Theda

Skocpol, eds., *Bringing the State Back In* (pp. 317–43). New York: Cambridge University Press.

————. 2000. "Brazil's Decentralized Federalism: Bringing Government Closer to the Citizens?" *Daedalus* 129, no. 2:145–69.

Tavares de Almeida, Maria Hermínia. 1983. "O sindicalismo brasileiro entre a conservação e a mudança." In Bernardo Sorj and Maria Hermínia Tavares de Almeida, eds., *Sociedade e política no Brasil pós 64* (pp. 191–214). São Paulo: Brasiliense.

Tironi, Eugenio. 1988. "La acción colectiva de obreros y pobladores." In Jaime Gazmuri, ed., *Chile en el umbral de los noventa: Quince años que condicionan el futuro* (pp. 71–93). Santiago: Planeta.

Tornell, Aaron. 1991. "Are Economic Crises Necessary for Trade Liberalization and Fiscal Reform? The Mexican Experience." In Rudiger Dornbusch and Sebastian Edwards, eds., *Reform, Recovery, and Growth: Latin America and the Middle East* (pp. 53–73). Chicago: University of Chicago Press.

Valenzuela, Arturo, and Alexander Wilde. 1979. "Presidential Politics and the Decline of the Chilean Congress." In Joel Smith and Lloyd Musolf, eds., *Legislatures in Development: Dynamics of Change in New and Old States* (pp. 189–215). Durham, N.C.: Duke University Press.

Waisman, Carlos. 1987. *Reversal of Development in Argentina: Postwar Counterrevolutionary Policies and Their Structural Consequences.* Princeton, N.J.: Princeton University Press.

————. 1992. "Argentina's Revolution from Above: State Economic Transformation and Political Realignment." In Edward C. Epstein, ed., *The New Argentine Democracy: The Search for a Successful Formula* (pp. 293–318). Westport, Conn.: Praeger.

Waterbury, John. 1990. "The Political Context of Public Sector Reform and Privatization in Egypt, India, Mexico, and Turkey." In Ezra Suleiman and John Waterbury, eds., *The Political Economy of Public Sector Reform and Privatization* (pp. 293–318). Boulder, Colo.: Westview Press.

Wilkie, James W., Enrique C. Ochoa, and David E. Lorey, eds. 1990. *Statistical Abstract of Latin America.* Vol. 28. Los Angeles: University of California, Los Angeles, Latin American Center Publications.

World Bank. 1993. *Argentina: From Insolvency to Growth.* Washington, D.C.: World Bank.

————. 1996. "Trends in Developing Economies." Retrieved from www.worldbank.org/countries. Uruguay.

4

Legacies of Injustice
in Italy and Argentina

PAOLA CESARINI

The question of "the legacy of fascism" . . . has to include the analysis of
the "collective memory" and of the multiple ways in which politicians
and societies responded to and learned from the fascist experience.

Juan Linz, "Fascism Is Dead: What Legacy Did It Leave?"

Alla mancanza di una storia condivisa, é la giustizia a sopperire
investendosi del compito improprio di riscriverla (In the absence of a
shared history, justice intervenes, investing itself with the improper
task of rewriting it).

Oscar Giannino, "La mala Italia non guarisce in procura"

At least since the southern European "wave" of the 1970s, political scientists
have enthusiastically engaged in studying the causes and mechanisms of
democratic transition. As the number of countries embarking on democratization increased, scholars progressively shifted their interest toward "democratic consolidation."[1] And many attempted to account for the variation among
different countries' rates of "progress" toward well-functioning Western-style
democracies. More recently, however, scholars have come to recognize that
"democratization in many countries involves contradictory or arrhythmic
patterns" (Agüero and Stark 1998, ii). Some have also acknowledged that a

significant number of so-called "consolidated" democracies around the world appear as "partial" or "incomplete" (Collier and Levitsky 1997). This, in practice, means that these regimes display nondemocratic features in selected institutional realms,[2] and that, while durable, they are also faulty (Agüero and Stark 1998, 9). In this new light, democratization can no longer be considered as a teleological process, immune from contextual variables, that starts with authoritarian breakdown and necessarily results in either consolidation or authoritarian backlash. It is rather a democratic regime's lifelong project that occurs in fits and starts,[3] incurs temporary setbacks, coexists with "faultlines" (Agüero and Stark 1998), and affects different institutional realms to different degrees.

This view of democratization poses, of course, all sorts of problems to political scientists from both a theoretical and a methodological point of view. However, it also offers promising new avenues of research (Agüero and Stark 1998, 11), challenging scholars, for example, to compare democratization across different institutional realms, sort out its "informal" from its more "formal" aspects (O'Donnell 1996), and embrace a "historical perspective that tries to discern the new from the old" (Agüero and Stark 1998, 11). In this context, political scientists, especially those working on Latin America and Europe, are becoming increasingly interested in how new democracies come to terms with their authoritarian past. While many typically analyze the influence of formal structures inherited from previous dictatorships, the lingering influence of traditional or conservative groups, and the enduring cultural and psychological legacies of authoritarianism (see also Elster, Offe, and Preuss 1998; Bermeo 1992; Hite 2000), others zero in on the so-called "politics of retribution" (see Aguilar 1996; Nino 1996; Elster 1998; Osiel 2000). In so doing, they attempt to explain, often successfully, how and why postauthoritarian democracies choose different paths in dealing with agents of previous regimes[4]— especially with those responsible for "administrative massacre."[5]

Relatively few scholars, however, are venturing to formulate concrete hypotheses on the *long-term* influence of choices about the past upon the shape of the new democracies. This chapter, in contrast, attempts to do just that, claiming that different choices made by new democratic rulers to deal with their country's authoritarian past have significant impact on democratization outcomes. More specifically, this essay argues that *postauthoritarian democratic rulers' different strategies, commitment, and ability to mark "a period of decisive break from their own pasts"* (Osiel 2000, 4; italics added), *to generate "myths of refounding," and to remold social memories of state institutions and state-society relations deeply affect citizens' trust in justice and, in turn, their trust in the new democracy.*

To illustrate the argument, the chapter contends that the choices made by post–World War II Italy and post-1983 Argentina in dealing with their authoritarian pasts account for why these countries' citizens—for the most part—fundamentally distrust justice and regard their democracies as "incomplete." Choosing justice as the focus of analysis is not entirely casual. Despite renewed interest in "transitional justice,"[6] the topic remains—per se—largely understudied in the democratization literature (Holston and Caldeira 1998, 263). This is rather unfortunate, since one of the most effective ways in which a new regime can signal its commitment to democracy is through the "establishment of credible courts and other impartial institutions for arbitrating disputes and ensuring that those who lose can sometimes win" (Levi 1998, 90). Conversely, failure to deliver or "democratize" justice—the state power that ordinary citizens have perhaps the most direct contact with—sends to society the message that the new regime's ways are suspiciously similar to the old one's and therefore that democracy cannot be trusted.

The argument applied here to Italy and Argentina finds a clear echo in the cases of Chile and Spain, analyzed elsewhere in this volume. It also potentially applies to post–World War II France (see Koreman 1999) and much of postcommunist eastern Europe (see Borneman 1997), which unfortunately fall outside this volume's regional focus. Italy's and Argentina's stories, however, stand in clear contrast with the case of Portugal, where the argument presented here is confirmed in reverse. There, in fact, citizens' trust in democracy is quite solid, thanks to the fact that Portugal's new democratic leaders—who found themselves in a situation similar to Italy's and Argentina's—took far greater advantage of the room to maneuver that was endowed to them by the transition. As a result, the process of settling accounts with the past in Portugal, "although short-lived and diffuse, . . . marked a durable break in the political culture of the country's social and political elite" (Costa Pinto 2001, 90) and freed political confrontation from the old demonizing dichotomies that continue to characterize Italy and Argentina. Also contrary to what has happened in Italy and Argentina, the Portuguese are able to confront their country's past with a sense of serenity and closure.

Some Definitions

Social memories[7] refers here to the intersubjective collective representations or claims about the past (Ben-Yehuda 1995). Such memories are "social" in as much as they provide common assets inherited by a society as a whole and offer somewhat "general and homogeneous versions of the past" (Aguilar 1996, 33) that help make sense of the environment each individual is steeped in. They are "both a common discriminating experience (this was right, that was wrong) and a 'factual' recollection—a seemingly veridical narrative— of the group's past 'as it really was'" (Cruz 2000a, 2). As argued by Aguilar, this is a clearly "Durkheimian" notion, in the sense that social memories are held to be distinct from individual memories but, at the same time, constitutive of the latter (Aguilar 1996, 33). They are, however, neither immutable nor immune from agency. In line with most of the literature on the subject, this chapter holds that social memories—at particular times similar to Collier and Collier's "critical junctures"[8]—are amenable to reshaping, often in response to memory entrepreneurship by political leaders. In other words, the past is "neither totally precarious nor immutable, but a stable image upon which new elements are intermittently superimposed" (Schwartz 1991, 234).

Trust is a relational concept, usually among people. Trust between citizens and the state is somewhat different from interpersonal trust, due to reasons that cannot be discussed at length here (see Hardin 1998). Suffice it to say that, to trust the state, citizens need, at a minimum, to believe that it will not act against them. In Hardin's (1998) words, "[V]ery often, all that is needed for government to work is for citizens not actively to distrust it" (11). Here, trust occurring between citizens and the state is taken to assume three different forms. Calling *A* the average citizens, and *I* the state, or an institution thereof, *A* is most likely to trust *I* when:

- *A* is in a position to predict that *I* will do (or not do) *X* because it is in *I*'s interest to do (or not to do) *X* (*instrumental trust*);
- *A* has sufficient knowledge about *I*'s record to reasonably expect that *I* will do (or not do) *X* (*reputational trust*); and
- The nature of *A*'s identification with *I*[9] is such that *A* is willing to offer "quasi-voluntary compliance" (Levi 1998, 52) to *I*'s authority (*social trust*).

Finally, *justice* here is intended to comprise the concepts of both *judiciary power* and *judiciary functions. Judiciary power,* in general, is that set of state institutions whose main task is to exercise *judiciary functions* (Pizzorusso 1990, 7). These, in turn, generally consist of

- Ensuring that the rules of the game that a society chooses to regulate itself are fairly, consistently, and, if need be, coercively applied and that they consequently enable citizens to formulate clear expectations in their interaction with fellow citizens and vis-à-vis the state

- Guaranteeing that any conflict among citizens, among state powers, and between citizens and the state is resolved quickly and peacefully
- Ensuring that deviant behavior is detected early and swiftly sanctioned according to the law in a nondiscriminatory fashion

Transitional (or retroactive) justice refers to new democracies' decisions to prosecute, bring to trial, and eventually punish leaders of previous authoritarian regimes, as well as others who committed human rights violations in its name. The term also includes *retributive justice*, which refers more specifically to the recognition, rehabilitation, and compensation of victims of the former authoritarian regime (Elster 1998).

Social Memories of Authoritarianism, Trust, and Democratization

At a highly theoretical level, this chapter argues that democratization outcomes depend on citizens' trust in the new regime. This trust, in turn, is critically shaped by the new democratic leaders' ability to break with the past, create myths that allow citizens' identification in the new regime, and remold social memories of state-society relations. This argument relies on three interlinked hypotheses:

1. It is in new democratic rulers' power, at least to some extent, to come to terms with their country's authoritarian past through willful policies and actions.
2. Effective democracy requires citizens' trust, and the path chosen by new democratic rulers to confront the past has profound implications for the development of citizens' trust in the new regime.
3. Coming to terms with the past also entails reshaping social memories of state-society relations to serve the needs of the present,[10] and such memories may indeed be subject to manipulation.

Let us take these claims in order. That new democracies may effectively deal with their authoritarian past through willful policies and actions is nothing new. Elster, Preuss, and Offe (1998) have already convincingly rejected the "structuralist" view on authoritarian legacies, according to which "the post-breakdown formation of a new social and political order is largely . . .

governed by . . . the deadweight of the past, continuity, inertia—factors which are at best slowly and marginally altered by institutional innovations and rational actors' decisions" (292). In other words, change in postauthoritarian democracies must be, at least to some extent, agent driven (see Levi 1997b) unless we "reduce agents to more or less 'cultural or structural dupes' [who have] no choice at all" (Rothstein 2000, 489). But it is not only change that requires agency. As Thelen (1999) argues, stability too—"far from being automatic—may need to be actively sustained politically" (38).

Allowing for agency, however, does not mean that new democratic rulers are fully unconstrained in their decision making. Rather, it means that their policies and actions are "path-dependent" (North 1990, 100)—that they may run up "against the unwillingness of many to sanction a break with the past, while other alternatives [are] legitimized when practical or intellectual precedents for them [can] be found in previous experiences" (Berman 1998, 380). In other words, while new democratic rulers must confront novel problems within old institutions—and with a "tool kit" (see Swidler 1986) largely established under authoritarian rule—democratization outcomes are not necessarily predetermined by the past. On the contrary, such outcomes should be interpreted as the result of a complex, bidirectional interaction among history, institutions, and agents. In Katznelson's (1997) words, "Structures and actors make democracy, and democracy remakes structures and actors" (97).

Once established that new democratic rulers are, if willing, actually able to confront their authoritarian past, the next question is: Why would they do so? They would because "changes in collective memory, through official efforts to revise historical understanding, can have monumental consequences for social and political structures" (Osiel 2000, 55). They also would because how a country's past is "officially" (re)interpreted influences social trust in and identification with a novel mode of rule. Finally, they would because, as shown by Ben-Yehuda (1995) and Schwartz (1991), careful manipulation of the past can be a powerful tool to entice citizens' legitimation of a brand new regime.

The link between democracy and trust is rather well established in the political science literature (see Tyler 1998; Braithwaite and Levi 1998) and therefore need not be discussed at any length here. The same applies to the connection between strong microfoundations and thriving democratization (see Toqueville 2000; Putnam 1993), where microfoundations are generally understood as citizens' full knowledge and active exercise of their rights (and obligations) vis-à-vis the state. In addition, this chapter claims that rights and obligations are not the only stuff microfoundations consist of. At least according to Tyler, in fact, citizens' *trust in* and *identification with* their state institutions are also important microfoundations of democracy. In other words, to effectively exercise their democratic rights, "citizens" must also (1) not be afraid to do so and (2) perceive those rights as being worth exercising because they mirror "just" and generally accepted social values (see also Rothstein 1998). In this context, scholars working on Latin America have shown time and again the causal relation between weak microfoundations (including lack of trust in the state apparatus) and "faultlines" of democracy (Agüero and Stark 1998) or degradation of democratic quality (Cruz 2000b).

The connection between citizens' trust in new democracies and the different paths chosen by new democratic rulers to deal with their countries' authoritarian past, however, is less recognized in the literature and may thus require some clarification. Political scientists have rarely focused on the connection between social memories of authoritarianism and the rebuilding of the trust and social solidarity that are indispensable to democracy.[11] Sociologists, anthropologists, historians (Connerton 1989; Douglas 1986; Geary 1996; Passerini 1987; Rowe and Schelling 1991), social psychologists (see Pennebaker, Paez, and Rimé 1997), and even lawyers (see Osiel 2000; Sarat and Kearns 1999), in contrast, often have. Their work abundantly illustrates that how the past is socially remembered (through the mechanisms of collective memory) has important implications for the beliefs, values, and identity of a society and the functioning of its institutions. In other words, how a recently installed democracy comes to terms with an old "tyranny" may well be the "constitutive act of the new order" (Connerton 1989, 7)—an act that (re)shapes the bonds of social trust and solidarity that are essential to democracy. As Timothy Garton Ash (1995) notes, "[T]here is a striking correlation between the degree of facing up to the past, . . . and the state of progress from dictatorship to democracy" (21–22). The link connecting the two is—as we contend here—the development of citizens' trust in the new democratic regime.

There is, however, another reason why social memories, citizens' trust in the state, and democratization are closely linked. While not all three kinds of trust mentioned above (i.e., instrumental, reputational, and social) rely on backward-looking considerations, it so happens that the most conducive to effective democratization—*social* and *reputational* trust—certainly do. In particular, the development of social trust in new democracies, which requires just enough identification with the new regime and its values so that citizens are willing to offer "quasi-voluntary compliance" to its authority, is largely dependent on the paths chosen by new rulers to come to terms with their country's authoritarian past.

But let's proceed in order. The first kind of trust this chapter made reference to is *instrumental* trust, a bond that may be cultivated by means of institutional reforms aimed at creating strong incentives for public servants not to act against citizens. However, even when the reforms are carried out, instrumental trust is bound to be less beneficial to democratization than trust founded on a more normative basis.[12] Furthermore, "it is probably not the formal institution as such that people evaluate, but its historically established reputation in regard to fairness and efficiency. What matters is the collective memory about the actual operations of the institutions" (Rothstein 2000, 493).

And this leads to *reputational* trust. Information about an institution's record is generally difficult to come by. In the case of brand-new institutions it is practically impossible. Citizens of new democracies, therefore, can rely only on their own (or some kind of "remembered") experience with similar institutions operating during, or before, the authoritarian period. The social traumas associated with authoritarianism, however, are likely to encourage a certain initial diffidence toward any new institutions rather than trust. This diffidence, in turn, is more likely to turn into "active distrust" the more continuities a new democratic regime's institutions appear to display with their authoritarian predecessors[13]—that is, the more the present resembles the past.

By way of contrast, *social* trust relies less on the past and more on "a set of institutions and social values with which people identify," as well as on a state that shows willingness to trust its citizens.[14] Authoritarian regimes, of course, do their utmost to destroy social trust. For fear that citizens' associations outside direct state control might turn into opposition groups, they systematically chip away at the country's "social capital" by compelling civic organizations to come under their corporatist aegis or perish. Furthermore, authoritarian regimes actively force their own preferred values upon society and manifest open distrust of their citizens, the general idea being that every citizen is suspected of disloyalty to the regime unless proven otherwise. Clearly, then, new democracies cannot count on their predecessors to leave behind a great deal of social trust in the state. They must create their own on an entirely new basis.

One way to do so, as some scholars argue, is to generate a powerful "myth of refounding" that, by drawing a clear separation with the authoritarian past, breaks the cycle linking citizens' trust in the state to its past performance and, in so doing, shapes a primitive, but untainted, bond of trust between citizens and the new democratic entity. As Osiel (2000) indicates, such a myth (or myths) may center on concrete events or documents (e.g., criminal trials of former dictators, truth commissions, the drafting of a new constitution) as well as on strategic discursive and symbolic practices. At least in the short run, and together with intelligent institutional design, the formulation (or resurrection) of such myth(s) may provide the most readily available and effective basis on which to rebuild the bond of trust between state and society that is essential to democracy.

The chapter's final claim is that coming to terms with the past is essential to democratization and that the reshaping of the well-ingrained (and often traumatic) social memories of the state and state-society relations associated with authoritarianism is a more effective means to do so, at least in the long run, than institutionalized "forgetting." To begin with, confronting the past in postauthoritarian settings is beneficial to democracy because it offsets undemocratic regimes' strenuous, conscious and well-organized efforts to mold state-society relations according to their needs, mostly through ubiquitous ideological propaganda, active resocialization programs, repression in both the public and the private spheres, and, of course, violence. Not surprisingly, the repressive policies of authoritarianism usually bequeath enduring and traumatic legacies to new democracies, such as a national sense of uprooting, loss of identity, "shame, guilt, silence and injury" (Axelrod 1984, 67), and a general reluctance to express one's opinion or participate in associational life. In short, authoritarianism powerfully undermines civic microfoundations. One way to rebuild them, as Osiel (2000) suggests, is to subject those responsible for state violence to trial. Such events, in fact, may provide "a 'theatre of ideas,' where large questions of collective memory and even national identity are engaged" (3) and in turn lead to interpretations of the past that favor societal healing and restore civic microfoundations. Many trials of former dictators[15] appears to have been staged largely for this purpose, namely to provide a severely traumatized and alienated society with a chance to confront its recent past and "derive from it common lessons for the future" (19).

Efforts to bring authoritarian rulers to trial are obviously based on the belief that social memories can, at least to some extent, be manipulated into new myths to serve the needs of the present. But can they really? According to a number of illustrious scholars, yes. Schwartz (1991), for one, shows that, within certain boundaries, George Washington's "democratic" image was progressively rediscovered over the years to serve the needs of an increasingly democratizing U.S. polity. Ben-Yehuda (1995), on the other hand, reveals how the "Masada Myth" was largely fabricated (upon a real historical event) by politicians, intellectuals, and others in British Palestine and later in the state of Israel to provide a "central and national symbol of heroism for the new secular Zionist culture" and give "a strong sense of personal and national identity, as well as a feeling of continuity with the past," to young Jewish Israelis (307–9). Finally, Judt (2000) claims in strong terms that "the special character of the wartime experience in continental Europe, and the ways in which the memory of that experience was distorted, sublimated, and appropriated, bequeathed to the postwar era an identity that was fundamentally false, dependent upon the erection of an unnatural and unsustainable frontier between past and present in European public memory" (83–84).

Although definitely feasible, reshaping social memories is a contested affair. There is by now wide agreement among scholars that "collective memory" is a relevant arena of conflict in democratizing countries, where "memory entrepreneurs" fiercely oppose one another with competing (and often irreconcilable) reconstructions of the past to further their contingent political objectives. These rival entrepreneurs may include a wide range of actors, including government officials, political party leaders, key public opinion makers, and various citizens' organizations.[16] In short, "[T]he relationship between remembered pasts and constructed presents is one of perpetual but differentiated *constraint* and *renegotiation* over time, rather then pure strategic intervention in the present, or fidelity to (or inability to escape from) a monolithic legacy" (Olick and Levy 1997, 934). And while it is certainly possible for eager political entrepreneurs of new democracies to reshape social memories of the state and state-society relations according to their present needs, their actions not only are "path-dependent" but also may be severely constrained by other actors' bearing of competing interpretations of the past. When this happens, and no compromise seems feasible, postauthoritarian democratic societies may indeed remain deeply divided across cleavages of "memory" for long periods of time, with troubling consequences for the quality of democracy.

To summarize, the general argument of this chapter is that social memories are relevant to democratization outcomes because if the latter is to be "substantial" rather than merely "procedural" it must also entail persuading citizens of postauthoritarian societies that a true break with the past has in practice occurred and that the new regime can be trusted. In other words, democratization not only is a process projected into the future—a forward-looking agreement (Przeworski 1986, 58–61) among old and new political elites to rewrite the rules of the political game, as much of the political science literature maintains—but also is about the past. In particular, it is about socially confronting and reinterpreting the authoritarian past as a means of creating an entirely new basis upon which to rebuild the essential bond of trust between citizens and the state, a bond that authoritarianism severely undermined.

This essay, however, also pursues a more specific argument: that new democratic rulers' commitment and ability to confront the authoritarian past are particularly important to resurrect citizens' trust in justice, which, in turn, helps ensure that the new democracy will be a healthy one. It is to this more specific argument that the next section is dedicated.

Justice, Social Memories, and Trust

Holston and Caldeira (1998) write that "the courts constitute the crucible of the democratic rule of law without which there is no democracy" (282, italics added). The courts they refer to, of course, possess certain characteristics. According to Montesquieu, the judiciary—one of the three pillars of democracy—should be separate and independent from the other powers of the state, as well as check on their abuses. The judiciary is also supposed to *apply* the existing law to a particular situation, while the legislative branch is responsible for formulating new or modifying existing laws.[17] And whereas the executive branch is allowed to set and pursue its own policy goals—always, of course, in the respect of the law—the judiciary in a democracy is not supposed to formulate any policies of its own or to bow to policy mandates formulated by the executive (Pizzorusso 1990, 17–22; Larkins 1998). Finally, justice in a democracy is supposed to be administered by the same set of institutions (normally civilian courts) and according to the same established procedures, regardless of the nature of the case in question or the personal characteristics of the people involved. Consequently, special jurisdictions should be as limited as possible[18] and well defined on the basis of clear and circumscribed criteria of specialization (e.g., administrative tribunals or constitutional courts).

Unfortunately, under authoritarian regimes, justice systems are often completely overhauled to serve the interests of the dictators. Common authoritarian measures in the realm of justice are revision or suspension of established codes and procedures in order to allow prosecution of so-called "political" crimes in violation of citizens' civil and political rights; widespread indoctrination of magistrates (with heavy sanctions for those who refuse to go along); arbitrary creation or extension of special jurisdictions; impunity for loyal servants of the regime; and stuffing of the judiciary with faithful followers of the dictatorship. It is, therefore, understandable that citizens in a dictatorship often distrust, even fear, the justice system. And fear and distrust are among the most challenging legacies that an authoritarian regime bequeaths to a successor democracy.

The "justice" issues that surface on the new democratic leaders' agenda are numerous, complex, and particularly thorny. They can be divided into three general categories: institutional reforms, transitional justice, and citizens/justice relations. All, however, imply a double challenge: set up institutions of justice that are fair, impartial, independent, and efficient; and educate diffident citizens to avail themselves of such institutions. In other words, new democratic leaders must not only reform the justice system but also effectively reshape deeply ingrained social memories of authoritarian justice that inspire deep diffidence toward state institutions.

As a matter of certain urgency, postauthoritarian *institutional reforms* in the realm of justice must deal with the laws and codes adopted under the previous regime that are incompatible with democracy—a massive task. Codes, however, are not the only survivors of authoritarianism; judiciary personnel often need "rejuvenation" as well. Such "rejuvenation" is often hindered by the enormous obstacles involved in suddenly replacing large numbers of legal professionals or sanctioning everyone who sympathized with the previous regime (especially when the latter was popular and lasted many years). Other ailments of justice in postauthoritarian regimes requiring institutional reform typically include the judiciary's continued subjection to the will of the executive (see Larkins 1998); discrimination against (or favoritism toward) specific groups or individuals; proliferation of special jurisdictions without clear specialization criteria; and the restriction of judiciary personnel recruitment to privileged social elites. Institutional reforms are extremely important when it comes to justice. Their relevance is not only practical but also symbolic. Purging the judiciary and rewriting the codes, in fact, are measures that powerfully signal a commitment to break with the past and may encourage citizens to renew trust in the justice system. Failure to reform justice, in turn, may deter citizens from using the courts altogether, for fear that their case may be judged or prosecuted by judiciary personnel compromised with the former regime or by means of laws that are unnecessarily harsh or discriminatory.

When it comes to symbols, however, a new democracy's choices about *transitional and/or retributive justice,* which generally implies prosecution and public trials of leaders and human rights violators associated with the previous regime, are even more important than institutional reform. Transitional justice, in fact, despite its clear sui generis quality, inevitably sets the tone for how citizens perceive the new regime's overall ability and commitment to deliver justice. As Nino (1996) writes, "[S]ome measure of retroactive justice for massive human rights violations helps protect democratic values . . . , counteract a tendency toward unlawfulness, negate the impression that some groups are above the law, [and] consolidate the rule of law . . . [and] is necessary for consolidating democratic regimes" (x). Furthermore, a "traumatized society that is deeply divided about its recent history can greatly benefit from collective representations of the past, created and cultivated by a process of prosecution and judgment, and accompanied by public discussion about the trial and its result" (Osiel 2000, 39). Included in such benefits is a measure of trust generation between postauthoritarian citizens and the justice system under the new regime. Carrying out retroactive justice, however, is extremely tricky. The issue is so complex and treacherous that many countries choose to avoid it altogether for fear it might encourage a countercoup or even civil war. Moreover, there is no overall good recipe for going about it, as the courts often seem ill suited to the highly symbolic task of reshaping social memories of justice. Tribunals are, in fact, highly formal and complex procedural bodies designed to apply the law rather than rewrite history in all its subtleties. Moreover, their procedures leave very little room for victims to tell their stories or receive some kind of apology, and individual sentencing of perpetrators does not often meet victims' needs for some kind of restorative justice. In light of this, several countries have opted for extrajudiciary paths to transitional justice—paths that rely more on truth and reconciliation commissions and "traditional" courts (e.g., tribal councils, gatherings of elders) than on "official" judiciary bodies and that administer retributive more than punitive justice.

Finally, there is the problem of rebuilding a healthy *relation between citizens and justice,* which—in a nutshell—entails shifting people's mentality vis-à-vis the justice system from one of subjects who fear the judiciary to one of citizens who trust the latter to protect them, especially from the abuses of the state. This requires deep cultural and symbolic changes, such as in the realm of language. For example, as Alessandro Manzoni, Italy's foremost modern novelist, cleverly points out in his *I Promessi Sposi,* the use of Latin on the part of lawyers and judges can be perceived by ordinary people as an intimidatory device to deter them from demanding justice. While the courts nowadays seldom use ancient idioms, the jargon of justice often remains incomprehensible to most. Authoritarian regimes usually aggravate, rather than alleviate, the obscurity of official language—for example, by preventing the use of native or regional languages. New democracies may thus signal a break with the past through the introduction of new languages, forms of speech, and forms of symbolic expression in the administration of justice to facilitate relations between citizens and the courts.

Authoritarian regimes are quite skilled in crafting "situations in which people [cannot] trust anything or anyone, thereby eating into the social fabric at numerous points, and poisoning or breaking down relationships of solidarity" (Passerini 1987, 144–45). This is true for justice as well, especially in the case of dictatorships that encourage spying among citizens or discriminate against testimony from certain witnesses, such as women, minorities, or opposition militants. Making these acts illegal is not enough. Stronger symbolic acts are needed to rebuild trust among citizens and between citizens and the justice system. For example, after the fall of communism, some eastern European countries decided to ban former secret police informants from public office in order to clearly indicate the new regimes' intentions to break with the past.

Finally, the widespread violation of human rights under military regimes and the subsequent impunity that many perpetrators enjoy in postauthoritarian democracies create a "general ambiance of political threat, . . . which [leads] to an atmosphere of chronic fear [and to] feelings of helplessness, defenselessness, and impotence" (Lira 1997, 224). Like distrust, fear cannot simply be legislated away. Much stronger signals are required on the part of a new democratic regime to convince citizens that the new justice system will punish the same behavior that it rewarded in the past. For example, victims of abuses, often neglected during ordinary trials, stand to greatly benefit psychologically from being able to tell their stories in an "official" setting, and possibly to receive an apology. Finally, citizens' confidence in justice is often just as positively affected by official symbolic acts of retributive justice that preserve the memory of the victim for posterity, such as the imposition of lengthy jail sentences for perpetrators. Such retributive gestures are all the more necessary when national "pacification" needs compel new democracies to issue blanket amnesties for members of the old authoritarian regime.

To sum up, it can be said that citizens of postauthoritarian societies "most frequently encounter the scope and limits of democratic rule" (see Agüero and Stark 1998, ii) in their relationship with the justice system. As a result, they perceive a continuity between authoritarian and democratic judiciary practices and, in turn, distrust justice. Moreover, "the judiciary is not fully used as an effective channel for addressing social and legal grievances" (Frühling 1998, 254). And while institutional reforms are often carried out, they generally turn out to be insufficient to correct this state of affairs because they lack the symbolic and discursive elements necessary to reshape social memories of justice and thereby create trust between citizens and the judiciary.

■

Among the democracies that fit the description above are Italy and Argentina. There, despite many reforms since the democratic transition, citizens continue to consider justice as one of the least trusted, effective, and reliable state institutions as a result of postauthoritarian rulers' failure to clearly break with the past and remold social memories of authoritarian justice. Paraphrasing Holston and Caldeira (1998), it can be said that Italy and Argentina's leaders' "overwhelming failure to secure and communicate a sense of effective justice . . . renders [the justice system] an isolated and even irrelevant institution for most people" of both countries (274).

What factors account for citizens' distrust of justice in two "consolidated"[19] democracies such as Argentina and Italy? This question might be answered in several ways. Citizens' lack of confidence in the justice system could be traced to common cultural traits between the two countries, such as "Latin" heritage, temperaments, and languages; a legal "culture" based on civil law traditions and rigid formalism; and the predominant influence of the Catholic Church. Alternatively, lack of trust might be interpreted as the result of the comparable institutional reforms adopted by the two countries after the transition—comparable because Argentina essentially redesigned its justice systems on the basis of the post-1948 Italian model. Finally, citizens' diffidence toward the justice system could be explained as a consequence of self-interested choices on the part of new democratic leaders.

This chapter, however, prefers to focus on Italy and Argentina's choices with respect to their authoritarian past and on the consequences that such choices produced for citizens' trust in the justice system. More specifically, this chapter claims that both Italy and Argentina attempted—but ultimately failed—to integrate their reforms in the realms of justice with discursive and symbolic practices that convincingly signaled a break with the past and created a powerful founding myth for the new democratic regime. Without such practices, social memories of justice associated with authoritarianism failed to be reshaped, and citizens lacked solid ground on which to rebuild trust in a "democratic" justice system.

This being said, this chapter does not claim that a social memories approach is incompatible with institutional and rational choice theories or culturally based explanations with a different focus than social memories. Clearly institutional reforms, political actors' interests, and cultural legacies are all part of the explanation. However, good theories of democratization are less a matter of "artificial choice between key factors" (Katznelson 1997, 93) than a question of specifying "how variables are joined together in specific historical instances" (99). And at least in the case of Italy and Argentina (but hopefully also for other postauthoritarian democracies), this chapter claims that a social memories approach offers a much more compelling view of the dynamic relationship between structures, actors, and institutions while allowing the uniqueness of each country's historical path to emerge.

Italy and Argentina: Transitions from Authoritarian Justice

Between 1853 and 1930, Argentina's liberal state presented the characteristics of a limited democracy. This was the case for Italy as well from 1860 until 1922, the year of the "March on Rome." Both countries' justice systems were based, at least in theory, on classic liberal principles. In practice, however, the executive strictly limited judicial independence, magistrates were essentially drawn from a small elite, access to justice was restricted to the economically privileged, and judges applied the law in a rigidly formalistic manner. The courts, in other words, instead of checking the executive's authoritarian tendencies, were often "a legitimating force, upholding [illegitimate] laws and endorsing many questionably constitutional policies" (Nino 1996, 42). Consequently, upon their takeover, both the fascists and the Argentinean military could readily exploit the authoritarian traits that characterized the liberal state's justice system for their own aims.

Italy's and Argentina's authoritarian regimes nevertheless left a clear imprint of their own on the administration of justice. Both began, of course, with a suspension of constitutional principles of individual freedoms and separation of powers. In 1928, Mussolini formally established the Gran Consiglio del Fascismo as the supreme state institution by de facto neutralizing Parliament. In 1976, Argentina's Supreme Court officially "recognized the military's authority to modify and suspend the constitution" (Nino 1996, 54). The next logical step for both regimes was to "domesticate" the state for their own aims. Justice, of course, was one of the first institutions to be "domesticated" by Italy's and Argentina's authoritarian rulers. In 1923 Mussolini suppressed the Consiglio Superiore della Magistratura, eliminating any symbol of judicial independence. The military in Argentina had no similar institution to get rid of. Both regimes, however, adopted decrees that made it easier to dismiss members of the judiciary and to hamper their careers on purely political grounds. Judges suspected of unorthodox sympathies were swiftly fired and replaced with loyal ones. Finally, the death penalty for subversive activity was quickly reestablished in both countries.

Despite many similarities, there were also important differences between the two dictatorships' justice systems. While Mussolini created an entirely new judicial layer, the Tribunale Speciale per la Difesa dello Stato (Special Tribunal for the Defense of the State) to prosecute "political crimes," the Argentineans relied mainly on military courts. And while Mussolini made justice the object of some elaborate reform, the Argentineans failed to do so. More specifically, in 1930 the fascist regime adopted a new penal and civil code to limit the individual freedoms, reestablish the death penalty, curtail the rights of the defense, and strengthen the power of the prosecution. In 1931, a new law on public security greatly increased police powers, especially as far as the investigation of political crimes was concerned. The *Duce* also decided to limit the ability to independently initiate prosecution on the part of ordinary magistrates, in favor of representatives of the executive and the public administration (in particular, the *Prefetti*—a category notoriously faithful to the regime). In sum, the institutional legacy of fascism in the realm of justice was far greater than that of the Argentinean military. Later, in 1938, this sad legacy came to include a series of discriminatory, harassing, and punitive directives against Italian citizens of Jewish heritage, adding racial persecution to the already rich panoply of fascist repressive measures.

When it comes to repression, it is interesting that both Italy's and Argentina's dictatorships largely relieved the police from political tasks, preferring instead to delegate such matters to the fascist militia and the Triple A, respectively. For the latter, Rodolfo Walsh[20] provided us with valuable accounts. In both *¿Quien mató a Rosendo?* ([1969] 1984) and *Operación Masacre* ([1957] 1994), he powerfully illustrated how paramilitary units in Argentina were able to summarily execute suspected (and mostly innocent) *subversivos*, often in the total absence of any formal act of the judiciary, and without the latter being able to do anything about it, except validating the deed ex post facto. Using loyal followers as henchmen, however, required both Italy's and Argentina's regimes to find ways to ensure their impunity. To this end both the fascists and the Argentinean military stalled investigation of crimes; assigned controversial cases to loyal judges (or at the very least to judges who could be easily intimidated into submission); and ensured that known and notable assassins blatantly retained freedom, position, and privileges even in the face of formal arrest warrants issued by the judiciary authority. And in those rare cases in which a sentence could be imposed, a special amnesty would quickly take care of freeing the condemned perpetrators from serving any time in jail.

Human rights abuses and generalized impunity were particularly grave in Argentina. As vividly detailed in the Comisión Nacional sobre la Desaparición de Personas (CONADEP) report *Nunca Más* (1986), violations escalated in the face of absolute denial on the part of the regime and utter powerlessness on the part of justice. "Approximately eighty thousand *habeas corpus* petitions were filed during the military's tenure. Most of the petitions were summarily rejected, following orders from the Ministry of the Interior. The petitioner bore judicial expenses" (Nino 1996, 58). The Mussolini regime's atrocities were on a smaller scale, despite his long tenure. Paradoxically, then, the more totalitarian ambitions of the *Duce* counseled him to avoid waging an all-out war against his own citizens and to opt instead for more "discreet" harassment of the opposition in order to preserve widespread mobilization in support of the regime and, ultimately, popular enthusiasm for his personal leadership—a strategy that worked admirably, at least until the outbreak of World War II.

The psychological and material legacy of authoritarianism in Italy and Argentina was enormous. At the fall of both regimes, citizens had endured all sorts of injustice and abuse by the state, which had left them feeling powerless, cynical, distrustful, and traumatized. In Argentina, thirty thousand *desaparecidos* between 1976 and 1982 among a population of thirty-five million meant that almost everyone in that country knew a family that had been targeted by the military's "dirty war"—a brutal battle waged by an illegitimate government on its own people, who were left with little or no ability to obtain justice.

Although in Italy the number of the politically persecuted was smaller, fascist abuses went on for over twenty years. What traumatized Italians most, however, was the postarmistice 1943–45 period. These were the years in which World War II came onto Italian soil, split the country into two, and started a tragic civil war between resistance fighters and Mussolini's remaining followers—the radical *Repubblichini*, operating under the aegis of a Nazi-supported rump government called the Saló Republic or Repubblica Sociale Italiana (RSI). In 1943–45 the RSI distinguished itself for its ferocity and became equated in the eyes of many Italians with the brutal Nazi occupation of northern Italy (see Woller 1997). If in 1943 fascism's responsibilities included a failed war and years of relatively mild repression, after 1945 it had a bloody civil war on its hands, in the course of which any semblance of justice was effectively removed.

Following such experience of war, fear, and injustice, authoritarianism's fall in both Italy and Argentina raised inevitably great popular expectations of peace, economic well-being, and, most importantly, justice. On the wave of such expectations, both Italy and Argentina decided to bring their former dictators to justice. In Italy, the attempt at sanctions against fascism after 1943 consisted mainly of trials against prominent leaders of the Partito Nazionale Fascista (PNF), and widespread dismissal of state administrative personnel. In Argentina President Raul Alfonsín made a personal commitment to the "big trial" of the members of the military juntas that governed Argentina from 1976 to 1982. These experiences are worth examining at some length.

In Italy, mass demand for retribution characterized especially those areas of the north that liberated themselves and where a serious threat of popular justice existed. Prosecutors' actions, however, were made very difficult by a great dearth of magistrates uncompromised with the previous regime and enormous obstacles to the collection of evidence. Nevertheless, a few fascist criminals were brought to trial, and light was shed on the corruption of justice under the dictatorship—which had virtually granted impunity to those responsible for the most notorious political assassinations. The trials against fascists provided initially a few cathartic moments concretely marking the defeat of the authoritarianism and allowing the country to save face internationally. Most importantly, they turned out to be very significant for public perception of the incoming administration. Newspapers' accounts of the time show, for example, that the very first judgment conducted in Rome against the police chief and his assistant greatly pleased public opinion and gave a strong signal of the new state's credibility. While these trials certainly left a lot to be desired from a strictly juridical point of view, they were initially considered successful from a political one. They also undoubtedly stimulated a public debate over fascism that was long overdue.

Over time, however, the fact that the lower fascist ranks were prosecuted while those with the greatest responsibilities—especially the king, Vittorio Emanuele III—could not (because either unavailable or protected by the Allied military government) convince public opinion that, despite its stated intentions, Italy's new government wished, in fact, to prosecute low while indulging high. In addition, individual prosecution and sentencing of fascist criminals showed great inconsistency. In one instance, a fascist *gerarca*'s lover—who had not been proven to be guilty of any wrongdoing besides having been his adulterous partner—ended up being condemned to ten more years of jail than the *gerarca* himself, whose participation in human rights violation had instead been clearly documented. As a result, a big part of Italian society who had initially trusted that justice would be done swiftly and efficiently suffered a grave disappointment and disenchantment with the new course and leadership of the country. On many occasions, this led radical anti-fascists to take justice into their own hands—especially in the north of Italy, where hatred for the fascists ran very deep.

The purge of the Italian public administration followed a similar course of events. Following initial enthusiastic action, carried on largely upon the Allied Military Government's insistence, the Italian authorities soon ran out of steam. From most interviews conducted for this study, it clearly emerges that people at the time considered the purges as *una presa in giro*—a "joke"—on account of the ways in which these were carried out and the reintegration later on of many "purged" Fascists into their jobs. Italy's administrative purge thus represented a missed opportunity—a "critical juncture" in which what was *not* achieved ended up carrying greater meaning than what was in fact accomplished (cf. Woller 1997, 1998). Even more importantly, it became a powerful symbol of the country's inability to deal with its authoritarian past. Italy's new leaders' tacit decision "to evade (rather than confront) the painful and difficult traumas of a national self-evaluation and extensive punishments" (Domenico 1991, 9) disappointed many bitterly.

In the end, a 1946 amnesty terminated, for all intensive purposes, Italy's venture in transitional justice. A law adopted shortly afterwards allowed "judges to . . . invalidate most of the anti-fascist sentences that had been handed down since the inauguration of judicial sanctions" (Domenico 1991, 208). Even the PCI (Italian Communist Party), an initially enthusiastic supporter of the purges, supported the amnesty adopted by the De Gasperi government. PCI's acceptance was apparently motivated by its need to acquire a reputation for moderation and reasonableness as a party of government in the eyes of Italians and Allied forces alike. Contrary to what happened in Spain, however, the amnesty and its ensuing "forgetting" was not seen by the Italian public in terms of an agreement among political adversaries (Aguilar 1996) for future benefit but rather as a first test of the new regime's commitment and ability to confront the past—a test that Italy's leadership clearly failed. In sum, defascistization in Italy constituted "a process that began with a vague idea of punishment and became a policy to forgive, or at least try to forget—a transition from sanctions to exoneration and national loss of memory" (Domenico 1991, 202).

In postauthoritarian Argentina, public opinion focused more on demanding punishment for those responsible of human rights abuses than on a thorough administrative purge. Thus most people welcomed governmental efforts to address military impunity and especially President Alfonsín's open commitment to the *junta* trials. Such trials were publicly carried out and ended with a guilty sentence for most of those involved. As post-trial opinion surveys (Landi and Bombal 1995) clearly reveal, most Argentineans not only approved of the trials but also believed Alfonsín's claim that punishing the military was important for their country's democracy and for regenerating citizens' trust in the state. The initial positive effects of the trials were subsequently reversed by President Alfonsín himself and by President Carlos Menem later. Their joint action approved an amnesty for the condemned military leaders and a law of due obedience and *punto final,* which effectively prevented further prosecution of lower military ranks for human rights atrocities. Both decisions bitterly disappointed Argentineans and caused a marked loss of trust in the new democracy's institutions.

The past still remains an open wound in Argentina. Despite government attempts—in the best Nietzchean tradition—to arrive at an official agreement to forget and move on, citizen's trust in Argentina's justice is still heavily influenced by the handling of the recurrent "irruptions of memory" (Wilde 1999). This is exemplified by the fact that Argentineans largely welcomed the condemnation of Alfredo Astiz in France; Judge Garzón's request in Spain for the prosecution of fifty members of the military; and the outcome of a trial in Rome where Santiago Riveros and Carlos Suárez Mason were given life sentences for their responsibilities in the "disappearing" of Argentinean citizens of Italian heritage. As Horacio Verbitsky (2000) wrote, people in Argentina lament the paradox that human rights atrocities against fellow citizens appear to be punishable anywhere in the world except where they were committed. Thus also the recent attempts on the part of the Argentinean judiciary to reopen cases regarding the military's responsibility in the kidnapping of *desaparecidos'* children—a crime that is not covered by the amnesty—was greatly welcomed by a public still clearly intent on obtaining justice.

As discussed earlier, justice in postauthoritarian democracies does not consist solely of bringing former dictators to trial. Institutional reforms and better relations between citizens and the judiciary too are often part of a new democratic regime's overall plan to restore people's trust in the justice system.

In both Italy and Argentina, however, justice reforms were hard to come by (Ungar 1997; Prillaman 1998). As a result, clear continuities persisted in both countries' penal and civil codes and judicial procedures (Calamandrei 1956). For Italy, a legal scholar recently stated that "the organization of justice currently operating in Italy derives without interruptions from the one instituted under the Kingdom of Sardinia, in the period immediately following the elaboration of the *Statuto Albertino*" (see also Guarnieri 1997, 242)—that is, 1848. As a result, ordinary citizens were prosecuted on the basis of monarchic and fascist laws, even after 1945. The Italian press has often had a field day in reporting episodes of this kind, especially as far as the application of family law is concerned. Argentinean scholars also point to a substantial continuity (San Martino de Dromi 1995, 280) in the countries' laws and judicial organization since 1853. The most troublesome continuity after democratization, however, was in terms of personnel. In both countries, in fact, the administration of justice long remained in the same hands of those judges who had diligently served the authoritarian regime.

The most important reform in the realm of justice in Italy consisted in the enunciation by the 1948 constitution of those principles of autonomy and independence of the judiciary (especially vis-à-vis the executive) that were sorely missing in the past. In line with these principles, the constitution also revived the Consiglio Superiore della Magistratura—the body through which the Italian judiciary virtually governs itself—and created the Corte Costituzionale, which was assigned powers of judicial review. Unfortunately, the constituent assembly left it largely to the Italian legislative branch to adopt by law all those measures relevant for the establishment of these new institutions. Parliament did so only after great delays or not at all.

Rather than writing a brand-new charter, Argentina revived its 1853 constitution, performing the necessary adaptations in light of democracy's needs. The most important justice reform adopted in Argentina after re-democratization was the creation of a Consejo Superior de la Magistratura, largely designed on the Italian model. As in Italy, the Argentinean Consejo was concretely realized, with considerable delays, in 1999. A Supreme Court had already existed in Argentina before 1976. However, its renewed prestige after democratization was soon undermined by President Menem, who increased the number of judges in the Supreme Court in order to create a body more "friendly" to his political objectives. During his tenure, he also set innumerable obstacles in the way of those magistrates who tried to prosecute him, his family, or his entourage for corruption. Thus the same impunity assured in Argentina to human rights violators has been de facto extended to major corporations and grand public thieves.

The Italian judiciary's relation with the political class has also been a difficult one. In the 1990s, the Italian judiciary entered the limelight of Italy's political stage thanks to its prosecution of government corruption, which, in practice, brought down Italy's entire governmental class after World War II. Interestingly enough, this activism, though quite popular among the public opinion, was later condemned by conservative and right-wing politicians as an instrument of the "left." In a creative exercise of memory entrepreneurship, the action of the magistrates was compared by Silvio Berlusconi and others to partisans' "popular" justice in the aftermath of fascism's downfall. This bitter controversy over justice continues to dominate the Italian political scene to this day, with the result that Italians are now deeply divided between those who believe that the magistrates are heroes and those who instead think of them as villains.

Conclusion

This chapter argued that both Italy and Argentina ultimately missed the opportunity to convincingly break with the past and create a founding myth upon which to rebuild a somewhat collective representation of their difficult past and, in turn, to renew citizens' confidence in the new "democratic" justice system. While new democratic actors in Italy and Argentina were clearly constrained in what they could achieve by innumerable structural, cultural, and historical factors, popular expectations in the aftermath of authoritarian collapse[21] were sorely disappointed. Reforms were adopted. But to turn justice from a machinery "traditionally dedicated to the defense of the State, . . . into an instrument of defense of individual rights," institutional reform is insufficient. A profound cultural as well as historical introspection is needed (Giannino 1997, 3–9). In both Italy and Argentina this introspection was missing. Proving largely unwilling or unable to reshape the collective memory of authoritarianism, political actors in Italy and Argentina botched processes of transitional justice, designed institutions that could not satisfactorily gain citizens' trust, and failed to adopt symbolic and discursive measures to significantly improve relations between citizens and the judiciary. In the end, all this reinforced among ordinary citizens the notion that state institutions could not be trusted—even in times of democracy.

NOTES

1. Democratic "consolidation" is a vigorously contested concept. Available definitions range from minimalist—for example, no danger of immediate authoritarian backlash—to maximalist, whereby *consolidation* refers to increasingly complex political systems in which democratization also encompasses economic and social realms.

2. For example, while elections have been free and fair for quite a while, a new democracy may nevertheless still display nondemocratic features in selected areas of policy making or even cornerstone institutions of the new democratic regime.

3. Schedler (1998) speaks also of consolidation of "partial regimes," where the level of analysis is necessarily switched from regimes to subsystems.

4. Responses to this problem varied greatly among postauthoritarian democracies. While some countries chose institutionalized "forgetting" of the authoritarian past by granting wide-ranging amnesty to those involved in human rights violations, others attempted to bring all responsible individuals before justice, and still others promoted a policy of national reconciliation principally geared toward uncovering the truth about atrocities in exchange for pardon.

5. Osiel (2000) defines *administrative massacre* as a "large-scale violation of basic human rights to life and liberty by the central state in a systematic and organized fashion, often against its own citizens, generally in a climate of war—civil or international, real or imagined" (9).

6. Elster (1998) defines *transitional justice* as "political decisions [to pursue retroactive justice] made in the immediate aftermath of the transition to democracy and directed towards individuals, on the basis of what they did . . . under the earlier regime" (14).

7. For relevant literature reviews on social memory studies, see Olick and Robbins (1998) and Carr (1986).

8. Collier and Collier (1991) define *critical juncture* as "a period of significant change, which typically occurs in distinct ways in different countries and which is hypothesized to produce different legacies" (29).

9. This idea is taken from Tyler (1998). For him, personal identification with authorities arises in connection with the existence of a social bond between A and I that permits the former to draw "self-relevant information" from the latter (285).

10. Schudson (1989), however, indicates that the freedom to reconstruct the past is limited by three factors: "the *structure of available pasts*, the structure of individual choices, and the *conflicts about the past* among a multitude of mutually aware individuals or groups" (107).

11. For an intriguing take on the link between collective memory and cooperation, see Rothstein (2000).

12. Here, I agree with Tyler (1998) that democracy's stability can benefit only if most citizens agree to play according to democratic "rules of the game" on the basis

of "feelings of internal obligation," rather than on the basis of fear of punishment or material interest.

13. To make things more complicated, the initial diffidence toward a post-authoritarian democracy may be (as in eastern Europe) paradoxically accompanied by unrealistic expectations of democratization (e.g., redistribution, development, equality, and justice), so that, at the first sign of the new regime's inability to deliver, it is democracy per se—and not just a particular administration—that citizens may end up mistrusting.

14. Axelrod's (1984) arguments on the evolution of cooperation could apply here.

15. The Nuremberg, Eichmann, and Vichy trials are good cases in point.

16. See, for example, the activism of representatives of Holocaust victims engaged in the efforts to retrieve confiscated Jewish property or compensation for forced labor during the Nazi era, or of the relatives of the *desaparecidos* during the "dirty war" trying to get justice against the perpetrators of torture and disappearance in Latin America.

17. In practice, this distinction is less clear. Many countries (especially those adopting "common law") allow also ordinary judges to creatively "interpret" the law or, at a minimum, to freely select which norm best applies to a particular situation (should more than one norm be potentially applicable).

18. Military courts represent, of course, an important exception to this principle, being, as they are, special jurisdictions geared toward a selected group of persons. When their domain expands or interferes with civilian justice, however, it is a serious problem for democracy, as shown by many Latin American cases.

19. At least according to strictly procedural criteria.

20. Rodolfo Walsh was a journalist who from 1951 to 1977—the year in which he was "disappeared"—ceaselessly denounced politically motivated murders and justice's helplessness (or cooperation) with such arbitrary acts.

21. Note here that in Italy and Argentina, contrary to Spain and Chile, where the transition had to be a negotiated one, the virtual collapse of the regimes following military defeat left a much greater opportunity for change.

REFERENCES

Acuña, Carlos, Inés González Bombal, Elizabeth Jelín, Oscar Landi, Luís Alberto Quevedo, Catalina Smulovitz, and Adriana Vacchieri. 1995. *Juicio, castigos y memorias: Derechos humanos y justicia en la politica argentina*. Buenos Aires: Ediciones Nueva Visión.

Agüero, Felipe, and Jeffrey Stark, eds. 1998. *Fault Lines of Democracy in Post-Transition Latin America*. Miami, Fla.: North-South Center Press.

Aguilar, Paloma. 1996. *La memoria histórica de la guerra civil española (1936–39): Un proceso de aprendizaje politico.* Madrid: Alianza Editorial.

Ash, Timothy Garton. 1995. "Central Europe: The Present Past." *New York Review of Books,* 13 July, pp. 21–22.

Assman, Jan, and Czaplicka, John. 1995. "Collective Memory and Cultural Identity." *New German Critique* 65:125–34.

Axelrod, Robert. 1984. *The Evolution of Cooperation.* New York: Basic Books.

Banfield, Edward C. 1958. *The Moral Basis of a Backward Society.* New York: Free Press.

Barahona de Brito, Alexandra, Carmen Gonzaléz-Enríquez, and Paloma Aguilar. 2001. *The Politics of Memory: Transitional Justice in Democratizing Societies.* New York: Oxford University Press.

Bates, Robert H., Rui J. P. de Figuereido, Jr., and Barry R. Weingast. 1998. "The Politics of Interpretation: Rationality, Culture and Transition." *Politics and Society* 26, no. 2:221–56.

Baylora, Enrique A., ed. 1987. *Comparing New Democracies: Transition and Consolidation in Mediterranean Europe and the Southern Cone.* Boulder, Colo.: Westview Press.

Ben-Yehuda, Nachman. 1995. *The Masada Myth: Collective Memory and Mythmaking in Israel.* Madison: University of Wisconsin Press.

Berlinguer, Mario. 1944. *La crisi della giustizia nel regime fascista.* Rome: Migliaresi Editore.

Berman, Sheri. 1998. "Path Dependency and Political Action." *Comparative Politics* 30, no. 4:379–400.

Bermeo, Nancy. 1992. "Democracy and the Lessons of Dictatorship." *Comparative Politics* 24, no. 3:273–91.

Bianchi, Alberto B. 1996. *Dinámica del estado de derecho.* Buenos Aires: Abaco.

Bielsa, Rafael, and Eduardo Graña. 1996. *Justicia y estado.* Buenos Aires: Ediciones Ciudad Argentina.

Borgna, Paolo, and Margherita Cassano. 1997. *Il giudice e il principe.* Rome: Donzelli Editore.

Borneman, John. 1997. *Settling Accounts: Violence, Justice, and Accountability in Postsocialist Europe.* Princeton, N.J.: Princeton University Press.

Braithwaite, Valerie. 1998. "Communal and Exchange Trust Norms: Their Value Base and Relevance to Institutional Trust." In Valerie Braithwaite and Margaret Levi, eds., *Trust and Governance.* New York: Russell Sage Foundation.

Braithwaite, Valerie, and Margaret Levi, eds. 1998. *Trust and Governance.* New York: Russell Sage Foundation.

Calamandrei, Pietro. 1956. *Procedure and Democracy.* New York: New York University Press.

Carr, David. 1986. *Time, Narrative and History.* Bloomington: Indiana University Press.

Colarizi, Simona, and Leonardo Morlino. 1998. "Italy after Fascism: An Overview of the Fascist Legacy." In Stein Ugelvik Larsen, ed., *Modern Europe after Fascism, 1943–1980s,* vol. 1 (pp. 457–75). Boulder, Colo.: Social Science Monographs.

Collier, David, and Steven Levitsky. 1997. "Democracy with Adjectives." *World Politics* 49, no. 3:430–51.

Collier, Ruth Berins, and David Collier. 1991. *Shaping the Political Arena*. Princeton, N.J.: Princeton University Press.

Comisión Nacional sobre la Desaparición de Personas. 1986. *Nunca Más: A Report by Argentina's National Commission on Disappeared People*. Boston: Faber and Faber.

Connerton, Paul. 1989. *How Societies Remember*. New York: Cambridge University Press.

Costa Pinto, António. 2001. "Settling Accounts with the Past in a Troubled Transition to Democracy: The Portuguese Case." In Alexandra Barahona de Brito, Carmen Gonzaléz-Enríquez, and Paloma Aguilar, eds., *The Politics of Memory: Transitional Justice in Democratizing Societies*. New York: Oxford University Press.

Cruz, Consuelo. 2000a. "Identity and Persuasion: How Nations Remember Their Pasts and Make Their Futures." *World Politics* 52, no. 3:275–312.

———. 2000b. "Latin American Citizenship: Civic Microfoundation in Historical Perspective." Unpublished manuscript.

Dahl, Robert. 1971. *Polyarchy*. New Haven, Conn.: Yale University Press.

Diamond, Larry, ed. 1997. *Consolidating the Third Wave Democracies*. Baltimore, Md.: Johns Hopkins University Press.

Domenico, Roy Palmer. 1991. *Italian Fascists on Trial 1943–48*. Chapel Hill: University of North Carolina Press.

Domínguez, Jorge I., and Abraham F. Lowenthal, eds. 1996. *Constructing Democratic Governance: Latin America and the Caribbean in the 1990s*. Baltimore, Md.: Johns Hopkins University Press.

Douglas, Mary. 1986. *How Institutions Think*. Syracuse, N.Y.: Syracuse University Press.

Elster, Jon. 1995. "Strategic Use of Argument." In Kenneth Joseph Arrow, Robert H. Mnookin, Lee Ross, Amos Tversky, and Robert Wilson, eds., *Barriers to the Negotiated Resolution of Conflicts*. New York: W. W. Norton.

———. 1998. "Coming to Terms with the Past: A Framework for the Study of Justice in the Transition to Democracy." *European Journal of Sociology*, no. 39:7–48.

Elster, Jon, Claus Offe, and Ulrich K. Preuss. 1998. *Institutional Design in Post-Communist Societies*. New York: Cambridge University Press.

Feitlowitz, Marguerite. 1998. *A Lexicon of Terror: Argentina and the Legacies of Torture*. New York: Oxford University Press.

Fondazione Amici di Liberal, ed. 1997. *Ripensare la giustizia: Una proposta sullo stato di diritto*. Document 4. Rome: Atlante Editoriale S.p.A.

Frühling, Hugo. 1998. "Judicial Reform and Democratization in Latin America." In Felipe Agüero and Jeffrey Stark, eds., *Fault Lines of Democracy in Post-Transition Latin America*. Miami, Fla.: North-South Center Press.

Gambetta, Diego. 1993. *The Sicilian Mafia: The Business of Private Protection*. Cambridge, Mass.: Harvard University Press.

Geary, Patrick J. 1996. *Phantoms of Remembrance: Memory and Oblivion at the End of the First Millennium*. Princeton, N.J.: Princeton University Press..

Geddes, Barbara. 1994. *Politicians' Dilemma.* Berkeley: University of California Press.

Ghisalberti, Carlo. 1998. [2002 according to LOC]. *Storia costituzionale d'Italia 1848–1948.* Rome: GLF Editori Laterza.

Giannino, Oscar. 1997. "La mala Italia non guarisce in procura." In Fondazione Amici di Liberal, ed. *Ripensare la giustizia: Una proposta sullo stato di diritto.* Document 4. Rome: Atlante Editoriale S.p.A.

Guarnieri, Carlo. 1997. "Magistratura e sistema politico nella storia d'Italia." In Raffaele Romanelli, ed., *Magistrati e potere nella storia europea.* Bologna: Il Mulino.

Gunther, Richard, P. Nikiforos Diamandouros, and Hans-Jürgen Puhle. 1996. *The Politics of Democratic Consolidation: Southern Europe in Comparative Perspective.* Baltimore, Md.: Johns Hopkins University Press.

Gurr, Ted Robert, Keith Jaggers, and Will Moore. 1996. "The Transformation of the Western State: The Growth of Democracy, Autocracy, and State Power since 1800." *Studies in Comparative International Development* 23, no. 1:73–108.

Hagopian, Frances. 1993. "After Regime Change: Authoritarian Legacies, Political Representation and the Democratic Future of South America." *World Politics* 45 (April): 464–500.

———. 1996a. *Traditional Politics and Regime Change in Brazil.* New York: Cambridge University Press.

———. 1996b. "Traditional Power Structures and Democratic Governance in Latin America." In Jorge I. Domínguez and Abraham F. Lowenthal, eds., *Constructing Democratic Governance: Latin America and the Caribbean in the 1990s.* Baltimore, Md.: Johns Hopkins University Press.

Halbwachs, Maurice. 1980. *The Collective Memory.* New York: Harper and Row.

Hall, Peter, and Rosemary Taylor. 1996. "Political Science and the Three New Institutionalisms." *Political Studies* 44:936–57.

Hardin, Russell. 1998. "Trust in Government." In Valerie Braithwaite and Margaret Levi, eds., *Trust and Governance.* New York: Russell Sage Foundation.

Herz, John H., ed. 1982. *From Dictatorship to Democracy: Coping with the Legacies of Authoritarianism and Totalitarianism.* Westport, Conn.: Greenwood Press.

Hite, Katherine. 2000. *When the Romance Ended: Leaders of the Chilean Left, 1968–1998.* New York: Columbia University Press.

Holston, James, and Teresa P. R. Caldeira. 1998. "Democracy, Law and Violence: Disjunctions of Brazilian Citizenship." In Felipe Agüero and Jeffrey Stark, eds., *Fault Lines of Democracy in Post-Transition Latin America.* Miami, Fla.: North-South Center Press.

Inter-American Development Bank. 1997. *Latin America after a Decade of Reforms: Economic and Social Progress in Latin America, 1997 Report.* Washington, D.C.: Inter-American Development Bank.

Jaggers, Keith, and Ted Robert Gurr. 1995. "Tracking Democracy's Third Wave with the Polity III Data." *Journal of Peace Research* 32, no. 4:469–82.

Jelín, Elizabeth, Laura Gingold, Susana G. Kaufman, Marcelo Leiras, Silvia Rabich de Galperin, and Lucas Rubinich. 1996. *Vida cotidiana y control institucional en la Argentina de los '90.* Buenos Aires: Grupo Editor Latinoamericano.

Judt, Tony. 2000. "The Past Is Another Country: Myth and Memory in Postwar Europe." In Deák István, Jan T. Gross, and Tony Judt, eds., *The Politics of Retribution in Europe* (pp. 293–324). Princeton, N.J.: Princeton University Press.

Katznelson, Ira. 1997. "Structure and Configuration in Comparative Politics." In Mark Irving Lichbach and Alan S. Zuckerman, eds., *Comparative Politics: Rationality, Culture, and Structure.* New York: Cambridge University Press.

Kaufman, Robert. 1997. "The Next Challenge for Latin America: Growth with Equity; Reform of the State; Consolidation of Democratic Institutions." Unpublished manuscript.

Koreman, Megan. 1999. *The Expectation of Justice: France, 1944–1946.* Durham, N.C.: Duke University Press.

Krasner, Stephen. 1984. "Approaches to the State: Alternative Conceptions and Historical Dynamics." *Comparative Politics* 16, no. 1:223–46.

Landi, Oscar, and Inés González Bombal. 1995. "Los derechos en la cultura política." In Carlos H. Acuña, Inés González Bombal, Elizabeth Jelín, Oscar Landi, Luís Alberto Quevedo, Catalina Smulovitz, and Adriana Vacchieri, eds., *Juicio, castigos y memorias: Derechos humanos y justicia en la polítca argentina.* Buenos Aires: Ediciones Nueva Vision.

Larkins, Christopher. 1998. "The Judiciary and Delegative Democracy in Argentina." *Comparative Politics* 30, no. 4:423–42.

Larsen, Stein Ugelvik, ed. 1998. *Modern Europe after Fascism, 1943–1980s.* Vols. 1 and 2. Boulder, Colo.: Social Science Monographs.

Levi, Margaret. 1988. *Of Rule and Revenue.* Berkeley: University of California Press.

———. 1991. "Are There Limits to Rationality?" *Archives Européennes de Sociologie* 1, no. 32:130–41.

———. 1997a. *Consent, Dissent and Patriotism.* New York: Cambridge University Press.

———. 1997b. "A Model, a Method and a Map: Rational Choice in Comparative and Historical Analysis." In Mark Irving Lichbach and Alan S. Zuckerman, eds., *Comparative Politics: Rationality, Culture, and Structure.* New York: Cambridge University Press.

———. 1998. "A State of Trust." In Valerie Braithwaite and Margaret Levi, eds., *Trust and Governance.* New York: Russell Sage Foundation.

Lichbach, Mark Irving, and Alan S. Zuckerman, eds. 1997. *Comparative Politics: Rationality, Culture, and Structure.* New York: Cambridge University Press.

Linz, Juan J. 1975. "Totalitarian and Authoritarian Regimes." In Fred I. Greenstein and Nelson W. Polsby, eds., *Macropolitical Theory.* Vol. 3 of *Handbook of Political Science.* Reading, Mass.: Addison-Wesley.

———. 1998. "Fascism Is Dead: What Legacy Did It Leave? Thoughts and Questions on a Problematic Period of European History." In Stein Ugelvik Larsen, ed.,

Modern Europe after Fascism, 1943–1980s, vol. 1 (pp. 13–51). Boulder, Colo.: Social Science Monographs.

Linz, Juan J., and Alfred Stepan. 1996. *Problems of Democratic Transition and Consolidation.* Baltimore, Md.: Johns Hopkins University Press.

Lipset, Seymour Martin. 1959. "Some Social Requisites of Democracy: Economic Development and Political Legitimacy." *American Political Science Review* 53 (March): 69–105.

Lira, Elizabeth. 1997. "Remembering: Passing Back through the Heart." In James Pennebaker, Dario Paez, and Bernard Rimé, eds., *Collective Memory of Political Events.* Mahwah, N.J.: Lawrence Erlbaum Associates.

Mainwaring, Scott, and Timothy R. Scully, eds. 1995. *Building Democratic Institutions: Party Systems in Latin America.* Stanford, Calif.: Stanford University Press.

Mainwaring, Scott, and Matthew S. Shugart. 1997. *Presidentialism and Democracy in Latin America.* New York: Cambridge University Press.

Morlino, Leonardo. 1998. "Is There Another Side to the Fascist Legacy?" In Stein Ugelvik Larsen, ed., *Modern Europe after Fascism, 1943–1980s.* Vol. 1 (pp. 662–98). Boulder, Colo.: Social Science Monographs.

Morlino, Leonardo, and Katherine Hite. 1999. "Problematizing Authoritarian Legacies and Good Democracy." Paper presented at the Workshop on Authoritarian Legacies in Latin America and Southern Europe, 27 August, Arrabida, Portugal.

Nino, Carlos Santiago. 1996. *Radical Evil on Trial.* New Haven, Conn.: Yale University Press.

Nora, Pierre. 1989. "Between Memory and History: Les Lieux de Mémoire." *Representations,* no. 26:7–24.

North, Douglas. 1990. *Institutions, Institutional Change and Economic Performance.* New York: Cambridge University Press.

O'Donnell, Guillermo. 1994. "Delegative Democracy?" *Journal of Democracy* 5, no. 1:55–69.

———. 1996. "Illusions about Consolidation." *Journal of Democracy* 7, no. 2:34–51.

O'Donnell, Guillermo, Philippe C. Schmitter, and Lawrence Whitehead, eds. 1986. *Transitions from Authoritarian Rule.* Baltimore, Md.: Johns Hopkins University Press.

Olick, Jeffrey K. 1999. "Collected Memory: The Two Cultures." *Sociological Theory* 17, no. 3:333–48.

Olick, Jeffrey K., and Daniel Levy. 1997. "Collective Memory and Cultural Constraint: Holocaust Myth and Rationality in German Politics." *American Sociological Review* 62 (December): 921–36.

Olick, Jeffrey K., and Joyce Robbins. 1998. "Social Memory Studies: From 'Collective Memory' to the Historical Sociology of Mnemonic Practices." *Annual Review of Sociology* 24:105–40.

Osiel, Mark. 2000. *Mass Atrocity, Collective Memory and the Law.* New Brunswick, N.J.: Transaction Publishers.

Passerini, Luisa. 1987. *Fascism in Popular Memory.* New York: Cambridge University Press.

Pennebaker, James, Dario Paez, and Bernard Rimé. 1997. *Collective Memory of Political Events.* Mahwah, N.J.: Lawrence Erlbaum Associates.

Pizzorusso, Alessandro. 1990. *L'organizzazione della giustizia in Italia.* Turin: Giulio Einaudi Editore.

Prillaman, William C. 1998. "Judicial Reform and Democratic Consolidation in Latin America." Ph.D. diss., University of Virginia.

Przeworski, Adam. 1986. "Some Problems in the Study of Transition to Democracy." In Guillermo O'Donnell, Philippe C. Schmitter, and Lawrence Whitehead, eds, *Transitions from Authoritarian Rule.* Baltimore, Md.: Johns Hopkins University Press.

Putnam, Robert D. 1993. *Making Democracy Work.* Princeton, N.J.: Princeton University Press.

Rawls, John. 1971. *A Theory of Justice.* New York: Oxford University Press.

Romanelli, Raffaele, ed. 1997. *Magistrati e potere nella storia europea.* Bologna: Il Mulino.

Roniger, Luis, and Mario Sznajder. 2000. *The Legacy of Human-Rights Violations in the Southern Cone: Argentina, Chile, and Uruguay.* New York: Oxford University Press.

Rothstein, Bo. 1996. "Political Institutions: An Overview." In Robert E. Goodin and Hans-Dietrich Klingemann, eds., *A New Handbook of Political Science* (pp. 133–66). New York: Oxford University Press.

———. 1998. *Just Institutions Matter: The Moral and Political Logic of the Universal Welfare State.* New York: Cambridge University Press.

———. 2000. "Trust, Social Dilemmas and Collective Memories." *Journal of Theoretical Politics* 12:477–501.

Rowe, William, and Vivian Schelling. 1991. "Memory and Modernity: Popular Culture in Latin America." *Journal of Historical Sociology,* no. 228.

San Martino de Dromi, Laura. 1995. *Formación constitucional argentina.* Buenos Aires: Ediciones Ciudad Argentina.

Sarat, Austin, and Thomas Kearns. 1999. *History, Memory and the Law.* Ann Arbor: University of Michigan Press.

Sartori, Giovanni. 1997. *Comparative Constitutional Engineering.* New York: New York University Press.

Schedler, Andreas. 1998. "What Is Democratic Consolidation?" *Journal of Democracy* 9, no. 2:91–105.

Schudson, Michael. 1989. "The Present in the Past versus the Past in the Present." *Communication* 11:105–13.

Schwartz, Barry. 1991. "Social Change and Collective Memory: The Democratization of George Washington." *American Sociological Review* 56 (April): 221–36.

Swidler, Ann. 1986. "Culture in Action: Symbols and Strategies." *American Sociological Review* 51, no. 2:273–86.

Swidler, Ann, and Jorge Arditi. 1994. "The New Sociology of Knowledge." *Annual Review of Sociology*, no. 20:305–29.

Tarrow, Sidney. 1996. "Making Social Science Work across Space and Time." *American Political Science Review* 90, no. 2:389–97.

Thelen, Kathleen. 1999. "Historical Institutionalism in Comparative Politics." *Annual Review of Political Science* 2:369–404.

Tilly, Charles. 1999. "Processes and Mechanisms of Democratization." Unpublished manuscript.

Tocqueville, Alexis de. 2000. *Democracy in America.* Indianapolis, Ind.: Hackett.

Tyler, Tom R. 1998. "Trust and Democratic Governance." In Valerie Braithwaite and Margaret Levi, eds., *Trust and Governance.* New York: Russell Sage Foundation.

Ungar, Mark D. 1997. *Courting Justice: Rule of Law Reform and Democratization in Argentina and Venezuela.* Ph.D. diss., Columbia University.

Varas, Augusto. 1998. "Democratization in Latin America: A Citizen Responsibility." In Felipe Agüero and Jeffrey Stark, eds., *Fault Lines of Democracy in Post-Transition Latin America.* Miami, Fla.: North-South Center Press.

Verbitsky, Horacio. 2000. "Jaulas Vacías: El juicio de Roma y su significado para Italia y la Argentina." *Página 12*, June 18, p. 11.

Walsh, Rodolfo J. [1957] 1994. *Operación Masacre.* Buenos Aires: Planeta Argentina.

———. [1969] 1984. *Quien mató a Rosendo?* Buenos Aires: Ediciones de la Flor.

Wilde, Alexander. 1999. "Irruptions of Memory: Expressive Politics in Chile's Transition to Democracy." *Journal of Latin American Studies* 31:473–500.

Woller, Hans. 1997. *I conti con il fascismo.* Bologna: Il Mulino.

———. 1998. "The Political Purge in Italy." In Stein Ugelvik Larsen, ed., *Modern Europe after Fascism, 1943–1980s.* Vol. 1 (pp. 526–45). Boulder, Colo.: Social Science Monographs.

5

Historical Memory and Authoritarian Legacies in Processes of Political Change

Spain and Chile

PALOMA AGUILAR *&* KATHERINE HITE

One of the most basic yet elusive problem areas in the democratization debates is how democratizing regimes, in both formal and symbolic terms, attempt to confront, interpret, and frame their violent histories.[1] A rich cross-
disciplinary literature has emerged regarding the notion of "coming to terms
with the past," from slightly older traditions in history, literary and cultural
criticism, social psychology, and sociology to more recent explorations in
legal theory and political science. Within the former traditions, the literature
emphasizes historical memory as foundational to the nation-state, nonlinear
understandings of the progression of time (*tiempo presente*), and the inesca-
pability and reach of traumatic pasts into the current social and political
landscape.[2]

Recent social science scholarship has focused on the social and political
institutions in which violent pasts are embedded and on the appropriate political mechanisms for addressing the dictatorships' egregious human rights
violations in democratizing or redemocratizing regimes. This chapter will review select debates regarding the utility of such political mechanisms, from amnesty laws to regime-sponsored "truth telling," compensatory measures, and
trials of the past persecutors. We will also incorporate scholarly treatments

191

of discursive and symbolic action regarding the past in transitions from authoritarian rule.

Focusing on countries during the process of regime transition is crucial in several ways. As much of the literature has asserted, such periods are unusual and take place amidst instability and uncertainty, making legacies of the transition process themselves of importance to democratic practice. A peculiar legal process during the transition often occurs, one that Ruti Teitel (1997) has characterized as "transitional jurisprudence." Transitional jurisprudence may leave in its wake a series of judicial legacies: "Legal responses in periods of political transformation . . . play an extraordinary constituting role. . . . The conception of justice that emerges is contextual. . . . Responses to repressive rule inform the meaning of adherence to the rule of law. As the state undergoes political change, legacies of injustice have a bearing on what is deemed transformative." (2011–14).

Moreover, the uncertainty during the transition process regarding societal priorities and the desire to ensure the stability of the new regime above all else have often meant that transitional actors approve a series of instutitions that may very well serve the specific juncture yet come to be an obstacle to the functioning of a consolidated democracy (Shapiro 1996; Karl 1986). This chapter will primarily draw empirically from the processes of regime transition and coming to terms with the past in Spain and Chile, focusing on the interpretations and assumptions behind regime choices to implement or forego particular mechanisms, as well as to adopt or suppress particular discourses about historical memories and the traumas of the past.

There are obvious differences between the Spanish and Chilean cases in terms of the countries' historical moments of authoritarian installation, duration, and transition, as well as their regional and global political-economic insertion. In addition, Spain has faced the question of plural subnational identities, which has clearly added a series of tensions to the process of political change.[3] Nevertheless, the dynamics of partisan conflict that led to democratic regime breakdown, the durability and innovation of the authoritarian regimes under a single dictator, the important levels of economic success after serious economic crisis in the preauthoritarian periods, the levels of social support for the dictatorship, the cohesion of the armed forces,[4] an elite-led transition controlled in important terms by the authoritarian incumbents, and the survival of positive evaluations of the authoritarian periods among certain sectors of society all make the two cases useful for examining historical memory and the political mechanisms used to address violent pasts in comparative terms.

Moreover, it is clear that Spain has served as an important referent for Chilean authoritarians and democrats, from Pinochet's self-comparisons to Franco, to democratic Chilean political leaders' interest in the consensus-minded behavior of the Spanish political leadership during the transition. Spanish policies of consensus and national reconciliation have clearly had a "demonstration effect" on a range of cases to follow Spain, from the Southern Cone to eastern and central Europe.

The Spanish "pacification" formula was especially appealing to those societies that had been profoundly divided socially and polarized politically under previous failed democratic regimes. The Chilean left, in particular, observed with close interest socialist leader Felipe Gonzalez's eventual presidential victory in Spain's democratic consolidation, just as the Allende experience had influenced Spanish socialists a quarter- century before. Finally, we must note an inescapable irony as well as a lively set of dynamics between Chile and Spain regarding Spanish responsibility for the October 1998 London arrest of Pinochet.

We argue that while the lines of causality are dynamic and complex, the relevant variables for comparing Spain and Chile regarding coming to terms with the past include (1) the distinct histories and magnitude of the violence of the two conflicts; (2) the comparative time elapsed between repression at its most extreme and the transitions from authoritarian rule; (3) the contrast regarding the absence in Spain and presence in Chile of organized demands for accountability, most notably from local human rights groups and their transnational advocacy networks; (4) the residual strength of the dictatorships, including Pinochet as a living presence in the transition; (5) the dynamics of the opposition to the dictatorships, as well as the residual fears of conflict and backlash on the part of the new democratic leadership; and (6) the persistence of what might be termed "authoritarian values" among important sectors of the citizenry.

As this chapter will attest, some variables are quite similar for the two cases and others differ markedly. Spain and Chile contrast fairly strongly regarding the magnitude of the violence and the historical distance from the most repressive periods of the dictatorships. There is little to compare regarding the degree and influence of domestic and international human rights groups in the Chilean case and their absence in Spain. Yet there are important similiarities when we examine the latter three sets of variables, including the dynamics between the authoritarian and democratic elites and the degree of societal legitimacy that the former dictatorships possess in the Spanish and Chilean transition. This makes the comparison between Spain and Chile quite rich. In ways that transcend the Spanish and Chilean cases, the comparison also suggests that in a correlation of forces in which authoritarians continue to possess a significant presence, democratizers engage in excessively prudent institutional designs that discourage public debate.

Our chapter will examine each of the six sets of variables and then address the contrasts in political elite discourse and the public sphere regarding the past, historical memory, and human rights, as well as in policy choices regarding amnesty, truthtelling, compensation, and retroactive justice. These differences have had profound consequences in terms of the authoritarian legacies that continue to haunt specific social and political institutions and collectivities in the two cases.

Much of the historical neoinstitutionalist literature raises the importance of legacies for understanding political process (Collier and Collier 1991; Pierson 2000; Thelen 1999; Putnam 1993). Perspectives that recognize the role of institutional or cultural legacies are also careful to avoid determinism, subscribing to the motto "No legacy lasts forever" (Collier and Collier 1991, 33). The challenge is to explore why, at particular "critical junctures," political actors adopt a series of positions and institutions that prove resistant to change, whether they are due to the "increasing returns" they generate (Pierson 2000) or whether they contribute to initiating a particular pattern of political learning (Bermeo 1992; Jervis 1976; Hall 1993) that is difficult to modify once certain habits and routines have been adopted for a long time (March and Olsen 1989). As this volume argues, authoritarian regime legacies can condition the transition process and, in some cases, become a part of particular cultural and institutional practices of the new regime.

We would not argue that democratic political institutions are in any danger in Spain or Chile, nor are we suggesting that deliberate, comprehensive regime-sponsored political mechanisms for coming to terms with the past are necessary conditions for democratic stabilization. Nevertheless, we will suggest that for the Chilean case, the official discursive and behavioral dimensions of confronting the traumatic past contributed to civic disengagement and a narrowly bounded public sphere. This was particularly pronounced during the first decade of postauthoritarian rule, where the all-too-recent repressive experiences actively haunted the politics of the Chilean state and society. In the Spanish case, we would suggest that the absence of public debate about the authoritarian past through the last quarter-century has permitted political actors to manipulate that past as a political weapon.

In discursive terms, a crucial difference between the two cases is that in the Spanish case, key political elites from left to right reworked or reinvented their painful pasts to produce shared blame for the brutality of the conflict (Aguilar 1996). This rhetorical or discursive manipulation of historical memory was important in producing a broader political consensus around the terms of the Spanish democratic transition and consolidation. Consensus existed around mutual responsibility for the barbarity of the war (a great deal of death in the rearguard, acts of "uncontrolled" personal revenge on both sides). There was also a consensus regarding collective blame for the incapacity of the left and the right to coexist peacefully during the Second Republic (1931–36) and to tolerate political adversaries democratically.

On the other hand, there is no consensus in Spain concerning who is to blame for starting the civil war, nor around the significance of the forty years of dictatorship. There is no consensus around a narrative of the authoritarian past. For many, that past is seen as an era of economic prosperity and social peace that contributed to establishing democracy in Spain.

Within Spain, the Basque case is singular. The Basque nationalists extracted a lesson and interpretation of the civil war that was virtually the opposite from that of the rest of Spain. After the conflict, particularly, the Basque Nationalist Party (PNV) held that the civil war was imposed on the Basque Country and that the Basques could not remain on the margins of the war as they would have wished. Moreover, the PNV affirmed that it was the Basques who, in spite of their perspectives on the war, suffered the most throughout the war (aided in their belief of this by the powerful symbolic reference to the bombing of Guernica), including the greatest reprisals by the Franco regime. During the May 2001 Basque autonomous election campaign, the leader of the PNV demanded that the Spanish state apologize for the bombing of Guernica by Francoist forces sixty years ago. It was an attempt to advance the idea of a continuity between the current democratic regime and the Franco dictatorship.

This reading of history means that, far from feeling responsible or guilty for the war, the Basques have seen themselves as the principal victims of the war. Moreover, according to Basque nationalist discourse, given the actions against the Franco regime by their terrorist organization Freedom for the Basque Homeland (ETA), it is the rest of Spain who should be indebted to the Basques and not the reverse. In this sense, the Basque nationalists do not share the Spanish conscience of collective blame that inspires a spirit of consensus, negotiation, and compromise that has been present in other political parties and other regions of Spain.[5]

As in Spain, there is no consensus in Chile regarding the meaning of the seventeen-year dictatorship. Yet in Chile, unlike Spain, the notion of a collective historical memory that includes shared blame for the conflict and the violence has proved elusive and remote. While the Chilean left has repeatedly voiced a mea culpa for the errors of the 1970–73 Popular Unity (UP) government, Chilean right discourse has yet to retreat, even in part, from placing total responsibility for the end of democracy and its aftermath squarely on the shoulders of the left. The Chilean right has assumed a brand of triumphalism regarding both defeat of the Marxist left and fundamental transformations of the Chilean state and society under the Pinochet regime. In spite of the dramatic events surrounding the former Chilean dictator over the past four years, leading historic supporters of the authoritarian regime have failed to engage in any kind of critical self-reflection regarding either their contributions to the downfall of Chilean democracy in 1973 or the atrocities of the dictatorship.

On the contrary, the economic and social power of the dictatorship's historical supporters, combined with the extreme concentration of ownership of the media by such actors, have all contributed to a notable "lopsidedness" regarding placement of responsibility for both democracy's fall and the dictatorship's extreme abusiveness. Over the past two years, important public space has opened in the media to the victims of the repression, and the Chilean judiciary has now assumed its responsibility for investigating and prosecuting human rights criminals. More than one hundred military officials have been indicted for human rights abuses. Nevertheless, Chilean political elites from left to right have fundamentally failed to provide a "counterhegemonic" discourse that confronts the authoritarian-generated and sustained discourse of the "warlike" conditions under the Pinochet regime. For Chile, we would argue, this failure of even a minimalist consensus regarding past responsibility has contributed to the continued polarization of historical memory in ways that have hindered the development of a public sphere.

In the policy arena, we would argue that in Spain, the historical distance of extreme repression, the lack of a mobilized constituency to demand truth and accountability for the past, and the lack of international pressure to do so all contributed to the absence of what are termed "retrospective justice" policies. All but a small faction of extremely radicalized Basque nationalists (who supported terrorist attacks) accepted Spain's 1977 amnesty. A large segment of society supported the amnesty, which was more generous than many had anticipated and prevented trials for those responsible for human rights violations. During the transition, the priority was to empty the jails of political dissidents, including those who had fairly recently acted violently against the dictatorship (even though their acts had to have occurred before the democratic primary elections of June 1977). During the transition from authoritarian rule, given the fear of confrontation and the broad amnesty, no one even considered the possibility of judging the torturers.[6]

In Chile, on the other hand, the transitional administration of Patricio Aylwin and the Concertación (1990–94) advanced a program of national reconciliation in the form of an official truth telling, an emotional public apology from the head of state to all the victims of human rights violations, assistance for returning exiles, pardon and release of political prisoners, and compensation for families of the executed and disappeared. The "freshness" of the atrocities and the emergence and strength of a human rights community supported by the international arena contributed to such a program. Nevertheless, while such policies were clearly more far-reaching than those of the Spanish case, the Chilean Concertación government chose a cautious path, perceiving insurmountable constraints to revoking the 1978 amnesty law and to any form of executive-led retroactive justice policy. It took all four years of the Aylwin government to secure the release of the political prisoners of the Pinochet regime, and cases were still pending into the Eduardo Frei, Jr. (1994–2000) administration. The truth commission itself was also limited in scope.

While President Aylwin publicly sought voluntary cooperation from the armed forces and a proactive, human rights–minded judiciary in the reconciliation process, neither was forthcoming under his tenure. During the successor government of Frei, policies fostering national reconciliation were not a top priority. In fact, we would argue that progress on the human rights front and on a broader process of coming to terms with the past in Chile have occurred largely in spite of the postauthoritarian Chilean political leadership, not because of it.

Debates over Political Mechanisms for Confronting the Past

The world has witnessed the proliferation of state-sponsored efforts to acknowledge and condemn flagrant human rights violations committed under predecessor regimes. This proliferation stems from a combination of forces, from the evolution of an international human rights regime that places greater pressure on democratizing regimes to hold human rights violators accountable (Keck and Sikkink 1998) to increasingly sophisticated and supported local human rights groups. Moreover, it is clear that political actors have increasingly come to anticipate the virtual inevitability of, as well as the tensions surrounding, societal demands for truth and accountability. Politicians attempt to craft rhetoric and policies that harness such demands in ways they deem subordinate to their political interests.

Thus, in many countries experiencing processes of political change, sectors of society have expressed their desire and their sense of the need to judge those responsible for the repression and the violation of human rights committed under authoritarianism. Clearly among the most delicate and urgent issues during many of these transitions is deciding how to handle former agents and collaborators in human rights abuse, as well as how to address the needs of victims of human rights abuse.

The academic literature is divided around this crucial set of issues. A first group of authors insists that the priority in transitions is the stabilization of new democracies and that consequently any measure, symbolic or not, that may jeopardize such a process should be removed from the political agenda. This literature emphasizes the efficacy of such measures as pardons, amnesties, and policies oriented toward forgetting the immediate past, as they are the only possible mechanisms for encouraging reconciliation among sectors of society who were former enemies.

Samuel Huntington (1991) has touched on this debate in part in his book on "third wave" democracies. Huntington outlines the conditions he considers most propitious for bringing those responsible for the repression under the previous dictatorship to trial (208–79). He concludes that whether processes of political justice take place is not so much a question of moral debate as it is the effective distribution of power among distinct actors. In this sense, in the majority of cases Huntington analyzes, "Justice was a function of political power. Officials of strong authoritarian regimes that voluntarily ended themselves were not prosecuted; officials of weak authoritarian regimes that collapsed were punished, and they were promptly prosecuted" (228). In a similar vein, political scientist Bruce Ackerman (1992) argues that new and fragile democratic governments may possess the moral capital but lack the organizational capital necessary to implement retroactive justice successfully. In his analysis of the Argentine policies of retroactive justice, Ackerman argues that the length and volatility of the process undermined rather than strengthened the legitimacy of Argentina's democratic political institutions.

Theorist Stephen Holmes ([1988] 1993) develops a distinct set of arguments regarding the strategic interests of not pursuing political justice measures. "To avoid destructive conflicts," Holmes argues, "we suppress controversial themes [. . . , for] conflict-shyness is not merely craven: it can serve positive goals. By tying our tongues about a sensitive question, we can secure forms of cooperation and fellowship otherwise beyond reach" (19). The author forwards the notion of "strategic self-censorship," emphasizing the advantages of not publicly addressing questions on which there will never exist consensus and that nevertheless represent serious, even destabilizing, conflict arenas. According to Holmes, gag rules often allow political leaders and citizens to center their efforts and attention on resolvable problems rather than wasting their energies eternally debating quite problematic questions (27).

Among the detractors from the notion of trials of the past persecutors, theorist Jon Elster (1995) has developed a peculiar argument. According to Elster, if analysts hold the principle of equality among citizens as that which sustains democratic regimes, and given that it is ultimately impossible to determine the responsibility of all those implicated in diverse ways in the authoritarian repression (from enthusiastic participation to complicit inhibition), the most just course would be not to judge anyone. To do otherwise would violate the principle of equality. According to Elster, "[O]ne should target everybody or nobody. And because it is impossible to reach everybody, nobody should be punished and nobody compensated." Besides, "People cannot be held guilty for what they are forced to do." To resolve this, Elster proposes conceding to a "general amnesty" and to the abandoning of any attempt to indemnify the victims (566–68).

A second group of authors nevertheless emphasizes the ethical weight that must accompany all democratization processes and therefore the moral obligation the political regime bears to carry out what have been termed policies of "retroactive" or "retrospective justice,"[7] "political justice,"[8] or "transitional justice."[9] Chief among such proponents was an architect of Argentine president Raul Alfonsín's human rights policies, the legal theorist Carlos Nino. Nino (1997) claimed that retroactive justice strengthened "the moral consciousness of society . . . [to] help overcome the corporatism, anomie, and concentration of power that all too long have been hallmarks of Argentine society" (104). While Nino recognized the Argentine process as imperfect, such imperfections, he argued, came from an administration that had attempted to conduct a truth and accountability process precisely within the letter of the law, to reinforce the legitimacy of the historic Argentine constitution. Nino charged that those within the scholarly community who opposed retroactive justice rested their arguments primarily on grounds of short-term political self-interest, failing to recognize the contribution of retroactive justice efforts to an epistemic democratic community.

Within this group are many who, in addition to making normative claims, insist that retroactive justice policies are politically efficacious. First, such authors argue that merely purging the principal civil and military institutions of the dicatorship would remove institutional obstacles that block the effective functioning of the new regime.[10] In addition, public judgment of the violators would have a clear deterrent effect.[11] Moreover, the new regime can take advantage of the only opportunity it may have to demonstrate its strength and especially its autonomy from individuals and institutions of the past. Only by establishing differences from the previous regime can reformist elites gain the adherence of the range of groups who composed the democratic opposition (McAdams 1997).

Finally, this group maintains that the only way to avoid premature "disenchantment" with democratic institutions is by enacting measures of political justice and by reviving the memory of the repressed. Impunity of human rights violators can cause significant sectors of society to disassociate themselves from the new regime, which will contribute to the partial exhaustion of democratic legitimacy or, at least, to the snail-like pace of democratic consolidation.[12]

Legal theorist Mark Osiel (1995) argues that trials of past persecutors can and should do more than lend ethical and political legitimacy to democratizing regimes. He claims that trials can become the dramatic discursive stages on which state and society debate the past, albeit in a highly manipulated fashion. Osiel's work is far more explicit than many regarding the deliberative democracy he has in mind as he advocates trials in the face of past "administrative massacres." Trials, Osiel argues, can, if properly crafted, lay the groundwork for a true public sphere in which citizens feel free to express discord as well as consensus about what went wrong and who is to blame for the human rights violations of the past. Trials thus become mechanisms for establishing historical memories that serve as foundations for a tolerant-minded national identity and a rich plurality of political beliefs.

Given the complexity of these issues, it is quite frequent to encounter authors whose arguments can be placed in more than one camp. Osiel, in fact, provides virtually as many challenges to his arguments that trials may contribute to a deliberative democracy as he does evidence to support his claims. Carlos Nino (1997) defends the idea that "some form of retroactive justice for massive human rights violations undergirds a more solid base for democratic values" (7) and that "all punishment produces worthy consequences in terms of preventing similar acts [in the future]" (288). Yet Nino also recognizes that "the value of prosecuting may be limited and should be balanced with the objective of preserving the democratic system," for this "is a prerequisite of prosecution and its loss is a necessary antecedent to massive violations of human rights" (288).

Holmes ([1988] 1993) swings the other way to some degree in a discussion regarding the drawbacks of amnesties:

> To remove all issues of high moral importance and assign them to individual conscience or even to the courts may make democratic politics unbearably bland and useless as an arena for national self-education. . . . [T]he strategy of avoidance can excacerbate pent-up tensions, eventually engendering terrorism or a revolutionary explosion by denying legitimate expression to deeply felt beliefs. . . . Indeed, a policy of self-gagging may eventually produce a culture where the threat of violence or secession is a common political tactic. (56)

Adam Przeworski (1995) also addresses the question "How can unarmed civilians administer justice over those bearing the arms?" According to Przeworski, transition leaders must attempt to arrive at an agreement that never again will certain limits be transgressed. Once this agreement has been established, all efforts must be made to further the guarantee of this pact, given that it is the only way of avoiding future violations of human rights. As Przeworski points out from a rational action perspective, "such an accord can be realized only if the political actors who have the capacity to violate it hold that it is more beneficial to comply, given the sanctions that others would inflict if they decide to renege on their commitment. As such, human rights can be maintained only as a result of an equilibrium in the political game among relevant political forces" (16).

In almost all cases, the danger to which the authors who show certain reticence regarding political justice processes refer is, obviously, the possibility that such processes will produce a coup d'état, especially in those cases where authoritarian power resided with the military. Holmes ([1988] 1993) provides the classic example: "A newborn government is especially unlikely to survive if forced to make controversial decisions about historically intractable problems" (28). We would argue that while there is no question that at least sectors of the military engaged in muscle-flexing exercises that were meant to threaten democratizing regimes in Argentina, Brazil, and Chile during the transitions in the Southern Cone, fears of another military coup were irrational. Such fears represent a legacy of authoritarianism in which memories of the coup, together with the residual strength of the armed forces, continue to produce an exaggerated fear of the unlikely. This is not to deny the crises that democratizing regimes confront when the armed forces refuse to cooperate. Yet as much of the literature on civil-military relations in the Southern Cone has documented, military coups never took place in the absence of powerful civilian forces who "went to the barracks."[13]

Much of the political science scholarship on the question of holding the military accountable downplays its importance or advisability in the face of what might be termed a hierarchy of other priorities, including the economy, social welfare, and international credibility. This downplaying has meant less scholarly attention to the ways in which short-term risks of civil-military tension may be worth the long-term gains of decisively subordinating the military to civilian authority while vesting the citizenry actively in such a process. This is not a direction, for example, that Przeworski develops. In his game-theoretic equation, Przeworski begins with the working premise of a strong, cohesive, autonomous military, an uncertain political society, and a weak civil society.[14]

There is evidence that dynamics between political and civil society suggest alternative premises. In Argentina, it is clear that Alfonsín could count on the backing of the majority of the Argentine citizenry, who could and did mobilize to support the president in the face of military insubordination. This relationship between Alfonsín and the citizenry weakened as Alfonsín retreated from the bold and unprecedented accountability process he had launched. In Uruguay, the traditional political parties advocated what has been termed a "politics of forgetting." The Uruguayan political class largely resisted organized civil society efforts to revoke amnesty for the military. Such political elite resistance, coupled with a discourse and behavior condemning the human rights movement, clearly weakened citizens' demands for truth, acknowledgment, and accountability (de Brito 1997). In Chile, during the commencement of the democratic administration, when mass graves of the "disappeared" were discovered and the bodies exhumed, the Chilean polity and citizenry grew increasingly sympathetic to calls for accountability (Lira and Loveman 1999). Nevertheless, in Argentina, Uruguay, and Chile, governments evoked or maintained military-advocated amnesties, which some scholars have provocatively termed an "institutionalized manifestation" of social amnesia or oblivion (Jelín 1998).

Short of trials as retroactive justice, scholars and polities have advocated truth telling as a "second-best" political mechanism for coming to terms with the past (Hayner 2001). In the past two decades, dozens of truth commissions have been established in countries around the world. Like trials, properly designed and "marketed" truth-telling processes can contribute to societal acknowledgment, awareness, and debate. Truth commission reports have often become national best-sellers, indicating societies' desires for officially recognized accounts of the painful details of their histories. While the official truth presented in such reports is by definition incomplete and contested, truthtelling processes have become increasingly innovative as mechanisms for constructing historical memories. As will be discussed below, the Chilean Truth and Reconciliation Commission has served as an efficient but minimalist model in this vein.[15]

Policies involving compensation for the victims of human rights violations represent another mechanism for coming to terms. Such policies generally take two forms. The first is direct economic or material recompense, including monthly pensions to families whose loved ones were killed or disappeared, educational benefits, and exoneration from military service for young men from victims' families. The second form involves symbolic public expressions, including monuments, street names, plaques marking particular sites (i.e.,where clandestine detention and torture took place), and commemorative dates.

Within the Southern Cone, policies have varied regarding compensation, ranging from a policy of no compensation in Uruguay, to moderate levels of compensation to families of the dead and disappeared in Chile, to a fairly high level of compensation in the aggregate in Argentina (de Brito 2001, 132).[16] In Spain, victims of human rights violations were difficult to compensate, given the time that had passed. Nevertheless, the government offered both symbolic and material reparations, including pensions to survivors of the repression and to families of victims who had died and economic compensation based on years in jail. In any case, the combination of budgetary limits during fragile transition years and the difficulty of defining the reach of compensation make compensatory policies quite problematic. Moreover, for the victims, such measures inevitably produce a limited compensatory effect.

Explanations for the Absence or Presence of a "Politics of Memory"

Drawing principally from the Spanish and Chilean transition experiences, this chapter will now focus on the primary dimensions and parameters that condition political elite approaches to a politics of memory in moments of transition from authoritarian rule. We argue that while there are some similarities, there are also fundamental contrasts between the Spanish case and the Southern Cone cases that tend to force the issue of political justice into the public sphere for the latter. This does not mean that Southern Cone state-crafters would not prefer to follow the Spanish example. Rather, Southern Cone political leaders face a set of dynamics that make it difficult to avoid political justice measures. The range of such measures is wide, and political and social actors battle discursively and behaviorally to assert their preferences regarding the most appropriate political mechanisms to address the past.

The Magnitude of Violence Exercised by the Dictatorship

In transition moments, the *magnitude* and *scope* of participation in past state violence emerge as defining features of the political process. While it is im-possible to claim a clear correlation between the scope of such violence and the level of transitional government response in policy terms, there are two key dimensions in terms of magnitude and scope on which past violence in Spain and the Southern Cone differ considerably. The first is the context of civil war in Spain contrasted with the "dirty wars" of the Southern Cone. Explicit fratricide took place during the Spanish war years, and the violence inflicted by the victorious Franco dictatorship in the war's aftermath was largely conducted in public and legal, albeit condemnable, terms. The mili-tary regimes of the Southern Cone exercised undeclared war, and the bulk of the human rights atrocities were officially denied and clandestine. While the March 8, 2001, Chilean appeals court decision to reduce the charges against Pinochet from homicide and kidnapping to a "cover-up" of such crimes was less than the prosecution had hoped, the cover-up charge symbolizes the distinction we draw between the Spanish and the Southern Cone cases.

Second, while both the Spanish and Southern Cone regimes engaged in arrest, torture, exile, and execution, the Southern Cone dictatorships also engaged in the practice of "disappearance." This notorious distinction, we would argue, has weighed particularly heavily on the moral, political, and legal consciousness of agents and institutions of the postauthoritarian Southern Cone regimes. In Chile, the question of the disappeared was the primary focus of the 1991 executive-appointed truth commission and 1999–2000 Round-table, key legislative debates, and recent Chilean court decisions—the chief expressions of Chilean government policies regarding truth and justice.

Defining the impact of the violence solely on the basis of the scope of the violence is virtually impossible. If in Argentina, for example, one calcu-lates that the number of murdered and disappeared under the dictatorship is as many as thirty thousand (an impossible statistic to confirm given the systematic hiding of the cadavers), in countries such as Uruguay, Chile, and Brazil the numbers are far less, which undoubtedly influences the magnitude of the trauma.[17] On the other hand, it is clear that it is not just a question of statistics, as the character of the repression itself also contributes to explaining the level of social trauma and, as such, society's need to know the truth and to demand accountability for the violence. While murder and forced disappearance clearly constitute heinous crimes, it is impossible to establish a hierarchy of the social and psychological effects of the range of human rights violations for those who continue to suffer their consequences.

Nevertheless, there is an important contrast between an authoritarian regime involved in a planned "dirty war" strategy, as in the Argentine and Chilean cases, where the dictatorships systematically hid that they were carrying out arrests, torture, and assassinations of thousands of people considered disaffected from the regime, and a declared civil war, as in the Spanish case, with its series of mass firing squads and summary trials against a defeated force. While there has been a good deal of debate regarding what societies knew and did not know, the behind-closed-doors nature of systematic human rights violations in the Southern Cone contributed to both the denial and the longevity of such practices. The psychological effects of an undeclared war, of assassinations with neither proof nor witnesses[18] and, above all, without a body to whom pain is surrendered,[19] differ, and the political consequences differ as well. As human rights scholars such as Aryeh Neier (1998) have argued, the clandestine character of the atrocities in the Southern Cone and Brazil make the need for investigation and public acknowledgment of the crimes all the more necessary.

It is not that in Spain there were no clandestine arrests, torture, or even deaths under strange circumstances in the decades following the 1940s, but it is certain that a good part of the repression occurred openly and under the protection of legislation. Such legislation included the use of the death penalty (that in the last ten years was scarcely applied, if we exclude the death warrants executed a few weeks before Franco's death), as well as the ability to temporarily suspend rights. While the Argentine, Brazilian, Chilean, and Uruguayan dictatorships employed state-of-siege and states-of-emergency clauses, the regimes also clandestinely kidnapped and tortured, in many cases to death, thousands who were never publicly tried.

Another fundamental aspect of the magnitude of the repression consists of determining whether the repression can be considered a "crime against humanity" or genocide, a systematic and deliberate act against a clearly delimited social, economic, ideological, or ethnic group. It seems evident that the line between this kind of crime and others of distinct magnitude is not always easy to distinguish. Nor is it sufficiently clear, as Przeworksi (1995) reminds us, what should be understood by "human rights," given that its content is the result "of a contingent historical compromise, not something given." "The central question," argues Przeworski, "is how to maintain this compromise, or to put it prescriptively, how to construct a political system in which such a compromise is always respected" (15).

In Chile, President Aylwin attempted to champion a platform of reconciliation through truth, focusing investigation of the truth on those who had been killed and disappeared under the dictatorship. Aylwin commissioned highly respected members of Chilean society, including citizens from the Chilean right, to investigate the individual cases of the executed and disappeared and to prepare a report for public release. In addition, Aylwin charged the commission with presenting an overall account of the history and context of the atrocities, as well as a set of recommendations for compensation and for policies that would contribute to a human rights culture in Chile. Over approximately five months, a staff of some sixty human rights advocates, lawyers, psychologists, historians, and other analysts gathered written documentation and personal testimonies concerning the dead and disappeared.

While human rights organizations and others representing the victims of the atrocities offered full cooperation, the victimizers did not. The commission lacked the power to subpoena witnesses. Moreover, in a somewhat ironic sense, the entire investigation took place behind closed doors, and the public report provided no names of those held responsible for the crimes. Aylwin argued that, given the lack of due process, the names of the accused could not be released and that the separation of powers in a democracy required the courts to decide criminality. Given the then-overarching record of judicial complicity in upholding the military-imposed amnesty, and given that the majority of the executions and disappearances fell within the amnesty law, the truth commission's failure to offer a more complete historical account proved limited in coming to terms with the past.

Nevertheless, Aylwin personally released the truth commission report in a moving and nationally televised public address. In the name of the state, the president apologized to the human rights victims and their families and sought their forgiveness. Aylwin exhorted the military to make amends for their actions. He criticized the judiciary for failing to uphold the rule of law and demanded future court action. For a moment, it appeared that members of the former authoritarian regime and their sympathizers were on the defensive. Yet three weeks after the public release of the report and Aylwin's appeals, leftist extremists assassinated the outspoken right-wing leader and senator Jaime Guzmán, a political and legal architect of the Pinochet regime. The Chilean right successfully used Guzmán's assassination to stymie efforts to engage the public in a collective exploration of Chile's historical memories.

Several years would pass before key Chilean institutions of the state would be forced to return aggressively to the question of the magnitude and scope of human rights atrocities under the dictatorship. Nevertheless, even in moments in which little official action took place on human rights, the government could not avoid addressing the question of the disappeared. In 1993, Aylwin proposed legislation that would trade anonymity for information regarding the fate of the disappeared. In 1995, President Frei proposed virtually the same. Both executive proposals failed. The Chilean legislature also formed task forces to formulate proposals regarding the disappeared. In June 1998, a multiparty Senate Commission on Human Rights, Nationality, and Citizenship proposed both that the courts' mandate to investigate disappearances be unrestricted by any statute of limitations and that secrecy be granted to those officials who came forward with information regarding the whereabouts of the disappeared. This proposal failed as well, rejected by both the relatives of the disappeared, who saw this as granting the violators impunity, and the Chilean military, who were concerned about the ending of the statute of limitations.

Through the 1990s, Chilean presidents consistently argued that under a democracy institutions must respect the separation of powers of the state and that it was the Chilean courts' role to determine whether or how to prosecute those accused of grave human rights offenses of the dictatorship. Before Pinochet's October 1998 arrest, a handful of cases had successfully been tried in Chilean courts. Almost without exception, these were cases that fell outside the 1978 amnesty law, from the Letelier case to cases of torture and execution in the 1980s. With the Pinochet arrest, however, the Chilean judiciary began actively to reinterpret the 1978 amnesty law regarding the disappeared. Judges claimed that disappeared victims fell outside the amnesty law because they constituted "permanent crimes."[20]

As such reinterpretations began to mount, the Chilean armed forces as an institution became increasingly anxious to negotiate a compromise to stave off potentially significant numbers of prosecutions. In response to the military's concerns, on August 31, 1999, Chilean civilian defense minister Edmundo Pérez Yoma created the twenty-four-member Mesa de Diálogo

(Roundtable). The Roundtable's chief mission was to retrieve information regarding "where the bodies were buried."[21] The major result of the Round-table, in which both lawyers for human rights victims' families and military officials participated, was a proposal for legislation demanding that the military produce a report on the disappeared, to be submitted to the president within six months' time. Like the previous executive and legislative commissions, the Roundtable proposed that those who came forward to provide information on the disappeared be kept anonymous. The proposal sparked public controversy. Nevertheless, the executive advanced and the legislature approved the Roundtable's proposal. As will be discussed below, in January 2001, the military did produce a report. While the Chilean public largely judged the report unsatisfactory, the document was also unprecedented, as it was the first time the military publicly admitted responsibility for disappearances.

Thus a key difference between the Spanish case and the Southern Cone cases has been the magnitude and scope of violence, including the legal as well as moral context in which the violence was exercised. In Argentina, society continues to be riveted by stories of children born to women political prisoners, children whose mothers were disappeared and who themselves dramatically surfaced upon occasion after years of search by their surviving family members. Argentine military officers who once thought they were through with human rights cases against them were rearrested for baby kidnapping. In Uruguay, one of the most publicized cases of the 1990s involved a former female political prisoner who gave birth while under detention and continued an extremely painful, elusive search for her missing daughter. In March 2002, after more than two decades of search, Sara Mendez found and confirmed her son's identity in Buenos Aires. For the first time since the 1985 transition from military rule in Uruguay, the current Uruguayan president publicly committed himself to expending resources to contribute to this search. In Chile, the ghosts of the disappeared have persisted as thorns in the side of those arguing that society must "move on," and the Chilean judiciary, executive, and military as institutions have had to respond.

The Proximity of the Repressive Moment

An equally important though similarly difficult-to-gauge variable of the context for transitional government policies toward the repressive past is at what moment the most intensive repression took place. In this sense, there are important differences regarding the Spanish case in which the most brutal repression ended thirty years before Franco died, and the Argentine, Brazilian, Chilean, and Uruguayan cases.

Proximity of the repressive moment contains at least two dimensions. First, it has a clear influence on the willingness of authoritarians to abandon power. Even when amnesty and other exculpatory laws and measures are seemingly in place, repressors are reluctant to face the uncertainty of a new regime led by enemies. Thus, when repressors are very much alive in transition moments, the "freshness" of the repressive experience proves more fraught for transitional governments.

Second, as Przeworski (1988, 1993b) suggests, as time passes, fewer direct victims remain to demand justice. Pzreworski argues that generational variables are crucial to the perceived intensity of the repressive moment and the transitional government's subsequent addressing of the repression in policy terms: "Where repression had been massive and brutal and *the memory is still vivid in the life of the same generation*, the issue of personal immunity may be without solution. Even the electoral victory of political parties representing interests of the authoritarian power block does not provide sufficient protection for individual members of the apparatus of repression" 1993b, (74, italics added).

On the other hand, the generational question is proving salient in a very distinct way in Chile today, where there have been significant generational turnovers within the military and judiciary as institutions. These turnovers have allowed greater room for political justice measures, as military officers are less subservient to the previous regime and as judges are increasingly appointed by the democratic regime.

Nevertheless, as several scholars have noted, the relationship between time and memory, particularly traumatic memory, is exceedingly complex. For both individuals and collectivities, memory is associational—that is, memories are triggered in ways and at moments that are often difficult to predict. Traumatic memories may be stimulated by otherwise mundane phenomena. Argentine sociologist Elizabeth Jelín (1998) argues that memories are located in such social spaces as sites and dates—places where torture occurred, or anniversaries of traumatic events, for example. Memories of trauma that occurred long ago can be recalled as if the trauma occurred only recently.

This makes legislating on traumatic pasts to bring closure exceedingly difficult. In August 1998, the Chilean government finally succeeded in securing the congressional votes necessary to end September 11, the anniversary of the coup, as a national holiday. This was an important symbolic victory for all who held the date as a tragedy. As part of a compromise with the Chilean right, the Congress legislated a day of reflection and unification during the first week of September, reserving the 11th as a military moment. On September 4, 1998, Archbishop Errázuriz held a mass attended by Chile's highest public officials to initiate a Day of Unification. With Pinochet's subsequent arrest, the first week of September 1999 passed with no official or unofficial attempt to recognize a day of unification. Given the circumstances, a unification day was simply out of the question.

In September 1999, triggered by the sixtieth anniversary of the end of the Spanish civil war, there was a frustrated parliamentary attempt to agree upon a text condemning the July 18, 1936, "military uprising" and recognizing the injustice done to the exiles. Left-wing, Basque nationalist, and Catalan nationalist parties introduced the proposition to the Parliament. The governing right strongly opposed the text, and it was not approved. Several analysts have noted how strange it seemed that a similar text had not been presented in earlier years when the Socialist Party (PSOE) was in power (Juliá 1999, 20). The majority of the groups that supported the legally nonbinding proposition adhered to the need to "recuperate the historical memory" that had been lost during the transition.

A series of differences do exist that separate the Basque case from that of the rest of Spain. Given the existence of a terrorist organization that was inflicting serious casualties on the regime, the repression that state security forces exercised in the Basque Country was higher than in any other region during the final years of the Franco regime. This explains why there were more demands from the Basque zone for a clean break from the authoritarian regime, for purges and the "dissolution of the repressive bodies," than in the rest of the country. The uniqueness of the Basque case contributes to understanding why among the Basques there is, as will be shown below, the greatest degree of disenchantment with democracy (especially among the nationalist electorate) due to the type of transition (pacted, reformist, lacking either trials or purges, and with important degrees of institutional continuity).[22]

The Absence or Presence of Organized Demands for Truth and Accountability

One of the most stark contrasts between the Spanish and the Southern Cone cases is the absence in Spain of an organized, visible human rights movement under the dictatorship, a movement that cannot be ignored by transitional government leaders. We would argue that the presence of such a movement proves to be a necessary (though not sufficient) condition for transitional government political justice policies. This variable gains increased saliency in a transformed international context, in which an international human rights regime has emerged that influences, albeit quite unevenly, political justice measures by governments around the world.

In this last democratic wave, societies have repeatedly evoked the cry "Never again." Nevertheless, it is not always evident what underlies this maxim. In the Spanish case, it has been clearer than in other cases that the historical event referred to by the slogan is the civil war and thus that "Never again" refers to fratricidal conflict. The conscience of fratricide, clearly, is a given only in societies with a sense of pertaining to the same *demos*. In plurinational states, such as the Spanish, this basic ascription is not a given, especially among the Basque nationalists. They extract a distinct lesson, adapted from their perception of national identity. As such, their "Never again" refers to the Basque fratricide, a framing that limits the possibilities of seconding the politics of "Spanish" consensus and that foments, on the contrary, attempts to create a united Basque front (Aguilar 1999).

In some Latin American countries, "Never again" has an added significance, namely the rejection of the preceding dictatorship. This added significance can be explained in part by the Southern Cone presence of nongovernmental organizations (NGO) that sprang up under the dictatorship to demand both an end to the atrocities and a return to democracy and the rule of law. In Argentina, the Mothers of the Plaza de Mayo became symbols of a global human rights ethic and of the nation's demand for democratization. In Chile, the Catholic Church lent tremendous authority to what would become one of the most sophisticated human rights movements in the hemisphere.

Nevertheless, human rights organizational demands for a "Never again" linking an end to the atrocities with the return to democracy as well as human rights have resonated somewhat ambivalently across the Southern Cone. In Argentina, "Never again" is above all concentrated on the brutal authoritarian regime, which, in contrast to the Chilean and Spanish cases, proved unable even to govern effectively in the economic arena.[23] The Chilean case is quite different, where in ways similar to the Spanish case, the authoritarian regime received significant levels of social support. Moreover, with the return to democratic rule, Chile's largest human rights organization, the Catholic Church's Vicariate of Solidarity, consciously diminished its public presence, ceding its work to official institutions.

Over the past two decades, human rights organizing has become both more sophisticated and more transnationalized. Unlike the context in which the Spanish transition from authoritarian rule took place, the contexts for the Southern Cone transitions have been ones in which international NGOs and, albeit less consistently, governmental institutions have placed pressure on transitional governments to evoke political justice policies. Pinochet's London arrest—a product of years of sustained individual and NGO efforts and the authority of a Spanish magistrate—symbolizes the new significance of human rights concerns and influence. There is no question that the arrest forced an entirely unanticipated series of debates and actions both within the Chilean state and between the Chilean state and society. What had been considered the unthinkable—holding Pinochet accountable for the authorship of human rights crimes—indeed became possible. Moreover, Spanish judge Baltasar Garzón's investigation reaches throughout the Southern Cone. Thus the concerted actions of the human rights movement clearly contribute to structuring the parameters in which political justice policies are conceptualized and implemented.

The Residual Strength of the Dictatorship

Authoritarian institutional capacities to control the process of political change and to impede political justice measures have been important variables regarding how democratizing regimes come to terms with past human rights violations.[24] In Spain, as Felipe Agüero (1995) recounts, "the majority of the military were against measures that would alter the fundamental characteristics of Francoist institutions" (22–23). In addition, given that the Spanish transition emerged from within the regime, it was also "characterized by important continuities," and "one of the most visible elements of continuity [was] the army, which did not suffer the purges that were subjected in Greece, Portugal, or Argentina" (22–23).[25]

The possibility of easily identifying the protagonists of the repression is fundamental to being able to try them. It is not the same when the body responsible is a visible collectivity, such as the armed forces in many Latin American cases, as when it is isolated individuals within the security forces. In Spain, once the extremely repressive postwar period had passed, particular members of the police and national guard committed isolated acts of torture. They did not represent a deliberate, systematic policy of physical elimination of the opposition.

In Chile, there was no greater symbolic authoritarian legacy over the 1990s than Pinochet himself. While formal authoritarian enclaves, embodied in the 1980 constitution, continued to represent clear roadblocks to human rights legislation, Pinochet's constant visibility and assertion in the public sphere contributed to silencing rather than engaging debates on mechanisms for coming to terms with the past. As commander-in-chief of the army, Pinochet's "interventions" in politics were generally confrontational. Nevertheless, in the months before his October 1998 arrest, the man who had retired from the armed forces to become senator for life had clearly begun to reflect upon and plan for his own legacy. Immediately before his arrest, images of Pinochet in the Chilean press and media were of a grandfatherly figure in a three-piece suit, and he publicly blessed the congressional move to end September 11 as a national holiday. Pinochet wanted to be remembered as a savior of the country, and it seemed that he had also become interested in being remembered in more peaceful terms.

A good deal of the power Pinochet enjoyed in the postdictatorial years stemmed from his ability to maintain absolute unity within the military as institution. In addition to the formal powers granted to the military by the 1980 constitution, such intramilitary institutional cohesion created a perceptible sense of military autonomy and a dubious correlation of forces between civilian and military institutions. Clearly, the relationship between Pinochet and his men came with benefits for both, while, on the contrary, a breakdown of the relationship potentially carried enormous costs, particularly in the area of human rights and accountability for the past.

Cracks between Pinochet and the new generation of military high officials did begin to surface with the appointment of commander-in-chief of the army Ricardo Izurieta. While Izurieta defended Pinochet and protested the judiciary's actions against him, the new army commander also showed greater willingness to admit that "excesses" had been committed under the dictatorship. Izurieta led the armed forces to discuss the situation of the disappeared with human rights lawyers, and he supported the armed forces' preparation of a document on the disappeared. In this document, the military recognized that between 1973 and 1989, security forces executed and disappeared 985 people ("Los datos" 2001). The report offered gruesome details on how Chileans had been killed, including the claim that at least 120 Chileans had been thrown from helicopters into the sea. Since the report's release, it has become apparent that the military both omitted a great deal of information and "doctored the facts" to attempt to avoid several pending disappearance cases. Official, institutional recognition of involvement in atrocities, nevertheless, was unprecedented.

The breakdown of absolute unity between Pinochet and the military as an institution came on January 23, 2001, during Chilean Supreme Court investigating judge Juan Guzmán's questioning of Pinochet in Pinochet's home. In a dramatic reversal of his previous position, Pinochet claimed that regional commanders who had participated in the "Caravan of Death" murders and disappearances had acted independently of his orders and that he was not responsible for the crimes they had authored.[26] This refusal to accept responsibility for the actions of his subordinates triggered public repudiations of Pinochet by former Pinochet loyalists. The most damning was the account offered by retired general Joaquín Lagos Osorio, who during the period of the "Caravan of Death" case was the Division I army commander, in charge of the area in which many were executed. Lagos claimed that Pinochet had been well aware of the heinousness of the acts committed and had ordered Lagos to alter his report of the incidents.[27]

It would appear, therefore, that the residual effects of a powerful authoritarian legacy are weakening in Chile. Nevertheless, the authoritarian enclaves securing military autonomy from civilian authority remain enshrined in the 1980 constitution. Together with an electoral system that overrepresents historic supporters of the dictatorship, authoritarian incumbents have decisively shaped the parameters for political justice mechanisms.

Democratic Political Forces in Opposition and in Government

Linked to the question of the residual strength of the military as a political force is the actual strength of those who opposed the military during the dictatorship and are now in democratic leadership positions. As stated above, in cases of reform and not *ruptura*, the democratic government is often weak and perceives itself as possessing little room to maneuver. In some senses, amnesty laws in both Spain and the Southern Cone symbolized the perceived correlation of forces between democrats and authoritarians. The Spanish Amnesty Law of 1978 granted amnesty to both victims and executioners, the latter of whom had very little public visibility. The Chilean government's upholding of the military-imposed Amnesty Law of 1978 reflected the Concertación's calculation that it did not possess the force in government to confront those responsible for grave human rights violations.

Both the type of oppositional activity under the authoritarian regime and the degree of social support for such activity are also quite important. For example, in the Spanish and Argentine cases, extremists committed terrorist acts whose victims on several occasions had no links to the dictatorship. This produced an important level of social rejection of acts of "political revenge," and it contributed to a certain "sharing of the blame" and to amnesties and mutual pardons.

In Chile, political prisoners from the Pinochet regime received relatively little public sympathy. Playing on heightened public security fears under the newly democratic regime, the political right indiscriminately condemned the prisoners as terrorists who deserved harsh punishment. Moreover, the right consistently linked legislative decisions regarding the fate of the political prisoners to policies regarding truth and accountability for human rights violations, essentially equating the prisoners with the military persecutors. Pardons for the political prisoners, the Chilean right argued, should be accompanied by a blanket amnesty for the military (Lira and Loveman 1999; de Brito 1997).

In Spain, after a series of partial pardons, the 1977 newly democratically elected Parliament voted to approve an Amnesty Law substantially broader than previous amnesty measures. On the one hand, this law encompassed all politically motivated crimes against the dictatorship (including those in which blood was spilled).[28] On the other hand, Article 2 of the Amnesty Law also included the following clauses: "e) Crimes and misdemeanors that could have been committed by the authorities, functionaries and agents of public order, whose motive or investigative occasion and pursuit of the acts are included in this law," and "f) Crimes committed by functionaries and agents of public order against the exercise of persons' rights."[29] There was no social mobilization against the inclusion of these two points in the law, with the exception of radical Basque nationalist sectors, where the slogan "Dissolve the repressive bodies" has been and continues to be present in their demands.

In perhaps one of the greatest ironies of Pinochet's London arrest, many of the very men and women who had suffered persecution under the dictatorship, including then Chilean foreign minister José Miguel Insulza, found themselves in the position of defending their old enemy. Fearful of the reverberations from the military and the powerful Chilean right, the Frei administration came to Pinochet's defense. The Chilean government argued that as a former head of state, Pinochet was immune from prosecution abroad. Moreover, one of the key Chilean executive arguments before the London magistrates was that Pinochet should be held accountable in Chile, and while initially few believed this could happen, such a possibility began to increase. Indeed, while movement toward holding Pinochet accountable was erratic, since his return to Chile in March 2000, the Chilean judiciary stripped Pinochet of his parliamentary immunity, held him under house arrest, and booked him on cover-up charges. The Court ultimately found the eighty-six-year-old mentally unfit to stand trial. While most doubted the veracity of the ruling, it certainly proved a tremendous blow to Pinochet's own perception of the legacy he would bestow.

Interestingly enough, several reports surfaced that the Chilean government pressured Judge Juan Guzmán, Pinochet's interrogating Supreme Court justice, to arrive at a legal remedy that would prevent the former dictator's standing trial.[30] While it was clear that Guzmán had been pressured, even threatened, by Pinochet loyalists for his bold efforts to hold Pinochet accountable since Guzmán had first begun his investigations in January 1998, it is somewhat surprising that the Concertación would also bring such pressure to bear. Moreover, public opinion polls indicated that even in the midst of tremendous media and political leadership criticism of Guzmán for his initial ordering Pinochet under house arrest in December 2000, 50 percent of Chileans supported Guzmán's ordering Pinochet under arrest, while 33 percent opposed. When Chileans were asked if they would prefer a political accord to resolve the Pinochet case, only 43 percent supported such an accord, 38 percent were opposed, and 19 percent were undecided (Barómetro Centro de Estudios de la Realidad Contemporánea [CERC] 2000, 4).

Informal authoritarian legacies plague postauthoritarian elite political behavior. In the Chilean case, indictments of human rights criminals are proceeding in full accordance with the rule of law, despite loud calls from the Chilean right to reach a political accord to prevent them. Publicly the center-left government has resisted such an accord, yet former opponents of the dictatorship now in government continue to fear reprisals as justice is done.[31]

The Pervasiveness of Authoritarian Values

The traumas derived from civil confrontations and the desire that these should never happen again—the process of political learning generated in a positive sense—have clearly left their mark in postauthoritarian political culture. In many cases, the residual legitimacy of the dictatorships is related to an obsessive discourse of order and social peace, as if part of these societies fixedly subscribes to the Kantian maxim "I prefer injustice to disorder."

To analyze the strength of the legacies of the authoritarian regime, including the regime's capacity to boycott political justice measures, it is useful to examine the degree of social support the dictatorship possessed while in power, as well as how it is remembered in the postauthoritarian period. During the transition from authoritarian rule, Chilean national surveys asked supporters of the "yes" and the "no" votes in the 1988 plebiscite to state the reasons for their positions. Among those disposed to vote "yes" to support the dictatorship, 49 percent affirmed it was due to their desire to maintain "order and peace," 38 percent due to the "economic situation," 30 percent due to "Pinochet himself," and 16 percent due to "anti-communism." Nevertheless, among those who voted to reject the regime's proposal, 73 percent claimed it was due to the "economic situation," 57 percent due to "human rights," 39 percent due to "rejection of the Pinochet government," and only 21 percent due to a desire for a "return to democracy" (Varas 1991, 76). These responses hardly constitute a firm rejection of authoritarianism.

A brief analysis of the major polls conducted during the transition years in Spain reveals interesting contrasts between Spanish political culture as a whole and that found in the Basque Country. According to 1975 data from Fundación Fomento de Estudios Sociales y de Sociología Aplicada (FOESSA), the percentages of Spanish persons with an "authoritarian" or "liberal" disposition (according to indices elaborated by the researchers) were 51 and 49 percent respectively, while for the Basque Country the figures were 31 and 69 percent. When respondents were asked whether they agreed or disagreed with the statement "In Spain the most important priority is to maintain order and peace," the national average was 80 percent, while for the Basques it was only 67 percent. In the same vein, according to a later FOESSA report, while a total of 40 percent of Spaniards considered maintaining "order" preferable to "liberty," only 26 percent of the Basque and Navarra population felt this way. Only 17 percent felt "liberty" was a priority over "order," while the percentage of Basques and Navarros who felt the same was at a higher 25 percent. Second, while 29 percent of the Spanish as a whole declared themselves Francoist and 36 percent anti-Francoist, the percentages for the Basque and Navarra population were 10 and 56 percent respectively (FOESSA 1981, 154).

According to 1996 data from Latinobarómetro (cited in Lagos 1996), in Chile 67 percent of the population was partial to a "*mano dura*," while in Argentina it stood at 50.4 percent. In addition, according to Marta Lagos's (1996) analysis of this survey, those partisan to authoritarian regimes and indifferent to the type of regime totaled 26 percent in Argentina, 42 percent in Chile, and only 15 percent in Spain. With respect to the degree of net support of democracy, Spain occupied first place, Argentina second, and Chile sixth. Support for authoritarian regimes has strongly declined in Spain over time. While in 1990 such support stood at 8 percent of the population, six years before it stood at 21 percent. (Centro de Investigaciones Sociológicas

[CIS] 1984, 1990). Reasons for support for the dictatorship were quite similar to those of the Chilean case, tending to concentrate on questions such as peace, order, and economic development. In Spain, according to FOESSA studies between 1975 and 1981 (FOESSA 1981), 68 percent of those interviewed thought that during the Franco regime "there was order and peace," and 64 percent affirmed that "Spain developed economically" during that time (though it was also recognized that economic growth was quite unequally distributed within society). Nevertheless, 79 percent of the population also agreed with the statement that "it was a period of a lack of freedom" and 78 percent with the statement that it was also a period of "much repression" (FOESSA 1981, 590).

In Spain, as in Chile, the dissuasive experience of a polarized, extremely conflict-ridden democratic regime that fell to dictatorship was crucial to the reconfiguration of the new democratic regime, as well as to the degree of social support for authoritarian regimes. Guillermo O'Donnell's (1997) findings for Argentina parallel those of Spain and Chile: many Argentines remember the years immediately preceding the 1976–83 dictatorship as "a period of intolerable chaos, violence and uncertainty, such that whatever alternative that brought order seemed preferable" (140).[32] Nevertheless, the Argentine dictatorial experience seems to have strongly contributed to the citizenry's rejection of authoritarianism (see Hite and Morlino, chapter 2 of this volume).

While support or rejection of the Chilean dictatorship is articulated primarily along social or ideological cleavage lines, in the Spanish case cleavages follow lines of nationalist loyalties. In this sense, if in 1985, 17.7 percent of the Spanish population considered Francoism a "positive period for Spain," only 2.2 percent of the Basques felt the same. And while 37.4 percent of the Spanish population as a whole characterized the regime negatively, 50 percent of the Basques did. Regarding the feelings Franco's death produced, 21 percent of Spaniards expressed "sadness," while only 2.2 percent of the Basques said they felt such, and 26.8 percent confessed to feeling "happiness" (Aguilar 1998; CIS 1985a, 1985b). In this same year, Spaniards were asked in a broader study what degree of sympathy they felt for a range of institutions. Of the Spanish, 52.7 percent located the police in one of the five highest categories on a scale of 1 to 10, while only 6.4 percent of the Basques did the same. Regarding the Civil Guard the results were 53.7 percent and 4.9 percent, respectively, and for the military, 35.9 percent and 3.5 percent (Aguilar 1998).

Such a stark difference between the Basque (especially the nationalist) population and the rest of Spain in their evaluation of the forces of public order, makes it quite difficult to arrive at a consensual solution that satisfies all equally regarding the ethical and political arenas of coming to terms with the past. The Basque nationalist attitude was quite minoritarian, and it was also apparent that the rest of Spain felt there were real risks attached to purging the security forces. Not only had Spain suffered the famous coup attempt on February 23, 1981, but there were also other failed conspiracies (one of the most discussed was "Operation Galaxy," headed off in 1978),[33] as well as a significant number of violent actions by the extreme right, intended to impede any kind of "revanchist" or "rancorous" policy.

In addition to the experience of a failed previous democracy, it is clear that the experience of traumatic, fratricidal conflict in the past has contributed to intense desires within the body politic for stability, arguably at the expense of policies that threaten "to rock the boat." On the one hand, political elites and society have extracted positive lessons regarding the importance of compromise in democratic politics. On the other hand, the combination of memories of extreme conflict in the past and comparative "successes" in terms of the economy and social stability and order under authoritarianism appear to contribute to a minimalist agenda regarding political justice measures.

Conclusion

This chapter has examined major debates in the social science literature regarding the politics of memory and political justice in transitions from authoritarian rule, and it has related such debates chiefly to the Spanish and Chilean experiences. In this conclusion, we will attempt to account for the presence or absence of particular policies toward the past in the two cases, including trials, truth commissions, amnesties, and compensation. We will also note similarities and differences regarding how historical memory is publicly expressed.

A comparison of the Spanish and Chilean cases clearly shows notable differences among several independent variables that contribute to active, if constrained, political justice policies in Chile and the lack of such policies in Spain. These variables are the nature of the violence, including the clandestine versus "public" character of the repression; the historical proximity of the repressive moment; and the presence of international as well as national organized voices demanding accountability.

In spite of these differences, it was the similarities that made comparison of Spain and Chile attractive. First among these is the nature of the transition process, including the negotiation process between the still quite powerful supporters of the authoritarian regime and the democratic opposition. The strong residual power of the authoritarian incumbents makes political justice policies limited, even unlikely. Second, and related to the first, is the question of a continued, relatively high valorization of the performance of the dictatorships in both cases. This is especially clear in the Chilean case, yet even the latest Spanish official survey of December 2000 shows that a significant 46.5 percent of Spaniards still think the Francoist period "had good and bad things" and that another 10.5 percent perceive it as a "positive period" (CIS 2000).

Another set of quite suggestive similarities is revealed in Spanish and Chilean traumatic political memories. Spanish and Chilean citizens share historical memories of a failed and highly polarized democratic experience and high levels of violence. For the Spanish case, such violence included both a civil war and severe repression in its aftermath. For Chileans, the extreme violence came at the hands of the dictatorship. In both cases, there is a strong element of a painful and divided past that persists today. In the Spanish survey mentioned above, more than sixty years after the war, 51 percent of Spaniards consider that "the divisions and rancors" from the civil war have not been forgotten.

For Chileans, perhaps the attitudes toward Pinochet's arrest and pending return illustrate the persistent desire on the part of much of the citizenry to avoid facing the traumas of the past. In spite of the intense nationalism that Pinochet's London arrest triggered, a July 1999 survey found that 38 percent of Chileans thought Pinochet should not return to Chile. In a similar vein, pollsters found that while 67 percent of Chileans viewed the situation of the disappeared as important, Chilean society was far more divided regarding the advisability of continuing to address the problem. Forty-four percent were against discussing the question of the disappeared, while 47 percent were in favor of such discussion. Another example of continuing political polarization is shown in a May 2000 poll, in which only 5 percent of those supporting center-left president Ricardo Lagos considered Pinochet innocent of the human rights violations charges (a resounding 86 percent considered him guilty), while 55 percent of the supporters of rightist presidential candidate Joaquín Lavín considered Pinochet innocent. Moreover, it is quite striking that even in May 2000, given all the evidence mounted against Pinochet, 27 percent of Chileans polled considered Pinochet innocent, and another 16 percent were undecided (Barómetro CERC 2000).

This chapter has documented the persistence of the remnants of fear of polarization and the obsessive desire to avoid the repetition of the atrocities of the past. The *nunca más* of the Spanish case has related primarily to the fratricide of the civil war, while in the Chilean case, it has centered primarily on the disappeared. In both cases, the traumas of past polarization have contributed to a contemporary politics in which consensus is highly valorized, arguably at the expense, at times, of a richer public debate.

Nevertheless, while in both cases there is a strong emphasis on consensus politics, there is also an important difference. Discursively, Spanish political elites, from former Franco loyalists to Socialist Party opponents, adopted a language of mutual accountability for the violence, regardless of its historical accuracy. This is not to say that there is a widely accepted Spanish narrative of the past in all its dimensions, nor are we arguing that there should be. As has been represented recently in the Spanish Congress, it is not even clear how Spaniards should refer to the event that triggered the war (the version proposed by some parties of "fascist military coup" was not sufficiently supported),[34] nor was Francoism unanimously condemned by Spanish society even through the mid-1980s. Finally, not even the Spanish Church, in spite of the latest tendencies within the Vatican, has sought forgiveness for its undisputed complicity in the civil war ("La Iglesia española" 1999, 1, 38).

Dominant Chilean narratives of the extreme violence in the immediate aftermath of the coup have remained couched largely in a language of "response" to the "chaos" that the Allende years had wrought that had to be aggressively addressed by the armed forces.[35] Once the "mopping up" period of late 1973 and 1974 was over, the narrative continues, the more select, notorious atrocities were committed by one security agency, the Dirección de Inteligencia Nacional (DINA), or Directorate of National Intelligence, rather than by the armed forces as a whole. Thus, while greater detail regarding the extent and scope of the atrocities has emerged, the detail is typically framed by a justificatory narrative, and the atrocities are blamed on a select group portrayed as beyond the control and cognition of the regime itself.[36]

To conclude, there does not seem to be one approach with sufficient explanatory efficacy that allows us to recommend it here. It is difficult to pinpoint at what possible juncture, or even to what end, taking measures against those responsible for the dictatorship attains. The difficulties that emerge at the moment of attempting to establish strict causal links between the modes of proceeding upon certain paths during the transition and the operative outcome for democracy are enormous. In spite of these caveats, we defend the study of institutional and cultural legacies as appropriate ways to trace the consequences as well as the origins of the presence or absence of political justice measures in transitioning democracies.

In Spain after the death of Franco, transitional actors did not purge the civil and military institutions inherited from the dictatorship. Nor did they create truth commissions that investigated human rights violations that took place under the Franco regime. There were no celebrated trials against those responsible for the deaths, torture, and illegal detentions produced in the earlier period. Given this, it is clear that in spite of the many successes of political change in Spain, we must ask ourselves about the limits of the so-called "politics of consensus," including the questions of who remained at the margins of the much-touted "national reconciliation," and what repercussions these limits had for the process of the consolidation and institutionalization of democracy.

The framing of political mechanisms within the rubric of "coming to terms with the past" tends to skirt explications of intent. For many social science scholars, the decision to hold past human rights violators accountable appears to rest more heavily on the perceived immediate consequences for political stability and support for the transitional regime by those most reluctant to embrace democracy unconditionally. For such scholars and statecrafters, "coming to terms with the past" may favor policies of truth telling and amnesty. Clearly, there is no agreement among researchers regarding the consequences of amnesty, the politics of national reconciliation, and the subsequent absence of purges, trials, and truth commissions in relation to the functioning of democracy.

If it is not simple to establish causal relationships among these phenomena, it is even less simple to conjecture regarding what would have occurred had these measures been applied in Spain in ways similar to other cases. In spite of the difficulties, various authors have ventured to make claims regarding these absences and their relationship to the quality of Spanish democracy. According to some, the lack of political justice measures has produced a series of negative consequences regarding the functioning of Spanish democracy. According to others, the majority, there was neither a significant social demand for retroactive justice nor the circumstances at the moment that would have permitted more to be done than was done. The first group of authors tends to focus on questions like the Anti-Terrorist Liberation Groups and the behavior of the security forces during the transition, while the second group of authors focuses on the imposed limits on the process of change given the coup threat, and they emphasize Spanish democratic stability and the high degree of legitimacy.

What does seem clear is that an aversion to excessive risk, such as that which existed in the moment of political change as a consequence of traumatic memories of the civil war, can impose serious limits on the necessary calling to account. On the other hand, the fact of not having conducted political justice policies, rationalized on the basis of the impossibility of doing so given the correlation of forces upon Franco's death, has favored the rather abusive use by some political elites of the argument of a "received heritage," blaming an authoritarian past for inexcusable behavior under a consolidated democracy.

While there is clearly a relationship between concrete political justice measures and the broader and perhaps more philosophical issue of historical memory, the two are quite distinct from one another. In Chile, the transitional regime produced an official truth narrative, recognized as eloquent and synthetic yet far from complete. Moreover, this official narrative has failed to be incorporated into the dominant discourses, or even the texts, of other public socializing institutions, including the educational system. This becomes all the more important in debates regarding the intergenerational transmission of historical memory. While for older generations there may be little that will alter attitudes regarding the past and the meaning of "Never again," for the younger generations, how historical memory is presented, interpreted, and debated may very well be a key to formulating democratic values. The disjuncture between the policy measure of an—albeit limited—truth commission and the status of historical memory in Chile continues to be profound.

Beyond the academic debates regarding the presence or absence of authoritarian legacies, it is clear that both Spanish and Chilean societies perceive certain legacies as quite real. In the Spanish case, the December 2000 survey by the Centro de Investigaciones Sociológicas (CIS) documents that 67 percent of the population agreed with the claim that the imprint of the Franco era was still vivid (CIS 2000). In a similar vein, in a CERC May 2000 survey of Chilean citizens, only 22 percent perceived the military as subordinate to civilian authority (Barómetro CERC 2000).

NOTES

1. Some of the arguments for this chapter regarding the Spanish case are developed more extensively in de Brito, Enríquez, and Aguilar (2001). The book will also be published in Spanish by Istmo.

2. See, for example, Lowenthal (1985), Passerini (1987), Yarushalmi (1989), and Halbwachs ([1941] 1992).

3. In fact, it was the Basque nationalist forces that demanded the most radical form of *ruptura* from the authoritarian regime and that were the most suspicious regarding the aspects of continuity between the authoritarian and democratic regimes. The problems of "stateness" can flourish in transition periods, heightening the tensions of the process (see Rustow 1970; Linz and Stepan 1996).

4. Regarding the armed forces, there are clear differences between the Chilean case, which was definitively a military dictatorship, and the Spanish case, in which the army became more limited in its influence with the passage of time. Regarding the implications of authoritarian regime type for regime durability and transition, see Geddes (1999).

5. For a more detailed analysis of Basque nationalist historical manipulation of memory, see Aguilar (1998).

6. In those cases where the number of people imprisoned by the dictatorship was very high and where there was an active opposition with terrorist characteristics, one can argue, as in the Spanish case, that a kind of mutual and reciprocal amnesty takes place, which involves freeing all political prisoners (including those who have committed homicide) in exchange for a democratic oppostion that overlooks that human rights violations were committed by the authoritarian regime (Aguilar 1997, 97).

7. Carlos S. Nino (1997) was one of the first to coin this term, now commonly used in the literature on this theme.

8. See Kirchheimer (1961).

9. Concepts used by Kritz (1995) and by McAdams (1997).

10. This is precisely what Huntington (1991) terms "the praetorian problem," namely "how to reduce military involvement in politics and establish a professional pattern of civil-military relations" (209). For Adam Przeworski (1993a), authoritarian legacies are especially difficult to manage when they take place through a process of *"transition by extrication"*—that is, when authoritarian reformists are those who initiate regime liberalization. According to Przeworski, a crucial element is who controls the repressive apparatus during regime transition and what attitude the armed forces adopt regarding the previous regime (67ff.).

11. According to Nino (1997), in the Argentine case "the trials contributed to creating a public conscience about the horrors that can take place when democracy and the rule of law are shunted aside" (287). See also Jelín and Hershberg (1996) and de Brito (1997).

12. Opposing this kind of assertion, several have argued, especially in the wake of the Pinochet arrest, that if it were not possible to offer clear guarantees of impunity to the dictators, they would never voluntarily cede their power or hold democratic elections. This would effectively end one of the few peaceful transition routes.

13. See, for example, Stepan (1988); Lowenthal and Fitch (1986).

14. See, for example, Przeworski (1986).

15. Perhaps on the other end of the spectrum, the South African Truth and Reconciliation Commission (TRC) serves as an alternative model. The TRC conducted a less ordered but far more ambitious and public process, geared very deliberately toward constructing a truthful, expansive historical memory.

16. Before the legal expiration dates for filing expired, the Argentine Under-Secretariat for Human and Social Rights received over twenty thousand claims for compensation from families of the disappeared and executed and from former political prisoners. Over half of these claims have thus far been approved, while the rest are still pending. In addition, the Argentine Grandmothers of the Disappeared received $600,000 to disburse to families of missing children (U.S. State Department, 1999–2000).

17. Among others, see Informe de la Comisión Nacional sobre la Desaparición de Personas ([1984] 1997), Perelli (1992, 1994), Pion-Berlin (1994), Quiroga and Tcach (1996), and Weschler (1990). A comparative discussion of the repression statistics on the Southern Cone appears in Loveman (1998).

18. In Argentina, the survivors of the brutal torture sessions (especially in the Escuela Mecánica of the Navy) are very few. Some of them testified before the court during the 1985 trial of the military juntas. Until August 1998, it was not possible to air on broadcast networks some of the images from that trial. It is important to emphasize that thirteen years had to pass before Argentines were allowed to view recordings of the trial with sound, for until then only muted images were permitted. The documentary, entitled *The Day of the Trial*, "ESMA: El día del juicio," Editorial Perfil, broadcast on Canal 13, Buenos Aires, Aug. 24, 1988), had to be shown two times given the high numbers of the viewing audience—a symptom of the urgent need to know what really occurred under the military dictatorship. For an excellent analysis of the relationship of the imagery of the trial to memory debates in Argentina, see Feld (2002).

19. As one well-known Chilean writer recently reflected, "Of all the cruel acts of Pinochet, the act of forced disappearance of his adversaries has been, without a doubt, the most ferocious and merciless. Having had the power to mitigate their suffering, he has obstinately refused to reveal where the cadavers are hidden" (Dorfman 1998, 4).

20. For a useful explanation of the courts' interpretation of the Amnesty Law in relation to disappearance, see Human Rights Watch (2000).

21. For a description of the Mesa de Diálogo's mission and proceedings, as well as the full text of the Roundtable's proposal to the president and other human

rights–related documents, see "Declaración de la Mesa de Diálogo sobre Derechos Humanos," retrieved from www.noticias.nl/11sept/cl_mesa_13jun00.html.

22. According to surveys, Basques say they feel much less proud of the form the transition took (Aguilar 1999). In addition, recently it has been possible to note the questioning of that period among those from the moderate nationalist parties, Partido Nacional Vasco (PNV) and Eusko Alkartasuna (EA), when they refused to commemorate the twentieth anniversary of the Guernica Statute.

23. The Argentine "Never again" also supposes the rejection of fratricidal violence due to terrorist attacks of the past. Regarding different levels of social support for Latin American and the Spanish dictatorship, see Lagos (1996, 1997).

24. Guillermo O'Donnell (1996) has extensively analyzed those countries that, while in transition from authoritarian regimes, have remained in an intermediate zone in the democratization process. Thus, while such regimes possess many of the characteristics of classic democracies, they also lack other important characteristics. With the objective of distinguishing clearly among both types of democracy, O'Donnell proposes altering the seven classic attributes of a polyarchy as defined by Robert Dahl and adding others of his own design, including that politicians should not be subjected to profound constraints from certain actors and that certain actors should not have veto power, in a clear allusion to the military. Felipe Agüero (1995) argues that the "initial conditions" regarding the correlation of forces between civilians and the military are crucial for explaining the degree of control that both collectivities will exercise in the institutional design of the transition. Nevertheless, such a design could constrain but not determine the final result of such a relationship, as democratic governments reinforce their power and ultimately prove capable of imposing military reforms that remained pending during the delicate moment of political change.

25. Moreover, as Agüero (1995) notes, "[T]he Spanish generals and admirals who remained in their posts during the entire transition were those who had been formed in the years of the civil war of 1936–39. They had fought in the conquering army that defeated the Republicans and Reds, and were always committed to the defense of Francoist institutions and ideals against what were termed the anti-Spanish forces. . . . It was the duty of the military chiefs to guarantee the continuity of the fundamental principles of 'The Crusade.'"(23).

26. For a report of the exchange between Judge Guzmán and Pinochet, see "Pinochet declaró" (2001). For details of the October 1973 "Caravan of Death" case, in which seventy-five political prisoners were removed from their cells in northern and southern Chile and executed, see Verdugo (1989), and for updated information regarding those involved, see *La Tercera*'s Web site: www.tercera.cl\casos\ caravana\documentos.

27. On Lagos's account, see Minay (2001).

28. The extreme right, the Popular Alliance Party, and a good part of the armed forces rejected the law due to this clause. According to polls, the majority of society

supported a broad amnesty, but only the Basque Country contained respondents who generally supported an amnesty for those who had committed homicide during their political acts (CIS, 1977). Polling proved a good demonstration of the government's concern for society's sentiments regarding the amnesty, as the Unión de Centro Democrático (UCD) government contracted two other surveys concerning the theme (CIS, 1976a, 1976b).

29. Amnesty Law 46, 15 October 1977.

30. See, for example, Faiola (2001).

31. For an elaborated discussion of the political evolution of leaders of the former opposition to the dictatorship, see Hite (2000).

32. In fact, this stage turned out to be very useful in deciding how *not* to design the institutions of the new democracy (Aguilar 1996). The unpopularity of the republican period was also reflected in national surveys: In 1984, 21 percent of Spaniards thought that Francoism was the period where Spain had "been politically better in the last 60 years," whereas only 5 percent thought the same with respect to the Second Republic. Still, in 1990, as we have seen, 8 percent of the Spaniards continued to say the same of Francoism, whereas only 3 percent continued subscribing to the republican option (CIS 1984, 1990, respectively).

33. It is important to note that the mercy with which these frustrated coup participants were treated is best explained by the fact that the protagonists of both the 1978 and 1981 unsuccessful coups were practically the same.

34. "The main problem, not yet resolved and the one that should create awareness and inspire an occasion for a deep and general debate, is that the 1978 democracy continues without finding a perspective to narrate the past of the Spaniards, of all the Spaniards" (Jose María Ridao, *El Mundo*, 19 November 1999, 22).

35. For a good example of how the Chilean media transmit this narrative, see "Los datos" (2001).

36. Chilean psychologist and member of the Mesa de Diálogo Elizabeth Lira (interviewed by author, 3 July 2002) claims that the narrative of military violence as justified has weakened significantly and that the military leadership now adopts a narrative that "explains" rather than "justifies" the violence in the context of a chaotic moment.

REFERENCES

Ackerman, Bruce. 1992. *The Future of Liberal Revolution.* New Haven, Conn.: Yale University Press.

Agüero, Felipe. 1995. *Militares, civiles y democracia.* Madrid: Alianza Editorial.

Aguilar, Paloma. 1996. *Memoria y olvido de la guerra civil española.* Madrid: Alianza Editorial.

————. 1997. "Collective Memory of the Spanish Civil War: The Case of Political Amnesty in the Spanish Transition to Democracy." *Democratization* 14:88–109.

————. 1998. "The Memory of the Civil War in the Transition to Democracy: The Peculiarity of the Basque Case." *West European Politics* 121:5–25.

————. 1999. "La cultura política del País Vasco en el contexto español: Legados institucionales y culturales de los procesos de cambio políticos." Unpublished manuscript.

Barómetro Centro de Estudios de la Realidad Contemporánea. 2000. "Encuesta Nacional." Santiago, Chile. Retrieved from www.cerc.cl/encmayo00.htm.

Bermeo, Nancy. 1992. "Democracy and the Lessons of Dictatorship." *Comparative Politics* 24, no. 3: 273–91.

Centro de Investigaciones Sociológicas. 1976a. "Estudio No. 1093." Retrieved from www.cis.es.

————. 1976b "Estudio No. 1105." Retrieved from www.cis.es.

————. 1977. "Estudio No. 1139." Retrieved from www.cis.es.

————. 1984. "Estudio No. 1441." Retrieved from www.cis.es.

————. 1985a. "Estudio No. 1461." Retrieved fromwww.cis.es.

————. 1985b. "Estudio No. 1495." Retrieved from www.cis.es.

————. 1990. "Estudio No. 1908." Retrieved from www.cis.es.

————. 2000. "Estudio No. 2401." Retrieved from www.cis.es.

Collier, Ruth B., and David Collier. 1991. *Shaping the Political Arena: Critical Junctures, the Labor Movement, and Regime Dynamics in Latin America.* Princeton, N.J.: Princeton University Press.

De Brito, Alexandra Barahona. 1997. *Human Rights and Democratization in Latin America.* New York: Oxford University Press.

————. 2001. "Truth, Justice, Memory, and Democratization in the Southern Cone." In Alexandra Barahona De Brito, Carmen González Enríquez, and Paloma Aguilar, eds., *The Politics of Memory: Transitional Justice in Democratizing Societies.* (pp. 119–60). Oxford: Oxford University Press.

De Brito, Alexandra Barahona, Carmen González Enríquez, and Paloma Aguilar, eds. 2001. *The Politics of Memory: Transitional Justice in Democratizing Societies.* Oxford: Oxford University Press.

Dorfman, Ariel. 1998. "Que decidan las víctimas." *El País,* 2 December, 4.

Elster, Jon. 1995. "On Doing What One Can: An Argument against Post-Communist Restitution and Retribution." In Neil J. Kritz, ed., *Transitional Justice: How Emerging Democracies Reckon with Former Regimes.* Washington, D.C.: United States Institute of Peace Press.

Faiola, Anthony. 2001. "Pressures Mount to Avoid Pinochet Trial." *Washington Post,* 10 January, A15.

Feld, Claudia. 2002. *Del estrado a la pantalla: Las imágenes del juicio a los ex comandantes en Argentina.* Buenos Aires: Siglo XXI de Argentina Editores.

FOESSA. 1981. *Fundación: Informe sociológico sobre el cambio político en España (1975–1981).* Madrid: Euroamérica.

Geddes, Barbara. 1999. "What Do We Know about Democratization after Twenty Years?" *Annual Review of Political Science* 2:115–44.

Halbwachs, Maurice. [1941] 1992. *On Collective Memory.* Chicago: University of Chicago Press.

Hall, Peter A. 1993. "Policy Paradigms, Social Learning and the State." *Comparative Politics* 25, no. 3:275–96.

Hayner, Priscilla. 2001. *Unspeakable Truths.* New York: Routledge.

Hite, Katherine. 2000. *When the Romance Ended: Leaders of the Chilean Left, 1968–1998.* New York: Columbia University Press.

Holmes, Stephen. [1988] 1993. "Gag Rules and the Politics of Omission." In Jon Elster and Rune Slagstad, eds., *Constitutionalism and Democracy.* New York: Cambridge University Press.

Human Rights Watch. 2000. *When Tyrants Tremble.* New York: Human Rights Watch.

Huntington, Samuel P. 1991. *The Third Wave: Democratization in the Late Twentieth Century.* Norman: University of Oklahoma Press.

Informe de la Comisión Nacional sobre la Desaparición de Personas. [1984] 1997. *Nunca más.* Buenos Aires: Editorial Universitaria.

Jelín, Elizabeth. 1998. "The Minefields of Memory." *NACLA Report on the Americas* 32, no. 2:23–29.

Jelín, Elizabeth, and Eric Hershberg, eds. 1996. *Construir la democracia: Derechos humanos, ciudadanía y sociedad en América Latina.* Caracas: Nueva Sociedad.

Jervis, Robert. 1976. *Perception and Misperception in International Politics.* Princeton, N.J.: Princeton University Press.

Juliá, Santos, ed. 1999. *Víctimas de la guerra civil.* Madrid: Temas de Hoy.

Karl, Terry Lynn. 1986. "Petroleum and Political Pacts: The Transition to Democracy in Venezuela." In Guillermo O'Donnell, Philippe Schmitter, and Laurence Whitehead, eds., *Transition from Authoritarian Rule: Latin America.* Baltimore, Md.: Johns Hopkins University Press.

Keck, Margaret, and Kathryn Sikkink. 1998. *Activists beyond Borders: Advocacy Networks in International Politics.* Ithaca, N.Y.: Cornell University Press.

Kirchheimer, Otto. 1961. *Political Justice: The Use of Legal Procedure for Political Ends.* Princeton, N.J.: Princeton University Press.

Kritz, Neil J., ed. 1995. *Transitional Justice: How Emerging Democracies Reckon with Former Regimes.* 3 vols. Washington, D.C.: United States Institute of Peace Press.

"La Iglesia española elude pedir perdón por su implicación en la guerra civil." 1998. *El País,* 3 December, pp. 1 and 38.

Lagos, Marta. 1996. "The Latinobarómetro Media and Political Attitudes in South America." Paper presented at the annual meeting of the American Political Science Association, 29 August–1 September, San Francisco.

————. 1997. "Latin America's Smiling Mask." *Journal of Democracy* 8:125–38.

Linz, Juan, and Alfred Stepan. 1996. *Problems of Transition and Consolidation: Southern Europe, South America, and Post-Communist Europe.* Baltimore, Md.: Johns Hopkins University Press.

Lira, Elizabeth, and Brian Loveman. 1999. "Derechos humanos en la transicón 'Modelo': Chile 1988–1999." In Paul Drake and Iván Jaksic, eds., *El modelo chileno: Democracia y desarrollo en los noventa.* Santiago: LOM Ediciones.

"Los datos del Informe Rettig." 2001. *La Tercera,* 7 January.

Loveman, Mara. 1998. "High-Risk Collective Action: Defending Human Rights in Chile, Uruguay, and Argentina." *American Journal of Sociology* 104, no. 2:477–525.

Lowenthal, Abraham, and J. Samuel Fitch, eds. 1986. *Armies and Politics in Latin America.* New York: Holmes and Meier.

Lowenthal, David. 1985. *The Past Is a Foreign Country.* New York: Cambridge University Press.

March, James, and Johan P. Olsen. 1989. *Rediscovering Institutions.* New York: Free Press.

McAdams, A. James, ed. 1997. *Transitional Justice and the Rule of Law in New Democracies.* Notre Dame, Ind.: University of Notre Dame Press.

Minay, Sebastián. 2001. "No es de hombre en las FFAA eximirse de las responsabilidades." *El Mercurio,* 26 January.

Neier, Aryeh. 1998. *War Crimes: Brutality, Genocide, Terror, and the Struggle for Justice.* New York: Random House.

Nino, Carlos S. 1997. *Juicio al mal absoluto.* Buenos Aires: Emecé.

O'Donnell, Guillermo. 1996. "Illusions about Consolidation." *Journal of Democracy* 7:34–51.

————. 1997. *Contrapuntos.* Buenos Aires: Paidós.

Osiel, Mark. 1995. "Ever Again: Legal Remembrance of Administrative Massacre." *University of Pennsylvania Law Review* 144:464–704.

Passerini, Luisa. 1987. *Fascism in Popular Memory: The Cultural Experience of the Turin Working Class.* New York: Cambridge University Press.

Perelli, Carina. 1992. "Settling Accounts with Blood Memory: The Case of Argentina." *Social Research* 59:415–51.

————. 1994. "Memoria de sangre: Fear, Hope, and Disenchantment in Argentina." In Jonathan Boyarin, ed., *Remapping Memory: The Politics of TimeSpace.* Minneapolis: University of Minnesota Press.

Pierson, Paul. 2000. "Increasing Returns, Path Dependence, and the Study of Politics." *American Political Science Review* 94:251–67.

"Pinochet declaró que no ordenó ejecuciones." 2001. *El Mercurio,* 24 January.

Pion-Berlin, David. 1994. "To Prosecute or to Pardon? Human Rights Decisions in the Latin American Southern Cone." *Human Rights Quarterly* 16:105–30.

Przeworski, Adam. 1986. "Some Problems in the Study of Transition to Democracy." In Guillermo O'Donnell, Philippe C. Schmitter, and Laurence Whitehead, eds.,

Transitions from Authoritarian Rules: Comparative Perspectives (pp. 47–63). Baltimore, Md.: Johns Hopkins University Press.

———. 1988. "Algunos problemas en el estudio de la transición hacia la democracia." In Guillermo O'Donnell, Philippe Schmitter, and Laurence Whitehead, eds., *Perspectivas Comparadas*, vol. 3. Buenos Aires: Paidós.

———. 1993a. *Democracy and the Market.* New York: Cambridge University Press.

———. 1993b. "Democracy as a Contingent Outcome of Conflicts." In Jon Elster and Rune Slagstad, eds. *Constitutionalism and Democracy.* Cambridge University Press. pp. 59–80.

———. 1995. "Presentación." In Carlos H. Acuña, Inés González Bombal, Elizabeth Jelín, Oscar Landi, Luís Alberto Quevedo, Catalina Smulovitz, and Adriana Vacchieri, *Juicio, castigos y memorias: Derechos humanos y justicia en la política argentina.* Buenos Aires: Ediciones Nueva Visión.

Putnam, Robert. 1993. *Making Democracy Work: Civic Traditions in Modern Italy.* Princeton, N.J.: Princeton University Press.

Quiroga, Hugo, and César Tcach, eds. 1996. *A veinte años del golpe: Con memoria democrática.* Rosario, Argentina: Homo Sapiens Ediciones.

Rustow, Dankwart A. 1970. "Transitions to Democracy: Toward a Dynamic Model." *Comparative Politics* 2, no. 3:337–63.

Shapiro, Ian. 1996. *Democracy's Place.* Ithaca, N.Y.: Cornell University Press.

Stepan, Alfred. 1988. *Rethinking Military Politics: Brazil and the Southern Cone.* Princeton, N.J.: Princeton University Press.

Teitel, Ruti. 1997. "Transitional Jurisprudence: The Role of Law in Political Transformation." *Yale Law Journal* 106, no. 7:2009–80.

Thelen, Kathleen. 1999. "Historical Institutionalism in Comparative Politics." *Annual Review of Political Science* 2:369–404.

U.S. State Department. 1999–2000. *Human Rights Report on Argentina.* Washington, D.C.: U.S. State Department.

Varas, Augusto. 1991. "The Crisis of Legitimacy of Military Rule in the 1980s." In Paul W. Drake and Iván Jaksic, eds., *The Struggle for Democracy in Chile, 1982–1990.* Lincoln: University of Nebraska Press.

Verdugo, Patricia. 1989. *Caso Arellano: Los Zarpazos del Puma.* Santiago: CESOC, Ediciones Chile América.

Weschler, Lawrence. 1990. *A Miracle, a Universe: Settling Accounts with Torturers.* New York: Penguin.

Yarushalmi, Yoseph. 1989. *Zakhor: Jewish History and Jewish Memory.* Seattle: University of Washington Press.

6

Authoritarian Legacies

The Military's Role

FELIPE AGÜERO

The military dominated the authoritarian regimes of the 1960s and 1970s in Latin America and provided authoritarian rule with critical support in southern Europe. During and after the transitions from these regimes, the military in most cases imposed limits on democratic reforms, attempted to exclude itself from them, and contributed to inhibiting social and political actors from pursuing an unfettered democratization agenda. An assessment of the military's contribution to authoritarian legacies in successor regimes is therefore fully relevant and is central to a general discussion of these legacies. To what extent is the military a carrier of authoritarian legacies? This question suggests a focus on the ways and channels through which authoritarian features, whether more or less institutionalized, travel to and endure in successor regimes.

This approach, like any dealing with specific legacies, raises the question of how to distinguish authoritarian legacies initiated during the period of authoritarian rule from those that may have originated in processes and norms existing prior to that period. A related question—a counterfactual—is whether what may be identified as a legacy could have come about anyway in the absence of authoritarian rule. This in turn leads to the question of how to identify the location of legacies in terms of their origins, carriers, and more or less institutionalized presence in the current regimes.

These questions are particularly relevant with regard to the military because of the specific nature of the military institution, its organizational

233

peculiarities, and its historic role in coercion, state building, and public order. The military lends itself well to a characterization as a discrete carrier of authoritarian legacies, especially if it held important roles during authoritarian periods and if it emerged from authoritarian rule with considerable power. The military is a well-established bureaucracy, an inherently conservative institution, and as such is prepared to guarantee organizational and cultural continuity. Through it, the past may persist more than in other institutions. But because of all these traits, the military may be made too easy a culprit in a search for authoritarian legacies, and special caution should therefore be applied. The analysis should also take into account the historically changing relations among the military, the state, and dominant social and political elites in order to ascertain the role of the military as a legacy carrier relative to other actors and institutions.

Identifying legacies, as well as tracing the process through which they travel temporally, is certainly a complex enterprise.[1] Legacies comprise various pasts, and their origins are found in different periods and come from different contributors. Legacies may include discrete institutions and practices but often involve diffuse cultural norms and orientations or hidden, yet widespread, perceptions that affect behavior. There also are distinct circumstances and junctures that result in distinct consequences. Policies, practices, laws, reforms, and discourses promoted or undertaken during a distinct period of authoritarian rule are a case in point.[2]

Our inquiry may be formulated in the following way: How do the historical organizational and value specificities of the military institution combine with its actual role and power in the authoritarian regime and during its demise to carry over legacies into successor postauthoritarian regimes? In addressing this question I will first address issues related to the specificity of the military as an institution and its implications for the question of authoritarian legacies. I will then turn to the question of the military's role in actual authoritarian regimes. Finally, I shall focus on the importance of the manner of exit from authoritarian rule for the analysis of legacies. This exercise will lead me to conclude that the military's role in fostering authoritarian legacies is contingent upon the power balance between it and democratic agents, which is in turn influenced by the form of authoritarian rule and the manner of transition. If, for instance, this power relation over time yields a relatively weaker military, the military will seek accommodation in the new situation in ways that obscure traces of authoritarian influence on the polity. It may still exert, however, a deeper, less visible influence on attitudes and beliefs, stemming from a memory of fear and repression. In this, as in cases of a stronger military, its impact on the polity must be assessed in the context of its relations with the state and dominant social and political elites. My general assertion will be that the military is not per se an institution that functions as an authoritarianism carrier.

The Military Institution's Nondemocratic Character and Outlook

Few organizations are structured according to transparent democratic norms and procedures, even if they function within democratic polities. Some of the most powerful organizations in society, such as the Church, and especially the Catholic Church, corporations, banks, and many autonomous institutions within the state, operate in ways alien to democratic procedures and principles (Weber 1968; Bowles and Gintis 1987; Brysk 2000). The military is therefore not alone in its nondemocratic character as an organization.

The military's specific organizational features certainly make it more authoritarian than most other organizations it can be compared with, and it is no surprise that the literature has characterized military organization as authoritarian (Abrahamsson 1972). Other hierarchic organizations, such as the Leninist party, operated under the principle of democratic centralism, but even if this and other parties succumbed to the "iron law of oligarchy," there was at least the formal rule of elections, and the existence of "electors," "mandators," and "delegators" (Michels 1962).[3]

Large business firms and corporations are arranged in hierarchical and disciplined ways, although variation exists in organizational culture across modern firms in different countries. This feature of the internal organization of firms shows in the stark contrast between citizen rights in the polity and individual rights of employees within business organizations. Nonetheless, firms face some form of accountability, as they have shareholders to respond to and consumers and clients to satisfy in a market environment. In addition, profit seeking will lead them to innovation and ways of enhancing productivity, rendering them inherently less conservative. Even if "oligarchy" may set in both in parties and in firms, and even if their organizational practice may be alien to democratic principles, they may have at least some form of internal accountability.

The Church, and the Catholic Church in particular, is clearly hierarchic, demanding discipline and obedience from the clergy, even if it is much less able to enforce such behavior. Doctrinal truth and infallibility, claimed by the pope, enhance the hierarchic nature of the organization. Nonetheless, the Church includes collective instances for the approval of critical documents, such as the *Sínodo de Obispos,* and more so at the national levels, with the Episcopal Councils. Actual pluralism, based on international diversity and the existence of several religious orders, allows for different doctrinal interpretation in manners alien to the practices of an army.

Organizational features of the military, derived from its principal functions, make it a special case of nondemocratic institution. The military is an efficient instrument for the employment of legitimate violence by the state. This functional imperative imposes strict organizational principles such as obedience and discipline within a well-established hierarchical structure. All its parts are arranged to follow a single orientation provided by a high command. Logistics, operations, intelligence, personnel, and all the rest of the support structure, jointly with the force structure, are arranged hierarchically in such a way as to respond to a single individualized high command. Collective instances of deliberation—such as the general staff at various command levels—exist only for the purpose of providing technical, strategic or tactical advice to the individual commander they serve. There are, of course, differences across cases in the manner in which organizational structures, procedures and practices actually materialize.[4] But these differences do not contradict the core principles of hierarchy, discipline, and obedience to individualized command.

The military's organizational features make it an efficient instrument of democratic regimes in whatever circumstances necessitate the threat or actual use of violence or merely the use of a capable organization for emergencies of any sort.[5] On the other hand, these organizational features, which are essential to the existence of a modern military, may weaken or break down in periods of military-dominated authoritarian rule. Most cases in Latin America and southern Europe indeed featured one or another kind of breakdown of those organizational principles, as their militaries faced disputes over policy orientations or leadership succession. The practice by some armies of collectively deciding on their leadership succession, under no guiding principles, as occurred in the juntas of Argentina and Uruguay and in the years immediately prior to Garrastazu Medici's term in Brazil, or the more direct mechanism of leadership replacement by coups within the coup, such as occurred in Peru or Ecuador, directly violated those organizational principles and created enormous stress within the military. The breakdown of those principles in Argentina, leading to the army's near–self-destruction, have been well described by O'Donnell (1986b). The Colonels' regime in Greece was itself the expression of a "nonhierarchical" (Linz and Stepan 1996) military, which was ousted simultaneously with the reassertion of traditional military organization and political democratization. Portugal's transition was animated by a nonhierarchical military, which led to temporarily institutionalizing a collective military body for political decision making (the Council of the Revolution). Only Spain and Chile were able, in different ways, to maintain military core organizational principles and features largely unchanged.[6] In fact, the need to restore hierarchy, discipline, and obedience in the armies often was a rationale in the move to oust the military from power (Stepan 1988). In these cases, the end of military rule tended to bring about the retrieval of the essential principles of military organization. It is this retrieval, which leads to carrying over an unreformed and unpurged institution into the successor regime, that presents the military as a channel for enduring authoritarian legacies.

It is not only organizational features that make the military distinct; there are also the values and mentalities within it and radiating out from it. The military's authoritarian organization has been rightly connected to a certain kind of military "mind." Abrahamsson (1972), for instance, observed that "writings on the military mind fairly often reflect the idea that since the military organization is authoritarian rather than democratic, it fosters an authoritarian outlook" (93). Huntington (1957) had already highlighted this point, not in terms of an authoritarian outlook, but in terms of conservative values embedded in the military mind. In tune with Abrahamsson's observation, Huntington affirmed that "[t]he continuing objective performance of the professional function gives rise to a continuing professional *weltanschauung* or professional 'mind.' The military mind, in this sense, consists of the values, attitudes, and perspectives which inhere in the performance of the professional military function and which are deducible from the nature of that function"(61). In Huntington's view, the military mind adopts a view of human nature as primarily evil and selfish, prone to conflict based on opposed interests. Its view is pessimistic. "The man of the military ethic is essentially the man of Hobbes" (63). However, because charged with the enhancement of the security of the state, the military profession also seeks cooperation, organization, and discipline at a societal level. It is "basically corporative in spirit" and "fundamentally anti-individualistic" (64).

Huntington's view of the military mind and ethic, applicable to all modern professional military institutions, led him to a diagnosis of crisis in civil-military relations in the United States, based on the incongruence between the ethics of military professionalism and what he perceived as the prevailing liberal ideology in society. The solution that he proposed disclosed his own ideological preferences: such crisis could be overcome only with the shift to a dominant conservative ideology in society, one more congruous with the military ethic. In his own admission of preference, he rendered a description of military life and order that, while capturing some of its universal traits, also much resembled religious life. In this description, enraptured by the imagery of a monastic West Point contrasted with the more ordinary, chaotic, civilian neighboring village of Highland Falls, Huntington notes:

> On the military reservation the other side of South Gate, however, exists a different world. There is ordered serenity. The parts do not exist on their own, but accept their subordination to the whole. . . . The post is suffused with the rhythm and harmony which comes when collective will supplants individual whim. West Point is a community of structured purpose, one in which the behavior of men is governed by a code, the product of generations. There is little room for presumption and individualism. The unity of the community incites no man to be more than he is. In order is found peace; in discipline, fulfillment; in community, security. The spirit of Highland Falls is embodied in Main Street. The spirit of West Point is in the great, gray, Gothic Chapel, starting from the hill and dominating The Plain, calling to mind Henry Adams' remarks at Mont St. Michel on the unity of the military and the religious spirits. But the unity of the Chapel is even greater. There join together the four great pillars of society: Army, Government, College, and Church. Religion subordinates man to God for divine purposes; the military life subordinates man to duty for society's purposes. In its severity, regularity, discipline, the military society shares the characteristics of the religious order. Modern man may well find his monastery in the Army. (463)

While Huntington highlighted values and traits that were distinctly found in the military and that clashed with those of society, other authors pointed instead to a civilianizing trend in the military that originated in the growing impact of technology and managerialism in the organization. Janowitz (1971), for instance, highlighted a trend toward a convergence between civilian and military organization and presented a view of the military as formed by a combination of traditional, heroic leaders, managers, and technical experts. A changing organizational lifestyle would result in lessening the "total institution" character of the military, as well as its predominant pattern of authoritative domination. This view admitted, nonetheless, that the civilizing trend would be resisted by the military's inherently conservative outlook, a conservatism of form derived from the security imperative over the organization. The extent to which the shift to an all-volunteer force would slow the civilizing trend and reassert the distinctness of military organization remained open to debate.[7] The authoritative and heroic aspects of the military, with their accompanying codes of honor, in fact remained well entrenched. An invigorating debate between the heirs to the views of Huntington and Janowitz, focused on the United States, has noted the enduring distinctness of the military's cultural traits. From this, many scholars have warned about a widening gap between the military and civilian society, and a weakening of civilian control in the United States (Holsti 1998–99; Desch 1998).

A view of the nondemocratic character of military institutions in general is certainly applicable to the militaries in southern Europe and South America. A well-known study on the Latin American military, for instance, identified the fundamental historical traits in military professionalism and its foreign and domestic influences, as well as the evolution of regional brands of military mind and ethics. The study confirmed the military's arrogation of the notion of national interest and the military's self-identification as trustee of the national interest and national values (Loveman 1999). The preponderant role that the military assigned itself in interpreting the national interest and defending the national values took, in Latin America, the form of national security doctrines that strengthened in the Cold War period. A well-articulated vision of society organized as various "fronts"—all of which were deemed relevant to the military's specific mission—for the defense against enemies that employed a variety of weapons, most of them nonmilitary, gave the military institutions a rationale for at least the intention of and preparation for widespread involvement. The features of the military mind identified by Huntington were reinforced in these cases by ideological outlooks that directly contradicted fundamental assumptions of democratic civilian political supremacy and made them more prone to authoritarian political inclinations. The historical circumstances that made this kind of ideological development possible were not present everywhere. The Spanish military, for instance, did not develop this kind of doctrine under Francoism. Instead, its rationale for involvement emerged from the founding conditions of the Francoist state: a military victor in a divided society, with ample trustee roles formalized in the Fundamental Laws. In addition, a deep sense of religious mission made the army, *la Milicia*, a sort of modern domestic expression of the Crusades. The military was there to protect the "national essences" from what was perceived as the debilitating impact of a moral attack by materialism, pornography, and drugs (Agüero 1995; Bañon Martínez and Barker 1988).

The "values, attitudes, and perspectives which inhere in the performance of the professional military function," described above by Huntington, are common to most modern professional militaries. Some militaries (e.g., that of the Netherlands), following civilianizing trends, exposed to high levels of technical innovation in weapon systems and managerial techniques, and in the midst of highly democratized societies that have penetrated the military via, for instance, the formation of unions, have evidently experienced a lessening of the "total character" of the military institution. In other cases (Germany, Japan), a breach between military function and the values and attitudes that would purportedly inhere in them has been specially promoted as a result of a conscious decision to break with a militaristic past (Katzenstein 1996; Katahara 1999). Other militaries, instead, as in most of the cases considered here, added to the inherent connection between function and outlook by developing views about their enhanced domestic role in the polity. In the cases in Latin America, the gradual development of these values and attitudes coexisted with a range of political regimes during this century. The institutional patterns of "authoritative domination" alluded to by Huntington and their larger ideological reach did not stem solely from the organization's functional imperatives described by him. These were embedded in a broader set of historical circumstances connected to the military's historical role in state formation and building and the kind of domination alliances established early on.[8] Evidently, the ideological tenets described above made the military more prone to authoritarian politics, which materialized once the necessary structural and political conditions developed to create the coup coalitions that led to the installation of authoritarian regimes (O'Donnell 1973).

Military-Authoritarian Rule and Legacies

Authoritarian rule did not have the same impact across all the societies on which it was imposed. In some cases, authoritarianism lasted longer and left enduring imprints in social and economic or political transformations, as in Spain, Brazil, and Chile. In other cases, authoritarianism was shorter-lived and less institutionalized and was less able to enact enduring social, economic, and political transformations, as in Uruguay and Argentina. In Peru and Ecuador, military-authoritarian rule was not very long-lasting, but due to the orientation of its military elites it attempted significant transformations in the economy and the social and political structures of those countries.

On the other hand, the extent, method, and severity of suppression of opponents was the source of different legacies in human rights violations. The military regimes in Peru and Ecuador, for instance, were only mildly repressive and did not leave a legacy in this area that was specific to the military-authoritarian regime. Brazil, but especially Argentina, Chile, and Uruguay, applied variegated forms of repression and widely violated basic human rights. This legacy has been visible in all these cases. The persistence and worsening of human rights violations in successor regimes in Brazil and Peru may also be looked at as a legacy in terms of the perceived "legitimacy" of methods of suppression and public order maintenance to be utilized by the police and the military or of the powers and autonomy left for repressive agencies in situations of emergency. In Spain, the brutality of repression subsided over time during Francoism, in comparison to the South American cases, although the brutality of the civil war and the post–civil war years lingered in the memories of Spaniards across society (Aguilar 1996).

Regimes also varied according to the military's role in establishing authoritarian rule and in sustaining it and leading it. In Spain and Portugal authoritarianism civilianized over time, whereas in Greece and especially South America authoritarianism remained controlled by the military (Agüero 1995). Finally, they varied in the way in which they ended and the way in which the transition from authoritarianism ensued. All these, then, are the factors relevant to the assessment of the military as a carrier of legacies from authoritarianism: the military's role in authoritarian rule; the depth and endurance of reforms in the economy and the political system pursued during authoritarian rule; the extent, severity, and methods of political suppression; and the manner of exit and transition from authoritarianism.

According to these factors, cases differed in the military's ability to maintain authoritarian enclaves (Valenzuela 1992; Garretón 1995); to inhibit other actors and institutions from removing those enclaves and pushing for democratization; to occupy space in postauthoritarian state institutions and society; to exclude itself from civilian-imposed democratic reforms; and to influence the manner of resolution of human rights questions and, more generally, the range of permissible items that could be placed in the public agenda. This ability constitutes the military's place in authoritarian legacies. Many of these legacies consist of easily identifiable constraints embodied in laws or regulations, overt threats, or actions. However, the abilities exercised by the military also result in harder-to-identify fears and inhibitions that are internalized by other actors and that influence behavior and affect the policy agenda. The often blurry zone of pacts in the transition as well as of collective memories in post-transition political practice are factors that help nurture the production of inhibitions and fears that suppress conflict and debate (Bermeo 1997; Agüero 2002).

Close to its own institutional sphere, the military maintains and reproduces important legacies with restrictive impact on democratization. For instance, military law trespasses on civilian spheres, while the military often remains protected within its own system of military law and courts. The military may influence the national system and content of education but keeps its own educational system well guarded, even expanding, under its own oversight. Also, policies for state and administrative reforms fall well short of including the military, which maintains special administrative status and exempts itself and its organs from the rationalizing intent of these reforms. Military and defense budgets, as well as independent sources of military self-financing, remain in many cases far beyond civilian monitoring (Agüero 1999; Brenes and Casas 1998). The perseverance and growth of well-entrenched areas of autonomy also should be seen as distinct authoritarian legacies embodied in and maintained by the military.

However, the military could very well be stripped of many of its prerogatives and privileges and of its abilities to contain reform. This evidently depends on the power relations between a resistant military and democratic reformers, the existence of reform policies, and the willingness of leaders to pursue them. However, reformers often overrestrain themselves (Sain 2000). The military does not necessarily have to be a carrier of authoritarian legacies, although in practice it often is one as a consequence of restraints that reformers impose on themselves. The extent to which this excess of restraint is itself an authoritarian legacy—"cultural" or "psychological"—is in fact hard to determine. This difficulty should advise against viewing unspecified "legacies" as the cause of all failure to act in democratic directions. Instead, legacies should be viewed in the context of the influence of a power arrangement resulting from the transition, in which the main contributors include important civilian actors. Below I develop a view of civil-military relations as power relations and argue about the impact of founding conditions in successor regimes.[9] I then review the impact of transitions in the case of Latin American successor democracies, which sets the context for a view on the impact of military-related authoritarian legacies.

A Focus on Founding Conditions

Dominant approaches in the study of military-state-society relations have pointed to crucial relations of power between civilian and military actors and institutions.[10] This focus is quite useful in cases, such as those of Latin America and southern Europe, in which disputes over prerogatives, agenda setting, and pending issues from an authoritarian past have continued to mark civilian-military relations long after the transitions.[11] It is critical, then, to ascertain how civil-military power relations get patterned and structured from their initial, founding conditions. These patterns and structures greatly influence the most important features in the structure of civilian-military relations observable at later points in time. Initial conditions that shape the basic parameters in the distribution of power between the military, on one hand, and the civilian elites and the rest of society, on the other, help delineate the contours of that relationship for long periods and hence the characteristics of the political regime and its dynamics of change.[12]

The study of the nature and power distribution of civilian-military relations during a military regime, for instance, is facilitated by a clear view of the conditions that originated that regime, the political alignments that made it possible, and the institutional arrangements found in its early stages. Here, O'Donnell's analyses, such as that found in his *Modernization and Military Coups* (1973), remain paradigmatic. And just as a study of the conditions behind the founding coups of the military-authoritarian regimes of the 1960s and 1970s is essential to understanding civil-military relations in their midst, so is the identification of the founding conditions of other long-lasting periods of particular patterns of civil-military relations.

For instance, the shape of civilian-military relations in the period preceding the wave of militarism of the 1960s and 1970s was, in many cases, established by changes that occurred during the disruptive conditions of the 1930s, which were, in turn, expressions of the profound political, social, and economic changes affecting the region. In Chile, the basic features of the structure of civilian-military relations that prevailed for most of the century were greatly influenced by the manner in which the dictatorship of Colonel Ibáñez came to an end and the *civilista* reaction that followed. In Argentina, in turn, the manner in which the Yrigoyen civilian administration collapsed gave rise to a completely different pattern that opened the way to frequent military intervention. Later, the rise and demise of Peronist rule set in yet another pattern and dynamics, based on the military-promoted political exclusion of a large sector of Argentine society. In Peru, the mode in which the Alianza Popular Revolucionaria Americana (APRA) and the military violently collided early in the 1930s set a pattern and dynamics for the following three decades quite similar to the exclusionary pattern inaugurated with the fall of Perón in Argentina. In Venezuela, the manner of collapse of the Pérez Jiménez regime and the pacted arrangements by its opposition that preceded democratic inauguration strongly influenced the kind of civilian-military relations that prevailed there until the early 1990s, when elements of the pre–pact-making transition were eerily resurrected. Important junctures such as the ones just mentioned decisively helped to shape power relations between civilians and the military for long stretches of the political history of the century that just ended.[13]

While initial conditions set the stage and the contours of the power distribution within which the civilians and the military interact, it is also critical to acknowledge the importance of the actual use that these actors make of those conditions to either reaffirm or change them to their advantage. The actual interaction in which these actors engage with ideas, initiatives, mobilization, or incorporation of new power resources also influences the pattern of their relations and may eventually help to change it and its corresponding distribution of power. For instance, the decision to join the inter-American military system after World War II in most cases resulted in empowerment of the military, affecting the pattern of civilian-military relations. The activation of the military's moderating power by political elites in Brazil and the formation of broad political coalitions, such as that promoted by APRA and the Odriístas in Peru in the 1950s, are examples of initiatives that affect the power distribution involved in a particular pattern of relations. Other examples are the impact of the formation of broad opposition coalitions or a successful call to mass mobilizations by the civilian opposition under military-authoritarian regimes. A focus on the structuring impact of founding conditions must therefore be balanced by a consideration of the actual ability and willingness of actors to pursue initiatives that strengthen their position within the existing pattern or to try to shake off its constraining impact upon them. Such a focus is essential to ascertaining the existence and impact of authoritarian legacies, as well as determining their location, their institutional carriers, and the actors that make them endure.

Transitions and Institutional Outcomes

Civilian-military relations in South America and southern Europe evolved in diverse ways, with different power distributions between civilians and the military and different forms of institutionalizing civilian-military relations. Spain and Greece, for instance, successfully attained civilian supremacy much earlier than Portugal, and each followed a different path. Also within South America there have been differences in the extent to which countries have been able to remove the military from center stage in politics and attain a level resembling civilian supremacy. While Argentina has gone the farthest, that goal has remained more elusive for Chile, with the other cases in intermediate positions. Overall, compared to southern Europe, South America has been much less successful in structuring patterns of military incorporation within clearly democratic standards.[14]

Much of the difference may be accounted for by initial and founding conditions of the successor democracies: the manner in which the military exit took place, the main features of the transition, and the early institutional arrangements that gave shape to the new postauthoritarian regimes. The nature of the first postauthoritarian arrangement—the transition outcome—was greatly affected by the strength of the forces that helped produce it. The formal power position of the military and the level of its unity and assertiveness were determinant in shaping the contours of the first postauthoritarian arrangement. Less formal factors, such as the perception of each side's legitimacy and the more or less conscious view of different actors of what could make it into the agenda and the public discourse, also affected the initial power situation.

The first institutionalized postauthoritarian political arrangement helps shape the institutions that differentially empower the civilians and the military for the ensuing period, within which attempts to promote democratization take place. Once that arrangement is inaugurated, it becomes very costly to attempt to introduce changes in the new political regime. Unsatisfied actors will attempt changes nonetheless, but they are the ones who will have to bear the burdens of initiating action and rallying support. For instance, the inauguration of an unfettered democracy would place heavier burdens upon a military that, critical of the transition outcome, attempted to expand its own prerogatives at the expense of an already accorded distribution of power. Conversely, in an incomplete democracy in which, for instance, the military had entrenched itself with excessive prerogatives, the burdens of initial reformist action would be placed on civilian democratizers. This reformist action is costly for a number of reasons and often because it implies questioning more or less formalized guarantees previously given the military in the course of liberalization or during the transition.[15] Thus initial conditions unevenly empower political actors in their attempts to change or maintain the contours of the first, inaugural postauthoritarian arrangement.[16]

But however influential the starting conditions may be, actors that started out strong may gradually be subdued, and initially weak actors may recover and strengthen later in the process. In Spain, for instance, the subordinate position of the military in the transition did not settle the military question once and for all. It did facilitate a clean democratic inauguration, placing the burden of subverting this order on the military, but ultimately it did not prevent the growth of military assertiveness, which severely tested the democracy and postponed the sound affirmation of democracy. It took a failed coup attempt, civilian leadership, a democratically minded monarch, public support, and a set of specific policies to firmly advance military subordination to the democratic order. In Argentina, a transition initiated from the ashes of the armed forces' political and military defeat proved not to be an insurmountable impediment for later reassertion of the military. Here too, a failed military uprising became the turning point that, with other factors, facilitated military subordination, however problematically. In Uruguay, conversely, the controlling position that the military held during the transition and the limitations imposed on the first democratic settlement did not in the end hinder the subsequent advancement of democracy. In Greece, with initial conditions roughly similar to those of Argentina, democratization nonetheless proceeded much more smoothly, at a faster pace, and with greater success.

These cases suggest that even if initial conditions are critical in shaping the first transition outcome, the fortunes of the post-transition process are also affected by many other elements. If initial conditions exert considerable influence by helping shape institutions with power distribution consequences, it is then up to the actors involved to mobilize, garner support, and prepare internally to exert the special effort to change the situation in pursuit of goals they value. They may decide that they are not able to do this; that it is not worth the risks, or that the alternative does not appear to be so bad after all; they may decide to jump in the dark, take the risks, and bear the consequences. Institutional settings and resources, as well as programmatic constructs of what is thought to be possible and permissible, provide the constraints but also the opportunities, and it is up to the actors involved to utilize, exploit, or avoid them.

Regime Institutionalization and Military Political Strength: Revisiting Initial Conditions in South America

All South American authoritarian regimes were military regimes. This meant that a transition from authoritarianism would involve an extrication of the military from government and, consequently, a large military role in the transition.[17] The military found added incentive to influence the transition to secure protection from retribution for itself and its members prior to exiting, especially if it was blamed for the regime's failures and crimes.

Military regimes differed, however, with regard to their institutionalization. Institutionalization in a military-authoritarian regime is the establishment of formal rules that regulate the power structure within the regime and the assignment of government functions to nonrepresentative or semirepresentative bodies, including the armed forces. A good indication of the intent to institutionalize a regime is the adoption of a new constitution, as in Brazil in 1967–69 and Chile in 1980.

One important consequence of institutionalization was stability in the military leadership. By presenting a minimum set of rules governing intramilitary relations and relations between the military and government, leadership succession, a critical problem for nondemocratic regimes, acquired predictability. Usually this was accomplished by attaining some degree of separation between the military as institution and the government. Stability in regime and military leadership—the ability to maintain an unchallenged hierarchical structure and cohesion—strengthened a military's position during the transition.

In Uruguay, Peru, and especially Argentina, the absence of a separation between the military as institution and the government led to relatively more internal bickering and hence instability at the top. Leadership of the military and the regime was thus more uncertain than in Brazil and Chile, weakening the military's position when faced with regime transitions. Another, perhaps more important, consequence of institutionalization was that constitutions provided a framework for dealing with demands from the opposition without having to resort to improvised responses. This was the case in Brazil and Chile and clearly not in Argentina, Peru, and Uruguay, which failed to attain institutionalization. In these three cases, the military was forced to devise a plan for extrication that included reaching out to the opposition.

An important distinction in transition modes is the degree of strength with which the ruling military entered the transition.[18] This determines whether the military may proceed without compromise, imposing its own terms, or must reach out to the opposition to compromise on the execution of the transition. In Chile and Brazil, the military faced the transition from a comparatively greater position of strength. It did not need to compromise with the opposition; rather, the opposition was itself forced to submit to the terms dictated by the outgoing authoritarian regime.[19] The military could remain confident about well-entrenched regulations and mechanisms to secure guarantees for itself and its interests into the future. These factors were not present in Uruguay, Peru, and Argentina, where the military faced the transition from a comparatively weaker position. Uruguay and Peru were cases of compromise, while Argentina was a special case of attempted, but failed, compromise (see McGuire 1995).

In the cases of weaker militaries, the opposition obtained most of what it desired for the transition: free elections (except in Uruguay, where the military kept the most popular politician from running in the first election) and either a new, democratically approved constitution or the resumption of the previous democratic constitution. In Brazil and Chile, stronger militaries executed transitions without compromise. The opposition could not obtain the democratic process it desired and submitted itself to the authoritarian constitutions.

Expectations Raised from the Transitions

These modes of transition led to different expectations about the military's capacity to constrain successor democracies. There were expectations of greater military restrictions to democracy in Brazil and Chile,[20] which were deemed to have recommenced it with ugly "birth defects" (Karl 1990; Hagopian 1990).

The military would constitute an obstacle to a full resumption of democracy in the other cases as well, but the manner in which they sought extrication was expected to prevent them from imposing weighty restrictions on democratic government. Still, the fact that in Uruguay a pact had formally been reached in which the military had made demands for specific action by the successor government made democracy look constrained as well. In Peru, the military exited with a few guarantees for itself that gave it autonomy in specific circumstances and with the expectation that military matters would be dealt with carefully and in consensus with its leadership. As insurgency flourished during successor civilian democratic administrations, the legislation that the military passed right before its exit proved to be critical in allowing it to operate in complete autonomy in areas declared as being in a state of emergency. In Argentina, the military exited with no guarantees other than those it granted itself, which the successor government promised not to honor. Argentina was the only case in which the military exited with no standing legislation or agreement with successor forces to protect it. In sum, transitions led to expectations of severe restrictions on democracy in Chile and Brazil, moderate restrictions in Uruguay and Peru, and unfettered democracy in Argentina.

How did expectations from the transitions match subsequent situations? Argentina, Chile, and Peru remained in positions consistent with the expectations that arose from their transitions. A decade later, Argentina and Chile were at opposite positions in terms of military constraints on democracy: a high level of constraints in Chile and a low one in Argentina. In these cases of correspondence between expectations and subsequent situations, the impact of the transition appears most clearly and decisively. Chile and Argentina reveal a break with historic patterns in the involvement of the military in politics. Argentina broke with the historic pattern of military intervention in politics that took hold for most of this century. Chile, on the contrary, broke with the pattern of no military intervention or participation in politics established in the democratic period between 1932 and 1973. In Peru, two decades later, constraints were not as strong as in Chile and remained consistent with the expectation of moderate restrictions.[21] On the other hand, constraints were lower than expected over a decade earlier in Uruguay and in Brazil.

Legacies of Transitions and Legal-Institutional Factors

Transitions produce outcomes—postauthoritarian arrangements—that differentially empower the military and civilian officials and political elites for the postauthoritarian period. In Argentina, for instance, the transition outcome allowed for an assertive civilian attempt on the human rights issue and the initiation of military reforms. The military was put on the defensive. However, the very attempts at retribution and reform ignited a reaction in the military that allowed it to reassert itself, rebelling repeatedly in pursuit of its goals. In the end, military contestation was eliminated in Argentina because the government appeased the military with amnesties and pardons and because of the failure of the last rebellious attempt, which made it possible to rid the army of rebellious leaders. Further weakening of the military's political clout was aided by the imperatives of economic and fiscal reform (Franko 1994). This, however, would have been impossible without the institutional outcome of the transition, which returned unrestricted constitutional powers to civilian government facing a weakened military.

In Chile, on the other hand, the transition produced a postauthoritarian arrangement based on the authoritarian constitution, which assigned large prerogatives to the military. The burden of initiating reform to remove the military from positions of influence fell on the successor government. Reform attempts were tried repeatedly but failed because of the rigidities imposed by the constitution itself. Constitutional restrictions on the successor government found renewed support in the power of parties of the right in Congress. Former allies of the military in the authoritarian regime, representatives of these parties, jointly with the nonelected senators, denied the votes necessary for reforms.

In Peru, the transition left the military with much autonomy, especially in its capacity to intervene against subversion. Trying not to antagonize the military, the first successor government respected its autonomy and, by inaction, contributed in practice to expand it. After the transition, the military nurtured this autonomy and substantially expanded it, aided by the dramatic surge of subversive violence and the virtual freedom of action that civilian authorities gave the military, with the exception of the few attempts to the contrary during part of Alan García's failed administration. So much did this autonomy develop that, as Degregori and Rivera (1994, 14) convincingly argued, Fujimori's decrees on military role expansion did no more than match actual roles to prerogatives. It is perfectly conceivable, however, that military prerogatives could have been reduced had there been assertive action on the part of civilian administrations, lessening the impact of the transition. However, the view prevailed, especially during Belaúnde's successor administration, that civilian rule could best be stabilized by leaving the military alone.[22]

Turning to Uruguay, why couldn't the military sustain its aspirations on prerogatives well into the successor regime? The answer highlights the importance of legal-formal factors: in Uruguay, unlike Chile, the military failed to institutionalize an extrication from direct rule with an authoritarian constitution. In lieu of that, the military attempted to retain some of those aspirations in a transition pact. Other than the restoration of elections and the previous constitution, this pact did not produce a binding agreement, in part because there was no written document. Institutional Act 19, which followed the pact, established the continuation of the National Security Council for a limited time. Only Congress could have, as the military had desired, reformed the constitution to incorporate it permanently. In addition to the lack of a binding agreement or legal legacy, the military in the successor regime had to face up to the fact that during its rule it had antagonized all political parties, both the left and the two traditional parties. Therefore, other than on the issue of the *ley de caducidad*, the military in Uruguay, unlike Chile, had no allies among political parties, nobody willing to defend and promote its legacy. Expectations from the transition could have been satisfied had the latter expressed military demands in formal-legal, binding terms. The successor parties could have then tried to suppress those demands.

But it would have been costlier for them, since they would have had to assume the burden of changing a formalized agreement or law. Had the military succeeded in the constitutional referendum in 1980, as it did in Chile, a transition would most likely have taken a very different course.

Along with Chile, Brazil entered the transition with an authoritarian constitution and with a strong military that could afford to reject the opposition's campaign for a new constitution or direct elections. Why, then, did military influence erode?[23] Why did expectations from the transition not materialize as they did in Chile? Again, the answer lies with legal-institutional factors and demands a closer look at the authoritarian constitution of 1967–69. The constitution comprised several institutional acts passed by the military after 1964 and highlighted national security functions for the military. But it established the primacy of the president over the armed forces and contained "liberal" elements such as the existence of a Congress, political parties, and opposition. Military rule thus relied on the primacy of the executive and its ability to secure a majority for its support party in Congress. For this, the president empowered himself with an additional resource—Institutional Act No. 5 (IA5)—which allowed him to dictate emergency measures at his discretion. When the military decided to start a process of liberalization, it dropped IA5 and relied instead on specific decrees that could help it contain the rising electoral power of the opposition and its representation in Congress. We know that the government ultimately failed in the attempt to control the forces unleashed by its own liberalization process that resulted in the 1985 election of a civilian president.

Without the control of the presidency, the military no longer could resort to emergency decrees to secure its interests. Now it could only rely on the constitution, but the constitution did not specify any special guarantees for a military out of government. In addition, no constitutional clause stood in the way of reform or the drafting of a new constitution. Therefore, nothing impeded the new president from submitting in 1985 a constitutional amendment to enable the Congress elected in 1986 to produce a new constitution. A constituent assembly thus offered an open-ended process that could substantially alter the legal-institutional basis of military power. In Chile, on the other hand, the constitution made sure that military powers remained enhanced even if the military no longer controlled the executive. The Chilean constitution established high requirements for reform and specific military prerogatives in the National Security Council and was accompanied by organic laws of constitutional status that restricted presidential powers over the military.

The new centrality that the constituent process gave Congress in Brazil led the military to organize several ways of influencing its deliberations. While military influence in a constituent process obviously goes against the sovereignty of elected representation, it did at least signal that the military was willing to abide by its decisions. The constitution approved in 1988 reflected the military's influence on a number of issues but it also denied some of the military aspirations (Mesquita Neto 1995).

In sum, Brazilian civilian elites were freer to transform the military legacy than they were in Chile. The military in Brazil tried to maintain core elements of its power by influencing elected officials and negotiating with them instead of imposing a rigid legal-institutional legacy. This helps to account for the lessened prerogatives of the Brazilian military relative to expectations from the transition. Certainly, the weakness of political parties and the absence of party discipline (Lamounier 1996; Mainwaring 1999), peculiar features of Brazil's political system, facilitated the military's strategy of systematic lobbying on civilian officials. However, comparatively lessened prerogatives are not the same as absence of authoritarian legacies, as these legacies continue to endure in numerous areas, such as education, justice, and defense (see Pereira 1999; Zaverucha 1997; Rizzo de Oliveira and Alves Soares 2000).

■

This brief review shows that differences in the manner in, and extent to which, military power constrains new democracies have been strongly influenced by the mode of transition from authoritarian rule. In none of the countries considered were the patterns of previous periods of democratic rule simply reproduced in the new democracies. Chile and Argentina represent a stark break with previous patterns. In the other cases, the military's influence or form of participation acquired new traits.

The expectations raised from the transition on the level of restriction that the military would impose in new democracies were clearly matched in Argentina, Chile, and Peru. In Brazil and Uruguay, where military influence turned out to be lower than expected, the major factors were also related to the transition. The comparative exercise highlighted the importance of formal legal-institutional factors in the transition and the type of institutionalization attained by military-authoritarian regimes. Militaries were not able to sustain in the postauthoritarian regime the power and influence with which they entered the transition if their power was not backed by formal-legal arrangements. These arrangements unevenly raised the cost of action for contending actors in the process ensuing after the end of the transition. Clearly, for instance, it was harder for Chilean authorities to curtail military power, which was backed by an authoritarian constitution, than it was for Uruguayan or Argentinean authorities, who were not constrained by such arrangements.

It might seem somewhat of a paradox that formal-legal factors might play such a role, especially in South America, a region not known for exemplary rule of law. However, while these factors may not pervade all spheres of politics and society, they certainly take added importance in the regulation of relations between state institutions. And while this role is not indicative of a special regard for the law on the part of actors that had not too long before toppled legally established regimes, it does support the notion that institutions, and the legal-institutional arrangements that frame them, do indeed have important consequences.[24]

These considerations are also valid for the southern European cases. The collapse of the Colonels' regime in Greece allowed the new regime swiftly to create a new constitutional order. In Spain, the *reforma–ruptura* characterization of the transition pointed to the quite radical break with Francoism while proceeding from within its very institutions. The astuteness of reformers consisted precisely in utilizing the regime's own legal mechanisms to promote blanket reforms: a referendum to end the old and call for elections with constitution-making consequences. Reformers followed established legal routes to shake off any legal-constitutional constraints. In Portugal, on the contrary, the collapse of authoritarian rule led to a new constitution conceived under heavy military tutelage. The establishment of full democracy thus had to wait until those constraints were removed through constitutional reform. Since a deadline for these reforms had been set in the original constitutional agreement, constraints were in fact temporary, although their actual elimination depended on the actors' relative empowerment in the interim. These differences in southern Europe affected the nature and quality of their early postauthoritarian arrangements.

The legacy of military rule is particularly visible in all the South American cases. All of them faced severe restrictions from the military in the human rights area. Even the cases that appeared the most successful in terms of lesser military restrictions on democracy were unable to punish criminals and dispense justice. In addition, the full assertion of civilian control remains a distant goal. Even in those cases usually deemed most successful— Argentina and Uruguay—there remain areas where civilian officials have no access, such as military education, or where the jurisdiction of civilian courts is restricted, while jurisdiction for military justice remains broad. Also, military reform and modernization programs have for the most part been conceived and carried out by the military exclusively (Pion-Berlin 1997). And where they are in control, civilians often have been guided by a desire to reassure the military and to not initiate conflict with its goals and interests.

However, the impact of variables specific to the transition on the extent and manner of military influence in the new democracies should not obscure the role of other factors beyond the transition. Among them one should find, for instance, the economy and its effect on budgets; political parties, their ties to the military, and the policies they put forth; political violence; international variables; bargaining processes animated by actors with changing relative empowerment; and others that, all jointly, have affected the authoritarian legacy, strengthening or weakening it.

In Spain, for instance, a crucial power shift in favor of civilian democratic reformers came about as a result of the failure of the attempted coup of February 1981. The vast reform process in the military sector initiated by the Socialist government in 1982 further changed those power relations, irretrievably empowering civilian control. A good indicator of the magnitude of the changes that had taken place in a country that had experienced pervasive military power during long stretches of this century was the widespread discussion in May 2000 about replacing the traditional military parade celebrating Army Day with a simple celebration of Spain's participation in international peace missions. Spain's democratization and the accompanying empowerment of its political authorities completely eliminated any traces of the army as a carrier of authoritarian legacies.

In Chile, change in power relations had not gone far enough to eliminate constitutional traces of authoritarianism and the powers it gave the military. Nonetheless, they had changed enough to allow what had been deemed unthinkable: the military's recognition during the year 2000 of responsibilities in the violation of human rights under Pinochet's dictatorship and the arrest of General Pinochet in his own country for the crimes of kidnapping and murder of political opponents (Zalaquett 2000).

This chapter has proposed an analytical focus that considers the actual ability and willingness of actors to pursue initiatives that strengthen their position within the existing pattern or that shake off its constraining impact upon them. It has, at the same time, insisted that these actors' efforts must be viewed within the context of the structuring impact of founding conditions. Just as the impact of civilian-military relations on the shape of political regimes during the military-authoritarian period, or the preceding democratic periods, could find their founding conditions in the background to the coups of the 1960s and 1970s or the social disruptions of the 1930s, so may the postauthoritarian period find defining characteristics in the founding conditions of the transitions. However, it is the variegated set of factors involved in changing those conditions, rather than the military per se, that will be determinant in carrying authoritarian legacies over to successor democratic regimes. Those conditions will present different opportunities and constraints for the chances of ridding polities and societies of authoritarian legacies.

NOTES

1. All of the present may be said to be the result of the past. Still, what features of this past—namely authoritarianism—endure more vigorously in the present is precisely the purpose of an inquiry into authoritarian legacies.

2. For a recent discussion of these issues in a different context, see Katzenstein (1996).

3. For an extended discussion, see Held (1987). For a study of the relationship between a Leninist party and the military, with a focus on civilian control, see Colton (1979).

4. Armies may differ, for instance, in the extent to which command structures at lower levels are given operational initiative and autonomy in the field.

5. This instrumental character is often disputed by the military itself, whose ideological outlook has led it to perceive itself as a state power of equal standing with state authority emanating from democratic validation. This may in fact be one of the authoritarian legacies carried over by the military itself. The problematic nature of this instrumental character is inherent in the conceptualization of the military as a professional institution that, as such, requires a client. The client is society and the state, which also are its superiors, though not always recognized as such by military ideological outlooks developed from within the "national security" doctrines that pervaded Latin American militaries. For general statements of this question, see Feaver (1996, 1998).

6. Although other features were indeed altered as a consequence of participation in government. In Chile, for instance, the Junta de Gobierno maintained much power throughout the authoritarian period. In Spain, military chiefs participated in the council of ministers and in state administrative posts throughout the country. See Barros (2002) and Agüero (1995).

7. The civilianizing trend was argued more forcefully in Moskos (1978). For an assessment of contending perspectives, see Martin and McCrate (1984). For other more recent views, see Moskos, Williams, and Segal (2000).

8. This literature has been more successful in describing the forms of professionalism and the doctrines and ideological tenets developed than in providing a careful account of the historical determinants of the resulting patterns or civil-military relations and accompanying military "minds." See Loveman (1999). For a recent account of the role of the military in state formation, see López-Alves (2000).

9. I borrow much of the following two sections from Agüero (2001).

10. See, for instance, Huntington (1957), Abrahamsson (1972), Lowenthal (1986), Fitch (1986), O'Donnell (1986b), and Stepan (1988).

11. Indeed, this approach has been much used in the study of civil-military relations, both in well-established democracies and in civilian-controlled authoritarian regimes. In these cases, a focus on the scope and means of influence over decisions (such as that introduced in Colton 1979) and on the agenda dominating civilian-military interactions has proved to be quite useful. The approach, therefore, does not assume that the normal and typical state of relations is one of conflict. In fact, such cooperation must take place for democratic politics to institutionalize into stable regimes.

12. For a more general statement of this kind of approach, see Krasner (1984) and North (1990).

13. Collier and Collier's (1991) analysis of the political legacies of critical junctures in modes of labor incorporation could be applied to a study of the regime legacies of founding patterns of modes of civilian-military relations. A pathbreaking analysis in this direction has been initiated in López-Alves (2000).

14. This comparison is fully developed in Agüero (1995).

15. Although inaction also may be costly in the long run if it leads to erosion of popular support for these civilian groups and to the institutionalized fixation of excessive prerogatives for the military.

16. For similar kinds of path-dependent approaches, see Stark (1992), and Przeworski (1991). See also Cammack (1992).

17. The arguments in this section are more fully developed in Agüero (1998).

18. For other ways of classifying transitions in the literature, see Mainwaring (1992) and McGuire (1995).

19. The distinction of transition paths of *compromise* and *no compromise* is made in Bruszt and Stark (1992).

20. In Brazil, these expectations were confirmed after the lamentable circumstances of Sarney's assumption of the presidency, which frustrated the opposition's hopes of a sharper break with military rule. Sarney had been elected as vice president in the opposition ticket, but Tancredo Neves, the president-elect, suffered a stroke on the eve of the transfer of power and died a few weeks later. Until six months before the election, Sarney had headed the official party that supported the military. He then led a splinter faction to join the opposition. The alliance of Sarney's group with the opposition allowed for their victory in the electoral college. Neves's death, however, lessened the successor government's break with the past.

Sarney ruled with substantial military support, which helped him resist pressures to shorten his term. Also, the military intervened in a wide array of policy areas.

21. Fujimori's abuse of power and tampering with democratic procedures and institutions, especially around his second reelection, make it hard to view his regime as democratic. Nonetheless, formally, the military, even if in practice it colluded with the regime, did not enjoy as much autonomy and as many monitoring prerogatives as in Chile.

22. Fernando Belaúnde, elected president immediately after the military's exit, had refused to cooperate with the military's orchestrated transition and had been the president deposed in the coup of 1968. These experiences led him to deal cautiously with the military in his second administration, which in fact meant tolerating its autonomy.

23. I take the view here that military influence in Brazil has eroded significantly, but this should be seen relative to the early phases of the transition, particularly during Sarney's administration, and to the expectations that this transition raised about military influence in the future. Nonetheless, there is wide disagreement among scholars regarding the extent of this influence. While Hunter (1997) argues about erosion of military influence, Zaverucha (1994) argues the contrary. Authors who consider other dimensions, such as military courts and the militarization of justice, have emphasized enduring authoritarian legacies (Pereira 1999). See also D'Araujo and Castro (2000).

24. Mussolini was, after all, demoted by the Fascist Council, opening the way for the king to force him out of office. See Pasquino (1986) and Barros (2002).

REFERENCES

Abrahamsson, Bengt. 1972. *Military Professionalization and Political Power.* Beverly Hills, Calif.: Sage Publications.

Agüero, Felipe. 1995. *Soldiers, Civilians, and Democracy: Post-Franco Spain in Comparative Perspective.* Baltimore, Md.: Johns Hopkins University Press.

———. 1998. "Legacies of Transitions: Institutionalization, the Military, and Democracy in South America." *Mershon International Studies Review* 42, no. 2:383–404.

———. 1999. "Las fuerzas armadas en una época de transición: Perspectivas para el afianzamiento de la democracia en América latina." In *Control civil y fuerzas armadas en las nuevas democracias latinoamericanas,* ed. Rut Diamint. Buenos Aires: Universidad Torcuato Di Tella, Nuevohacer, Grupo Editor Latinoamericano.

———. 2001. "Institutions, Transitions and Bargaining: Civilians and the Military in Shaping Post-Authoritarian Regimes." In *Civil-Military Relations in Latin America: New Analytical Perspectives,* ed. David Pion-Berlin. Chapel Hill: University of North Carolina Press.

————. 2002. "Chile: Unfinished Transition and Increased Political Competition." In *Constructing Democratic Governance*, ed. Jorge Domínguez and Michael Shifter. Baltimore, Md.: Johns Hopkins University Press.

Aguilar, Paloma. 1996. *Memoria y olvido de la guerra civil española*. Madrid: Alianza Editorial.

Bañón Martínez, Rafael, and Thomas A. Barker, eds. 1988. *Armed Forces and Society in Spain: Past and Present*. Boulder, Colo.: Social Science Monographs.

Barros, Robert. 2002. *Law and Dictatorship: Military Constitutionalism and the Pinochet Regime in Chile, 1973–1989*. New York: Cambridge University Press.

Bermeo, Nancy. 1997. "Myths of Moderation: Confrontation and Conflict during Democratic Transitions." *Comparative Politics* 29, no. 3:305–22.

Bowles, Samuel, and Herbert Gintis. 1987. *Democracy and Capitalism: Property, Community, and the Contradictions of Modern Social Thought*. New York: Basic Books.

Brenes, Arnoldo, and Kevin Casas. 1998. *Soldados como empresarios: Los negocios de los militares en Centroamérica*. San José, Costa Rica: Fundación Arias y COSUDE.

Bruszt, László, and David Stark. 1992. "Remaking the Political Field in Hungary: From the Politics of Confrontation to the Politics of Competition." In *Eastern Europe in Revolution*, ed. Ivo Banac. Ithaca, N.Y.: Cornell University Press.

Brysk, Alison. 2000. "Democratizing Civil Society in Latin America." *Journal of Democracy* 11, no. 3:151–65.

Cammack, Paul. 1992. "The New Institutionalism: Predatory Rule, Institutional Persistence, and Macro-Social Change." *Economy and Society* 21 (November):397–429.

Collier, Ruth Berins, and David Collier. 1991. *Shaping the Political Arena*. Princeton, N.J.: Princeton University Press.

Colton, Timothy. 1979. *Commissars, Commanders and Civilian Authority: The Structure of Soviet Military Politics*. Cambridge, Mass.: Harvard University Press.

D'Araujo, Maria Celina, and Celso Castro, eds. 2000. *Democracia e forças armadas no cone sul*. Rio de Janeiro: Editora FGV.

Degregori, Carlos Iván, and Carlos Rivera. 1994. *Perú 1980–1993: Fuerzas armadas, subversión y democracia*. In Documento de Trabajo 53. Lima: Insituto de Estudios Peruanos.

Desch, Michael. 1998. "Soldiers, States, and Structures: The End of the Cold War and Weakening U.S. Civilian Control." *Armed Forces and Society* 24, no. 3 (spring):389–405.

Di Palma, Giuseppe. 1982. "Italy: Is There a Legacy and Is It Fascist?" In *From Dictatorship to Democracy*, ed. John H. Herz. Westport, Conn.: Greenwood Press.

Feaver, Peter. 1996. "The Civil-Military Problematique: Huntington, Janowitz, and the Question of Civilian Control." *Armed Forces and Society* 23, no. 2:149–78.

————. 1998. "Crisis as Shirking: An Agency Theory Explanation of the Souring of American Civil-Military Relations." *Armed Forces and Society* 24, no. 3:407–34.

Fitch, J. Samuel. 1986. "Armies and Politics in Latin America: 1975–1985." In *Armies and Politics in Latin America*, ed. Abraham F. Lowenthal and J. Samuel Fitch. New York: Holmes and Meier.

———. 1987. "The Theoretical Model Underlying the Analysis of Civil-Military Relations in Contemporary Latin American Democracies: Core Assumptions." Unpublished papers, Inter-American Dialogue.

Franko, Patrice. 1994. "De Facto Demilitarization: Budget-Driven Downsizing in Latin America." *Journal of Interamerican Studies and World Affairs* (spring): 37–73.

Garretón, Manuel Antonio. 1995. *Hacia una nueva era política: Estudio sobre las democratizaciones.* Santiago: Fondo de Cultura Económico.

Gillespie, Charles. 1986. "Uruguay's Transition from Collegial Military-Technocratic Rule." In *Transitions from Authoritarian Rule: Latin America*, ed. Guillermo O'Donnell, Philippe C. Schmitter, and Laurence Whitehead. Baltimore, Md.: Johns Hopkins University Press.

Hagopian, Frances. 1990. "Democracy by Undemocratic Means? Elites, Political Pacts, and Regime Transition in Brazil." *Comparative Political Studies* 23:147–70.

Held, David. 1987. *Models of Democracy.* Stanford, Calif.: Stanford University Press.

Hirschman, Albert. 1970. *Exit, Voice and Loyalty: Responses to Decline in Firms, Organizations and States.* Cambridge, Mass.: Harvard University Press.

Holsti, Ole. R. 1998–99. "A Widening Gap between the U.S. Military and Civilian Society? Some Evidence, 1976–96." *International Security* 23, no. 3:5–42.

Hunter, Wendy. 1997. *Eroding Military Influence in Brazil: Politicians against Soldiers.* Chapel Hill: University of North Carolina Press.

Huntington, Samuel P. 1957. *The Soldier and the State: The Theory and Politics of Civil-Military Relations.* New York: Vintage Books.

Janowitz, Morris. 1971. *The Professional Soldier: A Social and Political Portrait.* New York: Free Press.

Karl, Terry Lynn. 1990. "Dilemmas of Democratization in Latin America." *Comparative Politics* 23:1–21.

Katahara, Eiichi. 2001. "Japan: From Containment to Normalization." In Muthiah Alagappa, ed., *Coercion and Governance: The Declining Political Role of the Military in Asia.* Stanford, Calif.: Stanford University Press.

Katzenstein, Peter J. 1996. *Cultural Norms and National Security: Police and Military in Postwar Japan.* Ithaca, N.Y.: Cornell University Press.

Krasner, Stephen. 1984. "Approaches to the State: Alternative Conceptions and Historical Dynamics." *Comparative Politics* 16:223–46.

Lamounier, Bolívar. 1996. "Brazil: The Hyperactive Paralysis Syndrome." In *Constructing Democratic Governance: Latin America and the Caribbean in the 1990s*, ed. Abraham F. Lowenthal and Jorge I. Domínguez. Baltimore, Md.: Johns Hopkins University Press,

Linz, Juan J. 1970. "An Authoritarian Regime: Spain." In *Mass Politics*, ed. Erik Allardt and Stein Rokkan. New York: Free Press.

————. 1973. "The Future of an Authoritarian Situation or the Institutionalization of an Authoritarian Regime." In *Authoritarian Brazil: Origins, Policies, and Future,* ed. Alfred Stepan. New Haven, Conn.: Yale University Press.

————. 1975. "Totalitarian and Authoritarian Regimes." In *Handbook of Political Science,* ed. Fred Greenstein and Nelson Polsby. Reading, Mass.: Addison-Wesley.

————. 1978. *Crisis, Breakdown and Reequilibration.* Baltimore, Md.: Johns Hopkins University Press.

————. 1986. "Il fattore tempo nei mutamenti di regime." *Teoria Politica* 2, no. 1.

Linz, Juan J., and Alfred Stepan. 1992. "Political Identities and Electoral Sequences: Spain, the Soviet Union and Yugoslavia." *Daedalus* 121 (spring): 123–39.

————. 1996. *Problems of Democratic Transition and Consolidation: Southern Europe, South America and Post-communist Europe.* Baltimore, Md.: Johns Hopkins University Press.

López-Alves, Fernando. 2000. *State Formation and Democracy in Latin America, 1810–1900.* Durham, N.C.: Duke University Press.

Loveman, Brian. 1999. *For La Patria: Politics and the Armed Forces in Latin America.* Wilmington, Del.: Scholarly Resources.

Lowenthal, Abraham F. 1986. "Armies and Politics in Latin America: Introduction to the First Edition." In *Armies and Politics in Latin America,* ed. Abraham F. Lowenthal and J. Samuel Fitch. New York: Holmes and Meier.

————, ed. 1991. *Exporting Democracy: The United States and Latin America.* Baltimore, Md.: Johns Hopkins University Press.

Mainwaring, Scott. 1992. "Transitions to Democracy and Democratic Consolidation: Theoretical and Comparative Issues." In *Issues in Democratic Consolidation: The New South American Democracies in Comparative Perspective,* ed. Scott Mainwaring, Guillermo O'Donnell, and J. Samuel Valenzuela. Notre Dame, Ind.: University of Notre Dame Press.

————. 1999. *Rethinking Party Systems in the Third Wave of Democratization: The Case of Brazil.* Stanford, Calif.: Stanford University Press.

Martin, Michel Louis, and Ellen Stern McCrate, eds. 1984. *The Military, Militarism and the Polity: Essays in Honor of Morris Janowitz.* New York: Free Press.

McGuire, James W. 1995. "Interim Government and Democratic Consolidation: Argentina in Comparative Perspective." In *Between States: Interim Governments and Democratic Transitions,* ed. Yossi Shain and Juan J. Linz. New York: Cambridge University Press.

Mesquita Neto, Paulo de. 1995. "From Intervention to Participation: The Transformation of Military Politics in Brazil." Ph.D. diss., Columbia University.

Michels, Robert. 1962. *Political Parties.* New York: Free Press.

Moskos, Charles. 1978. "From Institution to Occupation: Trends in Military Organization." *Armed Forces and Society* 4:41–50.

Moskos, Charles C., John Allen Williams, and David R. Segal, eds. 2001. *The Postmodern Military: Armed Forces after the Cold War.* New York: Oxford University Press.

North, Douglass C. 1990. *Institutions, Institutional Change and Economic Performance.* New York: Cambridge University Press.

O'Donnell, Guillermo. 1973. *Modernization and Bureaucratic Authoritarianism.* Berkeley: Institute of International Studies, University of California.

———. 1986a. "Introduction to the Latin American Cases." In *Transition from Authoritarian Rule: Latin America,* ed. Guillermo O'Donnell, Philippe C. Schmitter, and Laurence Whitehead. Baltimore, Md.: Johns Hopkins University Press, 1986.

———. 1986b. "Modernization and Military Coups: Theory, Comparisons, and the Argentine Case." In *Armies and Politics in Latin America,* ed. Abraham F. Lowenthal and J. Samuel Fitch. New York: Holmes and Meier, 1986.

———. 1992. "Transitions, Continuities, and Paradoxes." In *Issues in Democratic Consolidation: The New South American Democracies in Comparative Perspective,* ed. Scott Mainwaring, Guillermo O'Donnell, and J. Samuel Valenzuela. Notre Dame, Ind.: University of Notre Dame Press, 1992.

O'Donnell, Guillermo, and Philippe C. Schmitter. 1986. *Transitions from Authoritarian Rule: Tentative Conclusions about Uncertain Democracies.* Baltimore, Md.: Johns Hopkins University Press.

Pasquino, Gianfranco. 1986. "The Demise of the First Fascist Regime and Italy's Transition to Democracy: 1943–1948." In *Transitions from Authoritarian Rule: Southern Europe,* ed. Guillermo O'Donnell, Philippe C. Schmitter, and Laurence Whitehead. Baltimore, Md.: Johns Hopkins University Press.

Pereira, Anthony W. 1999. "Virtual Legality: The Use and Reform of Military Justice in Brazil, the Southern Cone and Mexico." Paper no. 99/00–2, David Rockefeller Center for Latin American Studies, Working Papers on Latin America.

Perlmutter, Amos. 1977. *The Military and Politics in Modern Times.* New Haven, Conn.: Yale University Press.

Pion-Berlin, David. 1991. "Between Confrontation and Accommodation: Military and Government Policy in Democratic Argentina." *Journal of Latin American Studies* 23 (October): 543–71.

———. 1997. *Through Corridors of Power: Institutions and Civil-Military Relations in Argentina.* College Station: Pennsylvania State University Press.

Przeworski, Adam. 1991. *Democracy and the Market: Political and Economic Reforms in Eastern Europe and Latin America.* New York: Cambridge University Press.

Rizzo de Oliveira, Eliézer, and Samuel Alves Soares. 2000. "Forças armadas, direção política e formato institucional." In *Democracia e forças armadas no Cone Sul,* ed. Maria Celina D'Araujo and Celso Castro. Rio de Janeiro: Editora FGV.

Sain, Marcelo Fabián. 2000. "Democracia e forças armadas: Entre a subordinaçao militar e os 'defeitos' civis." In *Democracia e forças armadas no Cone Sul,* ed. Maria Celina D'Araujo and Celso Castro. Rio de Janeiro: Editora FGV.

Stark, David. 1992. "Path Dependence and Privatization Strategies in East Central Europe." *East European Politics and Society* 6:17–53.

Stepan, Alfred. 1986. "Paths towards Redemocratization: Theoretical and Comparative Considerations." In *Transitions from Authoritarian Rule: Comparative Perspectives,* ed. Guillermo O'Donnell, Philippe C. Schmitter, and Laurence Whitehead. Baltimore, Md.: Johns Hopkins University Press.

———. 1988. *Rethinking Military Politics: Brazil and the Southern Cone.* Princeton, N.J.: Princeton University Press.

Valenzuela, J. Samuel. 1992. "Democratic Consolidation in Post-Transitional Settings: Notions, Process and Facilitating Conditions." In *Issues in Democratic Consolidation: The New South American Democracies in Comparative Perspective,* ed. Scott Mainwaring, Guillermo O'Donnell, and J. Samuel Valenzuela. Notre Dame, Ind: University of Notre Dame Press, 1992.

Weber, Max. 1968. "Bureaucracy and Political Leadership." In *State and Society,* ed. Reinhard Bendix. Boston: Little, Brown.

Zalaquett, José. 2000. "La Mesa de Diálogo sobre Derechos Humanos y el proceso de transición política en Chile." *Estudios Públicos* 79: 5–30.

Zaverucha, Jorge. 1994. *Rumor de sabres: Tutela militar ou control civil?* São Paulo: Editora Ática.

———. 1997. "Prerogativas militares: De Sarney a Cardoso." *Monitor Publico* (Rio de Janeiro) 4, no. 12.

7

The Persistence of the Mano Dura

Authoritarian Legacies and Policing in Brazil and the Southern Cone

ANTHONY W. PEREIRA & MARK UNGAR

In Latin America, violence by the police—and its support by the law, courts, and state agencies—was an integral part of authoritarianism. But the transitions to democracy did not have the impact on police forces that they did on more prominent actors such as political parties and military high commands. *Police* here refers to state security forces responsible for domestic "law and order," which includes military and intelligence agencies as well as police forces. Public security policies and police use of an "iron fist" (*mano dura*) approach to law enforcement were not part of the transition negotiations, so the police did not face questions about their personnel, training, practices, orientation, loyalties, and responsibilities to other state agencies and the public—if they faced them at all—until later in the democratic era. As a result, practices such as the summary execution of criminal suspects have endured throughout the region. Only when public concern about police violence, corruption, and lack of accountability rose has police reform been enacted. But even when reforms have been put in place, police strength and insulation have prevented many of them from being carried out.

This chapter focuses on efforts by contemporary governments to reverse authoritarian legacies to state security forces, which are vital to the understanding of Latin America's new democracies.[1] These forces are made up primarily of police forces and military agencies with internal policing

authorities. The continuation of close links between the military and the police in much of Latin America and the military's domestic deployment do not
allow a neat analytical separation between the two. Throughout Latin America,
widespread abuses by these forces continue to be left unpunished as the
range of targets has expanded from political troublemakers to entire sectors
of society, particularly those that are "marginal." Institutional restructuring,
better-designed laws, and greater public involvement in demanding state protection of citizenship rights and the accountability of security forces are all
necessary to alter such conduct. Few changes measure the deepening of democratic standards better than the control of state security forces that have long
been instruments of repression and have acted with impunity.

The chapter examines such reform in Brazil, Argentina, Chile, and Uruguay, neighboring South American countries that have similar political histories and contemporary conditions. It first discusses assumptions about
policing and democratic transition, showing the extent to which practices associated with modern authoritarianism—such as repressive tactics and a
lack of judicial oversight—had already existed and in most cases were only
reinforced by recent authoritarian regimes. We argue that the weakness of
Latin America's contemporary democracies should be attributed not just to
the regimes immediately preceding them but also to earlier regimes—some of
them formally democratic—that diminished accountability and civil rights.

Examining contemporary democratization in the four cases, we then assert that the impact of the mode of transition was delayed and mediated by
"normal" post-transition politics. In particular, we found that public support
for and mobilization around police reform are crucial to its enactment and
success. In response to society's heightened postauthoritarian awareness
of the state's repressive potential (Sayan 1999),[2] the bulk of such reforms
in most countries have been based on restrictions of police power, including
removal of military control over police operations, purges of abusive officials,
new investigatory and oversight agencies, and restrictions on detention. But
with increases in economic inequality and violent crime throughout Latin
America, public safety and order have also become a priority. Because most
reform involves reductions in police power, forces seen as effective against
crime are generally less pressured to change than those seen as ineffective.
Most Latin American societies have a high tolerance for police excess if it is
seen as a price of effective crime control; citizens may be distrustful or even
scared of police power but "confident" in its effectiveness and fearful that
reforms will reduce it.[3] But when crime and police excesses increase simultaneously, citizens start to associate the police's power with their inability to

TABLE 7.1 Police Reform in Argentina, Brazil, Chile, and Uruguay after Democratic Transitions

Country	Mode of Transition	Degree of Police Centralization	Degree of Public Confidence in Police[a]	Extent of Police Reform[b]
Argentina	Collapse (1983)	Decentralized forces	16%	High
Brazil	Pact (1985)	Decentralized forces	33%	Medium
Chile	Pact (1990)	Unitary force	63%	Low
Uruguay	Pact (1984)	Unitary force	47%	Medium

[a] The question was, "How much confidence do you have in the police?" and the percentage is of those responding "a great deal" or "some" (Basanez, Lagos, and Beltran 1996: Table 27H).
[b] Qualitative assessment by authors on the basis of information summarized in Table 7.2.

control crime. Police officials are so involved in corruption and are so unaccountable, many societies realize, that reform is needed to improve their performance. This shift in opinion is most important for reform because it gives officials the political support to enact change. As Table 7.1 suggests, in fact, there is an inverse relationship between public confidence in the police and the level of police reform. Public confidence in the police is lowest in Argentina, where police reform after the transition has gone the furthest, and highest in Chile, where it has barely occurred at all.

Third, we find that the level of centralization greatly influences how, but not whether, police reform takes place. Police reform is a national issue in unitary states such as Chile and Uruguay, where the main police forces are national, but is a regional issue in the federal states of Brazil and Argentina, where the main police forces are under state (in Brazil) or provincial (in Argentina) governments. Reform in unitary states thus requires more political capital than it does in decentralized states, but unitary states also offer reformers the possibility to reengineer the country's entire set of security forces in one fell swoop. In decentralized states, the trade-off is reversed.[4] Even when sufficient political support for police reform does not exist nationally, reformers can succeed in one region. However, this creates internal discrepancies with piecemeal and heterogeneous changes that do not exactly encourage those states and provinces more resistant to change. A poorly implemented decentralization, in addition, may lead to greater abuse. Historically, centralization was promoted to make state services more effective. But because of the state's limited capacity, centralization tended to reduce its presence in outlying areas, causing a de facto decentralization in which local powers enforced the law. Contemporary democracies, in an effort to be both more efficient and more accessible, are now decentralizing many state functions. But this process may repeat historical patterns: when decentralization turns over administrative burdens to local governments unprepared to balance them with individual rights and societal demands, oversight of the police is likely to be weakened. When involving basic constitutional guarantees, therefore, decentralization may inadvertently increase abuse in localities with lower levels of accountability.

The Question of Authoritarian "Legacies"

The extent to which the behavior of state security forces in Latin America can be described as an authoritarian legacy is controversial for several reasons. First, it is not the deployment of violence itself that distinguishes an authoritarian from a democratic regime but rather the degree to which state violence is subject to a rule of law.[5] Democratic as well as authoritarian regimes employ violence against individuals and groups who appear to violate the legal order. Second, since levels of societal violence have risen in Latin America during the current democratic era, it is impossible to separate long-term historical patterns from contemporary pressures, which also cause violent state actions. Third, many opponents of authoritarian regimes blame current maladies on those regimes, sometimes indiscriminately, while many defenders of the old regimes commit the opposite fallacy by attributing current levels of state violence to the "disorder" permitted by democracies.

Discussing security forces and violence requires us to decide what does—and does not—constitute a democratic system of public security, exactly what was authoritarian about the security forces of undemocratic regimes, and what concepts and methods best explain the past's impact on the present. At one end of the methodological spectrum are broad conceptions of authoritarian legacies that see them as so pervasive and deeply rooted as to make significant security force reform after democratic transition virtually impossible. At the other end is the outright dismissal of the concept of authoritarian legacies and the view that electoral competition in new democracies will naturally induce similar patterns of reform despite countries' historical variations. Our own study of police reform in post-transition Argentina, Brazil, Chile, and Uruguay produces no evidence to support either of these two extreme views. While significant reform of the police has occurred in some countries, there is no discernible tendency toward institutional convergence across even these cases, which are neighboring countries that share a considerable number of historical and political characteristics. Similarly, the substantial variation across these cases suggests that democracy itself does not make reform of security forces natural or inevitable.[6] In contrast, we argue that such reform is determined by a combination of long-term practices (including authoritarian legacies),[7] democratic politics, and the degree of centralization of the security forces. Throughout Latin America, security forces have sunk their roots deep into the state, with practices and authorities that continue into democracy. In the wake of a quick collapse of authoritarianism, however, a new democratic regime has a better chance of reforming the police than a regime emerging out of a pact with authoritarian actors. In the new democratic era, reform will be shaped by political actors' responses to public opinion—but not necessarily in a way that reduces police power. Finally, democracies where the police are part of provincial government will have more opportunities and patterns of change than unitary states.

Because of the centrality of the state, the literature on state formation is as important as that on democratic transitions. Much of the state formation scholarship (Centeno 1997; Holden 1996; Karl 1997; Mann 1993; Migdal 1988; Peloso and Tenenbaum 1996; Rueschemeyer, Stephens, and Stephens 1992; Stanley 1996; Tilly 1992, 1998) sees authoritarian legacies as arising from multiple, accreting changes in state institutions.[8] Tilly (1992, 75) and Schirmer (1999, 96), for example, identify the separation of military and police forces as a central element of western European state formation as well as of the development of a modern conception of consent-based law. As Tilly (1998) writes, "If you had to judge whether a state was democratic or not on the basis of a single organizational feature, whether the police reported to the military or to civilian authorities would serve as an excellent guide" (223–24).

The state formation approach suggests that authoritarian regimes in Latin America from the 1960s through the 1980s reversed and postponed the separation between military and police forces. Such an argument rests on a counterfactual hypothesis: had civilian, democratic regimes remained in place in these countries during this period, the preexisting separation between military and police forces would have been maintained and extended. One test of such a hypothesis is Spain and Portugal, which share many of the same traditions and institutions as Latin America but which democratized earlier and were subject to the democratic influence of their European neighbors. (Latin America, in contrast, began to integrate much later and was influenced during the Cold War by policies that often strengthened the state's coercive capacities.) Such a comparison, in fact, shows that policing and military functions have been separated more clearly in the Iberian countries than they have in the four Latin American countries discussed here.

Much of the transition literature attributes the longevity of authoritarian legacies to the mode of transition to democracy (Agüero 1998; Haggard and Kaufman 1997; Munck and Leff 1997; and chapter 6 by Agüero, chapter 3 by Hagopian, and chapter 2 by Hite and Morlino in this volume). The politics of the transition are seen as constituting a "critical juncture" (Collier and Collier 1991) or moment of "punctuated equilibrium" (Krasner 1984) that sets parameters on subsequent institutional change. In our case studies, indeed, the extent of police reform does generally reflect the degree of control that the authoritarian regime had over the transition. Such control was highest in Chile and lowest in Argentina, with Brazil and Uruguay in between, an ordering that corresponds inversely to the low, high, and moderate degree of police reform in each case. However, these reforms were not part of the transition itself and instead were negotiated during the "normal" politics of the post-transition period. Furthermore, the reforms came late: thirteen years after the transition in Argentina, eight to ten years after the transition in Brazil, and four years after the transition in Uruguay. This suggests that the impact of the mode of transition on the police is less direct and substantial than it is on other policy areas. Since police practices have been built up primarily over the long-term process of state formation rather than during any specific regime, these practices are likely to remain below the radar in most transitions.

Case Studies of Authoritarian Legacies in Policing

In this section, we apply our three-part argument about policing and post-transition reform to Argentina, Brazil, Chile, and Uruguay. First, while the most recent authoritarian regime in each country made policing more repressive, more militarized, and less accountable to the public, it built upon a long tradition of repression and generally exacerbated preexisting tendencies rather than creating new institutions and practices from scratch. Authoritarian legacies in policing are thus more legacies of an authoritarian state than of a particular regime. In fact, similarly violent approaches can be found in countries without an authoritarian regime in the recent past, such as Venezuela and Colombia. Second, while variation in the mode of transition in the four cases helps account for the differential degree of post-transition reform, the impact of the transition was drawn out by the give and take of "normal" democratic politics. In particular, the enactment and types of reform have depended on changing levels of public support and mobilization. Third, the degree of centralization influences the formation of reform coalitions in each country, with reformers in decentralized polities (Argentina and Brazil) working on the provincial and state level and would-be reformers in centralized Chile and Uruguay trying to effect change on the national level.

While these conditions lead to different changes in each country and province, proposals usually center on ten major police reforms, listed in Table 7.2. Many of them focus on altering the police force itself, from personnel changes to new forms of training. Most others are the creation or strengthening of oversight bodies, such as the courts, ombudsmen, or civilian commissions. As Table 7.2 describes, the four case studies have different records of adopting these central police reforms. In line with Table 7.1, and our argument about long-term practices, democratic politics, and state structure, this table shows the contrast in each area of reform among the four case studies.

Brazil

The Brazilian case illustrates three important points about policing in new democracies. First, while the 1964–85 authoritarian regime made changes in police organization and deployment that remain in place today, the overall problem of violent and insufficiently supervised police forces is an old one. The military regime adapted preexisting institutions for its own purposes, and the tendencies of the police to be repressive, insulated from popular control, and subservient to political overseers were already well entrenched before the 1964 military coup. Second, our study shows that support for police reform from a chief executive—in this case, Brazilian president Fernando Henrique Cardoso—is insufficient for successful reform in the absence of strong public support. Third, Brazil shows how the degree of police centralization crucially affects the tactics of those advocating police reform and shows that decentralized states present both advantages and disadvantages to would-be reformers. Where police forces are decentralized and administered at the state level, as in Brazil, reform requires less political capital than it does nationally, enabling significant changes to be enacted in states such as São Paulo. But reform in such a polity will ultimately be a patchwork with little homogeneity. In the Brazilian case, in the early and mid-1990s improvements in the investigation of citizens' complaints of lethal police violence in

TABLE 7.2   Reforms of the Police in Post-Transition Argentina, Brazil, and Chile

Measures	Argentina	Brazil	Chile	Uruguay
Formal disassociation of police agencies from the military	Yes	Yes	No	Yes
Personnel purges	Yes	No	No	No
New disciplinary bodies and programs of police misconduct	Yes	Yes (São Paulo)	No	No
New programs of civilian input	Yes	Yes (São Paulo)		Yes
Reformed criminal code	Yes	No	No	Yes
Creation of ombudsmen (*Defensoría del Pueblo*) for citizen complaints	Yes	Yes (São Paulo)	No	No
Changes in police training	Yes	Yes	No	Yes
Restrictions of police detention authorities	Yes	No	No	Yes
Reorganization of police affiliation to enhance judicial oversight	Yes	No	No	Yes
Removal of police from military court jurisdiction	Yes	Partial	No	Yes

São Paulo existed side by side with violently repressive policing in the neighboring state of Rio de Janeiro.

Brazil's police forces are relatively decentralized and pluralized, reflecting the country's relatively low degree of internal conflict as a colony and nineteenth-century independent state, at least in comparison to Argentina, Chile, and Uruguay.[9] Aside from the small federal police force limited to specialized areas such as drug trafficking and border protection, the country's police are organized primarily at the state level. State police are split into two parts, the civilian police (*policia civil*) and the military police (*policia militar,* or PM), both of which are under the nominal power of the state governor. (The military retains substantial control over the budget, training, and equipment of the military police.) The military police are responsible for routine street patrolling, monitoring public order, and arresting criminal suspects. Once an arrest is made, the suspect is turned over to the civilian police, who run the investigation.

From colonial times to the present, Brazil's police have exhibited authoritarian tendencies. These include the habit of punitive policing, in which the officers administer corporal punishment when they apprehend suspects, and serving the immediate political interests of the government in power by regarding certain forms of dissent as criminal. These tendencies, whose roots lie in the slave-owning and imperial past, were nurtured by political leaders in the twentieth century. Colonial policing was relatively rudimentary. Vigilance was performed by unarmed civilian watchmen (*guardas*) hired by town councils, as well as local inspectors (*quadrilheiros*) appointed by local judges (Holloway 1993, 29). However, these officials had no more powers of arrest than ordinary citizens had and merely represented higher authorities. The development of the police as a separate state institution began in the early nineteenth century, in the era that culminated in Brazil's formal independence from Portugal in 1822. But the real foundation of Brazil's contemporary police forces came in the wake of an 1831 riot by the Guarda Real de Polícia, who were acting in sympathy with a rebellious army unit stationed in Rio. Following the suppression of this revolt, the Guarda was dissolved and replaced by the Corpo de Guardas Municipais Permanentes, which was designated the Corpo Militar de Policia de Corte in 1866 and the Policia Militar in 1920 (Holloway 1993, 88). Significantly, it was administered by the civilian Ministry of Justice rather than the military.

Major changes in Brazilian policing occurred in the 1920s, as increasing labor mobilization spurred officials to increase state capacity to control the working class. The creation in 1925 of the Delegacia de Ordem Politica e Social (DOPS) in the industrial state of São Paulo, later duplicated in other states, marked the advent of a police force specifically oriented toward the repression of government opponents and political dissidents. In 1928, São Paulo's Secretary of Justice and Public Security affirmed that the DOPS had managed to identify 102,654 of the state's 300,000 workers and was satisfied that there was no significant organization among them that could perturb public order (Pinheiro 1991, 111). The DOPS, along with other new and specialized police organizations, later became a pillar of the dictatorial rule of Getúlio Vargas (1930–45).

Significant changes in policing also occurred under the military regime of 1964–85. Bayley (1985, 65) observes that authoritarian regimes tend to centralize policing; during this period, de facto (if not de jure) centralization and militarization did in fact take place in Brazil. The military regime created the federal police and national intelligence service (Serviço Nacional de Inteligencia, or SNI, a sort of CIA and FBI rolled into one) and after 1967 placed the state police forces under the command of army generals in the war against "subversion." Civilian police forces engaged in "ostensive" (noninvestigatory) policing were folded into the PMs,[10] which were reorganized to fit a militarized conception of public security (Pinheiro 1996, 27), while the investigatory capacities of the plainclothes civilian police were relatively neglected.[11] U.S. training and influence played a role in this metamorphosis.[12]

The authoritarian regime reshaped the judiciary as well as the police. A 1965 decree removed all crimes against "national security" from the civilian judiciary and placed them in the hands of military courts. Thousands of civilians were prosecuted in these courts, some of them for offenses involving little more than the mere expression of anti-regime opinions. While the use of military courts to prosecute civilian dissidents ended with the military regime, military court jurisdiction over the military police was retained under democracy. A 1977 constitutional amendment transferred crimes carried out by military police against civilians from the jurisdiction of civilian courts to state military courts—a modification preserved after the transition.[13] In contemporary Brazil, all cases in which PMs are accused of human rights violations against civilians—except intentional homicides, transferred back to civilian courts in 1996—are still heard in state military courts, resulting in high levels of impunity in these cases.

Such an arrangement is particularly problematic because neither the state nor the local police are subject to consistent or strict disciplinary mechanisms. With a strong belief in the efficacy of lethal violence in fighting crime (Chevigny 1995, 161), police regularly intimidate, torture, kill, and "disappear" arrested suspects. Both civilian and military officers block judicial investigations and delay taking suspects whom they have shot to the hospital. Similarly, the police often fill out a "resisting arrest" form, which leads to an entirely different type of inquiry, and one that rarely involves formal charges. Although the police have thirty days to complete their investigation, this timetable is rarely kept and usually stretches out into months and sometimes years. Under the law, suspects not convicted within a certain time period once the investigation has begun cannot be punished at all. When suspects are police officers, this statute of limitations is used to allow them to remain unpunished, lending impunity to police acts.

Though the police are in charge of their own inquiries, prosecutors can perform their own investigations and indict officers. But this parallel investigation rarely occurs because some of the overworked prosecutors do not consider victims of police shootings a priority. When they do and cases reach the courts, convictions are rare, and those officers who are convicted are often given suspended sentences. In addition, the family of the victim may appoint an assistant to the prosecution, who participates in all levels of inquiry. But most families are not educated enough or are too fearful to take this procedure. Cases within the state military judiciary can take up to ten years, and many of the ineffective civilian courts are biased in favor of the police and have poor witness protection programs. The branches of government with constitutional "police power" over all security agencies have not exercised this power adequately. The national Congress and state legislatures have rarely taken action on police issues or enacted laws regarding police discipline.

Clearly, democratization—which has led to considerable improvements in political freedom and electoral choice in the country—has not solved the problem of unaccountable security forces in Brazil. However, particular incidents have generated demands for reform. In March 1997, for example, nine military police officers were arrested after a photographer videotaped them physically abusing motorists and trying to extort money from them at a roadblock set up to apprehend drug traffickers in a São Paulo suburb. The video—showing one policeman shooting at a car driving away from the roadblock, killing that car's passenger—was shown throughout Brazil and provoked considerable public anger. In addition, a police strike in ten Brazilian states in June–July 1997, marked by armed confrontations between the police and the military in some cities, helped persuade much of the public that carrots as well as sticks are necessary for improved police performance and that the police should be paid more if they are to adequately protect society.[14]

Despite this generally bleak picture, several reforms initiated under the democratic regime hold promise. State efforts to inculcate normative adherence to human rights among the police and citizens are important and likely to have an impact. The discussions surrounding the 1988 constitution, which amply recognizes human rights (see especially Title II, Chapter 1, Article 5), may result in increased societal awareness of the importance of rights and lowered public tolerance of police abuses. The 1996 promulgation of the

National Program for Human Rights under Cardoso was intended to have a similar effect (Presidência da República 1996). Among other things, it authorized the federal government to undertake a survey of cities and states in order to identify and restrict funds to those regions where human rights violations were particularly common. The plan also mandated the inclusion of human rights material in police academy courses, urged the improvement of methods of selecting, training, and disciplining officers, and advocated the immediate suspension of members of the police who engaged in violence against civilians. In the medium term, it suggested the creation of community councils to oversee police performance and the adoption by police of community policing tactics.

Cardoso submitted the plan to the national Congress, where opposition to many of its provisions quickly materialized, by legislators as well as by outside actors such as the military police. One of the first manifestations of this opposition occurred in September 1996, when the bill to transfer jurisdiction of police crimes over civilians to civilian courts was passed by Congress in greatly revised form, limiting the transfer to cases of alleged intentional homicide only. Six months after the National Program for Human Rights had been announced by the president's office, none of its measures in the area of public security had passed in the Senate (Human Rights Watch 1997, 81).

Despite the obstacles to police reforms at the national level, the state of São Paulo initiated some measures that have had success in reducing police violence. Several of these were internal to the state military police force. Training in human rights was initiated, new forms of community policing were implemented, and a mandatory counseling program was formed. In 1993, a Program to Retrain Police Involved in High Risk Situations (Programa de Acompanhamento de Policiais Envolvidos em Situações de Alto Risco [PROAR]) was created to remove police officers involved in fatal shootings from their beats, assign them administrative duties, and require them to undergo three months of psychological counseling before being evaluated for a return to street patrol. The police saw this as punishment because many of them had second jobs that they squeezed between patrol shifts but that were impossible to maintain with regular daytime administrative shifts (Human Rights Watch 1998b, 51–52). A different type of reform went outside the police itself and invited civil society to monitor police performance. Around the same time as PROAR's formation, the state government established the office of ombudsman for the police and appointed a well-known human rights activist to the position. In his first six months, the ombudsman received 1,247 complaints, of which 246 concerned police violence. The ombudsman gave the latter his top priority and asked authorities for more information in each case (Human Rights Watch 1997, 52).

Evidence suggests that these measures did have an impact on the propensity of the military police to kill civilians. Whereas a reported 1,074 and 1,470 civilians were killed by military police in the greater metropolitan area of São Paulo in 1991 and 1992 respectively, this figure dropped to 243 in 1993, 333 in 1994, 331 in 1995, and 106 in 1996 (Chevigny 1995, 148; Human Rights Watch 1997, 51). However, this decrease was not permanent. Data on police killings for the state of São Paulo as a whole, for which greater São Paulo city constitutes the largest component, indicate that the rate gradually climbed again until it reached 839 in 2000.[15] The last figure is still disturbingly high—the police in New York, a city comparable in size to São Paulo, killed 25 civilians in 1993 (Chevigny 1995, 67)—but it represents a significant decrease from the 1991–92 figures. The creation of internal and external mechanisms to make police officers accountable to superiors, the courts, and the public when they use deadly force appears to have influenced this sharp decline.

The case of São Paulo illustrates an important point about security force reform. Commitment to change on the part of top political leaders may not be sufficient for successful reform. While Brazil's president supported the National Program for Human Rights, Congress, with strong political ties to state governors and police and military institutions anxious to defend their own prerogatives and control, was able to block most of its provisions. Second, the weight of public pressure may compensate for lack of support at the top. In São Paulo, both the state governor and the mayor had reputations for being tolerant of police violence; the reforms described above were initiated after a prison massacre of October 1992 that evoked widespread public condemnation of police heavy-handedness. Third, a mix of both internal and external accountability mechanisms is likely to be more effective than exclusive reliance on one or the other.

In contrast with São Paulo, the state government of Rio de Janeiro dealt with authoritarian legacies in a way more injurious to human rights. In 1995 the state governor appointed Nilton Cerqueira, a former general who was active in the military regime's repression, to head the Secretariat for Public Security. Cerqueira initiated a policy of awarding "bravery" bonuses and promotions to military police officers, which in practice were given to those who killed criminal suspects, regardless of the circumstances. Police killings of civilians then doubled; one study indicated that between May 1995 and April 1996, at least 179 police officers were promoted and given bonuses for incidents involving the deaths of seventy-two civilians and six police officers. In some of these cases, autopsies suggested that the victims were killed in summary executions (Human Rights Watch 1998a, 92). Another study showed that prosecutors in the state military justice system did not prosecute the officers in 295 (98 percent) of the 301 cases in which the Rio PMs had killed civilians between 1993 and 1996, choosing instead to simply archive the cases—even with evidence of a summary execution (Cano 1999, 16). In 1998, the bonus and promotion program was discontinued, and Cerqueira stepped down. Since then, the Rio police have been planning to reform, focusing, as in Chile, on professionalization, efficiency, and improved social relations. The Undersecretary of Public Safety, Luiz Soares, says that the force plans to improve coordination between civilian and military forces, incorporate new technology, train officers "to become community police officers," and form committees with civil society groups. At the same time, he acknowledges that political opposition, police attitudes, the slow judiciary, and financial constraints will make these changes unlikely.[16]

In general, the prospects for the reform of the security forces in Brazil vary from state to state and come under cross-pressures of various kinds. At the same time that some analysts talk of the "militarization" of public security (Zaverucha 2000) due to the increasing intervention of the army into public security questions, there are also proposals to "civilianize" the military police and to abolish state military courts. But it is nevertheless clear that the increased power and autonomy of the security forces under military rule have endured under democracy. And a statist and authoritarian conception of the legal order, which approves of a "strong hand" against crime and tolerates the summary execution of criminal suspects, remains deeply entrenched among the public. Under such circumstances, Brazil's authoritarian legacies in the realm of public security are likely to impede reform.

Argentina

Of all four cases, Argentina's police have undergone the most significant post-transition reforms. Major purges of police and intelligence personnel, a decoupling of police and military forces, changes to the criminal code and laws, the creation of civilian boards, an improvement of judicial oversight, and alterations in police training all occurred in the 1990s, primarily in Buenos Aires Province and the Federal Capital (see Table 7.2). The country's transition to democracy had a greater impact on policing than in new democracies, since the quicker collapse of its authoritarian regime opened up greater prospects for institutional reform than did the pacted transitions of Brazil and Chile. However, the fact that such changes occurred a decade after Argentina's 1983 transition suggests that the impact of the transition mode on policing is neither direct nor inevitable and that reform is unlikely to be included in the transition pact itself. The type of transition may make police reform more likely, but its achievement must be obtained via "normal" post-transition politics.

As in Brazil, contemporary patterns of policing in Argentina are primarily the product of a long and gradual process of state formation rather than the innovations of a particular authoritarian regime. And like Brazil, Argentina demonstrates the significance of civil society mobilization and of a federal structure. Change has been enacted mainly in the Federal Capital and in the Province of Buenos Aires, due in part to strong mobilization by civil-society organizations against police violence and impunity. However, reform has been far slower in other provinces, where such mobilization has been less intense.

Since the time of Spanish rule, the power of the executive, the subservience of the judiciary, and the centrality of the security forces in Argentina have generated an authoritarian approach to policing that has continued in the post-1983 democratic period. In particular, a growing crime rate and public support for "law and order" have allowed many violent practices to continue. Much more than Brazil's 1964–85 or Uruguay's 1974–84 authoritarian regimes, though, Argentina's brutal 1976–83 dictatorship led to a broad, deeply rooted questioning of the role of the state security forces. A federal structure made up of autonomous provincial governments, as in Brazil, has also opened up challenges to authoritarian legacies.

In colonial Argentina, there were no professional police forces, and in Buenos Aires each of the city's eight subdivisions, *comisarías*, policed itself. An irregular rural police force began in 1755, quickly acquiring both summary power of judgment and a reputation for arbitrary abuse. In 1799, an armed force within the military was established to handle general security in the Buenos Aires area. In 1810, Argentina's first independent government created the Policía General and declared itself in charge of "monitoring order, public tranquility and individual security."[17] Upon independence, the government "began on a vigorous and rapid road to concentration of police power, a shedding of municipal and neighborhood structures, and the creation of a State Police" (Maier 1996, 133). In 1826, it created the Central Police Department in the city of Buenos Aires, along with daytime and nighttime police forces. The power of these and other security agencies increased as Argentina endured a prolonged period of civil war between the Unitarians and Federalists, much of it under the dictatorship of Juan Manuel de las Rosas (1829–52), whose main pillar of support was his own security agency.

The 1853 constitution brought an end to the civil war, and the federal judiciary and legal codes were established in the 1860s. But the courts were occupied during their first years with questions of federalism rather than of constitutional rights, while the new Supreme Court supported de facto governments and often limited judicial authority. In 1872, all police services were unified and the city of Buenos Aires took on more of the provincial police's duties. These bodies were run mainly by the military, but after Justo José de Urquiza's ouster of Rosas they began to be gradually subsumed under civilian control. When the capital city of Buenos Aires was ceded to federal jurisdiction in 1880 (hereafter "Federal Capital"), the province handed over its Central Police Department to the national government, which led to the establishment of the Capital Police and the Police of the Province of Buenos Aires.

Despite the cessation of hostilities, control of the population continued to be a top government priority. The first penal code was introduced in 1886 to help rein in growing crime rates, and the government began using punishments such as internal exile. Throughout the country, in addition, "punitive social control of the disfavored classes was carried out" by legislation of the provincial *caudillos* and their judges. A parallel urbanization occurred through increased powers for city police agencies through harsh laws and a criminal code based on the one in Spain that had been derogated there because it was based on "the most inquisitorial moment of Spanish penal process legislation of the last century and a half" (Zaffaroni 1994, 254–55). As a result, the constitution's guarantees of individual rights and accountability fell behind these public order and criminal policies.

As immigration and industrialization generated unrest at the turn of the century, the police adopted more professional training and technology and repeatedly clashed with groups such as the anarchist and socialist unions popular among southern European immigrants. In 1909, the Buenos Aires police killed eight and wounded forty in an attack on a labor demonstration. The notorious Tragic Week (Semana Trágica) of 1919, in which the military violently crushed an outbreak of labor agitation, began with the capital police's intervention in a strike of metallurgical workers. Such violence spawned anti-leftist vigilante squads that killed labor organizers and were a precursor to right-wing hit squads such as the Argentine Anti-Communist Alliance (AAA) of the 1970s. In line with these developments, the judiciary became more restrictive of habeas corpus, denying it in favor of police powers in cases of preventative detention, even though "it was obvious that judges could not ignore worsening police abuses" (Dromi 1985, 13). The Supreme Court upheld new internal exile laws, the 1902 Residence Law that gave the executive sole authority to expel or deny the entry of any foreigner, and the 1910 Social Defense Law.

After the military took power in 1930, the police became a pillar of repressive regimes legitimized by the judiciary. The police began to utilize wide-ranging powers, often through ordinances and "regulations" such as edicts, which continued during returns to formal democracy. Under Juan Perón's 1946–55 rule, the use of torture increased, especially as his government's popularity waned. Attempts were made after 1955 to eliminate such abuse, but it continued under the elected Radical governments of 1958–62 and 1962–66, when the military structured the police and ran its day-to-day operations. During this time, the Supreme Court upheld laws passed by de facto governments as long as they did not conflict with constitutional regimes' laws, and it rejected the habeas corpus petitions of arrested labor leaders placed in military courts. When the armed forces returned to power in 1966, the power of state security forces increased, and the police continued to train and operate under the military. The government demoted the constitution behind its "Revolutionary Objectives," created federal penal courts for those accused of revolutionary activity, and proliferated decrees that eventually became full-fledged laws. Rising violence and failing governments only quickened this repressive pattern. Left-wing guerrillas grew in strength during the 1973–76 Perón governments, while the AAA attacked leftists with "the active engagement of the Federal police."[18] The military took repression to new heights after its 1976 coup, when up to thirty thousand people were "disappeared" and "all three armed services had the full support of the security branch of the federal police, forming espionage networks and clandestine operations with each" (Centro de Estudios Legales y Sociales [CELS] and Americas Watch 1991, 7; Rock 1987, 363). The Supreme Court declared itself incompetent to investigate the whereabouts of "disappeared" persons and accepted laws that subjected civilians to military tribunals.

Despite the frequent regime changes between 1930 and 1983, authoritarian practices only became more entrenched in that time. Police edicts, widespread torture, the constitutionality of de facto regimes, the legality of de facto laws, the increasing power of provincial police agencies, the Supreme Court's near-complete support of military governments on police issues, and the executive's authority over internal security all created powerful authoritarian legacies for the post-1983 period. The military's repressive

1976–83 rule, its economic mismanagement, and its failed 1982 Malvinas invasion led it to suffer one of the most thorough purges and reorganizations in all of Latin America's democratic transitions. But even though the police were central to the 1976–83 government's practices, they enjoyed continuity in both structure and power after the transition. The Radical government of Raúl Alfonsín did improve police training, tighten internal discipline, and replace top police officials responsible for abuses during the dictatorship. But the government's main concern was to strengthen individual rights through *amparo* and habeas corpus guarantees. And amid Peronist obstruction in Congress, military unrest, and an economic crisis, this focus left little room for police restructuring. The majority of the population in the 1980s, in addition, was either ambivalent or in favor of maintaining strong police forces.[19]

Many authoritarian practices, as a result, continued into the 1990s. Even personnel from the authoritarian past found top positions in provincial police forces. Well-known ex-military officials such as Luis Patti, a mayor and gubernatorial candidate for the March 2002 elections, and Aldo Rico, a former military official who led a military uprising against the 1980s trials of the former junta leaders, have been police *comisarios* in Buenos Aires Province. A Secretary of Domestic Security in the 1990s, Adrián Pelacchi, the country's highest law enforcement authority, was an official for six years in the Superintendency of Federal Security, the police body specializing in kidnapping, torture, and killings during the 1976–83 dictatorship. He once stated that it is necessary to sacrifice individual liberties for better security (Verbitsky 1998, 3–4) and proposed returning legal validity to the spontaneous statements given to the police. Old approaches to training also continued. Training in the Policía Federal Argentina (PFA,[20] responsible for enforcement of federal laws and of all laws within the Federal Capital), for example, focuses on "respect for authority" on physical training, with civil rights education remaining "just on the surface, without conviction, to show to society," according to one official.[21] Neither of the two bodies that handles internal complaints— the Agency of Administrative Investigations or the Agency of Preventative Investigations—has "any independence. They can't do anything against *comisarios*. They can only take on small issues [and] individual problems."[22] The process behind periodic suspensions and dismissals remains secretive.[23] Combined with low salaries, such poor accountability and discipline have generated corruption in nearly every Federal Capital *comisaría*.[24] As it spreads to other state agencies, money extorted by the police makes reform "virtually impossible, as civil officials stand only to lose if they cooperate in prosecuting corrupt police" (CELS and Americas Watch 1991, 8).

Gradually, the internal security threat shifted from political ideology to common crime, fueling and fueled by the state's own tough criminal policies. The government of Carlos Menem (1989–99) built up its security apparatus through such measures as the formation of the Superintendency of Security following the 1994 car bomb destruction of the Federal Capital's Jewish Community Center (AMIA) and promoted wide powers for police agencies, particularly intent on allowing them to stop crime in the "precriminal" state.[25] After the personnel purges and rights guarantees under Alfonsín, the first police reforms in democratic Argentina were usually taken in response to specific incidents of abuse. In 1991, for example, the death of a seventeen-year-old in a police station prompted congressional modification of the Organic Law of the Federal Police to allow the police to detain a person only if there is reasonable suspicion of criminal activity (or when the person does not produce adequate identification) and to reduce from twenty-four to ten hours the maximum time allowed for such detentions. Menem vetoed the bill but was overridden. But substantial challenges to the police's authoritarian legacies only came later. As macroeconomic conditions stabilized at the expense of equality and employment, rising rates of violent crime created a widespread sense of societal breakdown that the police and courts were incapable of slowing. In Buenos Aires province, where the crime rate nearly doubled in the 1990s—from 76 crimes for every 10,000 residents in 1991 to 148.1 in 1997—the overwhelming majority in every poll considered it probable that they would be a victim of crime (Saín 2002, 85). Nationwide, the number of crimes jumped from 489,290 in 1991 to 1,178,530 in 2001, while the percentage of sentences actually dropped, from 18,938 in 1991 to 18,377 in 2001 (El Instituto Nacional 2002, 172–75). That is, well under 2 percent of crimes led to a conviction. In a 2001 Gallup poll, only 18 percent of respondents expressed confidence in the judiciary, the lowest rate since 1984 (Zommer 2001). Starting to believe that the police were too involved in corrupt activities to actually slow down crime, the public began to generate pressure for change.

For the PFA, pressure when autonomy was granted to the Federal Capital in the 1994 constitution led to a grassroots campaign for the elimination of the PFA's edicts, which are among its oldest and most unaccountable sources of power. Edicts are internal police regulations allowing for the arrest and detention of individuals for up to thirty days, based primarily on noncriminal behavior. The PFA's twenty-three edicts, which date back to 1772 but were created mainly since 1932, range from "scandal" and "drunkenness" to unlawful firearm possession. In reality, the edicts were used to detain "undesirable" individuals, such as youth, the unemployed, immigrants, transvestites, and political protesters. By the 1990s, the PFA was devoting approximately 60 percent of its resources to edicts and making approximately 153,000 annual arrests under them. But as they failed to slow increasing crime, the edicts began to come under scrutiny. Then, in 1994, the new national constitution gave the Federal District status as a province, generating a wide citizen movement to push for the elimination of the edicts in the new province's first constitution. Battling heavy pressure from the PFA and the national government, the constituent assembly—dominated by the opposition Radical and Frepaso Parties—approved the edicts' elimination. But a new code that replaced the edicts did not dampen the controversy. The police stridently resisted the change—in the first half of 1997, as the edicts were being phased out, they detained an average of 413 persons per day, which was a yearly average of 301,490. Then, in March 1999, President Menem issued a decree giving the PFA new powers very much like those of the edicts.

A parallel political shift was occurring in Buenos Aires Province, home to a third of the country's population, where the forty-seven-thousand-member provincial police agency is the country's largest force and continues many repressive and unconstitutional authoritarian-era practices. Argentina's constitutions have always granted "police power" to the provinces—an authority upheld consistently by the courts,[26] which have generally adopted a "broad" interpretation of "police power"[27] that gives police agencies wide legal authority. Such decentralization can make reform easier in progressive provinces or states; it also enables conservative provinces and states to preserve the status quo and the *mano dura* preferred by hard-liners. As in other countries, in addition, reform requires funds such as those to raise salaries in order to stem corruption. As the country's ongoing recession shrinks expenditures—the 1998 PFA budget was a quarter of what it was in 1995—the possibilities for improving training and technology become even more remote in every province.

In Buenos Aires Province, most residents have favored tough policing since 1983. Since the transition, in fact, provincial officers have been implicated in drug trafficking, extortion, extrajudicial killings, "trigger-happy" (*gatillo fácil*) shootings, the 1997 murder of photojournalist José Luis Cabezas, the 1994 AMIA bombing, and use of *submarino seco* ("dry submarine"), in which a detainee's head is placed in a plastic bag until the point of asphyxiation. Many of the police's most popular *comisarios*, in fact, were high-level officials during the dictatorship and as police officials favor a *mano duro* approach. As with the PFA, internal regulations changed little after the transition to democracy. Structure and preparation continue to be very militaristic, with the bulk of cadets' training dedicated "to marching, as if they were soldiers,"[28] while "the surest route to advancement into elite squads" seems to be violent confrontations with suspected criminals (CELS and Americas Watch 1991, 7). Edicts also give the police wide leeway in making arrests, and torture continues to be a common practice in police stations. Creating and overseeing an effective police force has apparently been regarded as too costly, leading to a "solution" in which individual officers extort funds by "taxing" crimes such as prostitution, gambling, and drug trafficking, thereby skirting the government's budgetary limits. With low salaries, many officers are among the estimated forty thousand employees of private security firms. A lack of oversight aggravates these patterns. The province's Human Rights Office functions as a type of ombudsman on rights complaints but does not have the political authority to press charges or the political authority to wrest changes from the government. The provincial legislature receives denunciations but does not conduct investigation and its Peronist majority is reluctant to undermine executive power. Congress's Human Rights Commission, which monitors state officials and develops educational material, has had little impact. The police act "for repression, not prevention. This is part of the history of the police, of decades of the same pattern."[29]

Since the mid-1990s, however, the population has grown skeptical of the force's ability to combat crime. The campaign to find Cabezas's killers, for instance, attracted strong support from the media and human rights organizations and made it the most striking example of public mobilization against police impunity of all four cases reviewed here. More broadly, citizen concerns over the police's excesses and effectiveness grew so much that they began to impinge on the political prospects of provincial governor Eduardo Duhalde, the 1999 Peronist candidate for president. Beginning in 1996, he began to formulate a complete restructuring of the force. In a plan designed by his Secretary of Justice and Security, León Arslanian—who led the trials against military officials of the 1976–83 dictatorship—Duhalde dismissed nearly five thousand officials and completely restructured the agency. Previously, the one centralized hierarchy was run from the provincial capital and divided into functional areas, such as personnel and judicial affairs. But the "new"[30] police force was decentralized into eighteen departments, coinciding with the province's judicial districts. Each department is run by an official who is directly accountable to the Secretary of Justice and Security, a civilian. The functional division also has changed, from one large force to an investigative police of around five thousand officials, a security police of about thirty-five thousand officers, and smaller agencies for transportation security and for the provincial penitentiary system. Popular participation has also been instituted through citizen forums at the community, municipal, and department levels. Furthermore, the provincial legislature has passed a new criminal code that, by creating oral trials and strengthening the authority of the public ministry, reduces the police's authority in the criminal penal process.

Because they challenge both authoritarian legacies and patterns ingrained during the democratic era, these changes have generated widespread and violent resistance. Many judges and elected officials, including the chair of the Senate's Security Commission, have opposed the changes. Reactions from the police have been particularly strong, involving attacks against political officials as well as among police officers. While a total of twenty-three officers died in the line of work in 1997, fifteen provincial officers were killed in acts of revenge by other officers in just in the first month of 1998 ("La guerra de los botones" 1998). The 1999 Buenos Aires provincial gubernatorial campaign revealed the reform's other vulnerabilities. During the campaign, Arslanian resigned because of attacks against the reform by the Peronist candidate, national Vice President Carlos Ruckauf, who associated police killing with justice, asserting that "the bullet that kills the delinquent" is "society's response to the bullet that kills innocent people" (Oteiza 1999, 7). Since the reforms do not lessen the power of the governor over the police, Ruckauf's victory immediately raised doubts over whether they would be enforced at all. The new governor favors restricting bail and widening the police's powers to question prisoners and to conduct random searches, and he appointed notorious military official Aldo Rico as the province's Chief of Security.[31] But even if Ruckauf held back from such policies, continuing increases in crime—robbery and assault rose by 46 percent between 1997 and 1999[32]— may alone lead to a popular clamor to scrap the reform in favor of more immediate action. Finally, the reforms do not create the oversight that roots out police abuses. The reform dismantled corrupt agencies, but unless it is accompanied by increases in the police's budget—of at least sixfold, according to analysts—corruption and police "dependence" on bribes will continue.[33]

So from early on, police power in Argentina has been an intrinsic part of political relations, institutional structure, and legal interpretations, forming a legacy rooted as much in nineteenth-century *caudillismo* as in twentieth-century authoritarianism. The fact that real change in the police did not happen until a decade after the 1983 transition shows that changes beyond those of the transition itself were needed to reverse authoritarian legacies. On the one hand, the Buenos Aires restructuring was far more extensive than any changes in Brazil, Chile, or Uruguay. Reforms were also made in certain provinces, such as Córdoba and San Luis, as well as at the national level by the ending of the PFA's edicts and by President Fernando de la Rúa's dismissal of 1,500 military and civilian intelligence agents in February 2000 ("New Argentine President" 2000). Since then, however, such developments have been in rapid retreat amid the economic crisis, the collapse of the de la Rúa administration, and levels of civil violence unprecedented in the democracy era. In particular, the June 2002 killings of demonstrators by the Buenos Aires provincial police, the vociferous counteraccusations among political officials, and a rash of widely divergent proposals will only aggravate the low accountability and inconsistent policy that allow authoritarian practices to continue.

Chile

As the mode of transition literature would suggest, Chile—where the democratic transition was most effectively constrained by the prior authoritarian regime—has experienced the least amount of post-transition reform of all of our cases. The main branch of the police force has not been formally separated from the military, remaining a branch of the armed forces. Nor has there been much change in officer training, oversight over the police, or public input. Military courts continue to have jurisdiction over cases in which members of the police have been accused of abuses against citizens. Even full presidential control over the head of the police forces has yet to be fully established. But while the effects on policing of Chile's seventeen years of Augusto Pinochet's military rule (1973–89) appear to be strong, even in this case we find that major aspects of police behavior are rooted in earlier periods rather than exclusively in recent military rule. Hence it confirms our assertion that authoritarian legacies in policing are primarily legacies of an authoritarian state and not of a particular regime. Second, the barriers to police reform in Chile seem higher than in the other two cases, both because public support for and mobilization around police reform are relatively low and because the centralization of the police forces means that a relatively large amount of political capital is needed for reform to be successful.

Chile is a relatively homogenous country with a tradition of early state consolidation and constitutional rule. Its police forces are centralized and, like those of Brazil, divided between an essentially military force (the Carabineros) and civilian investigative police (Investigaciones). Of the four cases discussed here, Chile has the most legalistic political tradition, and its police enjoy the most popular support (see Table 7.1). In addition, while police torture of criminal suspects is common, Chile has not experienced the level of lethal police violence that Argentina and Brazil have, and it has one of the lowest murder rates in the Americas, even though concern about public safety is relatively high (see note 6).

Together, centralization, a steady history of institutional expansion, public fear of crime, and a delicate political balance have led to very few reforms since the end of the military regime in 1990. Instead of explicitly challenging the police's authoritarian tendencies, the government has strengthened the Carabineros and other forces. While the provincial structure of Brazil and Argentina led to many more opportunities for police reform in those countries, Chile's centralized government has not allowed similar opportunities. While postauthoritarian patterns of abuse led to greater moves toward reform in Argentina and Brazil, the lack of such excesses in Chile has lessened the push for change. Finally, while the authoritarian governments were broadly rejected in Argentina and Uruguay, the high levels of support for Pinochet in Chile have also reduced political drive for changes that challenge state security forces.[34]

The Carabineros have a long history of centralization, growth, professionalization, and more concern about effectiveness than civil rights. Modern policing began after the 1891 civil war, when small agencies run by the national government were established in the capital of Santiago and nearby Valparaiso. Abuses and poor discipline, though, soon led to the army's intervention in these forces. National organization of the police started in 1903 with the creation of the Regimiento de Gendarmes and the establishment of the Escuela de Carabineros five years later. Military control and unification of diverse law enforcement agencies increased in the 1920s, particularly with the 1924 establishment of the Police School. The contemporary Carabineros were founded in 1927, when, under the first government of General Carlos Ibáñez, three different police organizations, including the Carabineros, were fused into one. These new Carabineros, while formally directed by the Ministry of the Interior, were considered to be military forces and could be put at the disposition of the Ministry of War at the president's discretion. In its first several years, in fact, the Carabineros "constituted the principal repressive instrument of the nascent national militarism" (Frühling 1997, 83). The Policia de Investigaciones were then created in 1933 and, like their counterparts in Brazil, have engaged in competition and conflict with the Carabineros due to overlapping jurisdictions and blurred lines between their functions and those of the military police.

Though Carabinero personnel were stationed throughout the country, the national government retained tight control over them. Between 1933 and 1963, it added onto the agencies a wide set of specialized forces, such as a youth agency, a hospital, an air patrol, and a forest agency, as well as a well-equipped and armed unit, the Grupo Móvil, designed to be used against demonstrations. In 1960 it enacted the Ley Orgánica de Carabineros, which removed the partial dependency on the Defense Ministry. Attention to the police and its needs continued during the leftist Allende government (1970–73), which was worried about the level of its political allegiance.

Many of the force's authoritarian practices, however, developed during the Pinochet years. When it took over in 1973, Pinochet's junta declared the Carabineros a military agency on equal footing with the three branches of the armed forces and a year later returned both the Carabineros and Investigaciones to the Defense Ministry. The Carabineros then expanded rapidly, adding on subagencies such as the Special Police Operations Group in 1979, an intelligence operation called the Dirección de Comunicaciones de Carabineros (DICOMAR) in 1983, and the Special Police Activities subagency in 1985. Military-Carabinero ties strengthened during these years as well, particularly around military intelligence training of Carabinero officials. In the year following the coup, nearly a third of reported rights violations were attributed to police officials. By June 1974, internal security authority reverted to the Carabineros and the newly created Dirección de Inteligencia Nacional (DINA, or Directorate of National Intelligence), which soon became responsible for both the most accumulation of intelligence and the most state killings. In 1977, DINA was eliminated and replaced by the Central Nacional de Informaciones (CNI), which also focused on leftist groups but was better able to keep its operations secret. The CNI clashed with DICOMAR, and when the kidnapping and killing of three Communist Party members by DICOMAR in 1985 led to protests, DICOMAR was dissolved and the Carabineros' chief resigned. After the Pinochet government was defeated in the 1988 plebiscite, it instituted many changes in the Carabineros before it handed over power to an elected government in 1990. It formalized the force's dependency on the Defense Ministry, gave an eight-year term of office to its directors, and, for the first time in the country's history, shifted the power for hiring, transferring, and dismissing top officials from the president to the Carabinero chief.

Upon taking power, the government of Patricio Aylwin initiated a series of basic reforms. It dissolved the CNI, reformed the Law of Security to reinforce democratic principles, and began citizen participation programs. It gave the Carabineros jurisdiction over the Arms Control Law and other laws and emphasized its professional nature and focus on "common crime." Since then, in fact, the democratic regime has added on new agencies, such as the 1993 establishment of a new Public Information and Security Agency to handle police intelligence, expanding a police force that had already been greatly enlarged by the Pinochet regime. The governments have also increased the budget and personnel of the Carabineros, more than did their authoritarian predecessor and, some say, beyond its own infrastructural capacity. As a percentage of the national judiciary, the police's budget has been far higher since 1990 than it was in the authoritarian regime's last five years.

Despite this attention, serious tensions have arisen between the Carabineros and the democratic regime. The governments of both Aylwin and his successor Eduardo Frei failed to transfer the agency back to the Interior Ministry, even under a compromise that would move only some of its functions. In 1992, the Carabineros rejected the evolving National Plan for Citizen Security, developed by a representative committee, primarily on the grounds that it was an incursion on police authority. In 1995, tension arose between Carabinero head Rodolfo Stange and President Frei over Stange's role in the cover-up of the 1985 killing of three communists by Carabineros. Although Stange eventually resigned, the fact that President Frei could not dismiss him, instead only asking for his resignation, highlighted the insulation of the police forces from the elected president, even when the head of those forces was implicated in a crime.[35] In addition, demands for extra security by municipalities have created conflict between local government and the police. Finally, the Carabineros have not fundamentally altered their system of discipline and complaints. Information about citizen complaints is not available to the public, and there are no internal agencies to investigate charges of abuses by officers. Given the Carabineros' role under authoritarianism, this lack of change is unusual. In a 1994 report entitled "Human Dignity as a Principle of Institutional Doctrine," in fact, the Carabineros barely mention the seventeen years of dictatorship at all.

In democratic Chile, crime consistently comes in as one of the public's three main concerns, sometimes ahead of health, poverty, education, and salaries,[36] with a vast majority of people believing that crime and violence levels are increasing. In addition, the police enjoy a level of citizen confidence far beyond any recorded in Argentina, Brazil, or Uruguay.[37] These two trends have created political incentives to expand and strengthen the police rather than to reform them or examine their authoritarian legacies. Similarly, while Chile's criminal justice system still violates due process rights, it is speedier and more efficient than most of its regional counterparts. Just over half of all prison inmates are unsentenced—a high level, but among the lowest in Latin America. If Chile's police were decentralized, then a shift in public opinion, police effectiveness, or the criminal justice system could open up opportunities for reform at the local or provincial level. Without the less likely occurrence of such a shift at the national level, the chances for long-term structural change are much dimmer in Chile than in the rest of the region.

Uruguay

Because some reforms were adopted relatively soon after the transition, Uruguay comes closest to fulfilling the predictions of the mode-of-transition literature. The Uruguayan military had a weaker position in the transition negotiations than did its Chilean and Brazilian counterparts. This weakness, along with public views of the military's rule as repressive and heavy-handed (in terms of torture and incarceration, not killings) led to demands for reform after its downfall in 1984. But as in Argentina and Brazil, police reforms were not actually part of the transition pact and were instead the product of rather cumbersome evolutionary politics. The stable party system, along with the distraction of several plebiscites on military amnesty, led to a delayed and more cautious approach to reforming security forces and criminal laws. But popular pressure for change kept reform on the agenda, and as in Chile, because of the country's unitary structure, that pressure was exerted at the national instead of the regional level. The first reforms were structural alterations and civil rights protections, and, as crime and police abuse increased in the 1990s, changes were made in the criminal justice system.

Policing has always been under the purview of the national executive in Uruguay, and until recently all security forces were usually run by the armed forces. The first known forces were established in 1730 by the governor of Rio de la Plata, and in 1797 the governor of Montevideo created an additional force in the territory. In 1827, two years after independence, a decree gave police agencies greater authority to apprehend suspects, and the prisons were put under their authority. But other regulations enacted the same year obliged police authorities to turn over "delinquents and information" directly to judges instead of to the government, as had been the procedure up until then. In 1829, the first Law of the Organization of the National Police laid out the organization and the command structure of the police, while a decree the same year placed a military colonel as head of the police. The police were officially transferred to the Interior Ministry, and the 1830 constitution further specified the police's powers.

Internal violence, political instability, and tension with neighboring Argentina and Brazil led to expansion of security forces and to separation of the growing police force from the military. The police expanded further along with the population boom in the latter half of the 1800s. An 1874 law reorganized the police in both the capital and the interior, adding the new position of *subcomisario* and redividing the police districts of Montevideo, the capital city. A new "Police Guide" was published in 1883, and in 1887 the Montevideo police was split into a Municipal Police and a Security Police.

As political and economic uncertainty increased at the turn of the century, the police were strengthened. The government formed the Security Squad in 1895 (renamed the Republican Guard in 1916) and the "antidisturbance" Metropolitan Guard in 1924, and in 1926 it reorganized many forces in its most comprehensive police reform to date. Under the reformist governments of José Batlle y Ordóñez (1903–7 and 1911–15) and the 1917 presidential power-sharing agreement, Uruguay did not experience the same levels of violent labor and social protest racking its neighbors at the time. Nevertheless, the economic downturn at the end of the 1920s and the split in the dominant Colorado Party did lead to a coup in March 1933 by a coalition of minority factions of the Colorado and National Parties and some industrial and agricultural interests. The de facto regime did not use the military for internal security violent repression; that task fell primarily to the police. A rash of strikes in mid-1933, for example, were met with mass arrests and use of torture on detainees. Many newspapers were shut down, while worker meetings and strikes were prohibited. Democracy was restored with the 1942 elections, but the police had gained many new powers during the previous nine years. By the 1960s, though, failure of both the Colorado and National Parties to turn around a deteriorating economy and halt sliding wages led to increased political and social polarization as well as labor movement radicalism. By the end of the decade, popular agitation prompted an increase in exceptional powers by the executive and an expansion of the military's domestic role. It also led to the emergence of the Tupamaros, an armed guerilla group started by rural laborers and organizers who responded to police suppression of their protests. The government reacted with tough law enforcement measures. In 1967, a decree formed the Department of Intelligence and Liaisons, and in 1971 the Organic Police Law unified the police and gave it national jurisdiction. But the police's inability to stop the Tupamaros led to ever harsher approaches, including dismissal of lenient police officials and the widespread use of torture. This approach was stepped up after the military assumed control in 1973, such as through a 1974 executive decree creating the Republican Guard Regiment under the command of the Montevideo police chief.

The transition to democracy in Uruguay began after the military lost a plebiscite in 1980, pushing it into negotiations with the parties that led to democratic elections in 1984. During this phase, though, human rights were not a central point of contention. The human rights movement was relatively small and not well connected with the parties, which themselves had been compromised by their cooperation with the military during its rule, and it had no grassroots domestic or international human rights connections. In particular, the popular mobilizations instigated by rights organizations clashed with the tone and priorities of the military-party talks. The Colorado Party "deliberately ignored" human rights and pursued "a two-track policy: on the one hand it publicly supported truth and justice, while on the other it made private arrangements with the military to prevent just these policies" (de Brito 1997, 91). As a result, the government of José Maria Sanguinetti (1985–90) had no clear rights policy or commitments. But there was enough public pressure to oblige it to address rights issues, leading to developments such as Law 16.011 of 1988, which gave every citizen the right to use an "action of *amparo*" to challenge the action of state officials that violated any constitutional rights (Freitas 1993). The 1985 Law for the Reintegration of the Exonerated (Ley de Reposición de Destitutidos) rehabilitated thousands of public employees and cut back military courts to their pre-1974 jurisdiction. The dominant post-1984 interpretation of the constitution's Article 253, which outlines the military powers, was restrictive; Congress, for example, interpreted "military crimes" as those committed only by military officials, and not civilians, as during the military era.

But most political attention in the first five years of democracy focused on the issue of amnesty. Sanguinetti's 1985 National Pacification Project (Proyecto de Pacificación Nacional) released all political prisoners and created a National Repatriation Commission to help reintegrate returning exiles. Aside from right-wing protests about excluding police and military officers, the law had wide public support. But dealing with the authoritarian regime's rights abuses proved more divisive and drawn out. In December 1986, as a series of accusations were to appear in court, Congress approved the government's Amnesty Law (Ley de Caducidad de la Pretensión Punitiva del Estado), in which "the State relinquishes the exercise of penal actions with respect to crimes committed until March 1, 1985, by military and police officials whether for political reasons or in fulfillment of their functions and in obeying orders from superiors during the de facto period"[38] But government stonewalling of human rights charges in the courts, officials' support of military claims over them, stalled investigations, and secretive congressional reports all led to the *Nunca Más* report written by human rights organizations and then to an April 1989 referendum to derogate the 1986 Amnesty Law. In the charged referendum campaign, harsh attacks were made by both sides, the government questioned the morality and patriotism of the repeal's supporters, the Electoral Court bent the voting rules against the supporters, and military officials issued dire warnings of potential unrest if it passed. These tactics caused the referendum to fail by a narrow margin, but the controversial conduct of the campaign—as well as major support for the measure in Montevideo—led to a sense, not of resolution, but only of more injustice.

Though immediate changes in personnel and affiliation were made to Uruguay's police during these first years, as in Argentina, its structure remained largely intact. In the Organic Police Law, which was enacted in 1972 and modified in 1980, the country's unitary police hierarchy—headed by the National Police (Policía Nacional [PN])—was made part of the executive branch's Interior Ministry. Under the National Police are two networks of law enforcement agencies. One network is made up of nineteen regional offices, *jefaturas*, including the largest one, in Montevideo. The other is composed of fifteen specialized agencies, including the Intelligence Police, the Crime Prevention Police, a Penitentiary Police, and an investigatory Technical Police. The Inspección Nacional de Policía was formed in 1992 to improve coordination among these functional and regional agencies, as well as their relations with the courts and the Public Ministry. Other agencies, such as the Narco-Trafficking Unit, were added as the police's work expanded.

While such expansion caused some concern, police agencies are not as politicized as they are in the rest of the region, so debate over their role has been less charged. But growing economic strains and debates over the state's role in the 1990s brought renewed attention to policing. In particular, increases in crime and in protests against police abuse prompted tougher anti-crime measures as well as increased officer accountability. In 1995, the government enacted the Public Security Law, which obliges officers to exercise a proportional use of force and to use weapons only as a last resort and charges those who fail to take action against serious crimes with a "crime of omission."

The law also includes many anticrime provisions, such as one that allows the placement of juvenile criminals in adult prisons.

Efforts were also made to improve prosecution of reported police crimes, which had long been channeled into an understaffed internal police investigatory agency that could only recommend disciplinary actions. The judiciary has also had a poor record of prosecutions. In 1999, for example, legal action was brought by the widow of a criminal suspect who died under suspicious circumstances while in police custody the previous year. The first court dismissed the charge against the main suspect, and an appeals court order for a new investigation was shelved by the prosecutor and a higher judge. Criticism of such actions led to gradual improvements in prosecutions. While only a few convictions occurred between the mid-1980s and the mid-1990s, in 1999 the Interior Ministry reported that the courts had investigated or convicted 179 officers, 117 of whom were charged with abuses while on duty.

This stepped-up legal accountability was part of a broader improvement of the criminal justice system. Because of excessive delays and poor public defense, up to 90 percent of prison inmates were untried in the early 1990s. Through parole and other programs, this percentage was reduced to about 75 percent by the end of the decade—the average for Latin America. As in the rest of the region, this high percentage was another product of the gap between the written law and its daily application. A 1980 statute says that a police confession obtained before the detainee appears before a judge and attorney (without police officers present) is invalid and that judges must investigate allegations of mistreatment. However, in the twenty-four-hour period in which police may hold detainees incommunicado before presenting them to a judge, practices such as threats and forced confessions continued to be common. While judges officially headed criminal investigation, their overloaded dockets and poor administrative support allowed this power to be gradually taken over by police officials. Cumbersome written procedures, an understaffed Public Defense Agency, and little public concern for detainee rights also caused a systematic breakdown of due process that allowed the police to dominate the criminal justice system. Uruguay's lack of a guarantee against self-incrimination further undermined due process rights.

As in other countries, realization of this structural abuse led to criminal justice reform. In 1997, Uruguay reformed its penal process code to ease the investigatory burden of judges to allow for speedier and more impartial trials, to strengthen the investigatory and prosecutorial authority of the Public Ministry, and to clarify the police's investigatory role. The new code also replaced written trial procedures with oral ones, since proceedings based on written documents submitted to judges are notoriously slow throughout Latin America and are biased in favor of the prosecution, which has better access to evidence and investigatory specialists. Oral trials were first introduced in 1990, but they were made optional, and most judges chose to stick with the written system. After the new code was adopted, however, budgetary problems and political disagreements delayed its implementation and will continue to do so until at least 2004. As in the other case studies, politics can derail even cautiously moderate reforms.

Because of economic problems and greater attention to accountability since the mid-1990s, there have also been efforts in Uruguay to streamline and decentralize police administration. The 1995–2000 Sanguinetti government set up an Executive Committee for State Reform to investigate and rationalize expenses and structures throughout the state, while the 1999 Ley Cristal (Transparency Law) criminalized abuses of power by government officials, such as the laundering of funds related to public corruption cases. For the PN, these changes have encouraged greater efficiency. In 2000, for example, the police planned to increase hours dedicated to crime prevention, to decrease recidivism by 1 percent, to increase by 5 percent the percentage of resolved cases, and to decrease by 12 percent the amount of time needed to relay information among law enforcement bodies (Comité Ejecutivo para la Reforma del Estado [CEPRE] 2001). Since 1998, in addition, the Inter-American Development Bank (IADB) has been implementing a comprehensive "Citizen Safety" project involving community crime prevention, improvements in police training and relations with community groups, campaigns against domestic violence, and creation of a new penitentiary center. As part of this wider effort, in 2000 Uruguay began a gradual police decentralization in order to optimize and maximize human and material resources primarily fortifying the nineteen local *jefaturas* with new equipment and updated technology. As discussed above, however, decentralization can undermine police accountability in localities with lower levels of accountability. Combined with an unstable economy, such plans may not lead to all of the improvements envisioned.

Conclusion

Many police practices in Argentina, Brazil, Chile, and Uruguay are not authoritarian legacies. Many forms of corruption, brutality, discrimination, and shoddy investigation began after the democratic transition and can also be found in countries that have not endured authoritarian regimes in the last few decades. Security forces everywhere abuse their authority and reflect the prejudices and limitations of the societies from which they draw their personnel. Even extrajudicial executions and legal impunity of security officials predate recent military regimes. Authoritarian regimes, of course, did carry out practices of widespread and often unprecedented terror and during the negotiations of the democratic transition downplayed the issue of policing.

But such actions were also part of a larger process of state formation. One of the more significant authoritarian legacies for the security forces in our four cases, for example, was the postponement of the separation of internal police institutions from externally oriented military forces—a separation that occurred earlier and was sustained in much of western Europe. Latin America's particular path of state formation was influenced by a range of factors, such as weak capitalist and middle classes, a prior tradition of military intervention, a history of internal conflict, and Cold War politics. But a militarized conception of public security was promoted by both civilian and military regimes, with institutional changes reinforced by an ideology that regards security forces as enforcers of the law who should work outside it to preserve order. Constitutions (such as that of Brazil) that give the military the ultimate responsibility to ensure "law and order" are but one meta-legal example of a mentality that has long pervaded everyday interactions between citizens and security force officials. As the militarization of policing and the *mano dura* approach developed, they acquired public support as well as reinforcement by the most recent military regimes. These are therefore legacies of authoritarianism in state-society relations and not of one particular regime. As governments face increasing popular pressure to control crime, it remains to be seen whether reforms will reinforce this essentially authoritarian approach to public order or strike out on a new path toward a more democratic legal order.

In each country examined here, there have been reforms of the security forces to make them more accountable to and less insulated from society. The significance of such reforms has been highest in Argentina, average in Brazil and Uruguay, and lowest in Chile—an outcome that corresponds roughly with democratic transition literature. Chile, where the authoritarian regime most tightly controlled the transition, has had much less reform than Argentina, where the authoritarian regime basically collapsed. But the impact of this variation—at least in the area of policing—is indirect, delayed, and mediated by postauthoritarian politics, especially in the cases where police forces are decentralized. As seen in Argentina and Brazil, the fate of police reform proposals depends primarily on public views of crime and the ability of politicians to exploit those views. It is thus too early to predict the long-term relationship between security forces and the public. Political support backed by durable coalitions will be necessary to continue and deepen the reforms.

The degree of centralization of the state is also a crucial factor in explaining the role of security forces in the transitions. In Chile, police centralization, low public concern over police actions, and a relatively high degree of public confidence in the police facilitated the persistence of a *mano dura* and denied reformers the political capital to affect change. In Uruguay, where the police are also centralized, a weaker authoritarian regime gave way to a civilian government that allowed some reforms. In decentralized Argentina, the impact of the transition on the security forces was also mixed, with reforms advancing in certain provinces more than in others but in most cases outpacing the political and financial capacity to implement them. In Brazil, where decentralization of the security forces at the state level has been most marked, significant police reforms have occurred in São Paulo but not on the same scale elsewhere. At the same time, the police in many states are more violent (measured by the killings of civilians) than they were under the authoritarian regime. Authoritarian legacies in policing can be overcome in Brazil and the Southern Cone, but not easily or quickly. To a significant extent, successful reform seems to have to come "from below," via public support and mobilization for change, in conjunction with opportunistic elected politicians who can exploit such civil-society pressure for their own advantage.

NOTES

1. Tanner (2000, 101) observes that most books on democratic transitions have completely ignored the police, without even listing them in the index.

2. At the time, Diego Sayan was the executive director of the Andean Commission of Jurists in Lima, Peru. He later became Peru's minister of justice.

3. We find that levels of violent crime alone do not correlate with the public's willingness to support police reform. Chile has the lowest homicide rate of the three countries analyzed here but the least public mobilization around and support for police reform. However, in a recent survey, 11 percent of Chileans said that crime and lack of safety were major problems facing the country, compared to 9 percent in Argentina and 6 percent in Brazil 9 ("Neighbors . . . and Friends?" 1998). Thus the per-

ception that crime is a problem (rather than reported crime) may turn public opinion against reform and instead toward hard-line policing. The poll was carried out between January and March 1998 by the Resource Associates Corporation (RAC) and Mori International of Princeton, New Jersey. The margin of error is 1 percentage point in Latin America as a whole and an average of 3.5 percentage points in each country. The poll was apparently not conducted in Uruguay.

4. An important recent work on Latin American decentralization is Willis, Garman, and Haggard (1999), which points out that formally unitary states may, in some areas, be more decentralized de facto than federal ones. However, in the area of policing, the degree of decentralization does correspond roughly with the unitary-federal divide.

5. Schirmer (1999) asserts that what distinguishes democratic legality from authoritarian forms of it is that in the former "the socially approved use of force" is "the distinguishing element of law" (96). But since authoritarian violence is often approved by many segments of the population, it is perhaps more precise to say that in authoritarianism citizen rights are "securitized" ("constantly subject to qualification and denial whenever they are deemed to be in conflict with the security interests of the state").

6. For an interesting contrast in the assessment of post-transition security forces, and in particular the question of the degree of military control of domestic policing, see McSherry (1997), Zaverucha (2000), and Norden (1996). The first two authors see the continued power of the military in domestic security arrangements in Argentina and Brazil respectively and attribute this to a failure by civilian political elites to establish effective civilian control over all aspects of the military's activities. Norden comes to a wholly different conclusion about Argentina. The disagreement is interpretive rather than factual and stems fundamentally, in our view, from different conceptions of (1) the proper baseline from which to measure changes in civil-military relations since the transitions and (2) the model by which contemporary realities should be judged or, in other words, what kinds of expectations are reasonable in judging postauthoritarian legacies.

7. Leonardo Morlino's (1997) injunction to be clear about legacies and his suggestion that they be broken down into legacies for and against authoritarianism at the level of regime institutions, elites, social groups, and masses (in both the short and the long run) are very constructive and consistent with the distinctions made here.

8. For the distinction between state and regime, see Fishman (1990). O'Donnell (1999, 134–35) emphasized that many of the problems of the quality of new democracies can be attributed to the nature of their states.

9. Argentina suffered from an extended period of civil war in its first half-century of independence. Uruguay experienced many armed struggles in the same period, including the Brazilian invasions (1825–28) and the Guerra Grande (1839–51). Chile, which unified under a strong state relatively early, had civil wars in 1859 and 1891. Brazil, in contrast, experienced a relatively smooth transition from colony to

independent monarchy to republic in the nineteenth century. While occasional secessionist movements were suppressed by the center, major civil war was avoided. This comparison seems to confirm Bayley's (1985) argument that a significant cause of police centralization is the violent resistance to central rule in the process of state formation (69).

10. The PMs were placed back under the command of appointees of elected state governors in 1982.

11. Interview with Congressman Hélio Bicudo, 23 January 1995.

12. Between 1959 and 1969, 641 Brazilian police officials received training in the United States or at the International American Police Academy in Panama. A program managed by the United States Agency for International Development (USAID) supplied equipment, management consulting, and training to police in Brazil and assisted in the creation of the Federal Police in 1965 (U.S. Senate 1971, 1–6). See also Huggins (1998).

13. Constitutional Amendment 7 of April 13, part of the so-called April Package. From Holston and Caldeira (1998, 269). The political circumstances of this measure are described in Costa Couto (1998, 203). The reform had been proposed as a bill by the executive but rejected in a congressional vote. President Geisel then closed Congress and decreed the measure as a constitutional amendment. The amendment largely stands today—a striking, specific example of an "authoritarian legacy" in the institutional realm.

14. Survey research indicates strong support in Argentina, Brazil, and Chile for devoting more resources to the police. In a poll taken between December 1998 and January 1999, 84 percent of Argentines, 89 percent of Brazilians, and 80 percent of Chileans agreed that the government should spend more on the police ("Free Market" 1999). The poll was conducted by Latinobarómetro, and the margin of error is 1 percentage point for the Americas as a whole and 2.5 to 4.5 percentage points for individual countries. No data were provided for Uruguay.

15. "Policia de SP" (2002). The 2000 figure is for the state of São Paulo as a whole, whereas the 1991–96 figures are for greater metropolitan São Paulo. With almost half the population of the state and much higher rates of violence than elsewhere in the state, the latter is the primary component of the former. The article cited above, covering police killings of civilians by the São Paulo police from 1991 to 2002, gave figures only slightly different from the ones from greater São Paulo city provided by Chevigny (1995) and Human Rights Watch (1998a, 93).

16. Luiz Soares, interview, 10 July 1999, Vera Institute, New York City.

17. See the *Official Registry of the Argentine Republic* (Buenos Aires, 1879), vol. 1. Although the town council gave some orders to the police, most came from the ruling junta. Sanguinetti (1992).

18. PFA official who spoke on condition of anonymity, interview by author, 13 December 1996.

19. In a 1994 poll, 60 percent of respondents favored giving more power to police agencies.

20. Officially, the PFA has always been a part of the Interior Ministry. But with the preponderance of military regimes, it was really directed by the military up until 1983. While Article 2 of the PFA's Organic Law places it in the Interior Ministry, Article 15 subordinates "the headquarters of the Federal Police to a superior official of the Armed Forces of the Nation."

21. Interviewed on condition of anonymity, December 1996.

22. Ibid.

23. Internal PFA disciplinary action takes one of four forms: warning, arrest, suspension, or dismissal.

24. In November 1997, for example, the killing of a police official exposed a ring of top officials involved in robbery and extortion (see "Policía contra policía" (1998).

25. When two officials of the PFA were detained in 1998 for torturing a detainee, their excuse that "he lives in a permanent pre-delictual state" was a common one (Verbitsky 1998, 3).

26. In 1869, the Supreme Court ruled in *Empresa Plaza de Toros v. Provincia de Buenos Aires* that "it is a fact and also a principle of constitutional law, that the 'policing' of the provinces is the responsibility of local governments . . . to safeguard the 'security, health and morality' of their populations."

27. In 1959, the Supreme Court said in *Russo v. Delle Dome* that it had "accepted a broad notion of 'police power' . . . [b]efore the pressing necessity to face the damages/risks created by this emergency situation and to reduce or mitigate its effects" (Herraiz 1970, 28).

28. Roberto Vásquez, Subsecretario de Seguridad de la Provincia de Buenos Aires, interview by author, 19 August, 1998.

29. Provincial Deputy Juan Carlos Lema, Chair, Human Rights Commission, interview by author, 1 December 1994.

30. Roberto Vásquez, Subsecretario de Seguridad de la Provincia, interview by author, 19 August 1998.

31. As a provincial police official, Rico was on record as saying that "it is necessary to kill [delinquents] in the street without any doubt and without having pity" ("El carapintada por la boca muere" 1998).

32. "Quieren usar custodios privados" (1999).

33. In addition, in February 1999, the provincial government formulated a plan to allow an increase from twenty-four to forty-eight hours in the time that the police can hold someone detained for identification and to ease the ability of the police to carry out inspections without previous court authorization.

34. This remains true even after the initiation of legal proceedings against Augusto Pinochet in early 2001.

35. Human rights lawyer Hector Salazar was also prosecuted in Chile's military courts merely for making remarks to the media to the effect that if he were a carabinero, he would not obey Stange. Salazar was charged with "sedition," showing how the legal apparatus can be used by defenders of a *mano dura* approach to policing. Sebastian Brett and Hector Salazar interview by author, 6 June 1998, Santiago, Chile.

36. In a Centro de Estudios Públicos (CEP)-Adimark poll, crime was given top priority among 58.6 percent of respondents, followed by health at 47.7 percent (CEP 1999).

37. In a 1996 poll conducted by Adimark, the directors of both the Carabineros and the Investigaciones received approval rates of over 70 percent, while 63.9 percent of respondents said that police officers were helpful.

38. *Diario Oficial, Documentos* (Uruguay) 325, no. 22295 (1981).

REFERENCES

Adelman, Jeremy. 1999. *Colonial Legacies: The Problem of Persistence in Latin American History.* New York: Routledge.

Agüero, Felipe. 1998. "Legacies of Transitions: Institutionalization, the Military, and Democracy in South America." *Mershon International Review* 42:383–404.

Basanez, Miguel, Marta Lagos, and Tatiana Beltrun. 1996. *Reporte 1995: Encuesta Latinobarómetro, 1996.* Mexico: Agosto.

Bayley, David. 1985. *Patterns of Policing: A Comparative International Analysis.* New Brunswick, N.J.: Rutgers University Press.

Benavides, Augusto Quintana. 1998. "Informe nacional: Control democratico de los organismos de seguridad interior en Chile." In Hugo Fruhling, ed., *Controle democratico en el mantenimiento de la seguridad interior.* Santiago: Centro de Estudios del Desarrollo.

Cano, Ignacio. 1999. *Letalidade da acao policial no Rio de Janeiro: A atuacao da justica militar.* Rio de Janeiro: Instituto de Estudo da Religião.

Centeno, Miguel. 1997. "Blood and Debt: War and Taxation in Nineteenth-Century Latin America." *American Journal of Sociology* 102, no. 6: 1565–1605.

Centeno, Miguel, and Fernando Lopez-Alves. 2001. *The Other Mirror: Grand Theory through the Lens of Latin America.* Princeton, N.J.: Princeton University Press.

Centro de Estudios Legales y Sociales and Americas Watch. 1991. *Police Violence in Argentina.* Buenos Aires: Centro de Estudios Legales y Sociales.

Centro de Estudios Públicos. 1999. "Social Study and Opinion Poll, April to May 1999. Special Topic: Detention of Augusto Pinochet and Elections 1999." Poll no. 295. Retrieved 14 May 2003 from www.cepchile.cl/ddet295.ingles.pdf.

Chevigny, Paul. 1995. *The Edge of the Knife.* New York: New Press.

Collier, Ruth Berins, and David Collier. 1991. *Shaping the Political Arena.* Princeton, N.J.: Princeton University Press.

Comité Ejecutivo para la Reforma del Estado. 2001. "Programa de Reforma del Estado (1995–2001)." Retrieved 14 January 2003 from www.cepre.opp.gub.uy.

Costa Couto, Ronaldo. 1998. *Historia indiscreta da ditadura e da abertura: Brasil 1964–85.* Rio de Janeiro: Editora Record.

De Brito, Alexandra Barahona. 1997. *Human Rights and Democratization in Latin America: Uruguay and Chile.* New York: Oxford University Press.

Dromi, José Roberto. 1985. *Policía y derecho.* Buenos Aires: Ediciones UNSTA.

Dyzenhaus, David. 1997. "Legal Theory in the Collapse of Weimar: Contemporary Lessons?" *American Political Science Review* 91, no. 1:121–34.

"El carapintada por la boca muere." 1998. *Página 12* (10 March): 12.

El Instituto Nacional de Estadística y Censos. 2002. *Anuario estadístico de la República Argentina.* Buenos Aires: INDEC.

Fishman, Robert. 1990. "Rethinking State and Regime: Southern Europe's Transition to Democracy." *World Politics* 42 (April): 422–440.

"The Free Market Still Scores Highly among Latin Americans." 1999. *Wall Street Journal–Americas,* special supplement, January 31, 1–6.

Freitas, Ruben Correa. 1993. *Derecho constitucional contemporaneo.* Montevideo: Fundación de Cultura Universitaria.

Frühling, Hugo. 1997. "Carabineros y consolidación democrática en Chile." *Revista Latinoamericana de Política Criminal* 3, no. 3:81–116.

González, Gustavo Germán. 1971. *El hampa porteña.* Buenos Aires: Prensa Austral.

Haggard, Stephan, and Robert Kaufman. 1997. "The Political Economy of Democratic Transitions." *Comparative Politics* 29, no. 3:263–83.

Herraiz, Hector Eduardo. 1970. *Poder de policía.* Buenos Aires: Facultad de Derecho y Ciencias Sociales de la Universidad de Buenos Aires.

Holden, Robert. 1996. "Constructing the Limits of State Violence in Central America: Towards a New Research Agenda." *Journal of Latin American Studies* 28 (May): 435–59.

Holloway, Thomas. 1993. *Policing Rio de Janeiro: Repression and Resistance in a Nineteenth-Century City.* Stanford, Calif: Stanford University Press.

Holston, James, and Teresa P. R. Caldeira. 1998. "Democracy, Law and Violence: Disjunctions of Brazilian Citizenship." In Felipe Agüero and Jeffrey Stark, eds., *Fault Lines of Democracy in Post-Transition Latin America* (pp. 263–89). Miami, Fla.: North-South Center Press.

Huggins, Martha. 1998. *Political Policing: The United States and Latin America.* Durham, N.C.: Duke University Press.

Human Rights Watch. 1997. *World Report 1997.* New York: Human Rights Watch.

———. 1998a. *Los límites de la tolerancia: Libertad de expresión y debate público en Chile.* Santiago: Human Rights Watch/Coleccion Nuevo Periodismo.

———. 1998b. *World Report 1998.* New York: Human Rights Watch.

Karl, Terry Lynn. 1997. *The Paradox of Plenty: Oil Booms and Petro-States.* Studies in International Political Economy, No. 26. Berkeley: University of California Press.

Krasner, Stephen D. 1984. "Approaches to the State: Alternative Conceptions and Historical Dynamics." *Comparative Politics* 16 (January): 223–46.

Lopez Alves, Fernando. 1996. "The Authoritarian Roots of Liberalism: Uruguay, 1810–1886." In Vincent Peloso and Barbara Tenenbaum, eds., *Liberals, Politics, and Power: State Formation in Nineteenth-Century Latin America* (pp. 111–33). Athens: University of Georgia Press.

Loveman, Brian. 1993. *The Constitution of Tyranny.* Pittsburgh, Pa.: University of Pittsburgh Press.

———. 1998. "When You Wish upon the Stars: Why the Generals (and Admirals) Say Yes to Latin American 'Transitions' to Civilian Government." In Paul Drake and Mathew McCubbins, eds., *The Origins of Liberty: Political and Economic Liberalization in the Modern World.* Princeton, N.J.: Princeton University Press.

———. 1999a. *Civil-Military Relations in Spanish America: The Past as Prelude.* Paper presented at the Soldiers and Democracy in Latin America Conference, 19–20 February, University of California at Riverside.

———. 1999b. *For La Patria: Politics and the Armed Forces in Latin America.* Wilmington, Del.: Scholarly Resources.

Maier, Julio Bernardo José. 1996. "Breve historia institucional de la policía argentina." In Peter Waldmann, ed., *Justicia en la calle.* Bogotá: Centro Interdisciplinario de Estudios sobre Desarrollo Latinoamericana.

Mann, Michael. 1993. *The Sources of Social Power.* Vol. 2. *The Rise of Classes and Nation States 1760–1914.* Cambridge: Cambridge University Press.

McSherry, J. Patrice. 1997. *Incomplete Transition: Military Power and Democracy in Argentina.* New York: St. Martin's Press.

Mera Figueroa, Jorge. 1998. "Razones justificatorias y ambito de la jurisdicción penal militar en tiempos de paz." *Cuadernos de Analisis Juridico,* no. 40:15–77.

Migdal, Joel S. 1988. *Strong Societies and Weak States: State-Society Relations and State Capabilities in the Third World.* Princeton, N.J.: Princeton University Press.

Morlino, Leonardo. 1997. "Is There Another Side to the Fascist Legacy?" Paper presented at the first meeting of the Authoritarian Legacies Working Group, October 10–12, New York, Figure 1.

Munck, Gerardo, and Carol Skalnik Leff. 1997. "Modes of Transition and Democratization." *Comparative Politics* 29, no. 3:343–362.

"Neighbors . . . and Friends?" 1998. Wall Street Journal Americas.

"New Argentine President Orders Purge of Remnants of 'Dirty War.'" 2000. *New York Times,* 16 February, A2.

Norden, Deborah. 1996. *Military Rebellion in Argentina: Between Coups and Consolidation.* Lincoln: University of Nebraska Press.

O'Donnell, Guillermo, ed. 1999. *Counterpoints: Selected Essays on Authoritarianism and Democratization.* Notre Dame, Ind.: University of Notre Dame Press.

Oteiza, Eduardo. 1999. "Consecharás tempestades." *Clarín: Zona*, 8 August, 7.

Peloso, Vincent, and Barbara Tenenbaum, eds. 1996. *Liberals, Politics, and Power: State Formation in Nineteenth-Century Latin America*. Athens: University of Georgia Press.

Pereira, Anthony. 1998. "O monstro algemado? Violencia do estado e repressao legal no Brasil, 1964–1997." In Jorge Zaverucha, ed., *Democracia e instituicoes politicas brasileiras no final do seculo vinte*. Recife, Brazil: Bargaco.

Pinheiro, Paulo Sergio. 1991. *Estrategias da illusão*. São Paulo: Companhia das Letras.

———. 1996. "Préfacio: O passado está morto: Nem passado é ainda." In Gilberto Dimenstein, *Democracia em pedaços: Direitos humanos no Brasil* (pp. 7–45). São Paulo: Companhia das Letras.

"Policía contra policía." 1998. *Pistas*, June, 57–59.

"Policía de SP mata 68 civis por mes em 2002." 2002. *Folha de São Paulo*, 24 June, C1.

Presidência da República. 1996. *Programa nacional de direitos humanos*. Brasília, Brazil: Ministério da Justiça.

Przeworski, Adam. 1991. *Democracy and the Market*. New York: Cambridge University Press.

"Quieren usar custodios privados para prevenir y reprimir delitos." 1999. *Clarín*, 28 July, 38.

Rock, David. 1987. *Argentina, 1516–1987*. Berkeley: University of California Press.

Rueschemeyer, Dietrich, Evelyne Huber Stephens, and John D. Stephens. 1992. *Capitalist Development and Democracy*. Chicago: University of Chicago Press.

Rugendorfer, Ricardo. 1998. "La guerra de los botones." *Pistas*, no. 18 (13 February): 41.

Saín, Marcol Fabián. 2002. *Seguridad, democracia y reforma del sistema policial en la Argentina*. Buenos Aires: Fondo de Cultura Económica.

Sanguinetti, Esteban Adolfo. 1992. "Evolución histórica de la policía." *Mundo Policial* 22, no. 71:12–29.

Sayan, Diego. 1999. "The Development of a Culture of Rights-Claiming." Lecture presented at "The Rule of Law and Governance in Latin America", a conference at the Fletcher School of Law and Diplomacy. Tufts University, Boston, 15 April 1999.

Schirmer, Jennifer. 1999. "The Guatemalan Military Project: Legacies for a Violent Peace?" *Latin American Perspectives* 26, no. 2:92–107.

Slatta, Richard W., and Karla Robinson. 1990. "Continuity in Crime and Punishment: Buenos Aires, 1820–50." In Lyman L. Johnson, ed., *The Problem of Order in Changing Societies*. Albuquerque: University of New Mexico Press.

Stanley, William. 1996. *The Protection Racket State: Elite Politics, Military Extortion and Civil War in El Salvador*. Philadelphia: Temple University Press.

Tanner, Murray Scott. 2000. "Will the State Bring *You* Back In? Policing and Democratization." *Comparative Politics* 33, no. 1:101–26.

Tilly, Charles. 1992. *Coercion, Capital, and European States, AD 990–1992*. Cambridge, England: Blackwell.

————. 1998. *Durable Inequality.* Berkeley: University of California Press.

U.S. Senate. 1871. Committee on Foreign Relations. *United States Policies and Programs in Brazil: Hearings before the U.S. Subcommittee on Western Hemisphere Affairs,* 92d Cong., 1st sess., 4 May. Testimony of Theodore D. Brown, chief of AID public safety program in Brazil.

Verbitsky, Horacio. 1998. "Seguridad o libertad?" *Página 12* (22 February): 3–4.

Willis, Eliza, Christopher Garman, and Stephan Haggard. 1999. "The Politics of Decentralization in Latin America." *Latin American Research Review* 34, no. 1:7–56.

Zaffaroni, Eugenio Raúl. 1994. *Estructuras judiciales.* Buenos Aires: Sociedad Anónima Editora.

Zaverucha, Jorge. 2000. *Fragil democracia: Collor, Itamar, FHC e os Militares.* São Paulo: Civilizacão Brasileira.

Zommer, Laura. "Encuesta nacional de Gallup para La Nación: Sólo el 18 por ciento de los argentinos confía en la Justicia." *La Nación,* Sección Politica, 23 January 2001. Retrieved 23 January 2001 from www.lanacion.com.ar.

8

Latin American Citizenship

Civic Microfoundations in Historical Perspective

CONSUELO CRUZ

Like economic systems and philosophical constructs, polities are grounded in microfoundations. Democracies, at least in theory, ultimately rest on citizenries aware and in possession of their rights and duties. Even Dankwart Rustow, who thought that the spread of democratic institutions required only that "the vast majority of citizens" harbor no doubt about "which political community they belong to,"[1] assumed the prior existence of a citizenry.

This essay argues that Latin American political history has produced discursive formations that, by minimizing and even negating the principle of individual autonomy, impoverish regnant notions of citizenship and, by extension, weaken the microfoundations of the region's democracies.[2] I define a discursive formation as a series of rhetorical moves that together articulate the meaning of key political struggles and ultimately justify the content and consequences of their resolution. Citizenship, in turn, is defined as an ideal or model of political integration that generates a civic profile for the individual—that is, a coherent bundle of attributes that give him or her standing in the public sphere.

I posit a link between discursive formations and civic microfoundations because democracy depends on an array of cultural patterns, enumerated by Andrews and Chapman as "habits of mind, rituals of participation, and forms of dialogue between ruler and ruled."[3] Indeed, in a robust democracy some of these practices are so basic that they assume taken-for-granted status. A community of citizens, for example, lives by the notion that "speech" is supposed to "take the place of blood" and "acts of decision" are meant to "take the place of vengeance."[4]

I also argue that these everyday functions of citizenship—that is, the discursive practices that routinely energize a civic public sphere—ought to matter to democratization scholars on two counts. First, speech and acts of decision are at the core of "meaningful participation" in a democratic polity. Second, if meaningful participation requires citizens to be "communicatively competent individuals,"[5] then communicative competence becomes integral to such core issues as resource control, institutional design, and civil society development. In other words, it becomes necessary for scholars and political actors alike to ask, Who has the necessary resources—the skills, information, and time—to participate in democratic discourse? What are the norms of public debate? Can civil and political society thrive if these resources are poorly distributed and the pertinent norms are laden with intolerance?[6]

The historical impoverishment of Latin American citizenship is best illustrated if we begin by contrasting it to the republican model that Latin Americans themselves have invoked since postcolonial times and to the historical development of democratic citizenship in western Europe. This essay, therefore, first canvasses paradigmatic understandings of citizenship as well as the discursive formations and rhetorical practices associated with the struggles for citizenship in modern England. This discussion then serves as a reference point for a more detailed exploration of the discursive formations and practices that in postcolonial Latin America began to eclipse the individual dimension of citizenship. Finally, the essay links the deleterious discursive legacies of the postcolonial period to the microfoundational weakness and polarizing dynamics of the region's contemporary democracies.

Definitions of Citizenship and the English Experience

In the Greek classical conception, citizenship entails both the *right* to partake in the practice of collective decision making and the *obligation* to submit to its binding products. A citizen is thus one "who rules and is ruled." In the Roman alternative, citizenship is a legal *status*, so that a "citizen" is "someone free to act by law" as member of a legal community.[7] For Rousseau, in turn, "the essence of the body politic lies in the reconciliation of obedience and liberty," so the citizen is both subject and sovereign.[8] Finally, T. H. Marshall understood citizenship as a universal status entailing a series of rights. According to Marshall, these rights were vindicated in historical stages, as processes of capitalist differentiation loosened "bundles" of medieval rights and duties, engendered England's modern social classes, and led to the creation of the state's judicial, legislative, and social services.[9]

More recent accounts diverge significantly from Marshall's view.[10] Margaret Somers, for one, argues that citizenship did *not* originate as a status consisting of universal rights and duties conferred by the state. Somers's evidence points instead to social and political citizenship as a set of *practices* that emerged simultaneously with modern national labor laws and civil rights. In addition, her findings suggest that the enhancement of English citizenship was tied not to social classes but to political action, the source of which was identity—in turn shaped by political participation and discourse in non-state public spheres, community associations, and the family.[11]

If Somers is correct, then the crucial importance of discursive formations and rhetorical practices as conceived in this essay is rendered self-evident. But if Marshall wins the day, and the history of modern citizenship is indeed made up of a sequence of class-led struggles that enhanced the status of citizens, it is still the case that communicative competence was integral to those struggles and their outcomes.[12] In the eighteenth century, for example, the leadership of the English landed gentry championed the cause of civil rights through a series of rhetorical moves that simultaneously (1) recast the notion of "rights"; (2) engendered the imaginaries associated with the identities of the "state" and the "individual"; and (3) established the demarcations and reciprocities that kept the two identities distinguishable yet mutually dependent.

Moreover, once these rhetorical moves "formed" the discourse of civil rights, specific discursive practices privileged what we might call the "everyday truths and consequences" of this discourse. The civil rights discourse, for example, put in bold relief individuals' "freedom of movement"—a novel concept that Barrington Moore might have categorized as "subversive." This novelty, in turn, facilitated the construction of labor markets. Similarly, labor markets "empowered" laborers to "compete" for wages. And "wage competition" justified yet another novelty—namely the view of the individual as no longer deserving or in need of social protection.

These were all, to be sure, links in a historical chain of "real" event processes. But they were also the rhetorical moves of "communicatively competent individuals" bent both on making an overwhelming case for civil rights and on elucidating for themselves and for others the market logic that flowed from those rights. The gentry, in short, contributed to the historical-discursive formation of citizenship. The industrial middle classes, in the pursuit of their own visions and interests, did the same in the nineteenth century while fighting for political rights. And the laboring classes followed suit in their struggle for social entitlements in the twentieth.

The upshot of all this is that even if we take citizenship to be a time-enhanced status, the English social classes were themselves practical inventors of citizenship. The process was often conflictual and never linear, but this is, in fact, how the various classes became active owners of *individual* rights. For this reason, too, modern citizenship has at its core some "specified level of equality"; and while equality is never complete, as Thomas Janoski points out, "it most often entails an increase in subordinate rights *vis à vis* social elites."[13]

The Latin American Experience

Whether we take Marshall or Somers as our point of reference, it is clear that English citizenship was enriched with time. This was not the outcome of the crucial struggles that shaped Latin American citizenship in the early national era. If anything—partly because of the broader frame that organized political debate just prior to independence, partly because of the sequencing of the struggles themselves—Latin American citizenship gradually lost the robustness inherent in its republican model. In fact, the republican model itself came into play relatively late. At the close of the eighteenth century and in the early decades of the nineteenth, even the most heated creole disputes regarding the sources and institutions of legitimate authority took place within the parameters set by Iberian champions of royal absolutism and advocates of a constitutional monarchy. Like their Iberian counterparts, creole camps split on the issue of constitutional constraints on the monarchy but generally agreed on the inviolable status of the monarch.

This convergence proved crucial on several counts. To begin with, independist creoles did not articulate a clear and convincing case against the monarchical model of legitimation. The British colonies of the north, for example, came to repudiate the king of England himself after concluding that he too was a corrupt enemy of "liberty." Spanish American patriots, in contrast, continued to declare their sovereign "benevolent and wise." Indeed, because the royal sovereign remained a viable source of legitimate authority in the creoles' eyes, their rhetorical strategies and political action perennially targeted the apex of the political hierarchy. Liberals simultaneously argued for constitutional constraints on the monarchy and blamed their misfortunes not on their sovereign but on the "evil" men around his throne. Conservatives and liberals alike railed against the local *peninsular* officials who, in their view, humiliated and abused Spanish Americans against their king's benevolent will. And both liberals and conservatives fell to their knees when reaffirming their abiding commitment to the Crown during the Napoleonic crisis of 1808–12.[14]

The creoles' failure to delegitimate the king, in short, left ample space for the emergence of creole independist sentiment *without* a well-developed republican understanding of political authority. This was obvious in Mexico's Plan de Iguala, which declared the country's independence while explicitly calling on Ferdinand—or any other member of the Spanish royal house—directly to rule the aborning nation. And it was obvious in Central America, whose creoles were swept along by Mexican events yet repeatedly swore allegiance to the reigning monarch, popularly known as "The Beloved."

These persistent declarations of allegiance, too, would have serious consequences: once the Crown disappeared from the scene, creole elites had no other legitimating principles than those they had deployed rhetorically to buttress their case for a constitutional monarchy. This is why the same conservatives and liberals who on the eve of independence had upheld the monarchical principle of authority quickly turned in the wake of independence to the republican concept of the "popular will" in search of a new sovereign. And this is why liberals and conservatives alike were remarkably inclined to structure and regulate the pursuit of power through electoral channels.[15]

The recurrent, often violent electoral disputes that characterized postcolonial politics were in fact but a symptom of a destabilizing combination: elites' vital dependence on republican/democratic legitimation and those same elites' denigration of the existing *demos*. Not too long before independence, one of America's founding patriots, Simón Bolívar, explained to the Venezuelans that the failure of their First Republic (1810–12) was partly due to "stupid people who [did not] know the value of their rights." Later still, in 1819, Bolívar began to contemplate the formation of "a new aristocracy" of warriors and the creation of a government resembling a monarchy.[16]

Bolívar was not alone. As one scholar puts it: "According to Spanish-American elites, the true people had not yet been born." Indeed, from their perspective, the "true people" would have to be "created" by patrician governments whose enlightened policies might gradually produce acceptable replacements for the "urban riffraff" and the "ignorant peasants."[17]

At first glance, these founding elites seem hardly different from their counterparts in the United States, who harbored an ambivalent attitude toward the *demos*. But the American founders were also genuinely split on such key issues as suffrage precisely because they both feared and exalted the people. This is partly why one of the signal outcomes of North American postcolonial politics was the effective institutionalization of the checks-and-balances mechanism *and* a sacralized bill of rights.

By way of contrast, Latin American creoles managed to neglect and postpone the issue of individual rights,[18] in no small measure because they were able to articulate and impose an increasingly coherent discourse in which enlightened elitism figured as a necessary counterforce to the ignorant *demos* and the sinister factions that manipulated it. The origins of this discourse can be traced directly to the colonial view of the local polity as an organism whose "healthy" parts (the "honest" *vecinos*) must constantly struggle to dominate and exclude "unhealthy" elements from the public sphere in general and from its representative body (or *cabildo*) in particular.[19]

This discursive pattern remained unproblematic for as long as the arbitration and succession mechanisms supplied by the monarchical model were in place. Once these were removed, however, popular sovereignty and electoral procedure were both subsumed under the practices of the organic entities that had been at the center of the public sphere in the colonial regime—that is, *los pueblos* and their *cabildos*.[20] As Natalio Botana explains, the resurgence of organicism, even if in hybrid form, meant that the transitional period from 1810 to 1820 produced no clear republican resolution. If anything, in the subsequent period of national consolidation, from 1820 to 1840, there emerged a system that he aptly describes as "inverted representation."[21]

In this system of inverted representation, the principle of individual autonomy so closely associated with popular sovereignty was overwhelmed by the government's corporate will; and it was the ruler himself rather than the citizenry who acted as elector. In fact, to borrow another of Botana's apt phrases, inverted representation gave rise to the widespread phenomenon of "personalist hegemony," best exemplified first by the Rosas regime in Argentina and later still by the *Porfiriato* in Mexico (1884–1911).[22]

The Rosas case illustrates how all this actually worked in the politics of the day. Far from negating the principle of universal suffrage, Rosas expanded it. But he also employed a tactic that was common among the new nations of the region: he assembled a list of the persons he deemed "worthy" of "representing" the rights of the *patria*.[23] This process of selection and election from above harked back to the colonial distinction between "honest" and "dishonest" elements—a distinction that, as in colonial times, now served as a criterion for the granting or denial of standing in the public sphere. Drawing the distinction, in fact, became a central referent of competitive politics. Here again, discursive norms and strategies were key. Nowhere was this as clear as in Central America, where the discursive norm that had allowed the king's subjects to seek arbitration directly from the Crown was redirected to *El Público*, which was now assigned the role of grand arbiter.[24]

Unlike the royal arbiter, however, *El Público* was politically disorganized and bereft of institutional clout. This meant that this new arbiter was utterly incapable of rendering enforceable judgments. Nonetheless, competing political leaders persisted in seeking arbitration from *El Público*. Moreover, political rivals resurrected the dominant rhetorical strategy of colonial times as they set out to persuade *El Público* that they were virtuous while their rivals were "wicked" and deserving of "extermination."[25]

This rhetorical strategy had the perverse effect of forcing the various organic entities that actually made up *El Público* to reach polarizing moral judgments about the competing political leaders themselves. In fact, this rhetorical dynamic between leaders and followers promoted factional and violent mobilization. And this kind of mobilization, in turn, led liberals and conservatives to converge on the notion that in the clash between the forces of "light" and "darkness," evil men would naturally resort to "imposture" and promote "disorder" by "duping" the "naive" people—much as they had once duped the king.[26]

The interplay of these rhetorical norms and strategies gradually contributed to a distinct discursive formation. To begin with, both liberals and conservatives began to argue for "uniformity of opinion," since such uniformity would deny "harbor" to the "wicked."[27] In addition, both liberals and conservatives called for the "moral" education of the public[28] in a (futile) effort to prevent rivals from mobilizing the "populace." Finally, both liberals and conservatives developed a profound fear of "anarchy"; both warned of the dire consequences that would follow if people "delivered" themselves "to lavish plans and notions of inalienable rights"; and both predicted that great rewards would be reaped if "order" was established. As one liberal notable put it, "Good comportment and rectitude of intentions shall reestablish trust. . . . We shall enter a . . . new life, a new path; we shall navigate under the two stars of our purpose: forgetfulness of the past, brotherhood for the future."[29] By the 1840s, Central American competitive politics were premised on the claim that the *patria* was threatened from within by sinister forces bent on destroying its unity.[30] Even liberals perceived a vicious dynamic at play: "The *pueblos* have tasted excessive freedom, and public functionaries, demoralized by continuous revolutions, tend either towards despotism or towards dejection, and their subjects either toward servility or toward anarchy."[31] Even self-proclaimed conciliatory governments, by operating on the premise that the wicked thrived on "disorder," ultimately set out to eradicate "factions."[32] Their efforts proved counterproductive.[33] In retrospect, the reasons are clear. On the one hand, they upheld freedom of the press and speech as worthy of defense. On the other hand, they drew sharp limits around these freedoms in hopes of preventing politicians from "abusing" the "innocence" and "simplicity" of the people.[34]

This contradiction became particularly pronounced in two types of situations. The first was when electoral outcomes were in dispute.[35] The second occurred when leaders responded to the generalized craving for "paternal order" by attempting to restore the nation's broken "familial ties."[36]

The familial metaphor, in fact, was paradoxically destabilizing because it captured both the growing consensus in favor of "strong leaders" and its underlying logic.[37] This logic relied on two key distinctions. First, proponents of iron-hand rule argued that it was possible to differentiate between "despots" who "usurped" authority and ruled according to "caprice" and strong leaders who ruled by "reason" and thus provided their followers with "paternal protection."[38] The second distinction was this: "order" and "liberty" were not incompatible because one could easily distinguish between justifiable and unjustifiable disobedience, since "only savages rebel against just authority." (This was an allusion to Carrera of Guatemala, who figured in liberal political rhetoric as a "hungry tiger" at the head of rapacious and terrorist "Indians.")[39]

In the context of this political-discursive formation, protecting the moral fiber of republican institutions stood out as the normative objective.[40] Seizing control of government, in turn, was the practical-strategic objective. The violent upheavals that flowed from this shared view of the "solution" to disorder are well known and need not be revisited here. Rather, what is pertinent to this discussion is the supporting logic of paternalistic governance and its implications for the concept of citizenship. First, the most immediate goal for national "paterfamilias" was to put an end to the "democratic frenzy."[41] Second, in this homogenization model of "familial" inspiration, the organization of authority in the *patria*—conceived as a natural-moral unit—could take one of two forms. In the paternal/filial variant, a benevolent "father" guided a nation of obedient "sons." In the fraternal alternative, loyal "brothers" chose a ruler from amongst themselves. The former idealized vertical lines of authority, the latter horizontal.

Both variants, however, depended on individuals' unremitting compliance and fealty—as opposed to a perpetual balancing between liberty and obedience. And neither tolerated arguments that might arise from conflicting interests or divergent opinions. Put yet another way, neither allowed for the *ambiguity* inherent in the notion of the individual citizen as both subject and sovereign. This missing ambiguity stunted "meaningful participation" through civic "speech" and "acts of decision." Two immediate reasons stand out. First, rather than build a public sphere for civic dialogue, "communicatively competent individuals" formed intransigent camps. Second, and just as important, camps proved vulnerable to *internal* discord precisely because elites diminished their own communicative competence by adhering to the discourse of familial cohesion, which strictly prescribed uniformity of opinion.

For these reasons, as well, elites simply could not get past their understanding of civil wars as "fratricidal" clashes—"abominations" for which no camp was willing to take any measure of responsibility. All guilt was to be laid instead at the feet of the national family's "anarchical" enemies. Conversely, the politics of opposition could be properly justified only as righteous rebellion against "tyrannical" usurpers of legitimate power.[42]

Linking the Past to the Present

This fixation with creating a docile, internally harmonious, and virtuous "people" was no Central American peculiarity. Well into the late-nineteenth century, elites throughout the region simultaneously revered the abstract notion of the popular will and entertained designs aimed at regenerating the "inferior" masses. In Argentina, reformers from the generation of 1837 to the generation of 1880 produced and refined the discursive formation of the "enlightened minority."[43] In Mexico, Bolivia, Colombia, Venezuela, Peru, and Chile, elites carefully crafted arguments for their own intellectual, moral, and political superiority. Indeed, everywhere they propounded their special ability to govern over a *pueblo* presumed incapable of discerning its own preferences and welfare.

The urban and rural upper classes in Mexico and Peru, for example, might be internally divided by competing economic interests. They might even suffer the periodic assaults launched on aristocratic dominance by up-start *caudillos*. But through it all, they shared an unshakable conviction in their own superiority over the *castas*. Meanwhile, Chilean progressives and conservatives alike contributed to the liberalization of commerce in particular and the expansion of markets more broadly (very much at the expense of the peasantry) but clung to the oligarchic nature of "good" government into the twentieth century.[44] (European democracies retained restrictive or oligarchic institutional features as well, but their elites failed to establish a dominant discourse of superiority, thwarted as they were by the sociopolitical and cultural processes associated with the expansion of citizenship.)

In fact, "enlightened" governments throughout Latin America set out once again to "civilize" and homogenize their societies. As one scholar has demonstrated in ample detail, both positivist and antipositivist rulers saw immigration, public health, labor laws, obligatory military service, and the public school systems as ways of redeeming the common people while eradicating "difference." Hence the elites' open combat (in racially and ethnically complex societies) with cultural pluralism. Hence also the vertical integration of public education systems and the schools' paternalistic mission: prevent the contamination of children as they came into contact with "social vices."[45]

The 1900s did not displace the paternalistic discursive practices that flowed from the historical formations of the previous century. To be sure, rulers everywhere failed to standardize the region's heterogeneous populations. But rather than diminishing the appeal of a centralizing, even authoritarian public administration, this failure actually led elites in the early decades of the twentieth century to redouble their efforts to administer the socio-moral development of the "people." Public school systems, for example, were increasingly centralized, even in federal republics like Mexico, Argentina, and Venezuela.[46]

The different "enlightened minority" discourses that came to prevail in Latin America also renewed old arguments in favor of paternalistic rule, whether oligarchic or *caudillista* in institutional form. The exalted place accorded to paternal authority, in turn, meant that if one managed to establish plausible distinctions, say, between "barbarous" and "cultured" *caudillos*,[47] then *caudillismo* could be salvaged in the face of disappointing or even vulgar exemplars.

Salvaging *caudillismo* was crucial. After all, the constitutions of Latin America's modern states failed to break completely with the traditional holistic view of society—a view in which the whole was assigned greater value than its parts. This implied that state and society were caught up in the uneasy coexistence between universalistic principles that rendered individuals equal before the law and hierarchical and organicistic values.[48] Modern *caudillismo* offered a practical resolution to this uneasy coexistence by incorporating the contradictory ideas of individual equality and organic primacy into the persona of the leader. Specifically, modern *caudillismo* relied on the traditional claim that a *caudillo,* as the group's "head," understands best the collectivity's sentiments and is thus uniquely qualified to direct its movements.[49] Populism itself, by relying on charismatic *caudillos,* obliterated the duality of the citizen as both "sovereign" and "subject." As Torcuato di Tella correctly pointed out over three decades ago, populism was a "political movement which enjoy[ed] the support of the mass of the urban class and/or the peasantry but which [did] not result from the autonomous organizational power of these two sectors."[50] The military dictatorships of the 1960s and 1970s, too, were direct beneficiaries of historical-discursive formations and practices that proposed rule by paternal sages (whether in uniform or suits) and large discretionary powers for rulers. And of course, they were also beneficiaries of the uneasy coexistence between individualistic and organicistic principles, precisely because in this hybrid context an individual citizen's civil rights could be easily demoted and even removed to make room for the primacy of the greater good. Moreover, this rhetorical maneuver was clearly rooted in the traditional distinction between healthy and unhealthy elements of the community. One need only refer to the Chilean experience under the Pinochet regime to confirm this observation.[51]

The microfoundations of today's democracies suffer under the weight of this accumulated past. Perpetually in the grip of fear—fear of societal violence, economic anarchy, authoritarian restoration, and unbroken electoral dominance by a popular rival—politicians are constantly concerned with power relations among the branches of the national government, between "the center" and the regions, and finally between social classes and among racial and ethnic groups.

In this context, the general dread of mass mobilization becomes resurgent, both in the living polities and in the democratization literature. Everywhere in the academy, prodemocratic Machiavellis have counseled caution and pragmatism during regime transitions,[52] pointing time and again to the destabilizing potential of "the masses" in consolidating democracies.[53] In Latin America, these concerns not only marginalize the issue of microfoundational soundness but combine to reinforce the qualitative degradation of democratic regimes, which, as O'Donnell has argued, results in the negative equilibrium point he calls delegative democracy.[54] At such a point of equilibrium, the state is relieved in an almost seamless way from the task of enforcing the citizenry's rights and duties. The immediate implications are dismal. For as Larry Diamond has shown, the effective expression and protection of political rights and civil liberties actually deteriorated between 1987 and 1994 in Latin America as a whole.[55]

Conclusion

I have argued here that the project of individual rights was postponed and marginalized in Latin America by historical rhetorical practices and discursive formations that privileged organic identities and paternal authority. In practical terms, this means that in times of conflict, individual citizens have been left exposed to the ravages of shifting politico-ideological winds, whether from the right or the left. It also means that new democracies remain keenly vulnerable to quality erosion. This intangible yet powerful authoritarian legacy can be transcended only through the kind of political-cultural transformation that asserts, in both word and practice, that a mass of citizens is not a mob and that citizen activism is not a riot. So rather than subscribe to the "myth of moderation," to use Nancy Bermeo's phrase,[56] we might turn to the work of conceptualizing and building a democracy characterized by a robust public sphere, an equitable distribution of discursive resources, clear rules of debate and mobilization, and citizens who know themselves as such.

There have been recent indications, here and there, that Latin Americans are capable of reinventing themselves. In the 1997 race for Mexico City's regency, the most striking novelty was Cuauhtémoc Cárdenas's differentiation strategy. As the Partido de la Revolución Democrática (PRD) candidate, he managed to outshine both his Partido Acción Nacional (PAN) and Partido Revolucionario Institucional (PRI) rivals by drawing on the discourse of the nongovernmental organization Movimiento Ciudadano por la Democratización. Specifically, Cárdenas created the campaign theme of *ciudadanización*. Difficult to translate, the term hints at a vision of city governance based on a set of citizen rights that often translate into mutual obligations binding the citizenry and the state. As proprietors of the public space, citizens are obliged to join forces with their accountable government in the fight against institutionalized graft, common criminality, and urban degradation.

There have been other promising signs. In Argentina, Brazil, Bolivia, Uruguay, and Ecuador, independent citizens' groups are increasingly drawing attention to government corruption and demanding accountability.[57] And politically motivated experimentation with antipoverty funds—in the context of economic restructuring and social dislocation—began in the 1980s in Mexico, Bolivia, Chile, Peru, and Colombia. The very fact that the results of these experiments varied according to civic self-awareness, empowerment, and skills at the local and regional levels,[58] reinforces the arguments made in this essay. Or, to borrow from Somers again, it buttresses the claim that citizenship is a set of *practices* that arise from the interaction between the national legal sphere and communities' political cultures. Thus the enhancement of citizenship is tied not to particular social classes but to action shaped by political participation and discourse in nonstate public spheres, community associations, and even the family.[59]

If in Latin America these spheres eventually produce individual citizens aware and in possession of their rights and duties, then the region's democracies may finally rest on firm foundations, and the twin phenomena of inverted representation and delegative democracy may just become a thing of the past. Thus far, however, promising signs remain just that: hints of a transformative potential—a potential perhaps sufficiently rich to vindicate at last the region's early claims to a republican future.

NOTES

1. Cited in John Waterbury, "Fortuitous By-Products," *Comparative Politics* 29, no. 3 (1997): 384.

2. For exceptional cases like Costa Rica, see Jeffery Paige, *Coffee and Power: Revolution and the Rise of Democracy in Central America* (Cambridge, Mass.: Harvard University Press, 1997); Deborah Yashar, *Demanding Democracy: Reform and Reaction in Costa Rica and Guatemala, 1870s–1950s* (Stanford, Calif.: Stanford University Press, 1997); and Consuelo Cruz, "Identity and Persuasion: How Nations Remember Their Pasts and Make Their Futures," *World Politics* 52, no. 3 (2000).

3. George Reid Andrews and Herrick Chapman, eds., *The Social Construction of Democracy, 1870–1990* (New York: New York University Press, 1995), 6.

4. J. G. A. Pocock, "The Ideal of Citizenship since Classical Times," in *The Citizenship Debates*, ed. Gerson Shafir (Minneapolis: University of Minnesota Press, 1998), 32.

5. John S. Dryzek, *Discursive Democracy* (New York: Cambridge University Press, 1990), 41.

6. Ibid., 40–42.

7. Pocock, "Ideal of Citizenship," 36, 37.

8. Anne Norton, *Reflections on Political Identity* (Baltimore, Md.: Johns Hopkins University Press, 1988), 29.

9. T. H. Marshall, *Class, Citizenship and Social Development* (Chicago: University of Chicago Press, 1977), 74.

10. Some scholars argue that citizenship does not eliminate class inequality — not even in advanced industrial democracies. There are scholars who have gone so far as to argue that citizenship actually generates inequity. See Evelyn Nakano Glenn's review of *Citizenship Today: The Contemporary Relevance of T. H. Marshall*, ed. Martin Bulmer and Anthony Rees, in *Contemporary Sociology* 26, no. 4 (1997): 460–62. Other scholars insist that Marshall made a "mistake" because while political and civil rights are fundamental this is not the case with redistributive social rights. Instead, the latter belong to the purview of "political compromise and bargaining." See Jytte Klausen, "Social Rights Advocacy and State Building: T. H. Marshall in the Hands of Social Reformers," *World Politics* 47, no. 2 (1995): 244–67.

11. Margaret Somers, "Citizenship and the Place of the Public Sphere: Law, Community, and Political Culture in the Transition to Democracy," *American Sociological Review* 58, no. 5 (1993): 587.

12. An example from Brazil illustrates the potential usefulness of hybrids blending Marshall and Somers. In 1934, the Brazilian state made primary education compulsory for children between the ages of seven and fourteen. The law of the land opened up the possibility for universal primary education. But since that point, it is local political action, regional identities and ideologies, and federal governmental capacity that have actually determined both the numbers of students who get through school and the quality of their schooling. "Schooling the Multitudes," *Economist*, 18 October 1998, 38.

13. Thomas Janoski, *Citizenship and Civil Society* (New York: Cambridge University Press, 1998), 9–10.

14. See Oscar Gregorio Velez, *Gobernantes y gobernados* (Buenos Aires: Ediciones Ciudad Argentina, 1998), 178.

15. See Antonio Annino, ed., introduction to *Historia de las elecciones en Iberoamérica, siglo XIX* (Buenos Aires: Fondo de Cultura Económica, 1995).

16. Torcuato Di Tella, *Latin American Politics: A Theoretical Framework* (Austin: University of Texas Press, 1991), 51–54.

17. Francois-Xavier Guerra, "Spanish-American Representation," *Journal of Latin American Studies* 26, part 1 (1994): 11.

18. See Iván Jaksic and Marcelo Leiras, "Life without the King," Working Paper no. 255, May 1998, Kellogg Institute, University of Notre Dame.

19. Consuelo Cruz, *World-Making in the Tropics: The Politics of Possibility and Fate* (New York: Cambridge University Press, forthcoming).

20. Natalio Botana, *El orden conservador: La política argentina entre 1880 y 1916*, 5th ed. (Buenos Aires: Editorial Sudamericana, 1988), xix–xxiii.

21. Ibid., xxiv.

22. Ibid.

23. Ibid.

24. The case of Costa Rica is an exception whose complex origins and dynamics are beyond the scope of this chapter but that I have explored in Cruz, "Identity and Persuasion."

25. "Mensaje que el Presidente del Consejo, Doctor José Nuñez, encargado del Poder Ejecutivo, presenta a la Asamblea Legislativa al abrir sus sesiones," 1834, *Revista de la Academia de Geografía e Historia de Nicaragua* 1 (1936–37): 293–99.

26. "Contestaciones al centinela de Nicaragua," hoja suelta, León, 6 May 1837, in *Catálogo de la Exposición Treinta Años de Periodismo en Nicaragua, 1830–1860* (Managua: Instituto Centroamericano de Historia, Universidad Centroamericana).

27. "Decreto de 26 de febrero de 1833, que dispone que se nombre una comisión que pase al Salvador, Honduras i (sic) Guatemala con el objeto de uniformar la opinión sobre reformas," *Revista de la Academia de Geografía e Historia de Nicaragua* 1 (1936–37): 273–74.

28. *Aurora de Nicaragua*, no. 2 (September 1837): 2.

29. "Discurso que en el Aniversario de la Independencia, 15 de Septiembre de 1838, pronunció el Ciudadano Miguel Larreynaga, Presidente de la Corte Suprema de Apelaciones," *Anales de la Sociedad de Geografía e Historia de Guatemala* 25, no. 2 (1938): 230.

30. "Diálogo No. 3 entre Militón y Sompronio, Militón Meneces, Sompronio Fernández (October 1843)." *Revista Conservadora del Pensamiento Centroamericano* 27, no. 134 (1971): 69–72.

31. Rafael Miranda, Consejo Federal, San Vicente, El Salvador, [No title], 28 December 1844, *Revista de la Academia de Geografía e Historia de Nicaragua* 1 (1936–37).

32. *Registro Oficia* (Nicaragua), March 1845.

33. Pedro Joaquín Chamorro, *Significado patriótico de los Convenios del 12 de Septiembre de 1856* (Managua: Tipografía La Prensa, 1939), 108–9.

34. José León Sandoval, "Al público," *Managua*, 22 September 1846, unpaginated.

35. Juan Ruiz, "Al público" (Rivas: Imprenta de la Libertad, 31 January 1844), *Revista Conservadora del Pensamiento Centroamericano* 27, no. 134 (1971): 93–94.

36. See Doroteo Vasconzelos, *El Presidente del Salvador a sus pueblos y a los demás de Centro América* (San Salvador: Imprenta del Triunfo, 10 January 1851); "Dictámen sobre el pacto de erección de un gobierno jeneral (sic) provisorio," Asamblea Constituyente, Comayagua, Honduras, 15 January 1848; *Correo del Istmo de Nicaragua, Prospectus* (León, Nicaragua: Inprenta del Estado, 1 May 1849); *Contestación del Jeneral [sic] Flores a la gaceta del gobierno de San Salvador* (San José: Imprenta de la República, 24 October 1850); *El presidente del Estado de Honduras a sus conciudadanos* (Comayagua, Honduras: Imprenta de José M. Sánchez, 2 March 1852).

37. "Estado de los pueblos al establecerse la República democrática," *Registro Oficial* (Nicaragua), 1847, *Revista de la Academia de Geografía e Historia de Nicaragua* 11, no. 1 (April 1951): 67–77.

38. *Correo del Istmo,* no. 4, León, 16 June 1849, reprinted in *Catálogo de la Exposición Treinta Años de Periodismo en Nicaragua, 1830–1860* (Managua: Instituto Centroamericano de Historia, Universidad Centroamericana, n.d.).

39. *El Progreso,* no. 5, San Salvador, 9 May 1850.

40. For an exposition, see "Un vicentino" [pseud.], *Reflecciones dedicadas a las Lejislaturas [sic] de los Estados sobre la nacionalidad de la República de Centro-América,* San Vicente, 1 January 1853 (San Salvador: Imprenta de Lievano, 16 March 1853), leaflet.

41. "Estado de los pueblos al establecerse la República democrática," *Registro Oficial* (Nicaragua), 1847, *Revista de la Academia de Geografía e Historia de Nicaragua* 11, no. 1 (1951): 67–77.

42. For an illustrative document, refer to the September 1838 issue of the Central American official publication *NRO.* Also, see "Discurso del Presidente del Congreso Federal, Diputado J. B. Basilio Porras, pronunciado al cerrar sus sesiones ordinarias de aquel Cuerpo, el 20 de Julio de 1838, y otros documentos," *Anales de la Geografía e Historia de Guatemala* 13, no. 3 (1937): 317–30.

43. For a discussion of the liberals' claim to unique competence and a (more sympathetic) account of the federalists' position, see Nicolas Shumway, *The Invention of Argentina* (Berkeley: University of California Press, 1992).

44. Tulio Halperín Donghi, *The Contemporary History of Latin America* (Durham, N.C.: Duke University Press, 1993), 74–150.

45. Carlos Newland, "The Estado Docente," *Journal of Latin American Studies* 26, part 2 (1994): 454–57.

46. Ibid.

47. Hugh Hamill, ed., *Caudillos* (Norman: University of Oklahoma Press, 1992), 5.

48. Sonia Fleury, *Estados sin ciudadanos: Seguridad social en America latina* (Buenos Aires: Lugar Editorial, 1997), 194–99.

49. This has been a theme common to different types of *caudillos*—Bolívar, Carrera, Sandino, Cárdenas, Vargas, Perón, Somoza García, Castro, Pinochet, Menem, Ortega, Fujimori, and Chávez.

50. Quoted in Michael Conniff, ed., introduction to *Latin American Populism in Comparative Perspective* (Albuquerque: University of New Mexico Press, 1982), 24.

51. For the "good versus evil" rhetoric of Chilean politics at the time, see Pamela Constable and Arturo Valenzuela, *A Nation of Enemies* (New York: Norton, 1991).

52. For example, Edward Mansfield and Jack Snyder, "Democratization and War," *Foreign Affairs* 74, no. 3 (1995): 95–97.

53. Nancy Bermeo, "The Myth of Moderation," *Comparative Politics* 29, no. 3 (1997): 306–7.

54. Guillermo O'Donnell, "Delegative Democracy," *Journal of Democracy* 5, no. 1 (1994): 55–69.

55. Cited in Michael Shifter, "Tensions and Trade-Offs in Latin America," *Journal of Democracy* 8, no. 2 (1997): 116.

56. Bermeo, "Myth of Moderation."

57. Shifter, "Tensions and Trade-Offs," 119.

58. Jonathan Fox, "The Difficult Transition from Clientelism to Citizenship: Lessons from Mexico," *World Politics* 46, no. 2 (1994): 151–84.

59. Somers, "Citizenship and the Place of the Public Sphere," 587.

9

Conclusion

Toward an Institutionalist and Cultural Synthesis

PAOLA CESARINI & KATHERINE HITE

In this conclusion, we review the chapters' contributions, discuss the policy implications of our findings, and indicate the challenges and opportunities that, in our view, remain open for exploration in the study of authoritarian legacies and democratization processes.

The collaborative project that led to the present volume had three main objectives. First, we sought to systematize a concept—that of authoritarian legacies—increasingly used (and misused) by scholars of democratization. Second, we wished to revive the rich cross-regional and interdisciplinary comparative tradition on Latin America and southern Europe, taking it, in particular, from the volume produced by John Herz twenty years ago. Third, the project sought to craft a theory effectively linking authoritarian legacies to specific democratization outcomes. While this volume satisfactorily achieves the first and second objectives, it also shows that most democratization stories with authoritarian legacies as central characters are likely to be too complex to be easily reduced to a few explanatory variables. Nevertheless, this volume's contributors demonstrate that it is possible to honor the complexity of political process while maintaining analytical rigor. The theories they propose represent important steps toward greater comprehension of authoritarian legacies and their influences on democratization.

Conceptualizing Authoritarian Legacies

In the introduction we offered a comprehensive review of the many conceptualizations of authoritarian legacies to date, outlining the ambiguity—and at times incoherence—of the work of various social science scholars who have approached the theme. In light of the very size of our review, critics might point out that the concept of authoritarian legacies appears too dangerously overstretched to be useful. To this, we would reply that this collection of essays proves that it is possible to tailor the conceptual frame of authoritarian legacies offered at the onset of the volume to a specific context or issue area, so that, depending on the research focus, we might speak of more specific legacies of fear, clientelism, *mano dura*, impunity, and so forth. The range of legacies examined here is quite vast, including the discursive frames of the postcolonial period that continue to affect today's political dynamics in Latin America's democracies; the severed bond of trust between the state and its citizens; the traumatic past of human rights violations and its associated impunity; the economic policies, institutions, and networks of interest representation left by dictators; the style of policing inherited from authoritarianism; and the military's patterns of authoritarian domination.

While our authors address diverse objects of inquiry, they all do so in a comparatively systematic fashion. In other words, the volume confirms that it is possible to afford a coherent treatment of authoritarian legacies across the board, although in practice, and by design, our authors focus upon different actors (i.e., the military, police, judges, politicians, party leaders, citizens), diverse observable facts (i.e., economic policies, police forces' standard operating procedures, transitional justice, citizens' civic culture), and dissimilar mechanisms of transmission of such legacies into successor democracies.[1] All the chapters in this volume, in fact, develop in three successive steps. First, they pinpoint the historical origin of the legacy in a specific authoritarian experience; second, they analyze the mechanisms of transmission to the successor democracy (which include identifying contingent historical configurations, carriers of authoritarian legacies with their preferences and constraints, and political agents' concrete behavior); and finally, they study the impact of such legacies on the macro level of state policies and institutions, as well as on the micro level of democratic citizenship. It is the attention dedicated to the second step that sets our authors apart from others who, in assessing authoritarian legacies, tend to choose an overly deterministic and teleological path-dependency approach—a method that, in our view, may lead to serious misunderstanding of the legacies' phenomena and, perhaps, to policy blunders. For example, the persistence of a violent political discourse that demonizes the political opposition has been mistaken for some form of political immaturity or primitive political culture, leading both scholars and politicians to offer paternalistic and antidemocratic recommendations (see Huntington 1968). Instead, as some of our contributors explain, it is often the case that a demonizing discourse is kept alive only when this is in the interest of specific political actors and that political discourse can be thoroughly "civilized" by a civil society that is determined to keep memory alive and politicians in check.

Another important contribution of this volume to the conceptualization of authoritarian legacies lies in our call to scholars (and especially to political scientists) to devote more attention to the legacies of passivity, trauma, fear, alienation, and cynicism as serious hindrances to good democracy. Virtually all the volume's contributors take us in this direction. Thus Cruz (chapter 8) emphasizes the profound historical reach of authoritarian elite rhetorical frames in which the discourse of a democratic citizenry is virtually silent. Cesarini (chapter 4) points to the power of "refounding myths" in mending the severed bonds of trust between citizens and the state. And Aguilar and Hite (chapter 5) insist on the explanatory power of official discursive dimensions of confronting traumatic pasts. These authors' arguments directly emphasize that to understand authoritarian legacies, it is important to analyze new democracies' different patterns of intersubjective collective behavior and communication. They urge deeper exploration of the power of discursive practices to mold and to reorient politics.

In addition, the authors in the volume who concentrate primarily on institutions, actors, and policies also address "informal" arrangements inherited from the dictatorships as important hindrances to deeper democratization. Hite and Morlino (chapter 2) write of "political party ideological and identity insertion," Agüero (chapter 6) of a "military mind" and of "harder-to-identify fears and inhibitions internalized by other (i.e., nonmilitary) actors," and Pereira and Ungar (Chapter 7) of new democratic governments' "cultural-symbolic pronouncements" and "ideologies" that institutionalize authoritarian patterns of policing. The classic objection to the consideration of "softer" variables is that they are hard to quantify—which they are. The methods used here to circumvent this problem vary. While some authors resort to careful process tracing and rigorous comparative techniques, others cross-reference "softer" with "harder" instances of authoritarian legacies both across time and across country. In general, however, our contributors show that the effort to tackle more "intangible" authoritarian legacies provides for more satisfactory explanations to an undoubtedly complex phenomenon—both in and of itself and in tandem with analyses of "harder" legacies.

Theorizing Authoritarian Legacies

While all our authors agree that institutional reforms constitute a fundamental catalyst of broader democratization processes, they also insist that these reforms are most effective when they are so crafted as to provide powerful symbols of democratic change in which collective cultural/psychological transformations can be nurtured. This seems to be the case for reform across the board. The contributors to this volume—who investigate such varied institutional realms as justice, the market, the police, and the military—all stress that even the most elegant of institutional reforms, per se, might well fail unless they are perceived by citizens as a powerful symbol of change and/or a true harbinger of a new—and different—democratic era. In other words, greater democratic quality also requires transformations at the micro levels of citizens' comparative perceptions of authoritarianism and democracy. Consequently, we suggest closer exploration of the day-to-day relationships among citizens, political society, and the state, particularly at the levels of socializing institutions and political elite/nonelite interaction. We encourage scholars to establish "a link between discursive formations and civic microfoundations . . . because democracy also depends on an array of cultural patterns" (Cruz, chapter 8) that are often taken for granted. We stress that democracy has a greater chance of taking root where postauthoritarian leaders are willing and able to invest in rebuilding citizens' trust in and identification with the state. In the same vein, we argue that for all citizens, but in particular for the younger generations, "how historical memory is presented, interpreted, and debated may very well be the key to formulating democratic values" (Aguilar and Hite, chapter 5). Finally, we submit that the greatest obstacle to a reform of the state apparatus in postauthoritarian regimes often lies in societies' high tolerance for excess on the part of public officials.

This collection emphasizes that to understand the persistence of authoritarian legacies in successor democracies, inertia-based explanations are insufficient. We argue that the political struggle to shape as well as resist democratic reforms needs to be put squarely at the center of any analysis of authoritarian legacies. In the volume, many forms of such struggle are examined, from the power battle for party hegemony that shapes political sociali-zation in a postauthoritarian democracy to the fratricidal discourse char-acteristic of Latin America politics since the postcolonial era; from elite actors' failure to reach a consensus on the "refounding myth" for the new democracy to society's inability to reach even a "minimalist consensus" re-garding past responsibilities for human rights abuses; from the struggle between soldiers and democratic agents to police cover-ups of abuse of citi-zens. Overall, however, our contributors agree that authoritarian legacies are essentially "policy, institutional, and political contexts or arenas," (Hagopian, chapter 3 of this volume) created by authoritarians, within which, or against which, political leaders wage battle. The outcome of this battle between democratic and antidemocratic forces is by no means obvious, and, as our contributors agree, largely hinges on the space, size, and intensity of civil society's involvement.

Our authors also seem to agree that political elites should by no means be the sole focus in the analysis of authoritarian legacies. A key factor is also the willingness of the citizenry to organize and voice dissent. In other words, authoritarian legacies are the product not only of a struggle among leaders but also of citizens' acquiescence. Pereira and Ungar's chapter (chapter 7) points most clearly in this direction when it asserts that policing reform in Latin America is often a product of public action and support for change—in conjunction, of course, with opportunistic elected politicians willing and able to exploit public pressure to their own ends. Aguilar and Hite (chapter 5), in turn, argue that civil society also bears great responsibility for the creation of a public sphere in which historical memories are debated openly and freely, in ways that both embrace "dissensus" and trump those maneuvering toward the destruction of political community. Cesarini (chapter 4), in a similar vein, points out that institutional reforms often constitute a dead letter if the pub-lic remains skeptical of, or uninvolved in, the new democratic regime's plans for change. Finally, Cruz (chapter 8) argues that the abatement of a political discourse that effaces the citizen not only is the responsibility of particular elites but also is greatly influenced by "action shaped by political participation and discourse in nonstate public spheres, community associations, and even the family." Citizens, in other words, have a key and autonomous role to play in the eradication of authoritarian legacies.

This is certainly not the first scholarly work to argue that "resurrecting" civil society is important for democratization. However, we believe that this volume may contribute to refine this somewhat vague concept. The "resur-rection" of civil society generally implies a citizenry that becomes aware of its rights and begins to exercise them, rather than one that attempts to act or acts and is thwarted. The contributors to this volume argue, however, that citizens need to feel safe to exercise their rights, to be convinced that their active involvement can effectively cause change. But how can a citizen feel safe to act when powerful authoritarian actors still maintain impunity, privilege, and ability to do harm openly? How can they think they can make a real difference if the law, in theory equal for all, in practice treats people unequally? How can they imagine a future as democratic citizens if the memories of the authoritarian past are held hostage through continuous manipulation? How can they be confident that they can make a difference if politicians are unresponsive or irresponsible, just as they were under authoritarian rule? How can they respect opposition when the latter is still depicted as an enemy to eradicate? All the chapters in the volume clearly affirm that authoritarian legacies are one of the greatest obstacles to the resurrection of civil society in postauthoritarian democracies.

Authoritarian legacies possess an uncanny ability to seep through even in the most "unconstrained" of transitions. As this volume shows, they may hang in the air of day-to-day communications and gestures, and they often adapt in chameleonlike ways to new administrations and arenas. Thus, while most of our authors argue that the mode of transition is an important predictor for the degree of influence of authoritarian legacies in a new democracy, it is not sufficient. As this volume shows, countries characterized by the same kind of transition may display quite different authoritarian legacies, as well as varied strategies for coping with them. For example, economic reform in new democracies may proceed in divergent ways, and at a different pace, even in countries that experience similar forms of regime change.

Furthermore, even in a transition brought about by military collapse, the military establishment may still be in a position to stifle democracy's efforts to gain control over the armed forces. Finally, since some authoritarian legacies predate the dictatorial experience, these may not be at all a part of the transition's negotiations, yet may nevertheless pass on to haunt the successor democracy. Thus, while the mode of transition is certainly a "critical juncture" as far as authoritarian legacies are concerned, it is not the sole responsible factor. The historical evolution of the preceding authoritarian regime certainly matters a great deal, too. And as some of the chapters here show, even certain traits of the colonial and liberal regimes that preceded the dictatorship may help explain the nature of authoritarian legacies.

In addition, this volume clearly shows that transitions often matter more for what they fail to do than for what they achieve. Official silence on authoritarianism's worst atrocities may be more deafening than a public trial of some perpetrators. The failure to eliminate reserved domains for economic and military elites may restrict the public sphere and prevent meaningful reform. Falling short of applying the law, or failing to apply it equally, may cause citizens to distrust the new democratic regime as much as the old authoritarian one. These clarifications notwithstanding, the mode of transition matters, especially when opportunistic political actors display an uncanny ability to manipulate the transition's meaning for their own interests. Their ability to do so constitutes, in our view, an authoritarian legacy whose survival can be traced directly to the mode of transition, rather than simply an "unforeseen consequence" of the transition. How "unforeseen" can it be when a former high-ranking officer of the military dictatorship puts his impunity on display as proof of the new democratic regime's vulnerability? Or when populist leaders gain consensus among societies whose wealth is still distributed as inequitably as under the dictatorship?

Finally, we submit that this volume suggests novel areas where authoritarian legacies may harbor. This bodes well for the extension of this volume's approach to other regions of recent democratization, such as eastern Europe and Africa. The main such novel areas of investigation are political party ideological and identity insertion, party accountability, and internal party organization. As Hite and Morlino argue (chapter 2), if parties are the most appropriate political interest aggregators and representatives—the political anchors of good democracies—then it is incumbent upon students of political parties to explore authoritarian norms, discourse, and behavior, as well as rules and procedures within parties and party systems in democratization processes.

The second area is economic reform. Hagopian (chapter 3) shows that prominent actors of authoritarian regimes may often thwart economic reform even after democratization. And in fact, in much of post-transition Latin America and eastern Europe, former authoritarians have been the biggest "winners" (Hellman 1998) in privatization programs, as patterns of conflict and accommodation—"old political rationalities" (Seleny 1999)—endure from the pretransition period.

The third area concerns human rights and transitional justice. Several chapters in the volume thrust human rights debates to the forefront of comparative political science analysis of democratization processes. Comparativists working on democratic consolidation have tended to underplay the question of how to come to terms with atrocious pasts, a question that nonetheless continues to assert itself, with tension-ridden consequences for interstate relations as well as relations between the state and society (de Brito,

Enríquez, and Aguilar 2001). These chapters argue that to eliminate authoritarian legacies stemming from an unresolved traumatic past, a democratic leadership must not shy away from debates regarding painful historical memories and that political society must engender a public sphere in which such memories are debated openly and freely, in ways that both embrace "dissensus" (Osiel 1995) and trump those maneuvering toward the destruction of political community.

The fourth and final area regards state-society relations. Both Cesarini (chapter 4), in the case of justice, and Pereira and Ungar (chapter 7), in the case of security forces, treat authoritarian legacies as elements embedded within both institutions and fundamental state-society structures and relationships. These authors use a range of methods to assess the formal-legal and the dispositional/lived experiential dimensions of these legacies. Their conclusions regarding the profound entrenchment of abusive institutions are arguably among the most worrisome of the chapters. This suggests all the more reason to analyze culturalist interstices between institutions and praxis.

Policy Implications

The authors in this volume offer a number of policy suggestions for the eradication of authoritarian legacies in the countries of Latin America and southern Europe. These generally call for a two-pronged (i.e., through both institutional and symbolic/rhetorical devices) strategy affecting the macro level of the state apparatus, the intersubjective level of state-society relations, and the micro level of citizens' perceptions and collective memories. The institutions/policy areas that, according to our authors, seem most in need of intervention are political parties, justice, income distribution, civil-military relations, and internal security. Of course, a realm of intervention that is key to the eradication of all types of authoritarian legacies—and that our authors mention several times in the volume—is that of education and culture, at all levels of schooling; public, private, and international sponsorship of the arts; and civil society initiatives. Often, in fact, the best answer to authoritarian cultural practices is not censorship but the shaping of effective democratic countercultures.

This being said, we must, however, recognize that the focus of the present volume is more theoretical than practical. Further, while our contributors offer a number of policy recommendations to deal with authoritarian legacies, they do so mainly for the relatively "older" postauthoritarian democracies of Latin America and southern Europe—those that underwent democratic transition in the 1940s, 1970s, and 1980s. Since then, however, many more countries have democratized, or redemocratized, in Latin America and in other regions. This book alone cannot therefore do justice to the subject of authoritarian legacies, especially as far as policy implications are concerned. We thus leave it to others to delve more into detail on the specific policy measures needed to overcome authoritarian legacies. We believe, however, that careful historical comparisons of the paths chosen by different postauthoritarian democracies in regions such as Africa or eastern Europe on the model of those undertaken here may shed light on the effectiveness of various strategies to eliminate continuing interference of authoritarian legacies in the practice and quality of today's democracies.

We are convinced that democratization is a lifelong project that may be subject to setbacks and impasses. For this reason, we have purposefully abstained from being either optimistic or pessimistic about the chances for improving democratic quality in political systems affected by authoritarian legacies. We have done so because, while it is true that tremendous progress has been made toward democratization in most of the postauthoritarian democracies examined in the volume, much still remains to be done even in countries that democratized decades ago.

Remaining Challenges

This volume offers a specific approach to the study of democratization, that of authoritarian legacies. This approach is not of our own invention, to be sure. Here, however, we strive to make it explicit and show that it can be constructively used to complement other theoretical frameworks (especially the various institutionalisms) in the analysis of democratization processes. We hope that others will attempt to apply our approach to complement rational choice theories, such as those relating to electoral behavior, institutional engineering, conflict resolution, and economic reform in democratizing countries. With this collection of essays, we wish to go in the direction recently undertaken in some Latin American studies circles: to conceive of democracy "as regimes that simultaneously display elements typical of electoral competitive regimes and elements that corrode the components of democratic citizenship" (Agüero and Stark 1998, 373) and make the study of democracy more interdisciplinary. As far as interdisciplinarity is concerned, the project on authoritarian legacies involved from the start sociologists, historians, social psychologists, economists, security experts, and human rights practitioners in our meetings as coauthors, advisers, reviewers, and select audiences.

We believe that the variety of subject matter contained in this volume effectively illustrates how an authoritarian legacy approach can be productively applied to virtually all areas of democratization—as long as it is done carefully. Certainly, much more should be written in areas such as education, elite behavior, and party organization. Thus we hope that other scholars will expand on our framework, filling the many gaps that we have certainly left open for investigation. In particular, we endorse the study of historical memory, or social memories, as one potential area for linking institutionalist, sociological, and cultural/symbolic approaches.[2] Social memories, in fact, can be a window on the dynamic relationships among culture, society, and institutions. Thus, for example, while Linz and Stepan (1996) still argue that institutional engineering is the most important variable in reconstructing or constructing democratic political order, they also concede that it must be extremely cognizant of memories that haunt the new order. There is great room for inquiry here, starting—for example—from the following questions: How can institutional engineering confront memories of authoritarianism while recrafting democratizing institutions? And how can institutional design promote the systematic confrontation of the past in future reform efforts? Is there a correlation between a politics of "forgetting" and the reemergence of traditional power structures in the new democracies? Can civil society's call for *la memoria* be interpreted as a form of nonacquiescence to the new democratic asset in which traditional power structures continue to predominate? How can debates regarding memory and nation be utilized toward more constructive struggles for democratic deepening?

The study of authoritarian legacies both affirms the hindrances to democratizing reforms and suggests alternatives to paradigmatic understandings of the limits of democratization. Closer analysis of authoritarian legacies may contribute to coming to terms not only with obstacles to democratization but with policies and programs far more cognizant of such obstacles and therefore perhaps more effective in their implementation.

NOTES

1. Thus, for example, while Agüero (chapter 6) insists on the pivotal importance of transition arrangement for the persistence of military reserve domains

under a democracy, Pereira and Ungar (chapter 7) assign to citizens' attitudes the primary responsibility for the survival of a *mano dura* approach on the part of the police in most of Latin America.

2. See the pathbreaking "Memorias de la represión" series edited by Elizabeth Jelín, especially her *Los trabajos de la memoria* (2002).

REFERENCES

Agüero, Felipe, and Jeffrey Stark, eds. 1998. *Fault Lines of Democracy in Post-Transition Latin America.* Coral Gables, Fla: North-South Center Press.

Cruz, Consuelo. 2000. "Identity and Persuasion: How Nations Remember Their Pasts and Make Their Futures." *World Politics* 52 (April): 275–312.

De Brito, Alexandra Barahona, Carmen González Enríquez, and Paloma Aguilar, eds. 2001. *The Politics of Memory and Democratization.* Oxford: Oxford University Press.

Hellman, Joel S. 1998. "Winners Take All: The Politics of Partial Reform in Post-communist Transitions." *World Politics* 50, no. 2:203–34.

Huntington, Samuel P. 1968. *Political Order in Changing Societies.* New Haven, Conn.: Yale University Press.

Jelín, Elizabeth. 2002. *Los trabajos de la memoria.* Buenos Aires: Siglo XXI.

Linz, Juan, and Alfred Stepan. 1996. *Problems of Democratic Transition and Consolidation: Southern Europe, South America, and Post-Communist Europe.* Baltimore, Md.: Johns Hopkins University Press.

Morlino, Leonardo. 1999. *Democracy between Crisis and Consolidation.* Oxford: Oxford University Press.

Osiel, Mark. 1995. "Ever Again: Legal Remembrance of Administrative Massacre." *University of Pennsylvania Law Review* 144:464–704.

Schamis, Hector. 1999. "Distributional Coalitions and the Politics of Economic Reform in Latin America." *World Politics* 51, no. 2:236–68.

Seleny, Anna. 1999. "Old Political Rationalities and New Democracies: Compromise and Confrontation in Hungary and Poland." *World Politics* 51, no. 4:484–519.

Contributors

Felipe Agüero is an associate professor in the School of International Studies at the University of Miami. He is the author of *Soldiers, Civilians and Democracy: Post-Franco Spain in Comparative Perspective* (1995) and co-editor of *Fault Lines of Democracy in Post-Transition Latin America* (1998).

Paloma Aguilar is a professor of political science at the Universidad Nacional de Educación a Distancia and at the Instituto Universitario Gutiérrez Mellado, both in Madrid. Among her publications are *Memory and Amnesia: The Role of the Spanish Civil War in the Transition to Democracy* (2002), previously published in Spanish (1996). Most recently she coedited *The Politics of Memory: Transitional Justice in Democratizing Societies* with Alexandra Barahona de Brito and Carmen González-Enríquez (2001). During the fall of 2001, she was the Tinker Professor at the University of Wisconsin-Madison.

Nancy Bermeo studies the breakdown, emergence, and consequences of democracy as well as the effects of formal institutions on political life. Most recently, she edited *Civil Society before Democracy* (2000) and *Unemployment in the New Europe* (2001), and authored *Ordinary People in Extraordinary Times* (2003). She currently teaches at Princeton University.

Paola Cesarini is a doctoral candidate in political science at Columbia University. Before pursuing her doctorate, Cesarini held positions at the World Bank and the United Nations. She has been a Fulbright Fellow, a Zuckerman Fellow, and an International Fellow at Columbia and has also received support from the Center for Historical Social Science and the Women's International Leadership Program. Cesarini has taught courses in political science at the State University of New York and New York University, and she has published several articles on southern Europe and Latin America in Italy. She is currently at work analyzing the impact of collective memories of transitional justice on democratic quality.

Consuelo Cruz is an assistant professor of political science at Tufts University, where she teaches political economy and comparative politics. Cruz has published articles in *World Politics, Comparative Politics*, and the *Journal of Democracy*, as well as in the *New Republic*, and the *Washington Post*. Her book *The Politics of Fate and Possibility: World Making in the Tropics* (forthcoming) explores the political-cultural factors that shape institutional democratic development in two paradigmatic cases of failure and success (Nicaragua and Costa Rica).

Frances Hagopian is an associate professor in the Department of Government and International Studies and a Fellow of the Kellogg Institute at Notre Dame. Her current research focuses on economic liberalization and political representation in Brazil, Argentina, Chile, and Mexico. Her *Traditional Politics and Regime Change in Brazil* (1996) was named a Choice Outstanding Book in Comparative Politics, and her articles on democratization have appeared in *World Politics, Comparative Political Studies*, and several other publications. Hagopian has taught at Harvard, Tufts, and MIT; she has held fellowships from the Center for Latin American Studies and Howard Heinz Endowment of the University of Pittsburgh, the Social Science Research Council and the American Council of Learned Societies, and Fulbright-Hays.

Katherine Hite is an assistant professor of political science at Vassar College. She is the author of *When the Romance Ended: Leaders of the Chilean Left, 1968–1998* (2000) and coeditor of *The New Politics of Inequality in Latin America: Rethinking Participation and Representation* (1997). Hite's teaching includes courses on Latin American politics, political psychology, social movements, and political violence. Her current research is on political elite manipulations of traumatic political memories, focusing on the politics of commemoration and the discourses and silences surrounding coming to terms with the past.

Leonardo Morlino is professor of political science, University of Florence, Italy; director of the Research Centre on Southern Europe, director of the Doctoral Program in Political Science, Florence, co-chair of the European Consortium for Political Research's Standing Group on Southern Europe, and member of the Committee on Southern Europe, Social Science Research

Council. From 1998 to 2001, he was president of the Italian Political Science Association. His recent publications include *Democrazie e democratizzazioni* (2002); *Scienza Politica,* with M. Cotta and D. Della Porta, (1989); and *Democracy between Consolidation and Crisis: Parties, Groups, and Citizens in Southern Europe* (1998).

Anthony W. Pereira is an associate professor of political science at Tulane University in New Orleans. He received his B. A. from Sussex University (U.K.) in 1982, and his M. A. and his Ph. D. from Harvard University in 1986 and 1991 respectively. Among his publications are *The End of the Peasantry: The Emergence of the Rural Labor Movement in Northeast Brazil, 1961–1988* (1997) and "Virtual Legality: Authoritarian Legacies and the Reform of Military Justice in Brazil, the Southern Cone, and Mexico" in *Comparative Political Studies* (2001).

Mark Ungar is an associate professor of political science at Brooklyn College of the City University of New York. His publications include *Elusive Reform: Democracy and the Rule of Law in Latin America* (2002), *Violence and Politics: Globalization's Paradox* (2001), and other articles and book chapters on constitutionalism, crime, and related issues. He has also served on the policy committees of human rights organizations and is currently working with legal rights groups in Latin America to organize national dialogues on judicial reform.

Index